D0334985

American Families and the Future: Analyses of Possible Destinies

The *Marriage & Family Review* series:

American Families and the Future: Analyses of Possible Destinies has also been published as *Marriage & Family Review,* Volume 18, Numbers 3/4 1993.

The Haworth Press, Inc., 10 Alice Street, Binghamton, NY 13904-1580 USA

Library of Congress Cataloging-in-Publication Data

American families and the future : analyses of possible destinies / Barbara H. Settles, Roma S. Hanks, Marvin B. Sussman, editors.
     p. cm.
     "Has also been published as Marriage & family review, vol. 18, no. 3/4 1993"–CIP galley.
     Includes bibliographical references.
     ISBN 1-56024-468-2 (hc. : acid free paper)
     1. Family–United States. 2. Family policy–United States. 3. United States–Social policy.
     4. United States–Social conditions–1980- I. Settles, Barbara H. II. Hanks, Roma S. III. Sussman, Marvin B.
HQ536.A5443 1993
306.85'0973–dc20
                                  93-26749
                                      CIP

American Families and the Future: Analyses of Possible Destinies

Barbara H. Settles
Roma S. Hanks
Marvin B. Sussman
Editors

The Haworth Press, Inc.
New York • London • Norwood (Australia)

American Families and the Future: Analyses of Possible Destinies

CONTENTS

SOCIAL AND ECONOMIC ISSUES

FAMILY PROCESS IN SHAPING THE FUTURE

Theoretical Issues in Researching Problem Solving in Families
Irv Tallman

ABOUT THE EDITORS

Barbara H. Settles, PhD, is Professor, Department of Individual & Family Studies, University of Delaware. Dr. Settles is immediate Past President of the Groves Conference on Marriage and the Family, Vice President for Public Policy for the National Council on Family Relations, Secretary-Treasurer of The Family Science Association, Program Chairperson for the Committee on Family Research of the International Sociological Association XXX Seminar, Council Member of The American Association of University Professors. She is also a member of The American Home Economics Association and The International Home Economics Association, and various professional honorary societies including Kappa Omicron Nu, Sigma Xi, and Phi Kappa Phi. Dr. Settles' research has focused on decision making and planning over the family life course, family life education, cost and quality issues in child and family care, families with special needs, gender, work and family. She received the 1992 American Home Economics Pennsylvania Avenue Fund Award for her paper on Changing Social Values and was one of the 75 national leaders in Home Economics honored by the Association on its 75th anniversary.

Roma S. Hanks, PhD, is Assistant Professor, Department of Sociology and Anthropology, University of South Alabama, Mobile, Alabama. Dr. Hanks is a member of the American Sociological Association; the National Council on Family Relations; the International Sociological Association, Research Committee on Aging; the Gerontological Association, Research Committee on Aging; the Gerontological Society of America; Phi Kappa Phi; and Kappa Omicron Nu. She has published and presented scholarly papers nationally and internationally in the areas of family/organization linkage, ethics, corporate mobility, family caregiving and inheritance. She serves on the Board of Associate Editors of *Marriage & Family Review.*

Marvin B. Sussman, PhD, is UNIDEL Professor of Human Behavior Emeritus at the College of Human Resources, University of Delaware; and Member of the CORE Faculty, Union Graduate School, Union Institute, Cincinnati, Ohio. A member of many professional organizations, he was awarded the 1980 Ernest W. Burgess Award of the National Council on Family Relations. In 1983, he was elected to the prestigious academy of Groves for scholarly contributions to the field, as well as awarded a life-long membership for services to the Groves Conference on Marriage and the Family in 1984. Dr. Sussman received the Distinguished Family Scholar Award of the Society for the Study of Social Problems (1985) and the Lee Founders Award (1992).

Expanding Choice
in Long Term Planning
for Family Futures

Barbara H. Settles

KEYWORDS. Caregiving, Choice, Decision making, Opportunities, Problem solving, Management, Risk, Equity, Life course, Generational relationships, Family planning

INTRODUCTION

We are living our lives around and among crises and challenges. Planning for our futures is done with an awareness of the many imponderables and the unknowns that shape our destinies. The responsibility, that individuals and their families have for shaping their own lives and providing for their futures, has become more important because of demographic, social, economic, and technological changes. In addition, families need to become more effective in influencing the larger society and bureaucratic institutions in terms of long term outcomes of policies and programs.

Barbara H. Settles is Professor of Individual and Family Studies, University of Delaware.

[Haworth co-indexing entry note]: "Expanding Choice in Long Term Planning for Family Futures." Settles, Barbara H. Co-published simultaneously in *Marriage & Family Review* (The Haworth Press, Inc.) Vol. 18, No. 3/4, 1993, pp. 1-36; and: *American Families and the Future: Analyses of Possible Destinies* (ed: Barbara H. Settles, Roma S. Hanks, and Marvin B. Sussman) The Haworth Press, Inc., 1993, pp. 1-36. Multiple copies of this article/chapter may be purchased from The Haworth Document Delivery Center. Call 1-800-3-HAWORTH (1-800-342-9678) between 9:00 - 5:00 (EST) and ask for DOCUMENT DELIVERY CENTER.

1

Although there is increased opportunity for choice and planning, families need new strategies for dealing with the complexities, changing situations, and finding the relevant and useful information critical to estimating outcomes and assessing the effectiveness of actions. The role of professionals and agencies serving families must be re-examined in light of these changes. Often, the assumption has been that experts' programs, or interventions could replace individuals and families in making decisions that direct long term outcomes. In fact, it is clear that work and community institutions have much shorter time lines and interests than the individuals and families who use these programs. When employers are dominated by the bottom line on a quarterly basis, government has only a yearly budget process, and voluntary, non-profit groups are funded on a project or contributory approach, their evaluation and planning activities are constrained and consideration of long-term outcomes are pushed into the background. The accounting of costs and benefits seldom includes consequences over the lifetimes of clients in these bureaucracies. It is well to remember that is the individuals and their families that absorb the costs of short falls in economic and social institutions.

The question of intergenerational equity has arisen in the debate over how our society should be serving the citizens. In families, one can clearly see that the generations are related and transfers and interdependence can be documented in a meaningful way. However, in programs which target individuals, the cohorts become the unit of analysis and the relationships among children, adults, and elders are framed as if they were separate groups not in interaction or tied together in their respective destinies. A number of the changes that have increased the choice for individuals and families have also brought them into contact with bureaucracies in new situations. Cooperative planning that involves shared expertise and which acknowledges the family's long-term stake in individuals is becoming more frequently institutionalized and even mandated. Understanding how families attempt to shape their futures, deal with uncertainty, and relate to other work and community institutions is increasingly central to family studies. Designing programs, interventions, and educating family scientists and practitioners require a more complete analysis of this area of everyday life.

The analysis presented in this chapter was developed from a larger project that addressed the difference in long term public policy at a general societal level and the needs families have to manage their own lives in a milieu of changing public policy, resources and programs, and their own modest resources in their families, work places, and communities (Settles, 1990).

The project produced several educational approaches and supported materials and evaluated their effectiveness in helping individuals and families become aware of long-term planning issues (Settles, 1990). It was interesting to do this investigation and to see how it played off against the researchers' and staff's own life experiences around and subsequent to the project. Everyone gained from the project an increased awareness of their own needs for long-term planning. For example, six years ago just after my graduate students and I submitted our application for the grant, my husband had his first fight with lymphoma and endured a rigorous chemotherapy regimen. Following this incident the project at the University of Delaware was funded and our research began a development program to help people in their 30's, 40's, and 50's become aware of needs and skills in long term planning. In my own situation, the conclusion of this project coincided with a reoccurrence of my husband's lymphoma and we made the serious decision to do a bone marrow transplant procedure. All the processes discussed in this paper were used because this particular treatment required the intense family support and involvement that the family futures project addressed. One does not depend upon the personal, anecdotal experience to develop theory or test it, but it is emotionally satisfying when the theory one recommends is applicable to real life and the strategy is, as anticipated, satisfactory.

It is within this context of theory, research, educational programs and the rich array of personal experiences that a commitment to planning for family futures has been forged.

OPPORTUNITIES AND NECESSITIES FOR PLANNING

In an information rich world, assessing, evaluation, applying information to specific problems are critical issues. Problems arise quickly due to the fast pace of societal and economic change. Families may need to discover whole new areas of information and to resolve these issues within the constraints of time, energy, and money (Settles & Foulke, 1989). Questions of fairness, equity, practicality and personal independence and responsibility frequently require attention in interactive planning for families.

Individuals consider the domains of personal, family, community, and work in evaluating opportunities. One of the concepts used in project, to help adults look at planning as an interactive process was to identify domains of life: personal; family; community; and work. Within these domains issues were examined from the perspective of:

- how choice can be expanded?
- whose interests need to be included in cost-benefit analysis?
- what resources are available?
- how does each domain impinge on the others?

Issues in the Personal Domain

Typical planning issues in the personal domain are decisions about education, health practices and careers. While these decisions usually are thought to entail the rights of individuals to make their own commitments, the impact of these choices on family and friends is considerable. Such decisions are based on personal goals, aspirations, expectations, and inter- pretations of the future that are heavily influenced by family and peers (Berke, 1991). The family may serve as a laboratory in decision making for its members, especially adolescents (Brown & Mann, 1990).

Most families recognize that plans and decisions made with adolescents shape their lives and opportunities, but may be uncertain as to how the consequences are specifically related to critical decisions. For example, choice of a math or algebra class at the beginning of high school is a fork in the road that determines occupational and social class opportunities in the United States. However, it may be seen as only a scheduling problem by both parents and counselors. Currently, a number of studies are focus- ing on critical pathways in adult life that modify personal decisions. Moen (1992) points out that women continue to have opportunities to reshape their multiple roles to improve life chances.

Issues in the Family Domain

In this analysis the family domain involves decisions about issues in- volving the people a person is close to related by blood, marriage, legal or emotional bond. While the definition of family has many important implica- tions for the relationship among work, community, and personal domains and heavy consequences for resources and opportunities from the point of view of planning, these conflicts over definition become the background against which plans are made and implemented (Settles, 1987; Rettig, 1987; Levin & Trost, 1992). Definitions of the family found in the workplace, for example, may limit access to health insurance or family leave but from the family domain those limitations are problems to be overcome and the unit our own group has defined as family still the planning unit (Settles, 1991). Similarly, if a community zoning prohibits non-conventional households from some neighborhoods, the group usually handles this limitation as a problem rather than as a rationale to restructure the household to fit the definition. Families can also deal with these conflicts by tailoring their public image to fit the demands of work and community but retaining a private life that varies from these expectations (Settles & Hanks, 1988). Child advocacy programs have had to face the issue of when such privacy should be broached in order to protect the child's interests (Feshbach & Feshbach, 1978; Schoeman & Reamer, 1983).

Issues typical of planning in the family domain include care giving of children, elders, and disabled, changing family composition and transitions, retirement, launching, sponsorship, and inheritance. One of the few areas of long-range planning for families that has been carefully researched is the planning or lack of planning for fertility and family size (Miller, B. C., 1987, Thomson, 1989). The importance of education and employment of women to these discussions supports a focus on these four domains. Much of the other research on family decision making resolves itself into examining couples and how they perceive who decides what (Kingsbury & Scanzoni, 1989). Dyadic processes stand in for the larger system and questions about sex role ideology and power have been the central concern.

Issues in the Community Domain

The community domain is both the context for personal and family problem solving and planning that provides resources, support, and limitations and an opportunity for individual and families to influence how the community develops its services and structure. From a familial or personal perspective if the near community does not provide sufficient opportunity, mobility may provide the options. The decision for relocation may involve changed life style, circumstances, environmental and economic factors (Settles & Berke, 1989). Community resources are essentially latent until a family accesses or until the community intervenes in the family's life. The facts of what services, environmental opportunities and networks are available may be quite different from the family's knowledge and perception of their availability (Unger & Powell, 1980; Pilisuk & Parks, 1983). Whether or not a locality is defined as a community is an interactive process and the sense of access that families have to regional, national, and even international resources is highly variable (Settles, 1990).

Issues in the Work Domain

In the work domain paid employment usually provides both a financial base and a social network. The participation of individuals and families in work outside the home relates many dynamic forces. In the United States the policy of providing health insurance and retirement pensions primarily through employers has vested the work domain with great power over the long-range prospects of families (Rock, 1992). Although resources created by individuals and families outside of wage and salary work are important alternatives and supplement the larger economic picture, non-wage productivity in the home has not been carefully examined and in our societal bookkeeping is not given a value (Vanek, 1974; Walker & Woods, 1976; Culley, Settles & Van Name, 1976).

Typical issues in the work domain that affect personal and family long-range planning are changing job and advancement opportunities, benefit changes, and balancing work and family demands (Menaghan & Parcel, 1990; Spitze, 1990; Mortimer & London, 1984). As dual employment has become the majority pattern, interest in developing better policies has increased, although in a world economy downward pressures on labor prices has made it more difficult for workers to influence the work place (Piotrakowski, Rapoport & Rapoport, 1987; Voydanoff & Donnelly, 1988). Traditional labor unions and professional organizations have not been effective means for families to affect the work domain to influence the impact of the workplace and uncertainty of employment has become prevalent across all families (Cornfield, 1990; Voyandoff, 1990). Legal changes, such as affirmative action, have had greater impact in recent years in moderating the work environment and policies.

REQUIREMENTS FOR PLANNING

Each domain–personal, family, community, and work–has special requirements for effective planning and for developing the skills to:

- adapt to changing circumstances;
- meet the challenge of unknown consequences; and
- make the most of unexpected opportunities.

Processes in Planning for the Personal Domain

At the personal level styles of gathering and processing information may affect the ability to make long-range plans. Enlarging one's world view and recognizing changed circumstances can be important factors in making plans that lead to accomplishing goals and dreams (Rettig, 1987).

Expanding choice often requires overcoming inertia and divesting from previous decisions that are no longer effective. Many decision models underestimate how much energy may be invested in defining previous strategies. Thompson and Bubolz (1986) suggest that the concept of energy needs to be more directly addressed in understanding family systems, especially on such issues as information use and changing strategies. Investigations of families with chronic illnesses have been particularly useful in illustrating the critical nature of how families manage the relationship with the formal supportive services (Hauser, 1990). These crises provide the researcher with a window of opportunity to follow how families handle high demand problems. One of the interesting findings is that compliance with recommendations from the medical community is not a simple matter of producing a better outcome. In interviews with parents of children with cystic fibrosis, the tendency of these parents was to continue all interventions, even after they were no longer recommended (Settles, MacRostie, & Lucca, 1986). Recently, Reiss (1991) has found that highly compliant patients in hemodialysis whose families were supportive of that approach were actually less likely to survive in advanced disease stages.

Processes in Planning for the Family Domain

Frequently, it is one individual who sees the possibilities for changes for his or her family. Couples and families vary greatly in their social processes and may not be attentive to some of their members' inputs on planning and revision of plans (Sillars & Kalblesch, 1989). Expansion of choice for families can be encouraged by understanding critical events and developmental sequences (Deacon & Firebaugh, 1975; Gross, Crandall & Knoll, 1980), bureaucratic processes (Sussman, 1991), and informal social support and networks (Anderson, 1982; Berke, 1991).

Processes in Planning for the Work and Community Domains

In community and work domains, expansion of choice is driven by political and economic processes. The creation of markets and development of services and products are macro-level events that affect choices available or unavailable in specific locations and work places. Influencing the outcomes of these events may be difficult even for those who have legitimate authority and responsibility to manage businesses and community organizations and government (Buss & Redburn, 1988). Both the work and community domains have some planning and policy formation activities, but many factors limit the efficacy of those planning devices and process (Zimmerman, 1988). Decisions in the social or economic context can either limit or expand area of choice for individuals and families.

Integration of Domains in Planning Processes

On a daily basis, tensions among personal goals and family values must be resolved with compromises all around. The border between family and the surrounding economic and societal institutions is one that is negotiated continuously (Schwartzman, 1982). The integration of these domains is a challenging process even for less difficult activities than abstract planning and implementation. For example, one's religious affiliation may suggest specifically how daily family life should be arranged (McNamara, 1988) or your neighbors might evaluate your child rearing and report you to a social agency for investigation. The presumption of abuse must be investigated, but the definition of abuse may be quite different for research and intervention (Cicchetti & Manly, 1990). Institutions may evaluate the same behaviors differently and you may find your family being targeted for help you may or may not want (Dunnington & Settles, 1991). The role of family science professionals in advising this negotiation process has grown in this century (Kaslow, 1987; Darling, 1987; Guerney & Maxson, 1990; Lapp, Diemert, & Enestveldt, 1990). In the process of integrating these four domains of planning clearly individuals and families have only partial control over those policies and programs on which they depend for long-term resources and support. Specifically, they must deal with many elements outside their manageable interest, either by trying to build relationships, contracts, and expectations or by developing alternatives and fall back positions.

For most families, living their lives independently is their ideal for the future. They imagine being grandparents living in comfort, visiting their children and grandchildren, and traveling leisurely. Because of a lack of financial resources, poor health or death of a spouse, reality may not match this vision. Lifelong planning involves the process of developing strategies for achieving goals determined during various phases of the life cycle. Planning to be independent and developing equitable interdependencies are both important components of strategies for self sufficiency (Settles, 1990; Sussman, 1991).

Most individuals prefer to maintain their independence (Kahana & Young, 1990). Many fear becoming dependent on others due to lack of resources or personal capabilities. It is important to recognize that dependency is a natural and normal part of human interaction (Schwartzman, 1982). The infant, the handicapped child or adult, the elder and the loved one, are appropriately dependent on others for important care and concern, but such dependency should not be seen as the only defining characteristic of family relationships.

Love, concern, and altruism as concepts, cannot be developed without real situations in which they can be properly expressed. These positive emotions and actions cannot exist in a vacuum. The cartoon picture of the Boy Scout pulling an unwilling elderly person across a street to do his good deed amuses us because it speaks to the problem of opportunity to give care and concern. Taking responsibility for both what one can do to help and what one cannot and should not try to do for another is an important process in normal family life (Walsh, 1980).

Just as dependence is a recurrent theme throughout the life course, our desires and needs for independence are felt from the first breath to the last. Small children need privacy and respect as much as their elders (Cohler & Geyer, 1982). The phrase, the least restrictive option, which has found favor in a new program for the developmentally delayed and functionally limited could well be used for everyone (Wilson, 1988). One should not have to sacrifice personal dignity to have one's dependency needs met.

While the issue is often poised in terms of dependence or independence, the only real option for most individuals is to live interdependently. Interdependence is a complex relationship of activities, demands, expectations that provide mutual support and a sense of equity and fair exchange.

TRENDS IN THE EXPANSION OF CHOICE

Sussman (1983) has pointed out that one can use intergenerational transfers as one of the indicators of this process of interdependence. In his analysis, the close match of personal preferences and attitudes to the legal codes and typical practices in inheritance suggests that there is an underlying social contract between generations. Although these expectations have served many generations well, there has been a number of demographic, social, and technological trends that have created the opportunity and necessity for looking at the relationships among generations in a different way (Hanks, 1991). Assumptions about the relationships among generations, the resources available, and the responsibilities of different social institutions have been altered dramatically in this century.

Demographic Trends

Demographic changes have provided new opportunities for more people. Longer lifetimes have provided the expectation and reality of more elders to interact with families over an expanded time frame (Glick, 1989a). Four and five generation extended families are becoming more common (Pitts, 1986). At the same time smaller nuclear family size has become more common and lateral kinship ties with siblings and cousins may be reduced (Glick, 1989b). Children are far more likely to have living grandparents than previous generations (Brubaker, 1990). Fewer, healthier children have changed the proportion of people in each cohort and given confidence to families that they will spend more time knowing their children as independent grown-ups than as dependent youngsters.

Until recently, family planning literature has primarily dealt with how the demographic shift to smaller families occurs (Thomson, 1989). Demographic models emphasized education, women's employment, and availability of contraceptive and abortion technologies as primary factors (Miller, B. C., 1987). However, the development of intervention programs to encourage smaller family size, required models for decision making and planning at a more micro-level. At this level of analysis, education and employment may be seen as markers for empowerment of women in the actual commitment to "completed" family size or as indicators of family investment in the generations and hence, greater value being given to the adult roles outside parenting (Teachman, Polonko & Scanzoni, 1987). According to Keyfitz (1983, p. 123), "Regardless of the deeper origins of low birth rates abundant evidence shows that information about birth control and access to contraceptives have been major causes of declining fertility in all countries." The success in China of the single child family policy in which mandates and social pressure have been institutionalized has also had consequences for legal regulation of filial responsibility when filial piety can no longer be taken for granted (Terrill, 1991). The planning of family size is an intriguing question that has both abstract and general components and it is implemented by the couple in the most intimate and private moment, which researchers can usually only reconstruct from consequences and the couples' perceptions of the events.

Although general health is improved, longer survival from more debilitating and chronic illness, accidents, and genetic conditions has created intense needs for care giving and support over many years (Strauss, 1984). For example, the marvelous advances in caring for Down's syndrome children have extended life expectancies so many parents are required to plan for how their adult child will be supported when they themselves are frail or die before their handicapped dependent (Mount, 1988).

In contrast to caring for an adult child, the frail elders, usually thought to be frequent among those over eighty years of age, may have outlived both close friends and family (Sanborn & Bould, 1991). These elderly people may also have outlived the plans and provisions they made which were quite adequate for the first decade or two of retirement. Survival and the quality of life in longer lifetimes have become major issues facing both individuals and the larger society (Hanks & Settles, 1990).

Changing Relationships Among the Generations

As these horizons are extended individually, the relationship among generations and cohorts is changing. The concept of the "Sandwiched Generation" has focused on the mid-life adult as caught between the elder's and the child's needs and has had a familiar feel and response for most adults (Miller, J. A., 1987). It is only one of the squeezes caused by shifting demographics. Developmental sequences and interdependent generations can be seen across the life course. In order to illustrate the complexities of interdependence four examples are presented to show how caregiving is affected by cohort and generational resources:

- the adolescent parent and caregiving;
- the parent and/or lover caring for the AIDS patient;
- the elder caring for the frail elder; and
- the youth caring for a dysfunctional parent.

Adolescent Parents and Caregiving

In the case of adolescent parents, concern is usually focused on the unmarried and younger mothers who frequently have little prenatal care and often have at-risk infants with low birth weights and other problems associated with such pregnancies (Miller & Moore, 1990). Fathers have only recently been addressed in research and programs for young parents (Taylor, Chatters, Tucker & Lewis, 1990). A large number of programs and research projects have attempted to prevent teenage pregnancy and to document the situation for these young parents (Adolescent pregnancy, 1986). New programs have intervention components dealing with life options and alternatives for both girls and boys.

Relatively youthful grandmothers who are raising these babies and continuing to support the young mothers may be problematic. In some studies, the findings have indicated that in the case where these grandmothers' own mothers reared their babies there may be subtle encouragement of youthful pregnancy or at least, a greater enjoyment of the grandchild and sense of responsibility to the child (Burton, 1990). The impact that early sexual maturity and lack of alternative opportunities has in creating this type of family is not as well understood. Because this situation has been viewed as a problem to be solved rather than as a partial solution to problems, there has been only limited advancement of thinking about this intergenerational set of transfers. Furstenburg (1991) discusses the complexity of social concern about adolescent pregnancy and parenting and the cost and benefits to youth and notes that he would not assume that any one couple makes these calculations when they have sex. Rather, he believes that it is the social context that defines the situation.

AIDS Care Giving

The AIDS epidemic has been a great revealer of problems in the health care system and the informal social support system. The control of tuberculosis, pneumonia, and maternal mortality, which occurred in the first half of the twentieth century, had reduced the likelihood of mid-life death in industrialized nations so that little attention was paid to adult care giving or prevention of disease (Cohen, 1992). The reemergence of these problems that has paralleled the AIDS epidemic has shaken our medical institutions (Bloom & Murrey, 1992). When AIDS was first identified as an epidemic affecting the male homosexual community, the stigma and social distance of the victims from mainstream institutions at first, provided an excuse for underestimating the total social and economic impact of this new malady (Segal, 1987). The gay communities in large cities, like San Francisco, rallied to develop alternative support and care giving strategies (Macklin, 1989). The use of peers and fellow patients to provide help became the models. As the epidemic has continued to claim victims, the greater burden has stressed these new institutions (Needle & Leach, 1988). Apparently, medical inventions to extend quality of life and perhaps extend life spans are being developed, but the chronic disease pattern of AIDS with shortened life times appears to be the near term outlook with a cure or vaccine only an outside possibility (Koff & Hoth, 1988; Anderson & May, 1992). As the disease affects and includes the broader population base, higher demand for care giving of both children and adults is now projected (Bloom & Carliner, 1988; Hutchinson & Settles, 1991). Kin and peers will be attempting to meet new problems and maintain care giving over longer time periods. Resources that might have been available for intergenerational transfers may be exhausted in the process. Governmental medical care programs often require "spend-down" of all resources and encourage family break-up in order to gain eligibility. In a recent study on AIDS care giving, Matocha (1989) found that middle class AIDS patients had more difficulty negotiating the system than those who had some experience with the welfare system and unemployment. In addition, to the peer model of care, the role of parents and siblings in caregiving for ill adults is becoming more important.

Elder Care by the Elderly

Longer life expectancy and the ability to control chronic conditions has revised the time table for being elderly. Some people have aging problems by mid-life, but for most seniors relative good health may characterize their lives throughout their seventieth decade and even beyond (Brubaker, 1990). When the question of who is caring for the older citizens is posed and families are faulted for letting other institutions have a role in care giving, the picture is of some young adult failing to respect their parents' needs (Jackson, 1988). Nothing could be farther from the common situation. Although the parents of adolescents may be beginning to have elder care responsibilities, in health, housing, and retirement transitions, it is far more likely that an elder will need care from a "child" who is also of retirement age. Adult children are cognizant of the subtleties of intention and follow a conservative and supportive profile (Hansson, Nelson, Carver, NeeSmith, Dowling, Fletcher & Suhr, 1990). Elders caring for elders create a delicate support structure that depends on mutual needs fulfillment and reciprocal resources (Hanks & Settles, 1990). Many elders enter institutional care because their care givers' health declines (Hooyman, 1990).

Youth Caring for a Dysfunctional Parent

Alcoholism in the family is a problem for about 10% of all children under the age of 18, and being raised in such a family is one of the most stressful conditions experienced by children (Roosa, Geusheimer, Short, Ayers & Shell, 1989). The information about how families influence substance abuse is fragmented and loosely defined, and focused on the child's use (Volk, Edwards, Lewis & Sprenkle, 1989). Recent research on drug and alcohol use specifically and dysfunctional families, in general, has indicated that many children experience a squeeze on their developmental resources. This may be because they prematurely take on major responsibility for the household due to their parents' poor adjustments and needs for care. While it is hard to picture a child handling food preparation, bill paying, and their siblings' needs, as well as comforting and providing specific assistance to the parents, this arrangement can stabilize families.

Temporary disability of parents due to accident, illness, unemployment, or family dissolution is frequently part of most children's lives. In this less extreme situation, the reversal of the flow of care giving and dependency relationships in childhood could be viewed positively as preparation for lifelong interchanges and reciprocity. Most parents would admit that their children provide a great deal of emotional support, even when there is no crisis. How much children are involved in planning and even decision making activities, or how these activities impinge on later care giving needs more research (Liprie, Hanks & Berke, 1992, Brown & Mann, 1989). In the elder abuse research, there is a suggestion that abusive care givers may have been abused or neglected in their youth by these parents and involved in abusive or violent adult relationships (Steinmetz, 1987; Phillips & Rempushr, 1985). However, whether or not the inverse of having had positive dependency relationships serves as a protective shield against abusive behavior is not as well supported.

Impact of Demographic Shifts on Planning

These four examples are only a small illustration of the implications of demographic trends. Planning for intergenerational equity requires dropping stereotypes about who is caring for whom and recognizes that most families are multi-problem families who meet the challenges as well as they can. Specifically two shifts have major importance in planning for the future of families. Changing life course trajectories and diversity in family structures have provided a different context for families in anticipating the future and selecting appropriate strategies.

Changing Life Course Trajectories

The generations' and cohorts' time dimensions have altered how closely a family follows a fairly typical family life cycle sequentially. Deviation from this typical time line has major consequences. For both men and women the articulation of goals is critical. For example, late marriages and late childbearing have had a major impact on financial planning and preparation for the retirement years. When later marriage and child bearing characterize the extended kinship group, the squeeze or "sandwich" generation is accentuated (Glick, 1989b). Older grandparents are not as available to give child care and may need more care themselves when the younger family is relatively early in the cycle of child rearing. Remarriage following divorce or widowhood also creates families with complex life trajectories (Glick, 1989a). A family may encompass many more elder relatives from both the current and previous marriages and children of quite different ages and needs.

Timing of life events has an impact on life opportunities and stages. For example early childbearing is often a barrier to education and career development (Aldous, 1990). The young parent, who has limited resources and skills, may find it increasingly difficult to deal with a child as he or she grows up. In a study of decision making and critical thinking, Liprie et al., (1992) found that many teenage mothers wanted more input into family decision making, but they were not perceiving long term consequences as important. The use of foster care and termination of parental rights leading to adoption are less common for young women at birth, but by their child's preschool and early elementary years, the stress and failure of informal support to handle problems has become evident and the use of foster care is more common.

Anticipation of retirement is another example of problems in long term thinking. Retirement planning could be enhanced in its effectiveness if young adults took some action in their twenties and thirties to keep some options available and make some regular, small investments, however most research finds that people can only contemplate serious planning effort about ten years before anticipated retirement (Hanks, 1990). Even then the exact starting point for planning is difficult to determine (Beehr, 1986). Today's early retirement and displaced workers find many retirees who have not had even this period of savings and investment and who will not have the earnings to make up the difference (Hanks, 1990). Their children may well find themselves with heavier filial responsibility although they do not realize that outcome may need to be addressed (Jackson, 1988).

Diversity of Family Structure

It may be that divorce and remarriage rates themselves are also a product of longer life expectancy (Settles, 1991). The changing family forms which individuals may participate in over the life course requires a more refined balance between individual and family plans. Custody, adoption, and foster care also impact on the long term futures of families and the form the family takes at different times. There are simply many more choices at each age and stage in the life course.

There is a greater diversity in household and family patterns than ever before. The working-parent family, the single-parent family, the blended family and intergenerational households have become more common. There is little evidence to suggest there are any long term trends that will markedly diminish this diversity. Changing perceptions and values regarding care-giving and the rights of handicapped and dependent adults have created new demands on family resources and time. Blended families, the marriage of persons who bring children from their earlier marriages with them, are increasing in number and challenging their relationships among step-parents, step children and all the relatives (Spanier & Furstenberg, 1987; Glick, 1989a).

Living too far into the future is a problem of timing. Waiting until a child is old enough to appreciate a vacation or other experience may simply mean that the opportunity is lost. Waiting for economic problems to be solved or careers to mature has frequently meant that fathers were not involved heavily in the early years of a child's life (Bernard, 1984). The more important role that fathers are taking, even before childbirth, in many secure families has changed the dynamics of care and expression in families (Palkovitz, 1992, Hanson & Bozett, 1987). The marginalization of fathers where there is teenage parenting and in divorce and separation custody arrangements apparently has tremendous negative consequences in lost opportunities and sponsorship for children (Taylor et al., 1990; Rettig, Christenson, & Dahl, 1991; Salt, 1991).

In family life education, the use of the concept of the family life cycle and developmental theory and findings has been used to help individuals and families anticipate change. The criticism of this approach and the dialogue with histories and demographers who advocate the use of a life course perspective that sees the individual across familial arrangements, households and other social relationships over the life span have not been resolved (Aldous, 1990). In any event, both individuals and families cannot depend on tradition to help them anticipate what the future will be like for them and must develop a theory for the future in order to estimate the impact of social change on planning.

Social Trends

Individuals and their families look to their futures in the context of societal values, institutions, opportunities and constraints. Larger institutions, control resources and incentives and constrain the choices at the micro-level of the family. Much of our theoretical analysis of family in the mid twentieth century was dominated by the theme that families were losing many of their functions to other institutions and responsibility for both the ways these functions were addressed and what plans needed to be made for the future (Burgess, 1950). As the century comes to a close and commentators of various political, philosophical and practical backgrounds attempt to analyze the current situations and predict the future, there is renewed argument over the status of family as an institution (Levin &

Trost, 1992; Settles, 1992). "Family values" has become the media rubric to encapsulate all the unease with social and political change. Overwhelming nostalgia for some desirable earlier age when families were strong and expectations were clear has overcome the discourse (Howard, 1981). The control of individuals by their families and by their families' ascribed class position in the community that is implicit in this reminiscence may not be as positively viewed at the micro-level of specific families. Increased opportunity for non-discrimination in jobs, housing, education, public accommodation and mobility are social changes that have opened up choices and included more families in shaping their own lives (Bolger, Moen & Downey, 1985). In reviews of mobility and immigration trends and effects prepared for subsequent issues of Marriage and Family Review (Settles, Hanks & Sussman, in press), the complexities of providing both freedom and security in society for families are examined in detail. Overall, an open society and free movement tend to be family friendly policies and encourage family initiated planning activities (Settles, in press).

Impact of Social Change on Planning

The overall impact of these changes has been to produce more alternatives, but individuals and their families may or may not be able to access choices in their specific situation. Even when a choice is not acted upon, the knowledge that there are alternatives changes one's attitude. The costs and benefits of social change affect families differently, but in this century provided more choice and opportunity to make decisions for the family's future. Three specific examples of the impact of social change illustrate how the choices available to individuals and families may be expanded or contracted depending on how social change is handled:

- targeted social policy;
- stable relationships;
- family empowerment.

Targeted Social Policy

First, at the macro level work and community institutions have been targeted and segmented in their programs to help individuals and families. The issues related to planning for the future have been pushed aside, in order to address current emergencies and labeled problems. The horizon addressed is, at the most, a yearly organizational planning cycle and more often a quarterly or a monthly bottom line. Long term consequences and cost-benefit ratios over the life course may be of interest to the academic hired to do a program evaluation, but the ordinary politics and economics of institutions do not lend themselves to anticipating consequences or supporting long term plans. Instead the system addresses identified crisis, highly visible problems, and responds to interest group pressures to manage and relocate resources (Zimmerman, 1988).

In the United States, national policies result in leaving to the family the problems of coordination of services, choice of support, and responsibility for outcomes and consequences (Aldous & Dumon, 1990). Instead of instituting many of the government programs that other developed nations use to address these family problems, the national consensus relies on either the private insurance or benefits in the workplace. The result is a wildly uneven distribution of resources across the generations, and from one part of the country to another and throughout the social structure. These family policies include a rich array of services and supports, that give some American families the best selection available in the world, and produce major gaps in service and over-served clients.

Stable Relationships

Second, families have more stability than most other social groups today. Family relationships are longer term and more involved than other friendships, organizational memberships, and communities. Families, often, stay together over the life course to reap rewards or consequences of earlier plans. Fiftieth wedding anniversaries have become regular standard part of news coverage. Glick (1989b) has documented the prevalence of the preference for familial arrangements over other life styles. Even when families experience launching of children, separation, divorce, remarriage, and death, plans made as a family continue to influence life styles. Examination of property settlements, child support, and spousal rehabilitation agreements illustrate replanning and the outcomes of previous approaches.

As new relationships and families are formed the number of individuals involved in long term planning increases. Determining whose interests must be represented in planning has become a problem. Children, dependent or handicapped adults and elders are more likely to be considered as members of the decision making and planning team today. Representing their interests when they cannot participate actively is an ethical challenge to both the family and community (Clavan, 1985; Schulz, 1985; Hanks & Settles, 1990).

Although families and individuals are faced with immediate crises and survival needs, families and individuals know that they will pay the consequences for current decisions and will still be around to know how things turn out. One of the problems of being single in our society is the lack of advocacy when one must deal with one of the larger institutions (Stein, 1983). Unless one has friends who are willing to take familial responsibility and who are authorized to exercise these roles lower quality institutional response occurs. For example, look at the other end of the following social exchanges:

- graduation from school–Who helps you getting a job? Where do you live until you find a career? Who takes your picture?
- discharge from hospital–Who takes you home? Who manages your recovery?
- parole from prison–Who will agree to receive you? Who makes the plan for probation?
- retirement or lay off at work–Who shares your destiny? Where do you turn for help or companionship?

Family Empowerment

Third, the family manages relationships with the larger society. The family is usually the first group to notice problems. Their skills in linking up to larger institutions impact on the quality of professional advice and help they receive. Focusing on familial empowerment has become the preferred strategy for both the professional community in family services and the policy makers in both the private and public sectors. Knowing the limits on both sides of the interchange between bureaucracy and family is critical. If the family boundaries are broached too often or for insufficient cause by interventions the integrity of the family for problem solving and planning may be impaired. The police and welfare workers know that poor judgment can expose a vulnerable person to injury or neglect. Empowerment is no substitute for reasonably friendly and adequate community and economic institutions. For families to take initiative in looking toward the future they must have some assurance that some stability, security, and responsiveness will characterize their environment. A noble rhetoric that has no substance quickly leads to discouragement and disillusionment.

Economic Trends

The economic changes of the twentieth century have radically shifted the relationship between individuals, their families and the workplace.

Until the renaissance, feudal life was based on tying the individual and family to the land and the power structure. The economic industrial revolution tied individuals and families to employers and industries for much of their lives and had a similar power over the specifics of daily life. Although the company town with its wake up whistle and company store based on script was on the wane, the sense of commitment to an industry, a corporation, a profession, or trade, was normal practice for most of the twentieth century (Hanks, 1990). As a true world wide economy has emerged in which it is as easy to move capital, through incentives, as it was to move labor, through immigration, the tie between the work organization and the family is becoming more attenuated (Piotrakowski et al., 1987; Voydanoff, 1990).

In order to alleviate uncertainty, families have made major changes in work force participation. More adults are involved in the workplace and paid employment. While many families have only one employed, paid worker, more than half of the families in the work force have the wife employed as well (Glick, 1989b). Employment is the central foundation for the quality of life and financial preparedness for most families (Kilty & Behling, 1986). Regularity, opportunity and stability are sought after characteristics in work.

In the two parent family working outside the home represents the new norm. Many perceived benefits–social, personal, familial, and economic–lead to achieving a desired lifestyle. For those families who are on the edge of the middle class life style or part of the working poor, these jobs are critical to simply surviving and maintaining their households. For women there has been additional motivation. However, choosing a career has provided many women with greater sense of security and independence, more control over their own lives, and greater choice for the future. Consequently, financial planning for retirement is more interesting to those in dual earner homes, because of the added resources and potential choices (Van Name, 1991).

Although employment of women has helped to maintain family economic strength as the baby boom generation matured, there are some disturbing trends in the employment scene toward lower paid, part time jobs, and fewer middle managers (Russell, 1982). Incentives for early retirement have caused disruptions in family plans and personal careers (Hanks, 1990). There has been a marked increase in low skill/low pay employment. To keep costs down, employers use fewer full time or permanent employees and more part-time, contract or temporary employees who do not create overhead benefit expenses (Winnick, 1988).

Impact of Economic Change on Planning

By vesting health insurance in the workplace, we have made some families captive of their specific employers and others have been left out entirely. Those who have chronic conditions or children with handicaps find they cannot afford to change health plans to take new employment opportunities. These problems of younger families are not a result of improving elder health care through "Medicare." Releasing families from the burden of elder medical expenses by extending some coverage to all of our elderly through governmental programs, is helpful when there are smaller families. However, vesting the coverage of those families who are thought to have employable members in the workplace does exclude many families from any dependable medical resources. Many young families are without adequate health coverage. Some young mothers find entry jobs provide no health benefits so that their families are worse off than when they are in government assistance programs (Rock, 1992).

In response to the changes in employment patterns–organizations are asked to respond to the impact of employment on family systems. Flex-time, cafeteria benefits, greater supports of day care, changes in use of sick leave, caring for sick children or the elderly, and maternity leave for one or both parents are widely suggested policies to support families (Galinsky, 1986). New trends in organizational and management theory and practice have added impetus to programs for balancing work and family issues. Both employers and employees are reassessing how the family-work interface can best be arranged. Obligations to each other are being redefined and families are needing to do more independent planning of their futures, because the organizations are not committed to using benefits to hold their work forces for life time employment.

Technological Trends

Technology has been a key to human life since the earliest documentation of our existence. Rapid technological changes and applications have dominated our recent history. The elder generation in this century has specialized in adopting new ideas and artifacts. Fashion and fad have accentuated our sense that the new is better than the old and that technology will provide a solution just around the corner. Fascination with the possibilities of technological discovery and innovation has dominated the understanding of the future. Incorporating a new technology is quicker and easier than adopting a philosophy to accompany the change. Some technologies are more flexible and accommodating to individuals than others. For example, current trends in the technological medical treatments have freed the patient from the requirement to be hospitalized to receive treatment. Portable technologies bring the family and household back into medicine and treatment. At a more mundane level, the development of disposal diapers, undergarments, medical products, feminine hygiene products has had a mixed response. First, these technologies have received universal acceptance, because of the way they address unpleasant care tasks. Second, they have been attacked for the unexpected consequences for trash disposal, handling and environmental impact.

Information for Decision Making and Long Term Planning

The need for diverse, accurate, and complete information has risen faster than most individuals and families can accommodate. Families need to become information sensitive and information rich if they are going to cope with new problems and anticipate opportunities. For example, finding appropriate treatment for a major illness may require access and understanding of innovative techniques that are new to the family doctor. Seeking out the best practice may be critical to assuring a good outcome. Situations differ in clarity, complexity, information requirements, and involvement of individuals. Questions of information and responsibility are critical to effective planning and adequate decision making.

Who has information? Professionals and the organizations they represent have information systems to update and interpret the technical findings in their field of endeavor. Families have critical information on resources, problems, and values that affect how such technical information can be applied to their situation.

How is the information interpreted? Interpretation of both kinds of information requires communication and shared planning. The old fashioned view of the professional prescribing a course of action and explaining it to the family no longer works in our modern society. Shared responsibility for outcome is needed for many of the complex interventions available today.

Who is responsible for decision outcomes and risk management in the planning process? With shared decision-making and planning both professionals and families are changing their view of responsibility and estimating and evaluating risks. One of the controversies in our public life is how government, private insurance agencies, and families will share risk taking and handle unexpected consequences. Families need to be aware of how any specific support group or service defines its contribution to sharing risk management before agreeing to such services. Families should evaluate whether or not the service or treatment is meeting their needs and take charge of their own situations.

Understanding and Connecting Short Term and Long Term Outcomes

The family and the individual lives with the consequences of action. No community or work group has ongoing responsibility for outcomes at the micro level. At the macro level, planning only structures opportunities and restraints. It does not and cannot provide individualized plans at the micro level.

Families make many decisions in partial ignorance or in situations where the complex factors involved are too extensive for easy or clear predictions about outcomes or consequences. Ignorance in complex situations does not imply a fault or deficiency with the family. Rather it is a lack of information, knowledge, or specific skills that needs to be addressed in the problem solving process.

Certainty typifies consumer choices. The need is well defined. The range of options are easy to identify. The costs of each approach are clear, and there are already developed guides for evaluation. Because it is unlikely that anything unexpected will happen, values can be implemented. The clear criteria for success allow "rational" choice. Uncertainty stems from both internal and external sources. Environmental and personal changes contribute to uncertainty. More complex decisions require provisions for changing probabilities and new information (Collingridge, 1983). Diverse strategies may be needed. Only what is known or can be reasonably projected is used in making the initial decision.

In a technologically sophisticated society, at least, three sources of ignorance are important to long range planning for family futures; the unknowable, partial prediction, and lack of access to information. In today's rapidly changing scientific and technical culture both professionals and families need to identify and face those elements in a decision or plan that are unknowable and develop strategies that can incorporate information as it is available.

One of the roles of professionals is to interpret to families the information about a course of action and consequences for the many moderately certain connections between cause and effect that have been shown to exist by research. The information necessary is available to make predictions and plans with a greater assurance of a good outcome. When prediction is uncertain, establishing fall-back and alternative plans as part of the process of decision making becomes essential. Lack of access to this knowledge about the relationship of a course of action to outcomes is a far more serious problem. In this case, ignorance is not the problem, but failure to seek and evaluate information can seriously jeopardize a family's future. Developing skills to find information when stressed can create empowerment in families. One of the most difficult prerequisites to increasing choice in life is a tolerance for complexity and loose ends. Many plans must be continuously reevaluated and altered if the goals desired are to be reached. Simple solutions and commitments usually are not effective in the long run.

It requires a great deal of energy and negotiation in families to plan, even a clearly ineffective decision may not be changed. Unwinding a decision requires: recognizing replanning opportunity; re-examining assumptions; divesting from earlier decision; evaluating current strategies; seeking new advice or consultants; establishing a new decision (Settles & Foulke, 1989). Families need to find ways to accommodate the ordinary chaos of change within their current reality. Individual families who are on the front edge of sociological and technological change are often flexible and adaptable, but finding the social support necessary to follow through may be more difficult. Organizations and institutions lag behind the implications of innovations and discoveries in their policies. Each technological change produces the opportunity for application and creates a challenge to traditional knowledge and ways of life. Early adoption of new technologies can provide the individual with windfall profits yet also carry risks of major failure.

SUMMARY

Social and demographic trends have provided the opportunity and security for more generational interaction and long range planning. However, the relationship between the individual and family life course must be reexamined and the relationship among the formal and informal support systems renewed.

Economic trends suggest that individual and family planning for the future is more necessary and complex because the economic and political organizations are not going to assume this role or provide continuity.

Technological discovery and innovation provide a continually changing milieu for choice and planning that requires constant monitoring and reassessment of decisions and commitments as new knowledge and techniques become available and more useful theories are created.

IMPLICATIONS FOR RESEARCH AND THEORY

Three separate lines of research are fundamental to supporting individuals and families in their long term planning activities. First, a basic inquiry documenting how families approach planning and which strategies and processes are most effective is needed. The problem solving, decision making, stress/coping literature can provide a starting point, but much more information is needed on who is involved in therapeutic and supportive plans, how such plans are implemented and modified and which issues are of concern to families. Second, families need better information on means-ends connections and risk factors. Meta-analysis of the findings of family and development studies could be especially useful to both family units and those who design and deliver programs to families. Third, educational and therapeutic intervention and social policy development could benefit from research on the learning of knowledge, awareness, and skills for planning. The efficacy and design of educational, therapeutic, and supportive intervention for empowering families to shape their own lives is sorely needed. Appropriate technology to support decision making, problem solving and planning are becoming available and feasible, but creative application and evaluation efforts are still in the infant stage of development. In a multifaceted effort to test both hi-tech and traditional adult peer education materials our research included video and computer products used both in home settings and group programs (Foulke, 1989; Settles & Berke 1989). One of the advantages of these new approaches is that information and decision processes can be directly modeled.

New paradigms and theories of family futures require attention to both what is investigated and how it is studied. A theoretical match among types of data is fundamental: individual, pair, family, and context. To elucidate how planning operates across the domains of the individual, family, community and work, it is critical to consider when aggregation of the data makes sense (Ransom, Fisher, Phillips, Kokes, & Weiss, 1990). If we focus on only the individual or the dyad many of the processes essential for theory building and effective intervention and support to planning activities are not evident.

IMPLICATIONS FOR PRACTICE
AND PROFESSIONAL EDUCATION

Professionals serving families have several challenges in both training and practice that come from an understanding of long range planning. While there has been interest in interdisciplinary teams and involving the family in intervention programs of individuals, there should be a parallel expansion of 'consumer' education of families to participate in teams when advocating for family members (Lapp et al., 1990). Educational programs can help professionals see events from a familial long term perspective, as well as the perspective of immediate intervention success. Cost benefit analyses and evaluation should include the unpaid time of family members and the costs of consequences to the family unit.

Ethical treatment can exist only when professionals are clear about what responsibilities they can indeed really fulfill and what the limits of their roles are in meeting client needs. When information can be interpreted in diverse ways, the ethically responsible researcher or interventionist must be forthcoming about how advice is being generated and amenable to clients seeking second opinions and alternative sources of information. The situations in which institutions take total charge of clients are likely to become fewer and fewer. Not only do families require ways to divest from ineffective plans, but their advisors need to develop skills in changing plans and reformulating strategies without telling themselves to be failures. Planning is continuous process including emotional content and free wheeling elements that is a multipurpose, multilayer process for these professionals and the families they serve (Reid, Rotering, & Fortune, 1989). Just as outcomes for couples and families are dynamic (Hill & Scanzoni, 1982), planning and problem solving in intervention is a continuous process.

Styles of management that properly include risk assessment have social policy implications (Thompson & Wildavsky, 1982), which should affect the way leaders in family services are educated. If institutions and programs are seen to be effective in changing the economic and social climate the skills of projecting long range consequences and replanning are needed at the institutional level as they are at the individual and family.

FOUNDATIONS FOR FAMILY ACTIVITIES
IN LONG RANGE PLANNING

Against the backdrop of these larger macro-level trends the family might appear to be a small and ineffectual group in which to vest responsibility for long-range planning. The public and professional debate about the future of the family have emphasized the fragility of the family and all the problems which poor family functioning has caused the greater society.

The time has come for the professions that deal with family concerns across the life course to come together to speak out against planning for our human service programs by label and division of interest. Families are not simply: families of deviance; families of cystic fibrosis or cancer; families of missing in action; elder care givers; at-risk-to-abuse families. They have both a multiplicity of problems and strengths.

Divisions by age, class, region of the country, economic and work status may be used to focus programs and provide resources but they often stand in the way of a truly equitous support system for families across the life course. At the societal level, we have tended to group families by identified problems and design programs to meet just that problem. Such programs have large infrastructures that serve to determine eligibility, set priorities for service, and monitor accountability. Referral and coordination of services are a major challenge to workers in these programs and often result in families experiencing conflict and gaps of service.

Economic situations and governmental family policy may change rapidly with little or no opportunity for families to adjust their plans (Dooley, 1982). For example, when the social security was reformed, the provision to support post secondary education for children of deceased parents was eliminated. Some high school students went to college early in order to be eligible, but most of those who had planned on that program had no fall-back position; it was too late to go back and build a personal insurance program. To encourage families to do long range planning, some stability in social programs is necessary. For all but the simplest kinds of plans, some element of risk is involved.

The relationship between risk-taking and success can range from those who never take risks to those whose greatest thrill is in the gamble. Risk aversive people either never take chances or get involved only in relatively sure things. In contrast, those who enjoy taking chances without a serious calculation of the risks involved, often lose, but are carried along by hope. Moderate risk taking behavior is associated with higher levels of success and achievement.

Traumatic events, whether natural or man-made disasters can put all families in jeopardy. In such extreme events, many of the traditional guidelines for decision making have to be ignored because of the overwhelming nature of the incident or the speed and urgency with which decisions must be made. Normal procedures and consensus building are temporarily shelved so that effective coordinated action can begin. With such severe restraints on time resources there is the need to conserve as much of the available physical energy as possible while directing it to the most critical needs. Crisis calls forth a real turning outward to informal and formal community resources and support. Without external resources and support, neither communities nor families could respond to the emerging conditions in crisis.

At the community level, both public and private sector resources are important to long term planning. Governmental agencies provide information and limited assistance for family problem solving. For some families, there is a reluctance to approach public agencies for information or assistance, whether for fear of stigma or a perception that such information will be inappropriate or provided only grudgingly. While these perceptions are often inaccurate, and the human service and health service organizations seek to be helpful, they are constrained by guidelines, eligibility requirements and fiscal limitations. The families can learn to assess these resources to be more effective planners.

At each stage of family life, we tend to experience predictable kinds of adjustments and challenges. Families can leave their decision making to one spouse for major action, they can share in making decisions either by compromise or by creative consensus and with the growth of children, even including their younger members' preferences in the factors that are included in the planning process.

If we are to provide better options for individuals and families in planning for their futures, we will need to take action to effect these larger policies. Developing plans for assuring intergenerational equity require that constituent groups develop consensus building strategies and integrated programs for the old and the young, the poor and the rich, the able and the disabled. As professionals in family studies we need to become aware of coalition building opportunities and linkages to improve our programs and policies for families and individuals. We also need to speak out against planning our human services programs by problem label and division of interest.

AUTHOR'S NOTE

This paper is based on an invited paper delivered at the American Home Economics Association preconference family life workshop, June 1989, Cincinnati, OH, and draws upon the research and program development materials supported by a grant from the Administration on Aging U.S.H.H.S. Grant #0090AM0219, "Interactive Planning for Family Futures," Barbara H. Settles, principal investigator. Working papers and reports are available from the University of Delaware, Newark, DE 19716.

REFERENCES

Adolescent pregnancy: testing prevention strategies. (1986). *Carnegie Quarterly*, *31*(3&4), 1-7.

Aldous, J. (1990). Family development and the life course: Two perspectives on family change. *Journal of Marriage and the Family*, 52(3), 571-583.

Aldous, J., & Dumon, W. (1990). Family policy in the 80's: Controversy and concerns. *Journal of Marriage and the Family, 52*(4) 1136-1151.

Anderson, C. (1982). The community connection: The impact of social networks on family and individual functioning. In K. Walsh (Ed.), *Normal Family Process* (pp. 425-445). New York: Guilford Press.

Anderson, R. M., & May, R. M. (1992). Understanding the AIDS pandemic. *Scientific American, 266*(5), 58-67.

Beehr, T. A. (1986). The process of retirement: A review and recommendations for future investigations. *Personnel Psychology, 39*(1), 31-55.

Berke, D. L. (1991). A cross-sectional analysis of network structure, support functions, and satisfaction with social support over the life course. Unpublished doctoral dissertation. Newark DE: University of Delaware.

Bernard, J. (1984). The good provider role: Its rise and fall. In P. Voydanoff, *Work and Family* (pp. 45-60). Palo, CA: Mayfield.

Bloom, B. R., & Murrey, C. J. L. (1992). Tuberculosis: Commentary on a re-emerged killer. *Science, 257*, 1055-1063.

Bloom, D. E., & Carliner, G. (1988). The economic impact of AIDS in the United States. *Science, 239*, 604-609.

Bolger, N., Moen, P., & Downey, G. (1985). *Family transitions and work decisions: A life course analysis of labor force reentry for mature married women.* Washington D. C.: American Sociological Association.

Brown, J. E., & Mann, L. (1989). Parents and adolescents' perceptions of participation in family decisions. *Australian Journal of Sex, Marriage, & Family, 10*(2), 65-73.

Brown, J. E., & Mann, L. (1990). The relationship between family structure and process variables and adolescent decision making. *Journal of Adolescence, 13*, 25-37.

Brubaker, T. (1990). Families in later life: A burgeoning research area. *Journal of Marriage and the Family, 52*(4), 959-981.

Burgess, E. W., & Locke, H. J. (1950). *The Family; from institution to companionship.* New York: American Book Company.

Burton, L. M. (1990). Teenage child bearing as an alternative life course strategy in multigeneration black families. *Human Nature, 1*(2), 243-254.

Buss, T. F., & Redburn, F. S. (1988). Reemployment after shutdown: The Youngstown steelmill closing, 1977 to 1985. In P. Voydanoff & L. C. Majka (Eds.), *Families and Economic Distress: Coping Strategies and Social Policy* (pp. 17-37). Newbury Park, CA: Sage Publications.

Cicchetti, D., & Manly, J. T. (1990). A personal perspective on conducting research with maltreating families: Problems and solutions. In G. H. Brody & I. S. Siegal (Eds.), *Methods of Family Research* (pp. 78-134). Hillsdale, NJ: Lawrence Erlbaum Associates.

Claven, S. (1985). Even if a deformed baby or a person in a long term coma is unable to make a decision for him or herself to remove life support systems, the family has no right to make the decision. In H. Feldman & M. Feldman

(Eds.), *Current Controversies in Marriage and the Family* (pp. 333-344). Newbury Park, CA: Sage Publications.

Cohen, M. L. (1992). Epidemiology of drug resistance: Implications for a post-antimicrobal era. *Science 257*, 1050-1055.

Cohler, B. J., & Geyer, S. (1982). Psychological autonomy and interdependence within the family in normal families in temporal context. In F. Walsh (Ed.), Normal Family Processes (pp. 196-228). New York: Guilford Press.

Collingridge, D. (1983). Hedging and flexing: Two ways of choosing under ignorance. *Technology Forecasting and Social Change, 23*, 161-172.

Cornfield, D. B. (1990). Labor Unions, Corporations and Families: Institutions competition in the provision of social welfare in corporations, businesses and families. *Marriage & Family Review, 15*(3-4), 37-58.

Culley, J. D., Settles, B. H., & Van Name, J. B. (1976). *Understanding and Measuring the Cost of Foster Care.* Newark, DE: Bureau of Economic and Business Research, University of Delaware.

Darling, C. (1987). Family life education. In M. B. Sussman & S. K. Steinmetz (Eds.), *Handbook on Marriage and the Family* (pp. 815-834). New York: Plenum.

Deacon, R. E., Firebaugh, F. M. (1975). *Home Management: Context and Concepts.* Boston: Houghton Mifflin Company.

Dooley, J. E. (1982, June). Decision making in environmental crisis situations. In H. C. Kunruether & E. V. Ley (Eds.), Proceedings of IIASA, The risk analysis controversy in institutional perspective (pp. 79-80). Laxemborg, Austria.

Dunnington, S. F., & Settles, B. H. (1991, November). *The influence of liberal versus conservative religious values and beliefs on families' area of choice.* Paper presented at the Theory Construction and Research Methodology Workshop, National Council on Family Relations, Denver, CO.

Feshbach, S., & Feshbach, N. (1978). Child advocacy and family privacy. *Journal of Social Issues, 34*(2), 168-178.

Foulke, S. R. (1989). *Planning in Mid-life: An Evaluation of A Videotape Program to Create Awareness of Decision Needs.* Unpublished doctoral dissertation, University of Delaware, Newark, DE.

Furstenberg, Jr., F. (1991). As the pendulum swings: Teenage childbearing and social concern. *Family Relations, 40*(2), 127-138.

Galinsky, E. (1986, May, 16). *Work and family life: Corporate and union response.* Unpublished paper presented at symposium. University of Delaware, Newark, DE.

Glick, P. C. (1989a). Remarried families, stepfamilies, and stepchildren: A brief demographic profile. *Family Relations, 38*(1), 24-27.

Glick, P. C. (1989b). The family life cycle and social change. *Family Relations, 38*(2), 123-129.

Gross, I. H., Crandall, E. W., & Knoll, M. M. (1980). *Management for Modern Families.* Englewood Cliffs, NJ: Prentice Hall.

Guerney, Jr. B., & Maxson, P. (1990). Marital and family enrichment research:

A decade review and look ahead. *Journal of Marriage and the Family, 52*(4), 1127-1135.

Hanks, R. S. (1990). *Family and Corporation Linkage in Timing and Control of Incentive Based Early Retirement.* Unpublished doctoral dissertation, University of Delaware, Newark, DE.

Hanks, R. S. (1991). An intergenerational perspective on family ethical dilemmas. *Marriage & Family Review, 16*(1-2), 161-174.

Hanks, R. S., & Settles, B. H. (1990). Theoretical questions and ethical issues in a family caregiving relationship. In D. E. Biegal & A. Blum (Eds.), *Aging and Caregiving: Theory, Research, and Policy* (pp. 98-120). Newbury Park, CA: Sage Publications.

Hanson, S. M. H., & Bozett, F. W. (1987). Fatherhood: A review and resources. *Family Relations, 36*(3), 233-240.

Hansson, R. O., Nelson, R. E., Carver, M. D., NeeSmith, D. H., Dowling, E. M., Fletcher, W. L., & Suhr, P. (1990). Adult children with frail elderly parents: when to intervene? *Family Relations, 3* (2), 153-158.

Hauser, S. T. (1990). The study of families and chronic illness: ways of coping and interacting. In G. H. Brody & I. E. Sigel (Eds.), *Methods of Family Research: Vol. 2* (pp. 63-86). Hillsdale, NJ: Lawrence Erlbaum Associates.

Hill, W., & Scanzoni, J. (1982). An approach for assessing marital decision-making processes. *Journal of Marriage and the Family, 44*(4), 927-941.

Hooyman, N. R. (1990). Women as caregivers of the elderly. In D. E. Biegal & A. Blum, *Aging and Caregiving: Theory, Research, and Policy* (pp. 221-241). Newbury Park, CA: Sage Publications.

Howard, R. L. (1981). *A Social History of American Family Sociology.* Westport, CT: Greenwood Press.

Hutchinson, K., & Settles, B. H. (1991, November). *A Proposed Conceptual Framework for HIV Self-assessment in Women.* Paper presented at the Theory Construction and Research Methodology Workshop, National Council on Family Relations, Denver, CO.

Jackson, M. A. (1988). *Filial Responsibility Attitudes of Adult Children Toward Early Retired Parents.* Unpublished master's thesis, University of Delaware, Newark, DE.

Kahana, E., & Young, R. (1990). Clarifying the caregiving paradigm. In D. E. Biegal & A. Blum (Eds.), *Aging and Caregiving: Theory, Research, and Policy* (pp. 76-97). Newbury Park, CA: Sage Publications.

Kaslow, F. W. (1987). Marital and family therapy. In M. B. Sussman & S. K. Steinmetz (Eds.), *Handbook on Marriage and the Family.* New York: Plenum.

Keyfitz, N. (1989, September). The growing human population. *Scientific American, 261,* 119-126.

Kilty, K. M., & Behling, J. H. (1986). Retirement financial planning among professional workers. *The Gerontologist, 26*(5), 525-530.

Kingsbury, N. M., & Scanzoni, J. (1989). Process power and decision outcomes among dual career couples. *Journal of Comparative Family Studies, 20*(2), 231-246.

Koff, W., & Hoth, D. F. (1988, July 22). Development and testing of AIDS vaccine. *Science, 241*, 426-431.

Lapp, C. A., Diemert, C. A., & Enestveldt, R. (1990). Family-based practice; discussion of a tool merging assessment. *Family Community Health, 12*(4), 21-28.

Levin, I., & Trost, J. (1992). Women and the concept of family (Family Reports 21). Uppsala, Sweden: Uppsala University.

Liprie, M. L., Hanks, R. S., & Berke, D. (1992). *Teen pregnancy: Decision making, critical thinking and locus of control.* Newark, DE: Final report Delaware department of public instruction, and University of Delaware.

McNamara, P. (1988). The new Christian right's view of the family and its social science critics: A study in differing presuppositions. In D. Thomas (Ed.), *The religion and family connection* (pp. 285-302). Salt Lake City, UT: Religions studies center, Brigham Young University.

Macklin, E. D. (1989). AIDS and families. *Marriage & Family Review, 13*(1&2).

Matocha, L. K. (1989). *The effects of AIDS on family member(s) responsible for care: A qualitative study.* Unpublished doctoral dissertation, University of Delaware, Newark, DE.

Menaghan, E. C., & Parcel, T. L. (1990). Parental employment and family life research in 1980's. *Journal of Marriage and the Family, 52*(4), 1079-1098.

Miller, B. C. (1987). Marriage, family and fertility. In M. B. Sussman & S. K. Steinmetz (Eds.), *Handbook on Marriage and the Family* (pp. 565-590). New York: Plenum.

Miller, B. C., & Moore, K. A. (1990). Adolescent sexual behavior, pregnancy and parenting: Research through the 1980's. *Journal of Marriage and the Family, 52*(4), 1025-1044.

Miller, J. A. (1987, January). The sandwich generation. *Working Mother,* 47-52.

Moen, P. (1992, March). A life course approach to women's multiple roles, health and well-being. *The Sociology of Aging Newsletter,* 8-12.

Mortimer, J. T., & London, J. (1984). The varying linkages of work and family. In P. Voyandoff (Ed.), *Changing roles of men and women* (pp. 20-22). Palo Alto, CA: Mayfield Publishing.

Mount, B. (1988, November, 2). *Personal futures planning: A person centered approach to service delivery.* Unpublished paper at the Conference on The Rights of Passage. Coordinating Council for the Handicapped Child of Delaware, Alfred I. DuPont Institute, Wilimington, DE.

Needle, R. H., & Leach, S. (1988). *The human immunodeficiency virus(HIV) epidemic: Epidemiologic implications for families.* Unpublished manuscript.

Palkovitz, R. (1992, November). Parenting as a generator of adult development: Conceptual issues and implications. Paper presented at the Theory Construction and Research Methodology Workshop, National Council on Family Relations Annual Meeting, Orlando, FL.

Phillips, L. R., & Rempushr, V. F. (1985). A decision making model for diagnosing and intervening in elder abuse and neglect. *Nursing Research, 34*(3), 134-139.

Pilisuk, M., & Parks, S. H. (1983). Social support and family stress. *Marriage & Family Review, 6*(1-2), 137-156.

Piotrakowski, C. S., Rapoport, R. N., & Rapoport, R. (1987). Families and Work. In M. B. Sussman & S. K. Steinmetz (Eds.), *Handbook on Marriage and the Family*. New York: Plenum.

Pitts, J. M. (1986, October, 4). Planning for tomorrow's elderly. *Economics Review*, 17-20.

Ransom, D. C., Fisher, L., Phillips, S., Kokes, R. F., & Weiss, R. (1990). The logic of family research. In T. W. Draper & A. C. Marcos (Eds.), *Family variables: Conceptualization, measurement and use* (pp. 48-66). Newbury Park, CA: Sage Publications.

Reid, W. J., Rotering, L., & Fortune, A. E. (1989). Family problem solving and therapy: A new look. *Family Therapy, 16*(3), 197-206.

Reiss, D. (1991, November). *Realignments in families of chronically ill patients: The death of the patient and the survival of the family*. Paper presented at the National Council on Family Relations Annual Meeting, Denver, CO.

Rettig, K. (1987). *A cognitive conceptual family decision making framework* (Tech. Rep. No. NCR116). MN: Family Resource Management Research Reporting Technical Group.

Rettig, K. D., Christenson, D. H., & Dahl, C. M. (1991). Impact of child support guidelines on the economic well-being of children. *Family Relations, 40*(2), 167-175.

Rock, M. S. (1992). *Analysis of variables Affecting Concern for future health planning in families*. Unpublished doctoral dissertation. Newark, DE: University of Delaware.

Roosa, M. W., Geusheimer, L. K., Short, J. L., Ayers, T. S., & Shell, R. (1989). A preventive intervention for children in alcoholic families: Results of a pilot study. *Family Relations, 38*, 295-300.

Russell, L. B. (1982). *The baby boom generation and the economy*. Washington, DC: Brookings Institution.

Salt, R. (1991). Child support in context; Comments on Rettig, Christensen & Dahl. *Family Relations, 40*(2), 175-178.

Sanborn, B., & Bould, S. (1991). Intergenerational caregivers of the oldest old. In S. Pfeifer & M. B. Sussman (Eds.), *Intergenerational and generational connections. Marriage & Family Review, 16*(1&2), 125-135.

Schoeman, F., & Reamer, F. (1983). Should child abuse always be reported. *Hastings Center Report, 13*(4), 19-20.

Schulz, D. A. (1985). The family has the right to make the decision to remove life-support systems if the affected individual is unable to do so. In H. Feldman & M. Feldman (Eds.), *Current Controversies in Marriage and the Family* (pp. 345-352). Newbury Park, CA: Sage.

Schvaneveldt, J. D., Lindauer, S. L. K., & Young, M. H. (1990). Children's understanding of AIDS: A developmental viewpoint. *Family Relations, 39*, 330-335.

Schwartzman, J, (1982). Normality from a cross-cultural perspective. In F. Walsh (Ed.), *Family process* (pp. 383-398). New York: The Guilford Press.

Segal, M. (1987). AIDS education. *FDA Consumer, 21*(7), 26-29.

Settles, B. H. (1987). A perspective on tomorrow's families. In M. B. Sussman & S. K. Steinmetz (Eds.), *Handbook of Marriage and the Family.* New York: Plenum.

Settles, B. H. (1990). *Interactive planning for family futures.* Final report Grant #0090AM0219, United States Department of Health and Human Services, Administration on Aging. University of Delaware, Newark, DE.

Settles, B. H. (1991, July). *Defining the family for the future.* Paper presented at The seminar of the Committee on Family Research of the International Sociological Society, Oslo, Norway.

Settles, B. H. (1992). *Changing social values.* Paper presented at the annual meeting of the American Home Economics Association, Denver CO.

Settles, B. H. (in press). The illusion of stability in family life; The reality of change and mobility. In B. H. Settles, D. Hanks, III, & M. B. Sussman (Eds.), Families on the Move. *Marriage & Family Review, 19*(1-4), The Haworth Press, Inc.

Settles, B. H., & Berke, D. (1989). *Jane and the job: A relocation simulation.* (Computer software). Newark, DE: University of Delaware.

Settles, B. H., & Foulke, S. R. (Eds.), (1989). *Family futures: A manual for peer leadership.* Newark, DE: University of Delaware.

Settles, B. H., & Hanks, R. S. (1988, May). *Personal privacy and dysfunctional autonomy: Defining boundaries.* Paper presented at the Groves Conference on Marriage and the Family. New Orleans, LA.

Settles, B. H., Hanks, III, D., & Sussman, M. B. (Eds.). (in press). Families on the Move. *Marriage & Family Review, 19*(1-4), The Haworth Press, Inc.

Settles, B. H., MacRostie, & Lucca, J. (1986, March). *Parental coping strategies in the management of cystic fibrosis.* Unpublished paper presented at the Second Annual Parenting Symposium. Philadelphia, PA.

Sillars, A. L., & Kalblesch, P. J. (1989). Implicit and explicit decision making styles in couples. In D. Brinberg & J. Jaccard (Eds.), *Dyadic decision making* (pp. 179-215). New York: Springer Verlag.

Spanier, G. B., & Furstenberg, Jr., F. F. (1987). Remarriage and reconstituted families. In M. B. Sussman & S. K. Steinmetz (Eds.), *Handbook of Marriage and the Family.* New York: Plenum.

Spitze, G. (1990). Women's employment and family relations: A review. *Journal of Marriage and the Family, 52,* 595-618.

Stein, P. J. (1983). Singlehood. In E. D. Macklin & R. Rubin (Eds.), *Contemporary family forms and alternative life styles: Handbook on research and theory.* Beverly Hills, CA: Sage.

Steinmetz, S. K. (1987). Family Violence: Past, present, future. In M. B. Sussman & S. K. Steinmetz (Eds.), *Handbook of Marriage and the Family.* New York: Plenum.

Strauss, A. L. (1984). *Chronic illness and the quality of life.* St. Louis, MO: Mosby.

Sussman, M. B. (1983). Law and legal system: The family connection. 1981 Burgess Award Address. *Journal of Marriage & the Family, 45*(1), 33-340.

Sussman, M. B. (1991). Reflections on intergenerational and kin connections. *Marriage & Family Review, 16*(1-2) 3-10.

Taylor, R. J., Chatters, L. M., Tucker, M. B., & Lewis, E. (1990). Developments in research on black families. *Journal of Marriage and the Family, 52*(5), 993-1014.

Teachman, J. D., Polonko, K. A., & Scanzoni, J. (1987). Demography of the family. In M. B. Sussman & S. K. Steinmetz (Eds.), *Handbook of Marriage and the Family* (pp. 3-36). New York: Plenum.

Thompson, J., & Bubolz, M. M. (1986, November). Energy in the family system. Paper presented at the Research and Theory Workshop of the National Council on Family Relations, Dearborn, MI.

Thompson, M., & Wildavsky, A. (1981, June). A proposal to create a cultural theory of risk. In H. C. & E. V. (Eds.), The risk analysis controversy in institutional perspective. *Proceedings IIASA.* Saxemburg, Austria.

Thomson, E. (1989). Dyadic models of contraceptive choice 1957 and 1975. In D. Brinberg & J. Jaccard (Eds.), *Decision making* (pp. 268-285). New York: Springer-Verlag.

Unger, D., & Powell. D. (1980). Supporting families under stress: The role of social networks. *Family Relations, 29*(4), 566-574.

Van Name, J. A. (1991). *Financial management practices of married single earner and dual earner families in Delaware.* Unpublished doctoral dissertation. Blackburg, VA: Virginia Polytechnic Institute and State University.

Vanek, J. (1974). Time spent in housework. *Scientific American, 231*(5), 116-120.

Volk, R. J., Edwards, D. W., Lewis, R. A., & Sprenkle, D. H. (1989). Family systems of adolescent substance abusers. *Family Relations, 38*, 266-272.

Voydanoff, P. (1990). Economic distress and family relations: A review of the eighties. *Journal of Marriage and the Family, 52*, 1099-1115.

Voydanoff, P., & Donnelly, B. W. (1988). Economic distress, family coping and quality of family. In P. Voydanoff & L. C. Majka (Eds.), *Families and economic distress: Coping strategies and social policy.* Newbury Park, CA: Sage Publications.

Walker, K. E., & Woods, M. E. (1976). *Time use: A measure of goods and services.* Washington, DC: American Home Economics Association.

Walsh, F. (1980). The family in later life. In E. A. Carter & M. McGoldrick (Eds.), *The family life cycle: A framework for family therapy* (pp. 197-220). New York: Gardner Press.

Wilson, N. J. (1988). *Long-range planning for the disabled. Working paper #10.1. Interactive Planning for Family Futures.* Unpublished manuscript. Newark, DE: University of Delaware.

Winnick, A. J. (1988). The changing distribution of income and wealth in the

United States 1960-1985: An examination of the movement toward two societies, "Separate and Unequal." In P. Voydanoff & L. C. Majka (Eds.), *Families and economic distress: Coping strategies and social policy* (pp. 232-260). Newbury Park, CA: Sage Publications.

Zimmerman, S. L. (1988). *Understanding family policy: Theoretical approaches.* Newbury Park, CA: Sage Publications.

DEMOGRAPHIC ISSUES

Recent Demographic Change: Implications for Families Planning for the Future

Teresa M. Cooney

SUMMARY. Because of dramatic reductions in mortality levels across the 20th century, most Americans today can anticipate living into old age. The predictability of a long-lived life today, however, is accompanied by increasingly diverse life opportunities and experiences. Partly as a result of reduced mortality, we have witnessed marked changes in marriage, divorce, fertility and employment patterns in recent decades. These demographic changes introduce both new chances and challenges for the life course of individuals. This chapter describes recent trends in mortality, fertility, marriage, di-

---

Teresa M. Cooney is affiliated with the Department of Individual and Family Studies, University of Delaware.

[Haworth co-indexing entry note]: "Recent Demographic Change: Implications for Families Planning for the Future." Cooney, Teresa M. Co-published simultaneously in *Marriage & Family Review* (The Haworth Press, Inc.) Vol. 18, No. 3/4, 1993, pp. 37-55; and: *American Families and the Future: Analyses of Possible Destinies* (ed: Barbara H. Settles, Roma S. Hanks, and Marvin B. Sussman) The Haworth Press, Inc., 1993, pp. 37-55. Multiple copies of this article/chapter may be purchased from The Haworth Document Delivery Center. Call 1-800-3-HA-WORTH (1-800-342-9678) between 9:00 - 5:00 (EST) and ask for DOCUMENT DELIVERY CENTER.

vorce and employment, and considers their implications for how individuals and their families plan and prepare for their later adult years.

KEYWORDS. Family demography, Mortality, Fertility, Marriage, Remarriage, Divorce, Employment patterns

INTRODUCTION

Several significant demographic changes have transpired over the 20th century that potentially affect how individuals and families approach their daily lives and relationships, and plan for their futures. At the forefront of these changes is the reduction in mortality and the subsequent increase in life expectancy. This demographic transformation has resulted in what Neugarten (1969) calls a more "normal expectable life cycle," meaning that compared to their predecessors, individuals today can more realistically anticipate and plan in advance for living a long life.

While important in its own right, reduced mortality also is significant because it provides a foundation for several other notable demographic changes occurring in this century. Among them are changes in marriage and divorce, fertility and labor force participation. Interestingly, although reduced mortality has *increased* the certainty of living a long life, in many ways it has *reduced* the predictability of life experiences in these other life domains. For example, because the chances of early death are lower today, married couples now confront a reduced risk of widowhood and heightened risk of divorce compared to their predecessors. Consequently, individuals today face greater diversity in marital patterns and statuses than did persons living early in the century. Similarly, because of increased longevity today, there is more variability in employment patterns than in the past. Rather than working right up until death at a relatively young age, as persons did early in the 20th century, today most people plan for a period of retirement at some point in late life. This plan usually consists of more time for leisure, but may also include options for subsequent careers. Greater diversity in work patterns is also evident for women today. With increased longevity and changes in fertility, a significant number of years have been added to the pre- and post-childbearing periods, thereby increasing women's opportunities for pursuing paid employment.

These examples illustrate how reduced mortality and extension of the average lifespan have created greater opportunity for individual choice in life situations and patterns–at least those involving marriage, fertility and employment. The choices made in all of these areas have a major impact on our long-term futures. Thus, it is important to recognize not only the chances of experiencing different life patterns and situations, but also how various experiences might affect our future well-being and security. In doing so, we can begin to anticipate and plan for some of the life situations that may lie ahead, and thus better prepare to cope with the likely consequences of these situations should they arise.

This paper reviews key demographic changes that have occurred in the areas of mortality, marriage, divorce, fertility and employment in the 20th century, in an effort to document the diversity of life experiences possible today. Projections of future trends in these areas are also presented to provide some guideposts for future planning. Finally, the implications of these trends for how individuals and families plan ahead for their personal and collective futures are considered.

MORTALITY AND LIFE EXPECTANCY

Average life expectancy at birth in the United States increased markedly–from 49 to 68 years–during the first half of the 20th century. Today, nearly four of five Americans are likely to reach age 65 (Seigel & Taeuber, 1986). Obtaining this milestone predicts even greater longevity; provisional data for 1990 indicates that by reaching the age interval 65-70, individuals can expect to live an average of 17.3 additional years beyond age 65 (National Center for Health Statistics, 1991). Moreover, the Social Security Administration (1982) estimates continued advances in reduced mortality, forecasting an average life expectancy of 76 years for the 1950 birth cohort.

Projections of future mortality and life expectancy depend on anticipated death rates and expected medical advancements. Under one scenario, if annual death rates drop continuously through 2050 at levels established since 1968, life expectancy at birth in 2050 would approach 100 years–up about 25 years from today (Seigel & Taeuber, 1986). In contrast, foreseeing no major medical or technological breakthroughs anytime soon and a 50% reduction in death rates between now and 2050, sets a high average life expectancy at birth in that year at 84 years (Social Security Administration, 1983). Currently, only 18% of deaths occur to persons over age 85; the corresponding figure in 2050 would be 43% given conservative projections (Seigel & Taeuber, 1986).

A major debate surrounding future life extension involves the issue of compression of morbidity. Because age and disability are highly correlated, the prospect of increased life expectancy raises the question of whether the years added to the average lifespan in the future will be characterized by good health or impairment. Currently, about three-quarters of the years individuals live beyond age 65 are disability-free. Yet, after age 85 this figure drops below 50% (Manton & Stallard, 1991). Thus, it is possible that as the individual lifespan approaches age 85, more of life will be spent in a disabled state. Yet, if reduced mortality is accompanied by reductions in morbidity in the future, chances of disability will not increase. Fries (1983), for example, argues that morbidity will become compressed around age 85 as the future average lifespan approaches that age. The disabled lifespan would thus decline.

In addition to the debate over the duration of dependence, many have questioned overall rates of disability in the future, given changes in morbidity in the recent past. Palmore's (1986) analysis of non-institutionalized elderly in the U.S. indicated reduced rates of bed disability, acute conditions and severe visual impairments between 1961 and 1981. But, he noted increases in injuries, visual and hearing problems. Crimmins, Saito and Ingegneri (1989), in contrast, examined data for institutionalized and community-dwelling populations and discovered increased rates of long-term (greater than 3 months) disability over the 1970s, but no change in short-term disability.

S. R. Zedlewski, R. O. Barnes, M. R. Burt, T. D. McBride and J. A. Meyer (1990) pose two scenarios regarding future disability. The first assumes that future reductions in mortality will not result in decreased disability. Thus, projecting current disability rates into the future, they estimate that 21.4% of the elderly will have some limitations of daily living activities in 2030, compared with 19.5% in 1990. The alternative scenario foresees declining morbidity along with mortality, resulting in a drop in limitations of daily living to 18.5% by 2030 (Zedlewski et al., 1990). These different scenarios do not pose dramatically different odds of disability for individuals in the future, predicting that about one person in five can expect to experience limitations in daily activities in later life.

The extension of life and the possibility of increased risk of impairment raises the issue of institutionalization and the elderly's need for special care in the future. Nationally representative data analyzed by Kemper and Murtaugh (1991) reveal that 43% of persons reaching age 65 in 1990 will experience a nursing home stay at some time in their lives. Furthermore, they estimate that for about 1 in 4 elderly, total lifetime use of nursing homes will exceed one year, and for almost 1 in 10 it will surpass five years. The chances of institutionalization are especially likely to climb if the duration of dependence increases in the future.

In discussing extended longevity, and chances of disability and institutionalization, it is important to note significant sex differences that exist. At birth today, female life expectancy exceeds that of males by 6.8 years (National Center for Health Statistics, 1991). Sex differences are reduced, however, once old age is reached. Still, at age 70, an independently functioning female can expect to live an additional 15.4 years–4.1 years longer than her male peers (Rogers, Rogers & Belanger, 1989). Yet, compared to men, women spend a greater portion of the extended lifespan disabled, and they experience a greater likelihood and duration of institutionalization (Kemper & Murtaugh, 1991).

The reduction of mortality and the routinization of death in old age has significant implications for how society and individuals plan for the future. Societal planning must focus on the health care system in particular, as increased longevity and numbers of elderly are likely to burden existing medical services (Siegel & Taeuber, 1986). For individuals, the increased certainty of living a long life also requires that they and their families anticipate and plan for personal care and security in old age.

The increased likelihood of living into old age, and the accompanying chances of experiencing at least some temporary bouts with disability and institutionalization perhaps have their greatest effect on individuals' financial planning and health care considerations. In coming years, an increasing share of the cost of elder care will probably be transferred from public sources to the aged and their families, since the former are likely to become increasingly strained by the dramatic growth in the elderly population (Weinraub, 1981). Currently, the average personal expenditure for health care services of the elderly is four times that of persons under age 65 (U.S. House of Representatives, 1983). The average Medicare enrollee pays over $1700/year in out-of-pocket health expenses (Congressional Budget Office, 1983). Furthermore, a one-year stay in an institution costs an average of $25,000 today, and is only partially covered by Medicare and other government insurance programs (Kemper & Murtaugh, 1991). Dramatic changes in government coverage are not likely in years to come either, given current budgetary problems.

Thus, it appears that individuals and their families–primarily offspring–will be forced to confront the planning needs associated with later life care. Already, about half of nursing home expenditures come from private sources (Letsch, Levit & Waldo, 1988), yet at the prices cited above it is unlikely that most families will be able to meet these exorbitant costs for any extended period. Thus, one option that is becoming increasingly necessary for families is that of investing in adequate medical insurance. Yet, many families do not realize the extreme cost of insurance for the aged, and the fact that these rates are mounting rapidly (Wiener, Ehrenworth & Spence, 1987).

If medical insurance is the option families choose, it is probably best for them to invest early in the chosen policies. This approach is likely to secure lower yearly premiums for the older individual. Also, purchasing the plan before the onset of old age and its associated health problems, is likely to result in fewer limitations in coverage due to pre-existing conditions.

Purchasing some type of long-term care coverage also is important as individuals possibly face an increased risk of disability and institutionalization. This issue is particularly critical for women, since they outlive men, and thus often lose their partners who might have provided in-home care for them. Long-term care options have increased in recent years. Today, individuals can choose from long-term care insurance, Life Care at Home policies, and many other types of plans. Most plans, however, are not without limitations. For example, some policies only provide for three to five years of nursing home care. In addition, policies often fail to factor in inflation, and by the time payment of benefits is required their value may have deteriorated (Kemper & Murtaugh, 1991).

Yet, regardless of these shortcomings, long-term care coverage is something an increasing number of families will need to consider in years to come. Cohen, Tell, Greenberg and Wallock (1987) claim that 50-80% of elderly today can afford some type of long-term care option if they are willing to spend some of their assets. They suggest that the care choices the elderly and near elderly make should depend on their perceived health risk, financial resources, and the importance they place on health and security.

MARRIAGE

The United States has witnessed dramatic changes in the timing and rate of marriage since the 1950s. Marriage rates have dropped steadily over this period, particularly at the ages typically reserved for this transition. In 1970, only one in ten women and approximately 20% of men remained never-married by ages 25-29, compared to over 45% of men and almost one-third of women in 1989 (United States Bureau of the Census, 1991). Median age at first marriage in 1987 had risen to 25.3 and 23.6 for men and women respectively, up approximately 10% since the 1950s (U.S. Bureau of the Census, 1991). As a result of current marriage trends (and divorce and remarriage trends which are discussed below), the proportion of adult life spent married is currently declining. Compared with women in 1945-50, women today spend approximately 20% less of their adult lives married (Espenshade, 1985).

While there is no question that the *timing* of marriage is later today than in the 1950s, there is less certainty whether the ultimate likelihood of marriage also has fallen. Rodgers and Thornton (1985) estimate that only about 90% of the 1954 birth cohort will eventually marry, compared with 95-98% of cohorts coming of age in the 1950s. Such long-range projections of marriage patterns depend heavily on the theories to which one subscribes. According to linear theories of social change, we are unlikely to see a shift in current marriage patterns anytime soon because the social factors that contributed to their development, for example increased female labor force participation and earnings power, and non-marital sexual activity, have been fairly steady. Cyclical theories, in contrast, view marriage behavior as responsive to such cycles as those produced by the economy and changes in cohort size. Accordingly, Easterlin and others predict earlier and more marriages in the 1990s than in recent years (Espenshade, 1985), since smaller birth cohorts will enter adulthood during this period and will face improved economic prospects compared to young adults of recent decades. Still, it is debatable whether future cohorts will use their improved economic position to marry and form families earlier, or to enrich their single lifestyle.

Either way, marriage patterns have significant implications for the persons experiencing them and their parents. For parents, marriage patterns are likely to affect the duration of dependency by children. To illustrate, today's parents can expect their offspring to live at home longer than in recent decades. Between 1970 and 1984 the proportion of persons aged 20-24 living with parents rose from 37 to 45% (Glick & Lin, 1986). This change can be mainly attributed to delayed marriage and extended schooling by recent cohorts.

If coresidence of adult offspring with their parents results in continued economic dependence on the part of children, at least for housing, utilities and food, then patterns of reduced spending and increased savings parents might have anticipated for their middle years may need to be postponed. Also, later marriage is closely connected with extended schooling. Thus, should future cohorts of young adults continue to delay marriage and pursue advanced education, an increasing proportion of parents may need to plan for the expenses of higher education for their offspring.

Delaying or foregoing marriage altogether raises planning concerns for young adults as well. First, along with later marriage in recent decades there has been an increase in non-marital cohabitation. The likelihood that young adults will ever cohabit is now over 40%. Yet, for most couples, cohabitation is a transient state (median duration of 1.3 years), with about 40% of such relationships ending in less than a year (Bumpass & Sweet,

1989). Consequently, more young adults can anticipate being involved in such unions in the future. Still, they should not expect cohabitation to provide long-term security, as the chances of being on one's own again and fully responsible for one's living expenses are high following the initiation of such unions. How one approaches spending and saving money while cohabiting is thus important to consider. Since the odds of dissolving the relationship relatively quickly are high, one might opt for as much economic independence as possible within the union. This includes maintaining separate banking accounts and avoiding the joint-purchasing of big-ticket items.

Young people also should consider the potential impact of current marriage trends for their long-range future planning. Given current marriage patterns, individuals today may best be advised to start saving for buying a home and retirement long before they ever marry. Because these tasks require long-term planning and action, the chances of managing them successfully today may be jeopardized if one waits until marriage to initiate them.

FERTILITY

Fertility trends have mimicked those of marriage in recent years, with birth rates dropping and a delay in childbearing. Today, the United States fertility rate hovers around 70 births per 1000 women of childbearing age–lower than at any point since the early 1900s, and significantly below the 20th century high of nearly 120 births in the late 1950s (National Center for Health Statistics, 1990a). In part, general fertility has fallen because greater proportions of women are postponing births beyond the prime childbearing ages. The median age at first birth today is approximately 23.7 for women, much above the century low of 21.8 in 1960 (National Center for Health Statistics, 1990b). Over 30% of women reaching age 30 in 1988 were still childless, compared with only 19% in 1975. Recently, however, older women have shown a steady increase in birth rates, with the rate increasing 43% between 1975 and 1988 for women aged 35-39 (National Center for Health Statistics, 1990a).

Despite recent surges in delayed childbearing, it appears unlikely that fertility rates will increase noticeably in the near future. As Rindfuss, Morgan and Swicegood (1988) document, childbearing delays in one's 20s typically result in reduced total fertility. Thus, these authors estimate that about one-fifth of the 1954 birth cohort will be permanently childless, a level almost matching that prior to World War II.

Bumpass (1990) also forecasts the maintenance of low fertility into the future. He anticipates a drop in both planned and unplanned fertility in coming years, based on persistent trends in such social factors as women's commitment to the labor force and high divorce rates. Furthermore, he expects significantly improved methods of contraception in the future, which will reduce currently high levels of unplanned fertility.

Estimates of family size for older women made by The Urban Institute (Zedlewski et al., 1990) also indicate marked changes over the next half century. Today, women age 65 have an average of 3.08 children. But, by 2011-15, this figure will drop to 2.00. The average number of children is expected to dip below 2.00 by 2016 and to remain at that low level at least until 2030 (Zedlewski et al., 1990).

Anticipated changes in fertility have serious implications for how individuals plan for their later lives. While delayed childbearing is typically considered beneficial for young couples because it provides time to gain financial security and establish relationship stability, it may create "life-cycle squeezes" during the couple's later years. Rossi and Rossi (1990) note that when childbearing is postponed until the mid to late 30s, couples are more likely to enter old age before their children have fully established their careers and achieved financial stability. Such parents may be faced with reduced resources and heightened needs before their children can help them and when they still have need for parental assistance. Conversely, early childbearing couples are likely to reach their peak earnings and savings when their children are young adults, and enter old age as their offspring reach their earnings' peak. Thus, the life cycle squeeze for these parents occurs early in the childrearing years, and, in old age, they are more comfortably situated. In terms of long-range planning, couples who postpone parenting may thus be well advised to save and plan for retirement more carefully than their early child-bearing peers, and to ensure means of independently supporting themselves without assistance from children in later life.

Total fertility also has implications for well-being and security in mid to late life. For parents, declining family size means a marked reduction in the number of adult children available to serve as informal supports for them in old age. For middle-aged adults, the trend suggests the possibility of increased burden in providing physical, emotional, and financial assistance to aging parents, as families will have fewer siblings to share these demands. In addition, family size partly determines when parents will experience a resource squeeze: compared to their contemporaries with large families, parents with fewer children will face reduced economic, emotional and time pressures during the childrearing years. But, in old age, they are less likely to receive support from their children (Uhlenberg &

Cooney, 1990). This relative lack of filial assistance could leave many elderly with small families without the resources required to meet the greater financial and physical demands of later life.

DIVORCE AND REMARRIAGE

Divorce rates have climbed throughout most of the 20th century. In the early 1940s, only about one in seven women could anticipate experiencing a divorce; by 1980, the odds had increased to about 50% (Espenshade, 1985; Martin & Bumpass, 1989). Recently, divorce rates have stabilized (Norton & Moorman, 1987), but primarily among younger couples. Growth rates in divorce among middle-aged and older individuals are still on the rise (Uhlenberg, Cooney & Boyd, 1990); during the 1980s the divorce rate for persons over age 50 climbed 15% (National Center for Health Statistics, 1992). Hence, future life-time expectancies for divorce may jump even higher than today's levels.

While divorce rates soared in recent decades, remarriage rates plummeted. Since 1965, remarriage rates for women have fallen 40-50%, depending on age (Uhlenberg et al., 1990). The 1970-1980 decline was sharp for men as well, with rates falling 58% for those under age 45 and 25% among the middle aged (Goldscheider, 1990).

Leveling off of divorce rates in the 1980s does not necessarily signal an end to high levels of marital disruption. Bumpass (1990) argues that a similar 15-year plateau occurred in the United States before rates accelerated in 1960. As noted, his work suggests that over half of unions formed today will eventually end in divorce. It is possible, however, that future divorce rates will be suppressed as a result of current cohabitation levels. That is, in the future, many unions may be dissolved after a period of non-marital cohabitation, whereas in the past these unions might have progressed to marriage and subsequently ended through divorce (Bumpass, 1990). Cohabitation could similarly reduce remarriage rates since previously married persons have higher cohabitation rates than never-married persons (Bumpass & Sweet, 1989). After experiencing failure with the institution of marriage, more and more persons in the future may settle for cohabiting unions rather than remarriage as the former become increasingly acceptable.

Some of the most striking changes in future marital status patterns are anticipated for middle-aged and older persons, given their exposure to dramatically different mortality, marriage, remarriage and divorce regimes across their lives, compared to today's elderly. It is projected that when female baby boomers reach middle age, a third will be living outside of marriage compared with only about one-quarter of middle aged women today. Furthermore, at ages 65-69, over 20% will be divorced, fewer than one in five will be widowed and about one in ten will have never married (Uhlenberg et al., 1990). Even more striking is Goldscheider's (1990) claim that the percentage of ever-divorced among retirees may more than double–to about 50%–in the next 20 years. Among men 55-64, there is expected to be almost four times as many divorced as widowed by the year 2000 (Uhlenberg, 1990).

The economic consequences of divorce pose major concerns when planning for one's future. Women, in particular, are affected by the financial setbacks of divorce. On average, they experience a 30% reduction in income (controlling for changes in needs) following marital dissolution, which is likely to persist unless they remarry. Conversely, the average man faces improved financial conditions post-divorce (Duncan & Hoffman, 1985).

The financial set-backs associated with divorce appear to endure for women as they move into mid and later life. Comparing 1985 Current Population Survey data for married, divorced and widowed women, aged 40 and over, Uhlenberg et al. (1990) found divorced women at greatest risk financially. Not only were they living closer to the poverty line than widows, despite higher rates of labor force participation, they also had fewer assets than widows, with particularly striking differences in home-ownership. Moreover, the economic consequences of divorce appeared almost as severe for women who had divorced more than five years prior to the survey as they were for recent divorcees. Thus, experiencing divorce at any point in adulthood has serious consequences for women's financial security in later life. Still, the divorced are not the only group of formerly married to face financial hardship. Smith and Zick (1986) report that older widows have about a one in three chance of falling into poverty at some point during widowhood.

The risk of marital disruption and its consequences must be confronted when planning for later life. Not only does divorce threaten most of the accumulated wealth young couples have, but the chances of rebuilding this wealth post-divorce are limited because of increased expenses and legal costs (Fethke, 1989). Fethke (1989) contends that even the mere anticipation of divorce may result in reduced savings by married couples. Later life financial preparations also could be seriously jeopardized by divorce, since shifting assets out of marital property may result in liquidity problems and lower rates of return on assets. Finally, the post-retirement situation of at least one partner is likely to be hurt because of pension division and loss of insurance benefits following divorce (Fethke, 1989).

Written marital agreements are becoming an increasingly popular way of protecting one's individual interests in case of divorce, although their legal status is questionable (Weitzman, 1981). These contracts usually address such economic issues as the division of income and property, responsibility for non-wage family work and earning money, and support of various family members. The need to re-evaluate and possibly revise such agreements as time passes and new situations arise has been emphasized (Havemann & Lehtinen, 1986). Weitzman (1981) provides helpful guidelines for and examples of such agreements.

While the economic impact of marital disruption is most severe for women, for men the social effects are especially significant and potentially problematic. National survey data indicate that compared to continuously married men, ever-divorced older men are less likely to have steady contact with their adult offspring and to consider them potential sources of support in times of need (Cooney & Uhlenberg, 1990). As Goldscheider (1990) notes, such effects could place men in a particularly vulnerable position in old age when income related resources lose importance and those resulting from family ties assume greater significance. Viewing children as a source of security in old age is, thus, something fewer men may be able to do in the future, given today's high divorce rates and widespread maternal custody. The potential loss of this valuable resource demands that men plan for other sources of support, perhaps more formal ones, in later life.

WOMEN'S LABOR FORCE PARTICIPATION

One of the most dramatic labor force transformations in this century has been the tremendous increase of women in the paid work force. Only 43% of women were employed in 1970, compared to over 57% today (U.S. Bureau of the Census, 1991). The most growth in labor force involvement has occurred among married women. While single women have always had high participation rates (about 75% in 1960 and today), rates for married women were low until recent decades. In 1960, only 30.5% of married women were employed, compared to 57.8% in 1989. Also, young children are no longer a strong deterrent to women's labor force involvement. In 1960, married women with preschoolers were only half as likely as their peers with school-aged children to be employed. This difference fell dramatically by 1989 as 58% of married women with preschoolers and two-thirds of those with school-aged offspring were in the labor force (U.S. Bureau of the Census, 1991).

As women continue to pursue advanced education and bear relatively few children, they are expected to at least maintain, and possibly increase their commitment to paid employment in the future. The U.S. Bureau of the Census (1990) projects that the rate of female labor force participation will climb 11% between 1988 and 2000. Predicted increases in labor force involvement are slightly higher for women of childbearing age.

Consequently, women's economic dependency within marriage should decline in the future, as it has in recent decades (Sorensen & McLanahan, 1987). Therefore, the economic blow women experience following marital disruption should be softened somewhat in years to come. Still, it is un- likely that unmarried women will fare as well as their male peers anytime soon, particularly if they have children, since gender disparities in pay have been steady for several decades (Cooney & Uhlenberg, 1991). Fur- thermore, women still contribute the majority of support and care for children following divorce and nonmarital births.

Women's increased labor force involvement is, however, likely to influ- ence their planning for later life. Hatch (1990) concludes that women's access to pensions and Social Security benefits will markedly improve in the future because of their current and projected labor force experience. In 1960, 60-year-old women, on average, worked 11 of 40 years of their adult life. In 1990 they had worked 16 years, and women age 60 in the years 2000 and 2010 are expected to have worked 20 and 26 years of adulthood, respectively (Goldscheider, 1990). This change is critical since future cohorts of older women are less likely to be married than current ones, and to have a husband's pension or benefits on which to depend. Still, neither women's rates of pension participation nor their pension earnings are likely to match those of men in the near future, given females' concentra- tion in jobs in the secondary labor market that is characterized by lower pay and inadequate pension benefits (Hatch, 1990). Thus, tomorrow's older women, particularly the unmarried, will face greater financial risk than men, although they should be better situated than elderly women today.

Finally, because women typically earn less than men, their retirement savings are likely to be lower, as are their chances of home-ownership and the accumulation of other resources that serve as valuable assets in old age. These inequities may require that women, especially unmarried ones, initiate long-range planning for old age long before their male peers do, to ensure adequate accumulation of resources by late life. Furthermore, since women can expect to live longer than men and experience more years requiring care and possibly institutionalization, their rate of savings should also be greater than that of their male peers.

RETIREMENT

Another significant change in 20th century work behavior involves men and the timing of their retirement. Recently, retirement for men has occurred at increasingly younger ages. Between 1972 and 1980, working life expectancy at age 55 fell from 7 to 5.15 years in low specialization occupations and from 7.5 to 6.6 years in high specialization ones (Hayward, Grady & McLaughlin, 1988). Thus, early retirement is now the norm, with over 60% of those eligible for early Social Security benefits accepting them at age 61 (Morrison, 1986). While nearly half of elderly men were employed in 1950, the same is true of only 16% of older men today. Given increased life expectancy, earlier retirement means that a greater share of the adult years is now spent retired. Retirement occupied only 7% of adulthood in 1940, compared with 25% today (Palmer & Gould, 1986).

Future patterns of retirement are difficult to project because of recent legislative action concerning Social Security benefits. In 1983, new Social Security Amendments were passed which gradually raise the age at eligibility for benefits. Many (Chen, 1987; Gohmann, 1990; Gohmann & Clark, 1989) question whether this legislation will alter future retirement scheduling. Yet, most recent research suggests minimal changes in retirement patterns in the future unless new work incentives and programs are initiated for the elderly. Gohmann and Clark (1989) argue that most of the response to the Social Security Amendments will come in the form of a shifting age at which the elderly move from full-time to part-time work. While a slight delay in full retirement may occur between ages 62 and 64, the probability of retirement at age 65 will likely increase. Thus, they expect a large share of future retirees to enter retirement early, without full Social Security benefits.

An extended retirement period is primarily of concern because of the reduced standard of living that usually accompanies withdrawal from the labor force. In 1980, the average per capita income for individuals aged 65 and older was only 75% that of persons aged 55-64 (Palmer & Gould, 1986). Retired persons spend a lower proportion of their reduced income on food, consumer goods, and recreation than the non-retired elderly. Yet, they spend a greater share on housing, utilities and medical care. Five percent of each dollar goes to medical expenses among this group, compared to only 1% for non-retired persons (McConnel & Deljavan, 1983). This fact raises concern for the financial well-being of the retired, as they face a longer retirement period in the future, and perhaps greater chances of disability and sky-rocketing health care costs.

More importantly, these figures pertain to averages, and thus gloss over added hardships a significant minority of the elderly population may confront. Economic disparities are wider spread in the elderly population than among the non-aged (Palmer & Gould, 1986). At greatest financial risk are average-income and near-poor elderly who depend heavily on Medicare, which covers only about half of medical costs and none of the expenses of long-term or acute care. Unexpected medical expenses and crises can put these groups on the brink of financial disaster. Individuals without pensions and widows also are prone to economic catastrophe in the retirement years. One prospective study that followed retired persons over a 10-year period found that almost 6% fell into poverty in the two years immediately after retirement. By 10-years post-retirement, 28% of non-pensioned widows and about 15% of other widows had bouts with poverty. Among the married, rates were 5% and 18%, respectively, for those with and without pensions (Burkhauser et al., 1988). It thus appears that those hurt most by recent Social Security legislation will be minorities, unmarried women and the near poor–groups for whom this income comprises the greatest portion of total wealth (Gohmann, 1990).

In sum, more elderly in the future face heightened risk for economic problems unless they rethink their plans for retirement timing, and plan well for economic support. Survey data collected by Louis Harris & Associates (1981) indicate that a significant portion of older Americans would prefer to maintain a role in the workforce in later life, despite having already retired. This finding suggests that much of the early retirement observed today is not completely voluntary and may result instead from such pressures as threats of layoff, reduced earnings increases, worker discouragement, infirmity and/or changing technology (Bass, 1988). Given the option to continue in a more flexible, age-appropriate job, many elderly would likely choose to continue being productive members of the labor force. Yet, there has been little societal-level action to increase employment opportunities for this group. Hopefully, in the future, government and private sector initiatives will make such options as retraining, flexible scheduling and career switches at mid to late life more feasible for the majority of the middle-aged and older population.

Until that time, most Americans will probably continue to plan for retirement as they have done in the recent past. According to Ferraro (1990), however, most adults do very little comprehensive retirement planning, and more recent birth cohorts are preparing even less for this life stage, through such actions as savings, pension preparation, and home ownership than did earlier ones. Thus, in his view, tomorrow's elderly will be even more financially vulnerable than today's aged population.

CONCLUSIONS

As we head into the 21st century, individuals and their families are confronted with a more diverse array of possible life experiences than has ever existed before. Changes in mortality and longevity, marriage, fertility and employment behavior discussed in this article, have created new opportunities for individual choice and variability in life course experiences. One important consequence of increased diversity is reduced certainty about what the future holds in store.

Thus, the need for flexible futures planning is greater now than in the past. In order to prepare effectively today, we must be aware of the full scope of possible experiences–both positive and negative–that lie ahead and the likely consequences of these experiences for our future well-being. Certainly, in such a context, planning for the future is neither easy nor pleasant. On the surface, anticipating and planning for the possibility of such undesirable events as disability or divorce seems cynical and possibly self-fulfilling. Yet, the high risk of such events occurring in one's life is very real. To deny their potential can only increase the chances of experiencing the setbacks associated with such situations should they occur.

In sum, this paper has reviewed a number of recent demographic changes that one's future plans might account for. To simplify matters these changes were presented as discrete, independent events. Yet, it is important to realize that in making long-term plans, we must also consider the effects of experiencing various combinations of these events in our lives. Accounting for a diverse, potentially complex life course is one of the major challenges future planning presents us.

REFERENCES

Bass, S. A. (1988). The role of higher education in creating economic roles. In R. Morris & S. A. Bass (Eds.), *Retirement reconsidered: Economic and social roles for older people* (pp. 222-231). New York: Springer.

Bumpass, L. L. (1990). What's happening to the family? Interactions between demographic and institutional change. *Demography, 27*, 483-498.

Bumpass, L. L. & Sweet, J. A. (1989). National estimates of cohabitation. *Demography, 26,* 615-625.

Burkhauser, R. V., Holden, K. C. & Feaster, D. (1988). Incidence, timing, and events associated with poverty: A dynamic view of poverty in retirement. *Journal of Gerontology: Social Sciences, 43,* S46-52.

Chen, Y. P. (1987). Making assets out of tomorrow's elderly. *The Gerontologist, 27,* 410-416.

Cohen, M. A., Tell, E. J., Greenberg, J. N. & Wallock, S. S. (1987). The financial capacity of the elderly to insure for long-term care. *The Gerontologist, 27,* 494-502.

Congressional Budget Office (March, 1983). *Changing structure of Medicare benefits: Issues and options.* Washington, DC: U.S Government Printing Office.

Cooney, T. M. & Uhlenberg, P. (1990). The role of divorce in men's relations with their adult children after mid-life. *Journal of Marriage and the Family, 52,* 677-688.

Cooney, T. M. & Uhlenberg, P. (1991). Changes in work-family connections among highly educated men and women: 1970-1980. *Journal of Family Issues, 12,* 69-90.

Crimmins, E. M., Saito, Y. & Ingegneri, D. (1989). Changes in life expectancy and disability-free life expectancy in the United States. *Population and Development Review, 15,* 235-267.

Duncan, G. J. & Hoffman, S. D. (1985). A reconsideration of the economic consequences of divorce. *Demography, 22,* 485-497.

Espenshade, T. J. (1985). Marriage trends in America: Estimates, implications, and underlying causes. *Population and Development Review, 11,* 193-245.

Ferraro, K. F. (1990). Cohort analysis of retirement preparation, 1974-81. *Journal of Gerontology: Social Sciences, 45,* S21-31.

Fethke, C. C. (1989). Life cycle models of saving and the effect of the timing of divorce on retirement economic well-being. *Journal of Gerontology: Social Sciences, 44,* S121-128.

Fries, J. F. (1983). The compression of morbidity. *Milbank Memorial Fund Quarterly/Health and Society, 61,* 397-419.

Glick, P. C. & Lin, S. L. (1986). More young adults are living with their parents: Who are they? *Journal of Marriage and the Family, 48,* 107-112.

Gohmann, S. F. (1990). Retirement differences among the respondents to the Retirement History Survey. *Journal of Gerontology: Social Sciences, 45,* S120-127.

Gohmann, S. F. & Clark, R. L. (1989). Retirement responses to Social Security changes. *Journal of Gerontology: Social Sciences, 44,* S218-225.

Goldscheider, F. K. (1990). The aging of the gender revolution: What do we know and what do we need to know? *Research on Aging, 12,* 531-545.

Harris, L. & Associates, Inc. (1981). *Aging in the eighties: America in transition.* Washington, D.C.: The National Council on the Aging.

Hatch, L. (1990). Effects of work and family on women's later-life resources. *Research on Aging, 12*, 311-338.

Havemann, E., & Lehtinen, M. (1986). *Marriage and families: New problems, new opportunities.* Englewood Cliffs, N.J.: Prentice Hall.

Hayward, M. D., Grady, W. R., & McLaughlin, S. D. (1988). Changes in the retirement process among older men in the United States: 1972-80. *Demography, 25*, 371-386.

Kemper, P., & Murtaugh, C. M. (1991). Lifetime use of nursing home care. *The New England Journal of Medicine, 324*, 595-600.

Letsch, S. W., Levit, K. R., & Waldo, D. R. (1988). National health expenditures, 1987. *Health Care Financial Review, 10*, 109-122.

Manton, K. G. &, Stallard, E. (1991). Cross-sectional estimates of active life expectancy for the U.S. elderly and oldest-old populations. *Journal of Gerontology: Social Sciences, 46*, S170-182.

Martin, T. C., & Bumpass, L. L. (1989). Recent trends in marital disruption. *Demography, 26*, 37-51.

McConnel, C. E., & Deljavan, F. (1983). Consumption patterns of the retired household. *Journal of Gerontology, 38*, 480-490.

Morrison, M. H. (1986). Work and retirement in an aging society. *Daedalus, 115*, 269-293.

National Center for Health Statistics (1992). Personal correspondence.

National Center for Health Statistics (1990a). Advance report of final natality statistics, 1988. *Monthly Vital Statistics Report, 39*(4), supplement. Hyattsville, MD: Public Health Service.

National Center for Health Statistics (1990b). *Vital statistics of the United States: 1988, Vol. 1, Natality.* Washington, DC: U. S. Government Printing Office.

National Center for Health Statistics (1991). Annual summary of births, marriages, divorces and deaths in the United States: 1990. *Monthly Vital Statistics Report, 39*(13).

Neugarten, B. N. (1969). Continuities and discontinuities of psychological issues in adult life. *Human Development, 12*, 121-130.

Norton, A. J., & Moorman, J. E. (1987). Current trends in marriage and divorce among American women. *Journal of Marriage and the Family, 49*, 3-14.

Palmer, J. L., & Gould, S. G. (1986). The economic consequences of an aging society. *Daedalus, 115*, 295-323.

Palmore, E. B. (1986). Trends in the health of the aged. *The Gerontologist, 26*, 298-302.

Rindfuss, R. R., Morgan, S. P., & Swicegood, G. (1988). *First births in America: Changes in the timing of parenthood.* Berkeley, CA: University of California Press.

Rodgers, W. L., & Thornton, A. (1985). Changing patterns of first marriage in the United States. *Demography, 22*, 265-279.

Rogers, R. G., Rogers, A., & Belanger, A. (1989). Active life among the elderly in the United States: Multistate life-table estimates and population projections. *The Milbank Quarterly, 67*, 370-411.

Rossi, A. S., & Rossi, P. H. (1990). *Of human bonding: Parent-child relations across the life course.* New York: Aldine de Gruyter.

Seigel, J. S., & Taeuber, C. M. (1986). Demographic perspectives on the long-lived society. *Daedalus, 115,* 77-117.

Smith, K. R., & Zick, C. D. (1986). The incidence of poverty among the recently widowed: Mediating factors in the life course. *Journal of Marriage and the Family, 48,* 619-630.

Social Security Administration (1982). United States Office of the Actuary, "Life Tables for the U.S.: 1900-2050." Actuarial study no. 87, by J. F. Faber, September.

Social Security Administration (1983). United States Office of the Actuary, "Social Security Area Population Projections" Actuarial study no. 88, by J. C. Wilkins, August.

Sorensen, A., & McLanahan, S. (1987). Married women's economic dependence, 1940-1980. *American Journal of Sociology, 93,* 659-687.

Uhlenberg, P. (1990). *Implications of increasing divorce for the elderly.* Paper presented at the United Nations International Conference on Aging Populations in the Context of the Family, Kitakyushu, Japan.

Uhlenberg, P., & Cooney, T. M. (1990). Family size and mother-child relations in later life. *The Gerontologist, 30,* 618-625.

Uhlenberg, P., Cooney, T. M., & Boyd, R. (1990). Divorce for women after midlife. *Journal of Gerontology: Social Sciences, 45,* S3-11.

United States Bureau of the Census (1990). *Statistical abstracts of the United States: 1990* (110th edition). Washington, DC: U.S. Government Printing Office.

United States Bureau of the Census (1991). *Statistical abstracts of the United States: 1992* (111th edition). Washington, DC: U.S. Government Printing Office.

United States House of Representatives (1983, February). *Background information on programs under the jurisdiction of the Committee on Ways and Means.* Unpublished report, Committee on Ways and Means.

Weinraub, B. (1981, April 16). Home care is pushed in Senate as alternative to institutions for the aged. *New York Times.*

Weitzman, L. (1981). *The marriage contract: Spouses, lovers and the law.* New York: The Free Press.

Wiener, J. M., Ehrenworth, D. A., & Spence, D. A. (1987). Private long-term care insurance: Cost, coverage and restrictions. *The Gerontologist, 27,* 487-493.

Zedlewski, S. R., Barnes, R. O., Burt, M. R., McBride, T. D., & Meyer, J. A. (1990). *The needs of the elderly in the 21st century.* Washington, DC: Urban Institute Press.

Present and Future Health Care
for an Aging Society:
A Proactive Self-Health Approach

Norma O. Doolittle
Stephanie D. Wiggins

SUMMARY. Numbers of elderly are increasing and those over 85 make up the fastest growing group in America. This aging trend is

Norma O. Doolittle is Associate Professor of Adult Health Nursing, College of Nursing, University of South Alabama, Mobile, AL 36688. Dr. Doolittle teaches both graduate and undergraduate students and is an active member in Sigma Theta Tau, National League for Nursing, American Nurses Association, National Gerontological Nursing Association Phi Kappa Phi. Stephanie D. Wiggins is Assistant Professor of Adult Health Nursing also in College of Nursing, University of South Alabama. Dr. Wiggins teaches graduate and undergraduate students and is active in Sigma Theta Tau.

[Haworth co-indexing entry note]: "Present and Future Health Care for an Aging Society: A Proactive Self-Health Approach." Doolittle, Norma O. and Stephanie D. Wiggins. Co-published simultaneously in *Marriage & Family Review* (The Haworth Press, Inc.) Vol. 18, No. 3/4, 1993, pp. 57-71; and: *American Families and the Future: Analyses of Possible Destinies* (ed: Barbara H. Settles, Roma S. Hanks, and Marvin B. Sussman) The Haworth Press, Inc., 1993, pp. 57-71. Multiple copies of this article/chapter may be purchased from The Haworth Document Delivery Center. Call 1-800-3-HAWORTH (1-800-342-9678) between 9:00 - 5:00 (EST) and ask for DOCUMENT DELIVERY CENTER.

predicted to have an impact as great as any economic or social movement in our history. The purpose of this paper is to briefly review health care issues and concerns for elderly; to discuss health care reform; to address strategies for self-health promotion, illness prevention, and optimum adaptation to chronic illness; and to propose individual and family participation in health promotion, based on Olson's (1988) theoretical constructs about family systems, and Orem's (1985) concept of care. The authors believe that individuals and families can play a significant proactive role in resolving the health care crisis.

KEYWORDS. Self-health, Self-care, Health care reform, Health care proposals, Family cohession, Adaptability, Communication, Caring

INTRODUCTION

Current demographic changes in America's graying society are unprecedented! While there are now over 33 million Americans age 65 and older, those over 85 make up the fastest growing group in the population. Between 1950 and 1980, the numbers of persons 85 and older increased 165% (Biegel & Blum, 1990). The current rate of increase for the older old group is six times that of the general population (Lonergan & Krevans, 1991). The impact of this aging trend by the middle of the 21st century "will have been at least as powerful as that of any of the great economic and social movements of the past" (Pifer & Bronte, 1986, p. 3).

The purpose of this paper is to briefly review health care issues and associated concerns for elderly health care; to discuss selected proposals for health care reform; and to discuss how individuals and families can promote positive health based on the three dimensions of Olson's (1988) theoretical constructs about family systems. These include family cohesion, adaptability, communication, and Orem's (1985) concept of self-care. It is the belief of the authors that individuals and families can be involved proactively in self-health improvement, thus playing a significant role in resolving the health care crisis in America. Such proaction has positive health implications for all age groups, especially for the elderly.

The 20th century has been characterized by unprecedented political and technological change. Today's elderly have helped to bring about the transition in the United States "from a peaceful, isolationist, horse-and-buggy society at the beginning of the century" to "an industrial society of awesome scientific and technical skills, the inventor of atomic power, and the most influential nation of the world" (AMA Council on Scientific Affairs, 1990, p. 1184). While concomitant goals of greater prosperity, improved living conditions, and better health have been realized by most Americans, concerns have risen sharply related to the current and predicted prevalence of chronic illness; limited access to health care; lack of insurance coverage; rising health care costs, especially for the elderly; and smaller ratios of those in the work force to growing numbers of older persons needing care. According to the World Health Organization's "Health for All by the Year 2000," resources for health will be evenly distributed and essential health care will be accessible to all people (Little, 1992). Major questions are: Who will pay for needed health care? Who will provide future health care? How may the present health care system be reformed to meet anticipated needs of the future? What role can individuals and families play to help resolve the health care crisis?

The growing prevalence of chronic illness is especially apparent in older population cohorts as they age. Nearly half of all noninstitutionalized persons over age 65 are limited by at least one chronic condition (Lubkin, 1986). Twenty-three percent of those 65 and older are disabled in one or more aspects of self-care; 40% of the 75 and older group have multiple chronic illnesses; and more than 40% of those 75 and older have dementia (Lonergan & Krevans, 1991). Most of the 85 and older group are widows who have multiple, debilitating health problems and either live alone or with relatives (Cantor, 1991). "Current projections indicate that the nursing home population will increase to two million persons by the year 2000 and will double again by 2040" (Strumpf & Knibbe, 1990, p. 218). Greater longevity and growing numbers of the elderly population, "who have a great need for health care services," have contributed significantly to the rising costs of health care (International Trade Administration, 1991, p. 441). According to Lonergan and Krevans (1991), the costs for health care of older persons with disability or chronic illnesses amount to "about $162 billion per year and is likely to double in the coming decade" (p. 1825).

Rising prices in the Medicare program prompted Congress in 1983 to pass legislation that changed reimbursement for hospital Medicare charges from retrospective real costs of services to prospective, preset dollar amounts according to diagnostic-related groups (Dougherty, 1989). This action, it was thought, would curtail exorbitant rising health care costs. Such results have not been realized. According to the Budget of the United States Government 1992 (1991), "spending on Medicare in 1992 will be $127.3 billion, 11.9 percent over 1991 spending" (p. 275). In efforts to improve health care program efficiency, the 1992 budget includes proposed constraints in payments for selected physician, hospital, and related services.

The fact that America's health care system is in a crisis state is well documented in the literature (Adams-Ender, 1989; Holahan, Moon, Welch, & Zuckerman, 1991; Morreim, 1988; Powderly & Smith, 1989; Starck, 1991; Veatch, 1988). According to Starck (1991), 37 million Americans have no insurance of any kind, intergenerational and socioeconomic inequities "characterize the system," and "prevention, health promotion, and long-term care are woefully inadequate" (p. 26).

CONCEPTUAL MODEL FOR SELF AND FAMILY HEALTH PROMOTION

Olson, McCubbin, Barnes, Larsen, Muxen, and Wilson (1983) described and utilized the concepts, family cohesion, adaptability, and communication to study family dynamics based on systems theory. While these concepts "emerged from a family therapy perspective" (p. 47), they may be used to examine "balanced" (p. 16) families.

Olson et al. (1983) defined family cohesion as "the emotional bonding that members have toward one another" (p. 48). This bonding involves "boundaries, coalitions, time, space, friends, decision making, and interest and recreation" (p. 48). As progress through developmental stages occurs, it is significant that family members connect, adapt, and communicate in each area in order to form unified, healthy systems. At the same time, each family member must progress developmentally in each area as they move toward maturity, independence, and the point of beginning a new family system.

Family adaptability is "the ability of a marital or family system to change its power structure, role relationships, and relationship rules in response to situational and developmental stress" (Olson et al., 1983, p. 48). Adapting family members use assertiveness, control, discipline, and negotiation. The healthy family is characterized by positive adaptation during anticipated and unexpected developmental changes. Positive adaptation is enhanced when biopsychosocial and spiritual dimensions of family members are "healthy."

"Positive communication skills (i.e., empathy, reflective listening, supportive comments) enable couples and families to share with each other their changing needs and preferences as they relate to cohesion and adaptability" (Olson et al., 1983, p. 49). It is the belief of the authors that open and positive communication is a key element to a healthy functioning family system. With effective communication, the core concept of caring is extended among all members of the family system.

Orem (1985) described care as "attention, service, and protection provided by persons in a society who are in a position that requires them to be 'in charge of' or 'take care of' others . . . signifies a state of mind of an individual characterized by concern for, interest in, and solicitude for another" (p. 9). This description succinctly describes the Judeo-Christian ethic for the American family caring and concern that fosters healthy development from birth throughout one's lifespan. Development in physical, emotional, social, and spiritual dimensions are necessary and are enhanced by healthy family relationships. Such healthy relationships are enhanced by caring, family cohesion, adaptability, and communication.

A model based on Orem's (1985) concept of care and Olson's et al. (1983) concepts of family cohesion, adaptability, and communication is presented in Figure 1. Individual and family practices related to caring, family cohesion, adaptability, and communication can lead to a healthier society, thus reducing the costs of health care for Americans.

Residents who live in urban, inner city, and rural communities often have diminished access to health care. Due to geographic location, health care benefits may not be communicated in a timely fashion and access to health care may be inadequate. It is within these areas that many of the lower socioeconomic individuals and high risk groups reside. Examples of such groups include pregnant teenagers without prenatal care, widows who have few or no family members to assist with their care, and the older old with multiple chronic disabilities. An imperative part of health care reform should include plans to address the needs of these groups.

OVERVIEW OF HEALTH CARE
REFORM PROPOSALS

Numerous proposals for health care reform have been developed by groups of health care providers and others (American Nurses Association, 1991a; Butler, 1991; Davis, 1991; Fein, 1991; Ginzberg & Ostow, 1991; Holahan et al. 1991; Roybal, 1991; Todd, Seekins, Krichbaum, & Harvey, 1991). Health care was a major campaign issue in the 1992 Presidential race, but plans presented by the candidates lacked detail.

Work of the Pepper Commission will be addressed briefly. Proposals by nursing and medicine, representing two of the largest health care service groups, will be discussed briefly. The proposal of the Heritage Foundation,

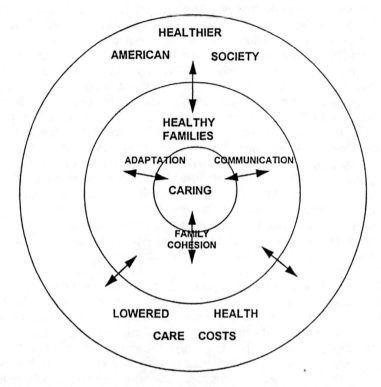

Figure 1. Conceptual model for self-health promotion within families

Washington, D. C. will be summarized because this proposal is congruent with the belief of the authors that individuals and families should assume more proactive roles in health care reforms. Through self-health promotion, illness prevention, and optimum adaptation to chronic illness, health care costs may be diminished.

Pepper Commission

Senator John D. Rockefeller (1991), Chairman of the Pepper Commission, explained the Commission's plan for health care reform. Recommendations are for actions toward health insurance protection for all Americans based on securing, improving, and extending job-based and public coverage programs now in existence. In addition to insurance coverage, the plan calls for a new federal program to replace Medicaid that would cover all uninsured individuals; coverage for employers based on private insurance tax credits and opportunities to acquire public coverage; plans for preventive and primary health care services and catastrophic care; and steps to enhance quality of care and cost containment.

Nursing's Health Care Reform Proposal

Nursing's "agenda for immediate health care reform" calls for basic and essential services to be available to everyone and to be delivered in familiar, convenient sites such as schools, workplaces, and homes (American Nurses Association, 1991a). To reduce costs, recommendations are for: managed care to be required in public plans and encouraged in private plans; growth of the health care system to be controlled "through planning and prudent resource allocation"; incentives to encourage consumers and providers to be more cost-efficient in exercising health care options; policies based on effectiveness and outcome research to be developed; and "unnecessary bureaucratic controls and administrative procedures" to be eliminated (p. 3). Long-term care provisions include "emphasis on the consumers' responsibility to financially plan for their long-term care needs, including new personal financial alternatives and strengthened private insurance arrangements" (p. 4).

Medicine's Health Care Reform Proposal

The American Medical Association proposed "Health Access America" as described by Todd et al. (1991). The proposal includes "six fundamental principles and 16 key points" (p. 2503). Principles are "improvements to the American health care system should preserve the strengths for our current system"; "affordable coverage for appropriate health care should be available to all Americans, regardless of income"; "particular efforts are needed to assure continued access by the elderly to affordable health care services"; "health care services should be delivered with high quality at appropriate costs"; "patients should be free to determine from whom and the manner in which health care benefits are delivered"; and "all physicians should be committed to the highest ethical standards in the delivery of care to patients" (p. 2504). Examples of the sixteen points of the proposal include the following: Medicaid reform to ensure all persons have access to needed care; health insurance provided by employers for "all full-time employees and their families, with tax help to employers" (p. 2504); state-level risk pools to ensure coverage to the medically uninsurable and others for whom individual health insurance is too costly or is unavailable; Medicare reform to address catastrophic benefits that would be funded "through individual and employer tax contributions during working years" (p. 2505); and expansion of long-term care financing through private sector coverage increases, tax incentives, and asset protection programs.

Heritage Foundation Health Care Reform Proposal

Butler (1991) recounted the proposal of the Heritage Foundation as calling for two principal steps: replacing "today's tax exclusion with a new system of refundable tax credits for health expenses," and establishing a "health care social contract" that would require, "by law," enrollment of all family members in a health plan for basic care (p. 2542). This plan proposes guarantee of basic health coverage to all Americans, regardless of employment status. Governmental assistance would be based on medical expenses as a proportion of income, and health care costs would be curtailed due to families seeking the best value for their money and avoiding overuse of the system. Refundable tax credits would provide strong incentives for individuals and families to stay as healthy as possible and to be more selective in their health care decisions. Overutilization of the health care system would be curtailed, thus reducing the current rise in health care costs.

PROPOSED STRATEGIES FOR SELF AND FAMILY HEALTH PROMOTION, ILLNESS PREVENTION, AND OPTIMUM ADAPTATION TO CHRONIC ILLNESS

As supported by cited literature, the rising cost within the health care delivery system, the issues surrounding equity of health care resources, the growing elderly population with chronic and debilitating illness, and the lack of preventive care represent frightening issues that must be addressed. All of these are important problems with repercussions that extend into intergenerational boundaries. Without the influx of possible solutions to these critical issues, poverty and illness are likely to flourish and compound existing concerns.

It is because of the pivotal nature of these issues that patchwork approaches will not be sufficient to propel health care in a positive direction for consumers and the nation. Proactive rather than reactive strategies must be the front line of defense for handling these delicate issues. With this mindset, health promotion, illness prevention, and optimum adaptation to chronic illness must be the ultimate goal. In order to accomplish these objectives long-range planning is essential. Although the initial planning and activation of plans during the transition may result in an outlay of significant dollars, the long-term benefits will result in a reduction in national health care expenditures and improved health care.

Prevention can be very powerful when placed into action. The focus of health care must propel the transition of change from restoration of health to illness prevention. According to the American Nurses Association (1991a), lack of preventive care has been an exorbitant cost for this nation in terms of individual lives and monetary expenditures.

If health promotion, illness prevention, and optimum adaptation to chronic illness are to occur, individuals must assume a greater responsibility. Through ongoing education, behavior modification toward the incorporation of self-care activities to maintain health and prevent illness may result in positive values and beliefs about health care practices. Proactive self-care education must emphasize the personal benefits attained when health care is a central focus throughout the lifespan beginning at conception. Because the human system is complex and interrelated, a balance between physical, psychological, social, and spiritual needs must be considered. In addition to individual efforts, Americans need to unite efforts in research, policy-making, and health care endeavors. Reforming health care is an exceptionally intricate task. A thorough assessment of the health care needs of the public must be the first step taken. Communication facilitates the entire change process from a health care system that is lacking in effectiveness and efficiency to a system ensuring access, effectiveness, and efficiency. The communication of this plan of action must include education on health and health promotion for individuals and families as well as knowledge about the influence of social and physical environmental factors influencing health. Incentives designed to encourage active self-care behaviors and adaptation to change on the part of consumers to promote optimum health and well-being is fundamental. A health care social contract enacted in an effort to ensure a preventive approach is necessary to assist in detouring astronomical health care expenditures for restorative care. Family efforts toward healthier life styles may serve as a viable part of the process of change. The boundaries established through a proactive approach to health will extend beyond that of the family to the larger geographical population. A shared interest and common goal to promote health and prevent illness may serve to establish an emotional bonding among Americans toward positive self-care behaviors. Olson's (1988) three dimensions–family cohesion, adaptability, and communication and Orem's concept of caring will serve as a framework to approach the assemblance of a workable health care reform for society. Each of these components can be directed toward the heart of formulating a solution to the health care dilemma. The following proactive strategies based on the Nurses Health Care Reform and the Heritage Foundation Reform are proposed for consideration.

Family Cohesion

A health care incentive program designed to encourage individuals to receive routine health, dental, eye, and ear checkups would be most advantageous. Just as in many states it is a requirement by law to have annual automobile checkups, it should also be a requirement for every individual to have annual examinations. Preventive measures are less costly than care for related illnesses and disability. Because of the danger of hearing loss, legislation should be enacted to curtail high decibel sounds that commonly endanger individuals, especially the younger generation.

Family participation visible in the role of caregivers must be rewarded by governmental support financially, socially, and psychologically. Many individuals are most willing to care for their family members but because of the high cost of living, the predominant scenario is that anyone who can work–must, in order to survive. Governmental programs designed to assist in the caregivers' well-being can be instrumental in decreasing costs of institutionalization of the elderly, diminishing elder abuse, and allowing better use of the health care professional. We, as a society, have become a world of high-technology in the midst of a definite crisis needing to return to high-touch for survival. The answer partially lies within each of us. Society as a whole must return to placing a high value on family and helping one another. It is our responsibility to take hold of the reins of society and critically review what is most valuable and advantageous. We have been ruled totally by our heart. What we see, we want, and what we usually want is costly. We must realistically grasp hold of other important things of life–family, friends, and good health.

Adaptability

Environmental changes should be designed to promote adaptation to good nutritional and exercise habits. Currently, the American society is operating in a mode that encourages poor health habits. A typical example relates to nutrition. Healthy choices are typically more expensive than non-healthy choices. Food product managers should make healthy food choices more affordable for the nutrition conscious consumer. Snack machine distributors should promote health food choices such as fruits and vegetables, and discourage the typical junk food purchases by placing higher prices on those selections. Other environmental considerations should be adapted in the work environment. Employers need to structure the work environment to reduce stress, emphasize good health habits through a balance of proper nutrition, exercise, social interaction, activity, and rest.

Health care programs should be developed based on the needs of the individuals within various geographical locations. The value of a well-designed health care delivery system is worthless if it has lost touch with specifically defined health care needs in the community it serves. Governmental rulings on the special health care programs and costs need to occur at the local level in order to assure congruence with needs of respective geographical area consumers.

Communication

Marketing strategies to communicate the dangers of harmful products such as tobacco, alcohol, and drugs should be enhanced. According to statistics obtained by the American Nurses Association (1991b), these substances account for a significant increase in health care expenses and restricted productivity. If elimination of these products is unrealistic or impossible, then high taxes should be placed on items that are hazardous to the health of consumers.

To promote emotional/psychological health, available community resources must be adequately marketed and easily accessible to all age groups. Health Care Centers designed to facilitate easy access to varied health care services are needed. Services available would need to include strategically located health care programs designed to meet physiological, psychological, social, and spiritual needs. Within this setting, consumer awareness booths providing easy-to-understand information about resources would be available. Health care advocates for individuals of all ages would be educated to assist, direct, and inform consumers of specialized services, health care options, and competitive costs. In addition, a return to home visits especially for the disabled and the elderly who may have difficulty in accessing health care services because of unavailable transportation or physical limitations is necessary. Nurses, physical therapists, and social workers have for several decades maintained home health visits. It is time for the physician to join the health care team once again in the home to meet the needs of those individuals who are home bound. This approach can assist in curtailing costly hospitalizations and inappropriate and unnecessary use of technology. A return to home care will also encourage individual and family involvement in maintenance of health that will contribute to self-health practices, thus reducing the need for costly medical care.

These strategies are congruent with stipulations addressed in the Health Care Reform proposals discussed in this paper. Through individual and family participation in proactive self-health approaches, the current health care crisis in America can be resolved and at affordable costs.

POLICY AND RESEARCH IMPLICATIONS

The agenda of the National Center for Health Services Research, when established in 1969, was to study access, quality, and cost of health care (Kane, 1991). Today, 22 years later, these three continue to be major concerns in America. Political groups, health care systems, research, nor any organization have been able to resolve the dilemmas. Therefore, careful attention should focus on ways individuals and families can contribute to better health.

Research is recommended in areas of self-health practices; acceptable allocation of resources according to needs of all cohorts within American society; effective strategies of communicating about, and delivering needed health care programs to all citizens; and programs to enhance affordable acute and long-term care. Health and wellness are desirable assets for any society's population. They are essential in managing health care cost in an aging society.

A health care reform has significant policy and research implications for health care professionals, hospitals, pharmaceutical companies, insurance companies, employers, and consumers. According to Deets (1991), policy implications directed at the medical profession, hospitals, and pharmaceutical companies are generated from a cost perspective; implications directed at business and industry employers are generated from a mandated employee benefits perspective; implications directed at insurance companies are generated from the possibility of a single pay system; and implications directed at consumers are generated from rationing of new technology, health care services, and limited access.

The future of health care for consumers will depend on research efforts directed at health promotion and illness prevention. A plan is needed to generate and disseminate knowledge to guide health care delivery and to develop an environment that is supportive of inquiry. Health problems caused by life-style, chronic illness, and the environment are and will continue to be responsible for illness, disability, and death. Therefore, research efforts need to be directed at minimizing or preventing behaviorally and environmentally induced health problems that compromise the quality of life and reduce productivity. According to the American Nurses' Association (1991b), "cancer, heart disease, arthritis, chronic pulmonary diseases, diabetes, Alzheimer's disease, and other diseases more prevalent during the middle and late adult years will produce major needs for individual and family adaptation and will command a major proportion of health resources" (p. 2). With this in mind, a research priority should focus on promoting health, well-being, and self-care activities among all ages, social, and cultural groups. In addition, research efforts should incorporate the design and evaluation of alternate models for health care delivery to enhance quality and cost effectiveness in meeting the health care needs of identified populations. The incorporation of Olson's adaptability dimension into the research arena could also be manifested through efforts directed at minimizing the negative influence of technology on the adaptive abilities of individuals and families enduring acute and chronic health problems.

CONCLUSIONS

Individuals and families, as well as the nation as a whole, must assume the responsibility of health promotion and illness prevention to contribute to a healthier nation with reduced health care costs. Political leaders need to listen intensely to the cry of the people in order to strategically plan for anticipated intergenerational needs. Unless reform of the current health care system is established and life styles are refocused on healthy practices, the rise of health care costs will continue. The burden on individuals, corporations, and the government at all levels will be intensified. America has the potential needed to avoid compounded crisis. Fruition of our potential is up to us, individually and collectively!

REFERENCES

Adams-Ender, C. L. (1989). *Health policy issues toward the year 2000. Perspectives in Nursing 1989-1991.* New York: National League for Nursing.

AMA Council on Scientific Affairs (June, 1990). Societal effects and other factors affecting health care for the elderly. *Archives of Internal Medicine, 150*(6), 1184-1189.

American Nurses Association (1991a). *Nursing's agenda for health care reform.* The American Nurse (Suppl. PR-3 220M). 1-24.

American Nurses Association (1991b). *Directions for nursing research: Toward the twenty-first century.* American Nurses' Association Cabinet on Nursing Research.

Biegel, D. E., & Blum, A. (1990). *Aging and caregiving theory, research, and policy.* Newbury Park, CA: Sage Publications, Inc.

Budget of the United States Government Fiscal Year 1992 (1991). Washington, DC: U. S. Government Printing Office.

Butler, S. M. (1991). A tax reform strategy to deal with the uninsured. *Journal of American Medical Association, 265*(19), 2541-2544.

Cantor, M. H. (1991). Family and community: Changing roles in an aging society. *The Gerontologist, 31*(3), 337-346.

Davis, K. (1991). Expanding medicare and employer plans to achieve universal health insurance. *Journal of American Medical Association, 265*(19), 2525-2528.

Deets, H. (1991). Health care reform has top priority. *Modern Maturity, 34*(5), 11.

Dougherty, C. J. (1989). Cost containment, drugs, and the ethics of health care. *Hastings Center Report, 19*(1), 5-11.

Fein, R. (1991). The health security partnership a federal-state universal insurance and cost-containment program. *Journal of American Medical Association, 265*(19), 2555-2558.

Ginzberg, E., & Ostow, M. (1991). Beyond universal health insurance to effective health care. *Journal of American Medical Association, 265*(19), 2559-2565.

Holahan, J., Moon, M., Welch, W. P., & Zuckerman, S. (1991). An American approach to health system reform. *Journal of American Medical Association, 265*(19), 2537-2540.

International Trade Administration (1991). *U.S. industrial outlook 1991–Health and medical services.* Washington, D.C.: U.S. Department of Commerce.

Kane, R. L. (1991). *The role of health services research: The link between cost and effectiveness in patient care and program management.* In J. C. Romeis & R. M. Coe (Eds). Quality and cost containment in care of the elderly. New York: Springer Publishing Company.

Little, C. (1992). "Health for all by the year 2000": Where is it now? *Nursing & Health Care, 13*(4), 198-201.

Lonergan, E. T., & Krevans, J. R. (1991). Special report a national agenda for research on aging. *The New England Journal of Medicine, 324*(25), 1825-1828.

Lubkin, I. M. (1986). *Chronic illness impact and interventions.* Boston: Jones and Bartlett Publishers, Inc.

Morreim, E. H. (1988). Cost containment: Challenging fidelity and justice. *Hastings Center Report, 18*(6), 20-25.

Olson, D. H. (1988). *Family types, family stress, and family satisfaction: A family development perspective.* In C. J. Falicov (Ed.), Family transitions: Continuity and change over the life cycle (pp. 55-79). New York: Van Nostrand Reinhold.

Olson, D. H., McCubbin, H. I., Barnes, H. L., Larsen, A. S., Muxen, M. J., &

Wilson, M. A. (1983). *Families what makes them work.* Beverly Hills: Sage Publications.

Orem, D. E. (1985). *Nursing concepts of practice* (3rd ed.). New York: McGraw-Hill.

Pifer, A., & Bronte, L. (Ed.) (1986). *Our aging society: Paradox and promise.* New York: W. W. Norton & Company.

Powderly, K. E., & Smith, E. (1989). The impact of drugs on health care workers and their clients. *Hastings Center Report, 19*(1), 16-18.

Rockefeller, J. D. (1991). A call for action the Pepper commission's blueprint for health care reform. *Journal of American Medical Association, 265*(19), 2507-2510.

Roybal, E. R. (1991). The 'U S Health Act' comprehensive reform for a caring America. *Journal of American Medical Association, 265*(19), 2545-2548.

Starck, P. L. (1991). Health care under siege: Challenge for change. *Nursing and Health Care, 12*(1), 26-30.

Strumpf, N. E., & Knibbe, K. K. (1990). *Long term care fulfilling promises to the old among us.* In J. C. McCloskey & H. K. Grace (Eds.). Current issues in nursing (pp. 217-225). St. Louis: The C. V. Mosby Company.

Todd, J. S., Seekins, S. V., Krichbaum, J. A., & Harvey, L. K. (1991). Health access America–strengthening the US health care system. *Journal of American Medical Association, 265*(19), 2503-2506.

Veatch, R. M. (1988). Justice and the economics of terminal illness. *Hastings Center Report, 18*(4), 34-40.

Intergenerational Issues
in Long Term Planning

Sarah Roberts Foulke
Finnegan Alford-Cooper
Sandra Butler

KEYWORDS. Caregiving, Direct cost, Indirect cost, Health care, Medical model, Filial responsibility, Planning, Retirement, Stress, Respite care, Planning

UNDERSTANDING LONG TERM PLANNING
AND THE NEED TO PLAN

For some families, long-range plans have been developed because a specific need has been identified. Specific needs are not limited to only handicapped children and their parents, the chronically or terminally ill. Most families plan to purchase a home, educate their children, or retire.

Sarah Roberts Foulke is Home Economics Program Leader, Cornell Cooperative Extension, Riverhead, NY. Finnegan Alford-Cooper is Associate Professor of Sociology, Assistant Director of Gerontology Graduate Program, Long Island University, Southampton, NY. Sandra Butler is Consultant, Southside Hospital, Caregiver Education Program, Bay Shore, NY.

[Haworth co-indexing entry note]: "Intergenerational Issues in Long Term Planning." Foulke, Sarah Roberts, Finnegan Alford-Cooper and Sandra Butler. Co-published simultaneously in *Marriage & Family Review* (The Haworth Press, Inc.) Vol. 18, No. 3/4, 1993, pp. 73-95; and: *American Families and the Future: Analyses of Possible Destinies* (ed: Barbara H. Settles, Roma S. Hanks, and Marvin B. Sussman) The Haworth Press, Inc., 1993, pp. 73-95. Multiple copies of this article/chapter may be purchased from The Haworth Document Delivery Center. Call 1-800-3-HAWORTH (1-800-342-9678) between 9:00 - 5:00 (EST) and ask for DOCUMENT DELIVERY CENTER.

All family members have needs and concerns, including even those who are currently independent and self sufficient. "Planning helps people link previous experience, current situations, and the future" (Rice & Tucker, 1986, p. 152). In a sample of 300 Delaware residents (age 25-60), over 70% reported being concerned about being able to maintain their independence at home (Settles, 1989). The necessity for developing care plans for elderly family members has been advocated by Seccome, Ryan and Austin (1978), and Clark (1987) has suggested that the elderly, themselves, be encouraged to plan for their futures.

Labor negotiations, an increase in personal wealth, and benefits supplied through government programs provided the opportunity to anticipate and plan for retirement and healthcare. However, events that occurred during the last decade impact the retirement outcomes for both current and future retirees. In the eighties economic events included bank merger or closings, the saving and loan scandal, insurance company collapses, a stock market crash, changes in the tax laws, corporate mergers, raiding of pension funds, downsizing of organizations through early retirement incentives, plant closing and lay offs, and increased insurance and health care costs.

Today there are fewer jobs existing in the manufacturing sector than just five years ago. Older workers are having to learn new skills and compete with younger workers for fewer benefits and available jobs. Now the possibility of being hired by one company and remaining there for the duration of one's work life is practically nonexistent. Employees and retirees are asked to pay part or all of their health insurance costs and are giving up benefits. Many individuals have given up health insurance or have postponed preventive procedures.

Many Americans believe that the 1990's will be financially tight. They feel that their own chances to save for their own retirement will be decreased because they are caught between the demands of educating their children and the need to help aging parents meet long term care and medical costs.

With mid-life adults, the development of life plans is an important practice if the goal is to remain independent in their later years. Differences exist not only in the extent to which the individual does or does not plan, but in awareness of the need to plan. Individuals differ in skills and outlook on planning because of cultural or personal norms about the desirability of planning (Scholnick & Friedman, 1987), familiarity with the context of planning, foresight and perception of control (Deacon & Firebaugh, 1988). Two types of planning exist: (1) prospective planning that emphasizes how life should be, and (2) projective planning in which the future is expected to be a projection from the present (Rice & Tucker, 1986). However, individuals tend to fantasize about the former while ignoring the latter. Planning as process can be anticipatory or opportunistic, short-term or long-term, simple or elaborate resulting in a written or unwritten scheme, program or method for goal attainment (Foulke, 1989).

CAREGIVING

On any given day over 17.6 million women and 12.7 million men, age 55 years or older, provide care to family, friends or neighbors. According to a study recently completed by The Commonwealth Fund (1992), 10.3 million women and 7.3 million men care for children, grandchildren, and great grandchildren. Among the married couples, 1.8 million women and 1.6 million men care for a sick or disabled spouse; 1.9 million women and 1.2 million men care for a sick or disabled parent; and 3.1 million women and 2.1 million men assist a sick or disabled friend or neighbor. In some cases, individuals are caring for more than one person.

Care for an elderly parent is provided by 5 million Americans of all ages, two thirds of which are 55 years or older. Next to the baby boom generation, the over sixty-five population is the fastest growing segment in society today. According to Census Bureau projections, during the last two decades of the twentieth century, the 65 and over population in America will have grown by 37%, while the under 65 will grow by only 15.6%. It is projected by the year 2000, the number of chronically disabled community-based elderly will grow by 31% (Cantor, 1991). Kin networks are becoming increasingly top heavy with more older family members than younger; and for the first time in history, the average married couple now has more parents than children (Cantor, 1991). As people live longer, more families are finding themselves faced with helping an aging parent, spouse, older relative or neighbor.

Elder care can be classified into two major categories: (1) home care where family or community resources may be utilized; and (2) institutional care. However, a description of elder care is not as clearly defined as child care. While child care usually occurs within a restricted period of time, about eighteen years, elder care has no defined time-lines. Neugarten described the phenomenon as "not the actual physical care of the parent (although that, too, is a critical issue), but the decision making in which the adult child or grandchildren participates, the social and emotional supports required (and given) and the sense of burden expressed by so many middle aged, especially middle aged women" (Brubaker, Cole, C., Cole, A. L., & Hennon, 1978). Among the complex issues to be addressed are assessing the family's willingness and ability to provide emotional, social, physical or financial support, the health of individual family members and their understanding and acceptance of the aging process.

Two modes of caregiving by families were identified by Shanas (1979). In "the shared-functioning kinship system" each family member provides assistance as needed. Under the second mode, "the substitution principle," members are available to provide care in serial order beginning with the spouse, followed by children, then more distant kin. However, Archbold (1980) suggests that caregiving follows three different patterns: (1) care provision, the caregiver identifies the needs and meets them; (2) care management, provided for by others while the caregiver supervises; and (3) transferral of responsibility, all caregiving responsibility is transferred to an agent or agency.

WHO GIVES THE CARE?

Historically the role of caregiver has been assigned to women (Abel, 1991; Brody, 1970; Hess, 1979; Morgan, 1969; Treas, 1977). In the nineteenth century, women spent a good part of their lives caring for the young and the dependent old family members. Disease, disability, and early death were common. Caregiving was a part of the female gender role and the cult of domesticity. Women were regarded as different and better suited than men for caregiving, and caregiving was one of women's innate talents. Women were encouraged to subordinate their needs to the needs of others, their family members, to be more selfless and more giving (Abel, 1991). In the nineteenth century women seldom worked outside the home after marriage, unless they were very poor. They relied on their male kinsmen's support and in exchange furnished care and were routinely expected to delay or give up work, or even marriage to care for sick parents and kinsmen. Because it was an economic and legal matter, women seldom had other recourse. With few hospitals, and doctors, women learned many medical skills and practiced them regularly.

This philosophy of woman as a natural caregiver has continued. Therefore, one might assume that the ideal family caregiver is the person not only readily available, but willing and able. To find a caregiver who meets these characteristics is more an ideal than reality. The past relationship between the parent and the adult child does not have to have been positive for the child to accept the caregiving role. "It appears that children respond not only to a loving parent but to a parent in need . . . if anything, care is given in spite of, not because of, the past relationship" (Horowitz, 1978, p. 6). It is estimated that today's woman will spend 17 years of adult life as mother of a dependent child and 18 years more as daughter of an elderly parent. In contrast, at the turn of the century women spent more than twice as many years as mother of a dependent child than as daughter of a dependent parent, 19 years with a child and only 9 with a parent.

In the last decade of the twentieth century, women are socialized to play much the same roles as their nineteenth century counterparts. Studies by Oren (1974) and Abel (1991), demonstrate that women tend to sacrifice themselves, and their own resources to care for family members. More importantly, they tend to regard the conflicts they experience between work and family caregiving as personal problems rather than a social problem. Consequently they try to find individual and personal solutions that do not impose on others. They sleep less, work more, spend their money and give their time to others. The implications for caregiving are clear. Women tend to take on caregiving single handed, they will define the situation as an individual dilemma and not seek large scale social solutions.

Mid-life individuals caught between childcare and eldercare have been dubbed the "sandwich generation." Although much has been said on behalf of the "sandwich generation" and the stress they experience, they are not the only caregivers. Spouses, as care givers, tend to be overlooked and overloaded. Fengler and Goodrich (1979), and Golodetz, Evans, Henritz and Gibson (1969) have indicated that spouse caring can be equally if not more stressful than parent caring, because caregivers were elderly themselves and had a significant number of illnesses of their own. Worcester and Quayhagen (1983) suggest that older caregivers may be more comfortable in the role than younger individuals because they are generally giving care to a spouse, not an elderly parent. Caregiving is an implied component of the marriage contract, many spouses carry the burden of care alone (Lurie, Robinson, & Barbaccia, 1984).

Approximately 70% of older persons in the U. S. have living grandchildren (Fewell & Vadast, 1986). Grandparenthood may expand to 20-30 years. Adult children are now likely to ask grandparents to assume part or total responsibility for their young children. The increase in divorce, female employment, teen pregnancy and drug addiction creates conditions where the services of the grandparent are sorely needed. Grandparents provide babysitting, direct financial aid to their adult children or buy gifts for their grandchildren. Other activities include assisting with educational expenses, serving as family historian or storyteller, mediating in conflicts between parents and their children as well as acting as a friend to their grandchildren (Fewell & Vadast, 1986).

The Commonwealth Fund study (1992) concluded after surveying

2,999 Americans age 55 and over, that while women are still the major providers of caregiving, men are taking on an increasing larger role. Half the men age 55 and over who have children or grandchildren, reported to interviewers of the survey that they care for them. The change in men's role as caregiver has been attributed by Butler to "women becoming more assertive and less likely to accept automatically the caregiver's role and men showing more interest in nurturing" (Teltsch, 1992, p. B1).

WHO IS AVAILABLE?

Archbold (1980) suggests that the caregiving role in the family has been automatically falling to the female sibling who has had the previous role assignment of oldest, most responsible, single or the closest one in proximity. Several significant changes have occurred which have influenced the availability of caregivers. The first trend was the increase in the number of females entering the work force. Many factors were involved in driving the trend. An increase in the divorce rate produced more single parent families. Rapid inflation impacted severely on lifestyles. To maintain the American dream many women returned to work. Seeking alternatives to staying home was further supported by the women's movement.

Secondly, the declining birth rate and spacing of children in later midlife also contributes to a decrease in the number of available caregivers. Women are postponing childbirth, having fewer children or choosing not to have children at all. Today, with more women interested in establishing a career before children, motherhood occurs at a later age. This means there will be dependent children in households later than in the lives of previous generations. This trend presents a very different problem: elongated age span between generations. The children of today's young and mid-life adults, when they are young adults in their late twenties and early thirties will not only be responsible for caring for one or more elderly family members, but face the prospect of caring for several generations age 60 and older. These responsibilities will occur at a time in the life cycle when family and career are developing and resources are limited. Postponing children is not the only reason mid-lifers have young children. Second families emerge from divorce. The blended family of children his, hers, ours is becoming a common family form. Children may have several sets of parents and grandparents, which raises questions about expectations of care giving and filial responsibility.

The third change that is decreasing the potential pool of providers is

AIDS. The increasing number of adults who have become HIV infected can no longer be relied upon for providing support to their elderly relatives. During the ten year period of 1981 through June of 1991, 182,834 documented cases of AIDS in the United States were reported. Since this disease can have an incubation period that can take up to fifteen years before it is detected, projections of the number already infected are tenuous. There is a growing concern by health officials over the increased number of women and teens who have become infected. How many teens are HIV positive, no one really knows; however in the past three years, the cumulative number of 13-24 year olds diagnosed with AIDS has increased 77% (Hanauer-Onyx, 1992). An unknown dimension to caregiving can be found in the gay community where younger men help partners afflicted with AIDS. Many individuals prefer to remain within their community, looking to that community for support during their illness. In a Delaware study, many respondents expressed a positive attitude toward caregiving, especially if the person lived near (78.6%) or if the individual moved into their household (71.5%) (Settles, 1989). However when asked would they be willing to extend care to someone with AIDS only 54.9% said they would *if* they were close to that person.

A fourth trend, limiting the number of young adults, is the increase among the young who die from acts of violence such as stabbing and shootings. Death by gun shot is the second leading cause of death for teens today. Already there is an indication that caregiving crosses the generations and no longer is the single role of the middleaged and elderly. Schools informally report more adolescent students involved with the care of elderly relatives. Tasks include elder sitting for a brief period of time, running errands, dispensing medications, and preparing meals, which are activities formerly performed by a nonworking parent.

There will be fewer younger members in the next generation, thus restricting the older generation's access to potential caregivers. There will not only be fewer caregivers, but those who will be caring will be doing it for a longer period of time. The profile of the typical caregiver and the amount of care, traditionally provided by families, will also change.

VIEWS AND EXPECTATIONS OF CAREGIVING

The extent of caregiving is influenced by particular circumstances of both caregiver and elder (Sivley & Fiegner, 1984). As the adult child ages, concern and worry about the parent, independent of health conditions, increases (Lieberman, 1978). Male children seemed less concerned about changes in their parents' health than were female children. Both Seelbach (1977, 1978), and Brody (1970) have studied filial expectations of adult children. Children tend to expect more from themselves and each other than their parents do, which offers one explanation of why caregiving can be so stressful.

A study of caregiving women in various counseling settings shows the major problems were to be time management and coping mechanisms, need for support (formal and informal), long term planning and personal issues vis-à-vis the care recipient and intimacy with caregiver (Smith, G., Smith, M., & Toseland, 1991). Overall, most of the specific problems cited by the caregivers involved conflicts regarding sharing responsibilities of caregiving while trying to maintain total control over the caregiving situation.

Whether or not giving care is viewed as a burden has been thought to depend on the social class of the caregiver. Lower class children consider caring for a parent less of a burden than middle class children (Lieberman, 1978). Earlier studies (Adams, 1968; Blenker, 1965; Schorr, 1960; Shanas, 1967; Sussman & Burchinal, 1962) show differences in mutual aid stem directly from social class differences. Working class or blue collar families tend to provide services whereas the middle class tend to give financial aid (Adams, 1968; Hill, Foote, Aldous, Carlson, & MacDonald, 1970; Sussman & Burchinal, 1962). "It may be that help is greatest at the extremes of economic situations . . . the poor need and seek help from their relatives, and the rich get it and give it in gifts and inheritance (Troll, Miller, & Atchley, 1979, p. 102)."

Parental expectations for help follow a different dynamic. Financial support is considered to be the responsibility of the government rather than the offspring (Seelbach, 1977). Request for housing is the most frequent referral problem that agencies handle (Simos, 1973), because feelings run strongly against doubling up in an adult child's household (Murrey, 1973). Most elderly want to remain independent, in their own homes, if possible (Shanas, 1961). Changes in expectations occur when the relationship between adult children and their parents begins to change. Such changes may be uncomfortable for both parties and can create feelings of misapprehension and resentment in both parties. The motivation to care for an elder may not only be out of love and concern, but also a sense of responsibility, duty, and guilt. Negative feelings about coping with an emergency, a crisis, or the inability to live up to one's own or one's parents' expectations may develop.

ISSUES IN CAREGIVING

Caregiving issues are influenced by ethnicity, perceptions, institutions, available resources, family history and the decisions that are made individually and collectively. They differ from family to family. Planning issues also include concerning choice as an active process, control, decision making, proximity, privacy, compensation, and legality. Plans and decisions are not the sole domain of the individual and the family, but are influenced by the existence and lack of institutional and public policies. Practical problems relative to long term planning that all caregiving families face concern: identifying the caregiver(s); defining the amount of caregiving; identifying personal and family needs; identifying current and future needs of the elder; and determining direct and indirect cost, associated with caregiving.

The bulk of caretaking is done informally by family members. The increase in social services to the elderly has been cited as evidence that families are abandoning their elderly. The family routinely provides social outlets, help in performing tasks of daily living and help in crises. The use of additional formal services is usually chosen because of further impairment of the care recipient, not family neglect. Stoller (1989) found that people who received more formal services also had more informal assistance mostly because they had more serious impairments.

ISSUES OF CHOICE AND CONTROL

In the early nineteenth century doctors made home visits, saw the place of care, interacted regularly with the informal caregivers, and were under the supervision, in some ways, of the home caregiver (Abel, 1991). When doctors became associated with hospitals and medical science was born, caregivers' roles changed. When patients and their caregivers began to go to hospitals and clinics to visit doctors, the physicians gained the control over defining the situation. Both care recipient and caregiver felt more helpless and out of control. New understandings of disease, helped to undermine traditional caregivers' authority. When caregivers and recipients fail to ask questions, to gain knowledge and so gain control, their choices are limited. The knowledge they have from experience and sharing is not legitimized because it didn't come from "science" or "medicine" (Rose, 1991). Family members were not even welcome in the hospital setting until recently. The nonmedical aspects of care were downplayed, disregarded, and considered insignificant. The psychological state of caregiver and recipient, the relationship between them, the activities of everyday living, and the environment of the elder were ignored.

Women are not given adequate choices about when they will begin to care for their elders, and how caregiving will intrude into their lives. "When the task becomes too much they cannot always choose assistance because it may not be available (Abel, 1991, p. 22)." The decisions that caregivers make reflect the lack of publicly funded services, not private, individual choices. A situation cycle has developed in which women provide significant amounts of care at little or no cost to others, therefore this care is largely unrecognized in any political agenda. Settles (1987, p. 174) maintains that "the areas of choice for the individual are affected by constraints in the society that may be modified by social process." The problem is getting caregivers to recognize and seek social solutions.

Atchley (1988) thinks that the merger of the ideal of the free market with unrelenting faith in progress with new technology and efficiency has undermined the social roles of the aged. Individuals earn money independent of their families, which diminishes an elder's economic control of younger adults. The economic condition of the elderly has changed significantly. The number of elders living below poverty level has dropped because of publicly funded maintenance programs and private retirement programs. Adult children do not have to financially support their elders, but they usually assist them with noncash goods and services.

With the technological changes new values emerged: an emphasis on individual achievement, progress, efficiency, greater reliance on machines. When mass production took over, age discrimination in the workplace had emerged. These technologies and values helped to shape people's world views, their explanations of the world around them, the 'natural order' of things. These world views, in turn, shape people's actions and social policies, the division of labor, and expenditures of public funds.

The value on individualism is evident in the shift of women caregivers' responsibilities, from depending on an entire network of kin, friends, and neighbors, to doing it alone with few community support systems. Emphasizing these values undermines community support of less able individuals, produces a piecemeal approach to health care, and a lack of control over cost and quality of that health care.

CAREGIVING AS A SOCIAL PROBLEM

The need for different types of caregiving situations dominates the social policy side of the problem. "Families and individuals may take action to change their relationship to other institutions, but the costs vary" (Settles, 1987, p. 174). Everyone wants to alleviate stress and burden on the caregiver and recipient, but this activity redirects attention away from ways to organize our society to give dependent people better lives and better care without causing inordinate sacrifice by their families. Unless caregiving is defined as a social problem we will not really find social solutions to the dilemmas, and caregivers will continue to see their situations as personal, with individual solutions. When politicians suggest returning to more family centered care of elders because of disenchantment with impersonal high tech care received in hospitals and nursing homes, they also emphasize reducing spending (Abel, 1991). Home care is not always cheaper than institutional care, if all costs are examined. Since the 1960's there has been a trend to de-institutionalize healthcare. Nursing home beds are seriously limited and patients are screened for admission. Mental patients are already deinstitutionalized even when there are no community services. Acute medical care has been radically altered with more outpatient surgical facilities and the expansion of home health care. Interestingly, as hospitals reduce nursing staff to cut costs, patients are also typically sicker and so nurses have more to do. In some instances, families are now encouraged to participate in the care. Fischer and Eustis (1988) studied the effects of DRG's on family caregivers. They found that DRG's increased the hospital bureaucracy. Caregivers expressed concern about hospital admissions, discharges and the quality of hospital care. People are discharged sooner and sicker from the hospital so caregivers must take over the initial care, as well as manage the paperwork for federal and local assistance, and plan the delivery of formal health care services. Clearly two competing forces are at work in public policy surrounding caregiving, understanding and supporting the caregiving experience versus the cost efficiency mentality of health and social services faced with an economic recession and soaring health care costs.

While informal care by kin may seem to be cost effective to governments it can be very costly to caregivers who must rearrange their work and family lives to fit their caregiving duties. Not everyone can accommodate to these social expectations. Caregiving is a lonely job, cutting a caretaker off from the rest of the world. He/she must act as service broker, managing a complex array of medical and social service eligibilities.

Anastas, Gibeau and Larson (1990) report that women caregivers spend about twice as much time as men in weekly caregiving. They also point to degree of disability and overall intensity of caregiving as the crucial variables in determining work conflicts. The women caregivers in this study had missed, typically, 35 hours of work a year because of caregiving.

About 20% of the women had thought about quitting their jobs because of caregiving demands. Fifteen percent had missed a week or more of work because of caregiving responsibilities. These working caregivers wanted more information and referral for eldercare, flexible working hours, reduced working hours with full benefits, and elder day care, cafeteria benefits, respite care, and job sharing.

O'Grady-LeShane, Kingson and Hopps (1988) found that early and late-life caregiving by women depressed the total retirement income of newly retiring women. In Stone and Short's study (1990) 29% of the caregivers had quit or adjusted their jobs to fit their caregiving responsibilities. White collar managerial positions may be more flexible than a blue collar job where the time clock is more rigid.

Miller and Eisdorfer (1989) also point out the importance of the quality of relationship between recipient and caregiver, the caregiver's values, the available resources, and any serious worsening of the care recipient status. These variables are difficult to access when families are held responsible for their elders' care. Frail elderly (over 85) and caregivers frequently have different perceptions of the caregiving experience resulting in lowered morale, stress and strain (Zweibel & Lydens, 1990). Both caregiver and recipient must participate together in caregiving decisions to the extent the disabled elder is able. Pratt, Jones, Sin and Walker (1989) studied autonomy in decision making among caregiving daughters and their mothers. They found that daughters were especially influential in decisions relating to health, finances and housing. Mothers perceived loss of autonomy in their decision making.

Some ethnic differences were found by Smerglia, Deimling and Banesi (1988). Black elderly were more likely than white elderly to be excluded from decision making about their own care by their adult children or spouses. Neither whites nor blacks reported being included in much decision making by formal resources. Parsons and Cox (1989) suggest mediation to resolve eldercare decisions. A social worker mediates between family caregivers and elders, helping them to separate emotions from issues, to discover the underlying mutual interests, to find and explore options.

Many of the studies on caregiver stress adopt the medical model for solutions often ignoring the social and economic forces creating the problem. The caregiver may be advised to use professionals, therapists, and doctors, or use sedatives or tranquilizers. Everyone wants the caregiver to feel better, but this may not be a realistic goal. The caregiver's role is demanding, and no amount of respite care takes away the sense of personal responsibility, affection and concern a caregiver will feel. The caregiver and recipient will have conflicting needs. Caregivers must face their fears of sickness, disability, dementia and death.

Stress is related more to a caregiver's emotional response and the relationship with the recipient than the number of tasks to be done. Their perception of the caregiver role determine whether or not they feel a "sense of burden" (Foulke, 1980). Even if home care services fail to relieve stress, they do perform a number of important functions. Services assist the caregivers in remaining in the public world, work, seeing friends, and having leisure time, and so minimize the costs to the caregiver in his/her life. In addition to helping caregivers adjust to burdens the goal should be to enable caregivers to have lives beyond caregiving.

While participants and leaders typically report support groups offer relief, a study by Toseland and Rossiter (1989) found no relationship between support group participation for the caregiver and improved coping skills, prevention of psychological problems or in enabling caregivers to do more for themselves. Killeen (1990) reports that caregivers in her study were most stressed by the constant and unrelenting demands on their time, the lack of information they had about available community services, the lack of communication they had with the elder care recipient, and having to face the inevitable death of the elder. Typically those caregivers coped by giving up time for themselves. Caregivers expressed needs for information about medicines and health care, help dealing with government bureaucracies, and current information about federal and local government regulations that affected them.

It is rather difficult to get caregivers to use respite care because of their overwhelming sense of personal responsibility for the care of the elder. In many areas there is a simple distrust of "strangers." Caregivers must feel confident of the respite care and feel a sense of satisfaction in choosing this alternative (Lawton, Brody & Saperstein, 1989). Seltzer and Mayer (1988) report a general difficulty of convincing primary caregivers to share responsibility in their study of a Boston eldercare program.

INSTITUTIONAL CARE

The health care system clearly favors reimbursement for services provided in hospitals and nursing homes. Physician directed lobbying groups/ advocacy groups like AMA, AHA, Blue Cross/Blue Shield have lobbied effectively because they have more resources available to them than non-medical/physician oriented lobbyists. Doctors favor institutional settings, because they know and were trained to operate in these settings and may be affiliated with these institutions.

The medical model is symmetrical with the nursing home as the setting for long term care of elderly in the US. The standards are modeled after hospitals. For example, the medical director of a nursing home has the same role as a hospital chief of staff, however, it is difficult to persuade physicians to visit nursing homes or to work full or half time as the medical director (Atchley, 1988, p. 345). Controlling the quality of care at institutions has become problematic. While there are rules for enforcement, there are limited inspection and enforcement funds. Nursing home space is at such a premium that enforcing license revocations would make waiting lists even longer.

MEDICAL-CAREGIVER RELATIONSHIP

The way the caregiver and recipient define their interactions with physicians is informative. Physicians tend to recommend a patient be viewed as a cluster of symptoms to control. Caregivers have to come to terms with the gradual loss of that individual and assertion of control over the afflicted person. The more information made available to the caregiver from the physician the better the adjustment. Caregivers need to know what to expect and to be able to consult professionals on a wide range of topics. When the physician is taken at his word, without question, control for the care is removed from the recipient and caregiver. Open questioning needs to be encouraged by medical personnel. However, Abel (1991) found that her informants relied on doctors to justify what they had already decided to do anyway. They did not generally want professional opinions otherwise. Physicians' recommendations were used to support limitations of elders' activities, like driving which caregivers think is dangerous. Having a diagnostic label gives caretakers control in getting family resources together to face the problem, to develop ideas for coping with demented elders. It allows them to get emotional distance by defining behavior as part of an illness they cannot control, and they can rely on a physician's authority when decision making is overwhelming and/or beyond their expertise (Abel, 1991).

Pfeiffer (1990) says caregivers need more adequate information about the progression of their elder's disabilities, more information about the care given, better means of financing long term care, more legal information on care of elders, and more information about their own normal emotional reactions.

When an elder is initially under the care of a physician, the caregiver and recipient tend to see themselves as nonauthorities in an acute care setting like a hospital, and therefore they take the professionals' word seriously. As the elder recovers and returns to the home, both caregiver and recipient begin to reassert their own authority, modifying the professional's recommendations, figuring out what works, and ideally, teaching it to the professional too, so he/she can share the knowledge later (Hasselkus, 1988).

Caregivers tend to override the professional when they believe their intimate, individual knowledge of the patient is better informed. It might be a good idea to work with caregivers to form a caregiving team so that everyone's expertise can be used openly. The caregiver can act as a monitor of the elder and can interpret the elder's concerns to the doctor when necessary (Coe, 1987). Caregivers do not expect physicians to provide for their own health, caregivers said they simply wanted the doctors' acknowledgment of the problems they are facing (Glasser, Rubin & Dickover, 1989).

Another difficult issue involves the increased use of high tech medical equipment in the home. Leader and Liebig (1988) raise questions about the overall costs and benefits of such programs. No one understands the effects of bringing sophisticated machinery into the home. Equipment is commonly used for last stage renal disease, transmission of antibiotics and chemotherapy, ventilation, hydration and feeding. All family members will be affected by the presence of this equipment. Caregivers may be reluctant to admit to or be unaware of their inability to use the equipment properly, and the effects on the care recipient are also largely unknown.

AT WHAT COSTS IS CAREGIVING BEING GIVEN?

Increasingly, overspent state budgets can't handle the projected increases in the costs of long term care. Health care rationing becomes a real possibility (Binstock, 1985). The growing gap between care costs and available resources may result in a two tier health care system in which poor people will not get high cost health care. Binstock (1985) believes that in the future a young person's life may be viewed as worth more than an elder's life. Should this trend occur control then passes out of the hands of the individual and the family to the physicians and institution.

Determining needs, whether they are those of the elder or the adult child and his family, is an individual issue. Regardless, there are both direct and indirect costs associated with those decisions. Some families deal better with the direct cost than the indirect costs associated with caregiving.

Direct costs are defined as any expense associated with providing basic necessities of life such as food, shelter, clothing, health care, transportation, plus any other out of pocket expenses incurred by the family. Such costs are influenced by differences in region, age, sex and standard of living.

There are also direct costs to the community and society for the expense of social services and program delivery to the elderly. Consider the wage earner who pays for both social security and Medicare through payroll deductions and programs for seniors through other taxes, but does not support an elderly relative. Employers also provide support through social security payments, taxes and may even pay retirement and health care benefits.

The indirect cost of caring for an elderly family member is not so easily recognized or measured as the direct cost. Perhaps the easiest approach is what economists refer to as the opportunity costs. A dollar value can be assigned to the income that the caregiver forgoes when staying home to give care. In addition dollar values can be assigned as if they were paid for alternative caregivers to certain caregiving activities such as shopping, food preparation, cleaning and bed making or in the practical nursing tasks of feeding, bathing, grooming, dressing or giving medication.

FILIAL RESPONSIBILITY

One function of the family is to care for its members. Today, it is generally believed that filial responsibility forms the base of the family's role to provide care for the parental generation. Seelbach (1977, p. 421) defines filial responsibility as: " . . . an attitude of personal responsibility toward the maintenance of parental well being: in short, the obligations of adults to meet their parent's needs." This concept finds its genesis in the biblical commandment "honor thy father and thy mother."

Butler, Lewis and Sunderland (1991) point out that filial responsibility refers to finances, as well as attitudes and beliefs about care of the elderly. Not until the Elizabethan Poor Laws were enacted did Western societies have laws regarding community assistance to elders and other needy people. Social Security, enacted in 1935, was based on the belief of inter-generational support, and Medicare and Medicaid further supported elders in our society. While most studies show that actual financial assistance by family members to elders is relatively small (however, richer people tend to give their parents more), there are no adequate studies measuring the actual costs of noncash goods and services exchanged by caregivers and recipients. Policy makers fear that greater availability of Medicare/Medicaid funds would cause a rush on their services, but, evidence from other nations doesn't confirm this (Butler et al., 1991, p. 39). Families continue to be involved with their elders in Denmark and Norway despite the lack of filial responsibility laws. Nowadays with a greater proportion of elderly and fewer caregivers there are problems.

Bulcroft, Van Leynseele and Borgatta (1989) surveyed filial responsibility laws in 50 states in 1988. Increasingly, the family has been identified as the natural caregiver, and this must be explored, especially since little financial or service support has been forthcoming to families. These authors most frequently found filial responsibility codes in family relations or support of poor sections of state statutes. Some laws are a decade or so old, and some are new. Thirty states had some kind of law about support of elders, varying: (1) in terms of who was named to be the caregiver (spouses, children, siblings, grandchildren); (2) methods of enforcement; and, (3) nature of support, financial, reimbursement, personal care, etc. Of twenty states without such laws, some had repealed them. There was no apparent geographic or demographic pattern. Arizona, Florida and other states with a high proportion of elderly are not more likely to have filial responsibility laws. Usually the law focuses on parents' responsibility to care for children, and vaguely refers to support of elders. Basically the thrust of most laws is that children should maintain their needy parents and elderly kin.

Some kin are not expected to contribute. For example, great grandchildren, nephews and nieces are not called to be caregivers by these laws. Similarly married women may be excluded. The most common order of caregiver responsibility in these laws is spouse, parents, children, siblings, grandchildren, and grandparents. Sometimes there are exceptions, such as Indiana, New Jersey and Rhode Island where children are not obligated to care for parents if they were abandoned or neglected as children. In Colorado and Montana children don't have to support intemperate, indolent, immoral parents. Most states have added a caution that children and other family members are only required to support parents if they are able to do so, but "sufficient ability" is never clearly defined (Bulcroft et al., 1989).

The hierarchy of support seems to be predicated on the idea of implied contract and reciprocal obligation between generations. Most of the attempts to force children to provide care have dealt with financial support. The definition of need is unclear as to requirements. Sometimes they seem to suggest that families are obligated to help with activities of daily living. Generally, the laws require families to reimburse and repay benefits paid by government agencies. While Medicaid funds cannot be recouped, there is variability across states as to whether other federal or state funds are collectable. Payment of support is usually a reimbursement to third parties. How an elder's need is established is not determined in any of these laws, and nowhere can an elder directly sue his kinsmen for support. Some states have specified courts to hear these cases. There is great variation in enforcing. When children live in another state it is particularly difficult to enforce. While all 50 states adopted the Uniform Reciprocal Enforcement Act in 1968 application is difficult due to terminology and lack of uniformity of laws as they apply to elders and filial responsibility.

Filial responsibility laws have not been tested and there is no agreement on the constitutionality of these laws. Most of the legislation seems to be aimed to support of social service agencies. The only successful constitutional argument suggested is that equal protection must be offered (14th Amendment). While the states have argued that there is an implied contract, since parents first cared for their children, then, later children must care for their parents. This interpretation ignores the voluntary nature of childbirth, and creates the duty of a child to support a parent that is not voluntary. Unsuccessful claims include lack of procedural due process, discriminatory classification claims, double taxation charges, and taking private property for public use without compensation (Bulcroft et al., 1989). Overall, these laws have not been enforced mostly because many people believe that liability for relatives undermines family relations and imposes unfair burdens. These laws may not be socially desirable, and may not be very productive financially.

EMERGING LEGAL ISSUES

The economic power of elderly people has changed in the US. The number of elders living below poverty level has dropped because of publicly funded maintenance programs and private retirement programs. Inflation has increased the value of homes. As a group, today's elderly are better off financially than at any other time in history. Adult children typically do not have to support financially their elders fully, but they typically do assist them, especially with noncash goods and services. The elderly are also living longer and needing more care for a longer period of time; placing the population of old old (85+) at risk for illness and disability.

Most individuals expect to leave an inheritance to their family or friends. However when long-term illness strikes prior inheritance plans are threatened. Assets gained over a lifetime are quickly eroded away in a short amount of time, to cover medical expenses and long term care. Public policy does not provide financial coverage or other support for all forms of illness. There is no consistency among states concerning spousal impoverishment laws.

A majority (62%) of the young and middleaged adults in the 1987 Delaware Household Survey (Settles, 1989) expressed concern about having enough money for medical expenses. Sixty-seven percent of those sampled had actually discussed wills, insurance or other financial arrangements with others. Such findings reflect the value society places on maintaining financial independence. However, in this same group half (52%) had not discussed medical care and treatment in case of serious illness.

Maintaining control over health care decisions has become an issue for public policy. The passage of the Patient Self Determination Act of 1991 supports the right of the individual to give advance directives concerning life sustaining decisions in the event of serious illness. In some states the living will must also be accompanied by a health care proxy that provides a medical power of attorney.

Because laws governing and protecting spousal impoverishment, financial and medical decisions are becoming more complex a new market has been created for a specialized area of law, elder law practice. Originally designed to assist families with estate planning, it now focuses on finding the loopholes of asset protection. This tends to raise ethical issues related to the intent of protected assets to provide for one's long term care, support the caregiver(s), or pass assets on to family members. It sheds new light on the definition of responsibility.

CONCLUSION

Clearly shaping public policy is complex. First of all, researchers in gerontology tend to focus on tasks involved in caretaking, rather than the intimate personal relations involved in family caregiving. The importance of the quality of relationship between recipient and caregiver, the caregiver's values, the available resources, and any serious worsening of the care recipient are difficult to measure but must be considered when families are held responsible for their elders' care. The role of professionals should be in mediating between family caregivers and elders, helping them separate emotions from issues, refine needs, discover the underlying mutual interests, and find and explore options.

Secondly, although many studies focus on the stress experienced by the caregiver, they often adopt the medical model for solutions ignoring the social and economic forces creating the problem. Caregivers need education about their elder's problems, how to care for themselves and for their elders. Formal recognition and appreciation in our society, coupled with financial and emotional support could make a positive difference. Even if services do not alleviate stress they do perform a number of important functions, they assist the caregiver in remaining in the public world, remaining at work, having leisure time, seeing friends, and so minimize the costs to the caregiver in his/her life.

Long term planning is not merely the acknowledgment of need, but it encompasses complex processes and systems given the current and projected demographics of an increasing aging population. With fewer resources in an economic crunch, crisis strategies rather than preventative oriented actions have become dominant. Conflict over perception of institutional responsibility has created ambiguity for families over personal responsibilities. Empowerment of the individual is the current response to give control to those who are directly affected by long term planning. The goal of empowerment is to enable a community to care for all its members through shared responsibility.

In order for informal caregivers to be empowered with knowledge, skills training, support and the availability of community resources, the social and health care systems must be secure enough to relinquish expert power so that the care receiver, family member and system provider can address needs as a team.

REFERENCES

Abel, E. (1991). *Who cares for the elderly?* Philadelphia: Temple University Press.

Adams, B. (1968). *Kinship in an urban setting.* Chicago: Marham.

Anastas, J., Gibeau, J., & Larson, P. (1990). Working with families and eldercare: a national perspective in an aging America. *Social Work, 5,* 405-411.

Archbold, P. (1980). Impact of parent caring on middle-aged offspring. *Journal of Gerontological Nursing, 6,* 79-85.

Atchley, R. (1988). *Social Forces and Aging.* Belmont, CA: Wadsworth.

Binstock, R. (1985). Health care of the aging: trends, dilemmas, & prospects for the year 2000. In C. M. Gaitz et al. (Eds.), *Aging 2000: our health care destiny: Vol. 2. Psychosocial & policy issues* (pp. 3-15). New York: Springer-Verlag.

Blenker, M. (1965). Social work and family relationships in later life with some thoughts on filial maturity. In E. Shanas & G. Streib (Eds.), *Social Structure and the Family.* Englewood Cliffs, NJ: Prentice Hall.

Brody, E. (1970). The etiquette of filial behavior. *Aging and Human Development, 1,* 87-94.

Brubaker, T. H., Cole, C., Cole, A. L., & Hennon, C. (1978). Forum on aging and the family: Discussions with F. Ivan Nye, Bernice L. Neugarten and Vera Mace. *Family Coordinator,* 436.

Bulcroft, K., Van Leynseele, J., & Borgatta, E. (1989). Filial responsibility laws: issues and state statutes. *Research on Aging, 8*, 374-393.

Butler, R., Lewis, M., & Sunderland, T. (1991). *Aging and mental health.* New York: Merrill.

Cantor, M. H. (1991). Family and community: Changing roles in an aging society. *The Gerontologist, 31*, 337-346.

Clark, P. G. (1987). Individual autonomy, cooperative empowerment and planning for long-term care decision-making. *Journal of Aging Studies, 1*, 65-76. (ERIC DATABASE, 88T2928, 197).

Coe, R. (1987). Communication & medical care outcomes: analysis of conversations between doctors & elderly patients. In R. Ward & S. Tobin (Eds.), *Health in aging: Sociological issues & policy directions* (pp. 180-193). New York: Springer-Verlag.

The Commonwealth Fund. (1992). *The nation's great overlooked resource: the contributions of Americans 55+* (Louis Harris and Associates, Inc.) New York, NY: Author.

Deacon, R. E., & Firebaugh, F. (1988). *Family resource management.* Boston, MA: Allyn and Bacon, Inc.

Fengler, A., & Goodrich, N. (1979). Wives of elderly disabled men: The hidden patients. *The Gerontologist, 19*, 175-183.

Fewell, R., & Vadast, P. (1986). *Families of handicapped children.* TX: Pro-Ed.

Fisher, L. R., & Eustis, N. N. (1988). DRG's and family care for the elderly: A case study. *The Gerontologist, 28*, 383-389.

Foulke, S. (1980). *Caring for the parental generation: An analysis of family resources and support.* Unpublished masters thesis, University of Delaware, Newark, DE.

Foulke, S. (1989). *Planning in mid-life: an evaluation of a videotape program to create awareness of decision needs.* Unpublished doctoral dissertation, University of Delaware, Newark, DE.

Glasser, M., Rubin, S., & Dickover, M. (1989). Caregiver views of help from the physician. *American Journal of Alzheimer's Care and Related Disorders and Research, 4*(4), 4-11.

Golodetz, A., Evans, R., Henritz, G., & Gibson, C. (1969). The care of chronic illness: The 'responsor' role. *Medical Care, 7*, 385-394.

Hanauer-Onyx, M. (1992, August 3). Teenagers and AIDS. *Newsweek,* pp. 45-50.

Hasselkus, B. R. (1988). The family caregiver's view. *Topics in Geriatric Rehabilitation, 4*, 60-70.

Hess, B. (1979, January 9). Family myths. *New York Times,* A19.

Hill, R., Foote, N., Aldous, J., Carlson, R., & MacDonald, R. (1990). *Family Development in Three Generations,* Cambridge, MA: Scherhman Publishing Company.

Horowitz, A. (1978). *Families who care: a study of natural support systems of the elderly.* Paper presented at the Thirty-first Annual Meeting, Gerontological Society, Dallas, TX.

Killeen, M. (1990). Influence of stress and coping on family caregivers' perception of health. *International Journal of Aging And Human Development, 30,* 197-211.

Lawton, M. P., Brody, E., & Saperstein, A. (1989). Respite care for Alzheimer's families: Research findings & their relevance to providers. *American Journal of Alzheimer's Care and Related Disorders and Research, 4,* 31-38.

Leader, S., & Liebig, P. (1988). High tech home care: a reexamination. *Caring, 7*(9), 4-7.

Lieberman, G. L. (1978). Children of the elderly as natural helpers: Some demographic differences. *American Journal of Community Psychiatry, 6,* 489-498.

Lurie, E., Robinson, B., & Barbaccia, J. (1984). Helping the hospitalized elderly: Discharge planning and informal support. *Home Health Care Quarterly, 5*(2), 25-43.

Miller, M., & Eisdorfer, C. (1989). Model of caregiver's willingness to provide care. *Caregiving, 8,* 10-18.

Morgan, M. (1969). The middle life and the aging family. *The Family Coordinator, 29,* 37-46.

Murrey, J. (1973). Family structures in the pre-retirement years. *Social Security Bulletin, 36,* 25-44.

O'Grady-LeShane, R., Kingson, E., Hopps, J. G. (1988). *Women and Social Security: An analysis of the economic impact of later life care giving: Final Report.*

Oren, L. (1974). The welfare of women in laboring families: England, 1860-1950. In M. S. Hartman & I. Banner (Eds.), *Clio's consciousness raised: New perspectives on the history of women* (pp. 226-244). New York: Harper & Row.

Parsons, R., & Cox, E. (1989). Family meditation in elder caregiving decisions: An empowerment intervention. *Social Work, 34,* 122-126.

Pfeiffer, E. (1990). Why caregivers need care, too. *Senior Patient, 2,* 30-32.

Pratt, C., Jones, L., Sin, H. Y., & Walker, A. (1989). Autonomy and decision making between single older women and their caregiving daughters. *Gerontology, 29,* 792-797.

Rice, A. S., & Tucker, S. M. (1986). *Family life management* (6th Ed.). New York: Macmillan Publishing Company.

Rose (1991). What is feminism? A reexamination. In E. Abel (Ed.), *Women's Work: Women's Knowledge.* New York: Pantheon, 649-656.

Scholnick, E. K., & Friedman, S. L. (1987). The planning construct in the psychological literature. In S. L. Friedman, E. K. Scholnick, & R. Cocking (Eds.), *Blueprints for thinking: The role of planning in cognitive development.* New York: Cambridge University Press.

Schorr, A. (1960). *Filial responsibility in modern American family.* Washington, D. C.: Social Security Administration.

Seccome, K., Ryan, R., & Austin, C. D. (1987). Care planning: Case managers assessment of elders' welfare and caregivers' capacity. *Family Relations, 36,* 171-175.

Seelbach, W. (1977). Gender differences in expectations for filial responsibility. *The Gerontologist, 17,* 421-425.

Seelback, W. (1978). Correlates of aged parents' filial responsibilities, expectations and realizations. *Family Coordinator, 27,* 341-350.

Seltzer, M. M., & Mayer, J. (1988). Families as case managers: a team approach for serving elders. *Generations, 12,* 26-29.

Settles, B. H. (1987). A perspective on tomorrow's families. In M. Sussman & S. Steinmetz (Eds.). *Handbook of Marriage and Family.* New York: Plenum Press.

Settles, B. H. (1989). *Interactive planning for family futures.* (Final Report for Grant # 0090AM219 USHHS). Newark, DE: University of Delaware.

Shanas, E. (1961). Living arrangements of older people in the United States. *The Gerontologist 1*: 27-29.

Shanas, E. (1967). Family help patterns and social class in three countries. *Journal of Marriage and The Family, 29,* 257-266.

Shanas, E. (1979). The family as a social support system in old age. *The Gerontologist, 19,* 169-174.

Simos, B. (1973). Adult children and their aging parents. *Social Casework, 18,* 78-85.

Sivley, J. P., & Fiegner, J. J. (1984). Family caregivers of the elderly: Assistance provided after termination of chore services. *Journal of Gerontological Social Work* (1/2), 23-24.

Smerglia, V., Deimling, G., & Barresi, C. (1988). Black/white family comparisons in helping and decision making networks of impaired elderly. *Family Relations, 37.*

Smith, G., Smith, M., & Toesland, R. (1991). Problems identified by family caregivers in counseling. *Gerontologist, 31,* 15-22.

Stoller, E. (1990). Family caregiving: What price love? *Journal of Long-Term Care Administration, 2*: 16-21.

Stone, R., & Short, P. (1990). Competing demands of employment and informal caregiving to disabled elders. *Medical Care, 6,* 513-526.

Sussman, M. B., & Burchial, L. (1962). Parental aid to married children: implications for family functioning. *Marriage and Family Living, 24,* 320-332.

Teltsch (1992, July 22). As more people need care, more men help. *The New York Times,* pp. B1, B4.

Toesland, R., & Rossiter, C. (1989). Group interventions to support family caregivers: A review and analysis. *Gerontologist, 29,* 438-448.

Treas, J. (1977). Family support systems for the aged. *The Gerontologist, 17,* 486-491.

Troll, L., Miller, S., & Atchely, R. (1979). *Families in later life.* Belmont, CA: Wadsworth Publishing Company.

Worcester, M. I., & Quayhagen, M. P. (1983). Correlates of caregiving satisfaction: Prerequisites to elder home care. *Research in Nursing and Health, 6*(2), 61-67.

Zweibel, N., & Lydens, L. (1990). Incongruent perception of older adult/caregiver dyads. *Family Relations, 39.*

Social Programs for Families in Poverty: Past Impacts and Future Prospects

Juanita B. Hepler
John H. Noble

KEYWORDS. Social programs, Family policy, Poverty

INTRODUCTION

The economic well-being of families is an important issue for our society. The programs we develop to assist and support families living in poverty are a reflection of our commitment to those, who for many reasons, are experiencing financial hardship. In this chapter we examine the impact of government programs on the economic well-being of poor families and discuss prospects for the future. We argue that:

1. Government programs during the past twenty years have reduced poverty.
2. Female-headed households have increased dramatically since the 60s, and a large number of these families live in extreme poverty.

Juanita B. Hepler is Associate Professor, Social Work Department, Boise State University. John H. Noble is Professor, School of Social Work, State University of New York at Buffalo.

[Haworth co-indexing entry note]: "Social Programs for Families in Poverty: Past Impacts and Future Prospects." Hepler, Juanita B. and John H. Noble. Co-published simultaneously in *Marriage & Family Review* (The Haworth Press, Inc.) Vol. 18, No. 3/4, 1993, pp. 97-123; and: *American Families and the Future: Analyses of Possible Destinies* (ed: Barbara H. Settles, Roma S. Hanks, and Marvin B. Sussman) The Haworth Press, Inc., 1993, pp. 97-123. Multiple copies of this article/chapter may be purchased from The Haworth Document Delivery Center. Call 1-800-3-HAWORTH (1-800-342-9678) between 9:00 - 5:00 (EST) and ask for DOCUMENT DELIVERY CENTER.

Many of the women lack education, job skills, and job experience. The problems appear to be most severe for blacks and other minority groups.

3. AFDC, the major government program providing cash benefits to families has been hampered because of controversy concerning the program. Real benefits have decreased since the 70s because of inflation and budget cuts. Many of the allegations against the program are not supported by research and the restrictive benefit levels seem detrimental rather than helpful.

4. Cuts implemented during the Reagan Administration have decreased the effectiveness of social programs for families and probably placed some children at greater risk for abuse and neglect.

5. The continuing recession in the 90s, rising poverty rates, and efforts by states to restrict or reduce welfare costs are creating further hardships for poor families.

6. The poor need jobs. Effective job training programs are an essential part of a successful anti-poverty program. The consistently high unemployment rate of black males is of special concern and may be a major contributing factor in the increase of black female headed households.

7. There are no easy, simple solutions to poverty. If we are committed to reducing poverty for families, we must be willing to commit extensive financial outlays during the initial stages. In the long run, the benefits to these families and society should exceed the costs. To ignore the problem means large numbers of people will endure extreme hardships and that many children will grow up in poverty with all the negative consequences for themselves and society.

8. Former President Bush and President Clinton made "family values" a major issue in their presidential campaigns. However, neither candidate demonstrated a strong commitment to reduce poverty for families.

To address these issues we draw from recent studies on demographic trends and changes in this country and government programs designed to help poor families.

GOVERNMENT ATTEMPTS TO REDUCE POVERTY

In the mid sixties, social programs experienced great expansion. There was a feeling of optimism that poverty could be substantially reduced or even eliminated in our society. Programs were developed and financial resources were allocated to provide job training, educational opportunities, community development and increased cash and in-kind benefits for low-income families. There was an emphasis on including minorities in these programs in order to help them become successfully assimilated into society. The mid-seventies saw a decrease in the growth of some programs as benefit rates were not adjusted for rising inflation. Consequently, the real value of benefits for programs such as AFDC declined (Danziger, Haveman, & Plotnick, 1986). By the 80s both the public and the government appeared disillusioned with the high cost of reducing or eliminating poverty. Inflation and the poor economy made increased funding seem less attractive. Furthermore, after 20 years of expanded programs, poverty had not been eliminated. Many felt that the "War on Poverty" had been a failure and a waste of taxpayer's money. With the election of President Reagan, there was a turnabout in federal policy towards the poor. The Reagan Administration attempted to eliminate or reduce funding for most social programs. While congress refused to go along with many of the proposed cuts, Reagan was able to essentially stop the expansion of federal programs (Bawden & Palmer, 1984). The late 80s and early 90s show a similar trend. The economy continues to perform poorly and there has been little expansion in social programs for the poor. In fact, many states have attempted to reduce welfare programs despite an increase in the number of people living in poverty (Morganthau, Lewis, McCormick, Wolfberg, & Washington, 1991).

EFFECT OF GOVERNMENT TRANSFERS ON POVERTY

During the past 20 years, the rate of poverty declined from 19% in 1964 (1 year prior to the War on Poverty) to 11-11.5% in the early seventies. Beginning in 1980, with the recession and cuts in social programs, the trend was reversed and the rate of poverty rose to 15% increasing to 15.2% in 1983. At present the poverty rate is over 13% and rising (Morganthau et al., 1991). It is important to remember that the reduction in poverty after 1964 was the result of economic growth and the increase in government cash and in-kind benefits (includes non-cash services such as food stamps and Medicaid) rather than the increased earning power of the poor (Danziger et al., 1986; Ellwood & Summers, 1986; Bawden & Palmer, 1984; Schiller, 1980a).

Although government benefits or transfers played an important role in reducing poverty, their effect was limited as a substantial amount of the funding went to programs not specifically targeted for the poor. Contrary to public opinion, it is the middle class rather than the poor who have most benefited from government transfers. During the past twenty years, the programs receiving the most funding and experiencing the greatest expansion were the social insurance programs (social security, Medicare, unemployment insurance, workman's compensation). In 1982, for example, social security benefits exceeded $13 billion dollars per month for 36 million individuals or families (Garfinkel & Holden, 1983). The middle class receives the highest benefits from these programs because of their higher incomes while working. Nevertheless, while the major purpose of social insurance is to maintain workers' incomes under certain circumstances (retirement, temporary unemployment, work-related injury) they have also helped to reduce poverty, especially for the elderly (Ellwood & Summers, 1986). The rate of poverty for the elderly dropped from 25% in 1969 to 15% in 1979. At the same time for all persons, the rate of poverty decreased only four tenths of 1% (O'Neil, 1986).

Programs targeted for the poor (AFDC families and SSI for the elderly and the disabled) showed less growth although they were expanded in the 60s. These programs are means-tested which means individual or family income must be below a specified amount to be eligible for benefits. In 1982, the total expenditures for the 30.6 million nonelderly poor were approximately 20 billion dollars, with the disabled receiving the larger benefits. These expenditures represented less than 2% of the federal budget for that year. In addition, states failed to adjust benefit levels for programs such as AFDC to adjust for inflation; that means the real value of these benefits decreased by approximately 30% between 1972 and 1980 (Ellwood & Summers, 1986). Furthermore, most of the increase in expenditures for cash assistance programs went to the disabled (approximately 2 million individuals) rather than to families (Danziger & Gottschalk, 1985; Ellwood & Summers, 1986; Schiller, 1980a). A similar pattern is evident at present. Because of the recession and budget deficits, states have opted to maintain current levels without adjustments for inflation, or they have reduced benefits or implemented more stringent eligibility requirements (CDF Reports, 1991). It is evident that these levels of expenditures for cash assistance programs, especially for families, could not have a very large impact on the prevailing poverty rate for the nonelderly.

REVIEWING PROGRESS SINCE 1964

The programs we implemented during the 60s and 70s were successful within their limitations (Ellwood & Summers, 1986). As previously discussed, most of the funds were allocated to social insurance programs that benefited the middle class and the elderly. Consequently, we see a large reduction in poverty for the elderly. Families received smaller benefits and their rate of poverty, especially for single-parent families remain high. The elderly and many people with disabilities are not expected to work, and we seem to experience less difficulty in providing funds for these individuals and their dependents. On the other hand, the nonelderly, especially single-parent families are viewed with suspicion and mistrust. While most Americans want to help children and see that their basic needs are met, they have difficulty providing cash assistance for able-bodied parents. There is the strong belief that jobs are available if individuals really want to work (Schiller, 1980a). Thus welfare recipients are viewed with distrust, and there is always the fear that providing too much assistance will increase their dependence on society and reduce their work incentive. Hence, there is considerable controversy surrounding programs such as AFDC, and funding for these programs has traditionally been at lower levels.

Because of conflicting feelings concerning the poor, the development and implementation of effective social policy is hampered. As Schiller (1980a) points out, we want to establish viable programs, because we realize that poverty is related, in part, to economic and social factors. But we also tend to believe the poor lack ability and motivation and have questionable morals (Schiller, 1980a). (These same sentiments were reflected by Alexis De Tocqueville in 1835, Public Interest, 1983). Critiquing the English Poor Laws, Tocqueville admitted that public charity is necessary for the aged, the sick, the very young and the insane. However, he was convinced that permanent public support will "breed more miseries than it can cure, will deprave the population that it wants to help and comfort, will in time reduce the rich to being no more than the tenant-farmers of the poor, will dry up the sources of savings, will stop the accumulation of capital, will retard the development of trade, will benumb human industry and activity, and will culminate by bringing about a violent revolution in the state, when the number of those who receive alms will have become as large as those who give it, and the indigent, no longer being able to take from the impoverished rich the means of providing for his needs, will find it easier to plunder them of all their property at one stroke than to ask for their help" (Tocqueville, 1835, Public Interest, 1983, p. 119). Many of our present attitudes are reflected in Tocqueville's passage, and even though poverty was reduced with the expansion of public assistance during the past 20 years, many Americans would not view this as success. Instead, a program that increased earning potential and self-sufficiency rather than dependence on public assistance would receive greater approval and support (Danziger et al., 1986).

THE REAGAN ADMINISTRATION
AND ANTIPOVERTY PROGRAMS

Considering Americans' ambivalent feelings toward the poor, the high costs of programs, and the slow growth of the economy, it is not surprising that the Reagan Administration found public and congressional support for halting the expansion of social programs. While growth in these programs had been curtailed, Reagan attempted to bring a halt to the expansion of all social programs and even to eliminate a number of them. He believed that economic recovery by itself would help the poor by creating jobs and higher salaries. A problem with this rationale is that many of the poor do not benefit from economic growth (female heads of households, the disabled, unskilled workers). In 1982 Congress gave President Reagan most of the cuts he asked for; however, few cuts were allowed in 1983 and 1984. Several criticisms were leveled against the budget cuts. First, the President showed little discretion in selecting programs to cut. Both successful and less successful programs were included. Another, and perhaps more serious criticism, was that most cuts were aimed at programs for the poor. We have seen historically that the largest expenditures were in the social insurance programs, yet most of the cuts were not directed at these programs. Over half of the proposed cuts were in income security, education, training, employment, and social services (Bawden & Palmer, 1984; Danziger & Haveman, 1981). According to Haveman (1982), the cuts increased the gap between the rich and poor. He cites a 17% cut in AFDC while Veterans Compensation received no cuts.

Reagan was not able to garner support for budget cuts after 1983 as the public and Congress came to the realization that the social programs had been cut as much as possible. At the same time, there was not and still does not appear to be any strong cry for increased spending or expansion of programs, perhaps due to the budget deficit and the present political environment. Consequently, while few people are happy with the present programs, including recipients, major changes seem unlikely without the stimulus of general discontent with the prevailing policies.

AID TO FAMILIES
WITH DEPENDENT CHILDREN (AFDC)

In this section we focus on AFDC, the only major federal program specifically designated to provide cash assistance to poor families. Of all welfare programs, it is the most controversial and has been accused of destroying the family unit, increasing the number of nonmarital births, and decreasing work incentives (we will examine the validity of these allegations in a later section). Because of strict eligibility requirements, only the most needy are eligible for benefits from this program. Bane and Ellwood (1983) found very few families on AFDC had incomes above the poverty level. There has been much controversy concerning the amount of money recipients receive. Is the amount excessive allowing families to enjoy luxuries and decreasing their incentive to work? Within federal guidelines, each state establishes a standard need level (minimum amount of money a family of four needs in order to meet their basic needs) and benefit levels. A look at benefit levels for 1986 shows variation across states with a range of approximately $823 per month for a family of four (one adult and three children) to a low of $144 per month (Skoro & Johnson, 1991). These differences appear to be related to regional per capita GNP and attitudes towards the AFDC program. According to Gramlick (1986) and Gramlick and Laren (1984), southern states have traditionally had lower per capita GNP and pay lower benefits to AFDC recipients. The northern states have a slightly higher GNP and pay higher benefits. Skoro and Johnson (1991) found little consistency across states in their assessment of need level for families and the actual benefit payments paid to these families. The authors report that only twenty states provide benefits equal to the need level they have established. Nor was there a correlation between need and benefit levels on the state level and the federal government's designated poverty level. Skoro and Johnson (1991) conclude that most states do not provide adequate benefits to meet the basic needs of poor families. And, as previously mentioned, AFDC benefits have not been adjusted for inflation, so that their real value has declined across regions. For example between 1989 and 1990 the real value of the maximum benefit level (family of three) decreased in 45 states (CDF Reports, 1990).

How effective is AFDC in removing families from poverty? Looking at the effects for public assistance cash benefits (includes AFDC, SSI, and general assistance), we find that the programs made strides in reducing poverty between 1965 and 1978. According to Danziger, Havemen and Plotnick (1986), 6.3 percent of the pretransfer poor were removed from poverty by these benefits in 1972. However, because of nonindexing of benefits, cuts in programs, and stricter eligibility requirements, effects of cash benefits have declined since 1978. Thus in 1983 only 3.4 percent of the pretransfer poor were removed from poverty by public cash assistance. Consequently, while there was an increase in the number of female-headed households, the number of these families receiving benefits remained relatively unchanged (Danziger et al., 1986).

GROWTH IN FEMALE HEADS OF HOUSEHOLD
AND THEIR RATE OF POVERTY

A major reason for the controversy surrounding AFDC is the rapid increase in the number of female heads of household and their corresponding high rate of poverty. (The frequent allocations concerning the association between the expansion in social programs and the increase in female-headed households will be discussed in a later section.) Prior to 1960, most families in this country consisted of two parents. This was true for both white and black families; however, after 1960 there was a substantial increase in the number of female-headed households with the greatest increase in black families. By 1970, 28% of black families were headed by females. This increased to 42% in 1983 and 53% in 1986. In 1960 8% of white families were headed by females, 12% in 1983 and 18% in 1986. Less data are available on Hispanics but they have also experienced increases from 21.5% in 1982 to 23.4% in 1989 (Garcia, 1991; McRoy, 1990; Wilson & Neckerman, 1986). Although more black families are headed by females, Garfinkel and McLanahan (1986) suggest that the recent rate of growth has been similar for both black and white families–(37%) for both groups between 1960-1970 and 40% for whites and 35% for blacks between 1970-1980. Ellwood and Summers (1986) report that before reaching eighteen years of age, 45% of the white children and 85% of the black children in this country will have spent some part of their childhood in a single-parent home.

The rate of poverty for female heads of household with children under eighteen years of age is high, especially for black families. In 1981, 67.7% of all black children in female-headed households were poor, while 42.8% of white children were poor. For children under age 6, the rate is even higher. In black families headed by females, 74.2% of the children were poor and 59.1% of the white children lived in poverty (Center for the Study of Social Policy, 1983). In 1989, the poverty rate for Hispanic female-headed families was 51.8% (Garcia, 1991) and in 1991, the overall poverty rate for female headed households was 53.4% (CDF Reports, 1991).

These are sobering statistics as the negative effects of poverty have been well documented (Center for the Study of Social Policy, 1983; Kimmich, 1985; Burt & Pittman, 1985). Child abuse and neglect, for example are more prevalent in low income families. According to Burt and Pittman (1985) the occurrence of abuse and neglect is ten times higher in families with incomes below $7,000 than in families with incomes above $25,000. While part of this is due to the lack of information on middle class families who tend to use private services, research also indicates a greater likelihood of abuse and neglect in low income families. Children in female-headed families are more susceptible to neglect and abuse. The fact that many of these families also receive welfare suggests poverty may be a major contributing factor rather than family composition (Burt & Pittman, 1985). The number of children living in poverty increased during the 80s and in 1990 more than 13 million children were poor. Large numbers of these children will receive child protection services before reaching adulthood.

Although the poverty rate is high for female-headed households, only about one-fifth of all poverty is related to changes in family composition (Bane, 1986; Gottschalk & Danziger, 1984; Danziger et al., 1986). Utilizing the Panel Study of Income Dynamics (PSID), a longitudinal survey including over 6,000 households, Bane (1986) provides an explanation for the low impact of these families on the overall poverty rate. She concluded that less than half of the poverty of female-headed and single person households is associated with their becoming independent households. In other words, many of these families were poor prior to the break-up of the family. This is especially true for black families. Almost two-thirds of the poor black families had been poor before establishing independent households. For white families, a different picture emerges. Of those who were poor, only about 25% had been poor prior to becoming female heads or single-person households. These findings suggest that much of the poverty within black families would not have been eliminated if family composition had remained stable but that family break-up is associated with poverty for white families. In a later section, we will discuss how enforcement of child support payments could help to alleviate poverty for white women but probably would not greatly improve the financial condition of most black families.

EXPLANATIONS FOR INCREASES
IN FEMALE HEADS OF HOUSEHOLD

We have discussed the dramatic increase in female-headed households and documented their high rate of poverty. We will now consider the causes for this increase. Again the evidence suggests there are different patterns for black and white women. For white women the growth is related to the increasing tendency for them to marry and then divorce, while for black women, the growth is related to a decrease in marriage and an increase in nonmarital births. The economic independence or labor force participation of white women appears to be a major factor affecting their divorce rate. For black women, the evidence suggests black male unemployment is an important factor contributing to a decrease in marriage (Garfinkel & McLanahan, 1986; Wilson & Neckerman, 1986; Wilson, 1984; Ellwood & Summers, 1986; Center for the Study of Social Policy, 1983; Bane, 1986).

Black male unemployment has been ignored as a cause of the increase in black female heads of household, but several authors suggest that their high unemployment rate is a severe problem that should be addressed (Ellwood & Summers, 1986; Center for the Study of Social Policy, 1983; Garfinkel & McLanahan, 1986; Wilson & Neckerman, 1986). Black unemployment has consistently been twice that of whites since 1960. It is especially high for black males and their participation in the workforce is declining. Approximately 74% of black males participated in the labor force in 1960, but this rate had dropped to 53.5% in 1982. Black males remain unemployed for longer periods than white males. In 1983, the average time was 19.8 weeks for black males and 16.6 for white males. The picture is also bleak for black male teenagers. Their unemployment rate has remained twice that of white male teenagers since 1960 (Center for the Study of Social Policy, 1983). The 1986 unemployment rate shows the same discrepancy: 6.0 for whites and 14.5 for blacks (McRoy, 1990). Again, limited information is available for Hispanics but the Hispanic male unemployment dropped from 16.3% in 1983 to 7% in 1989 (Garcia, 1991).

Explanations vary for the large differential between black and white male employment. On the one hand, educational levels of blacks are almost equal; therefore lack of education cannot explain the high unemployment rate of blacks (Center for the Study of Social Policy, 1983). If the problem is lack of jobs, why do whites continue to be employed at higher rates? Possible explanations include black male's increased participation in the military service, the loss of agricultural jobs, the recession, and lack of skills and job connections (Ellwood, 1988; Ellwood & Wise, 1983; Wilson & Neckerman, 1986). The severity of the problem suggests there is continued discrimination against blacks in the labor market. Illegal activities may also provide a partial answer. One study surveying black male youths in ghettos found that more than half engaged in criminal activity and approximately one fourth of their income came from these activities (Ellwood, 1988). Certainly, the devastating impact of substance abuse in black ghettos has been documented.

The high unemployment rates for black males could contribute to the increase in female heads of household. Several studies have documented the negative effects of unemployment on family stability (Bakke, 1940;

Ross & Sawhill, 1975; Garfinkel & McLanahan, 1986). Furthermore as Wilson and Neckerman (1986) point out, black males also have high mortality and incarceration rates. Consequently, the number of black men able to support a family is greatly reduced. Furthermore, the number of marriageable men available has declined for black women (there are approximately one million more black women than black men), while it has remained steady or increased for white women (McRoy, 1990).

FEMALE HEADS OF HOUSEHOLD
AND WELFARE DEPENDENCY

Public assistance programs such as AFDC are meant to provide temporary aid to families. Therefore, there is considerable interest in the length of time women receive AFDC benefits and a real concern that they will become dependent on the program. Bane and Ellwood (1983) using the PSID data provide us with important information on women's use of AFDC. They found that for approximately 75% of the women, AFDC assistance coincided with becoming heads of household. Almost half of these women became heads of household through separation or divorce, while 30% were unmarried when they became heads of household. Only 12% of the women entered the program as a result of decreased earnings. Contrary to public opinion, most recipients remain in the program for relatively short periods of time. Approximately half leave the program within two years. Those who participate in the program for two years tend to remain for long periods. Sixty percent of these women receive benefits for at least six years, and 17% receive benefits for over eight years. This last group of women uses the bulk of AFDC resources.

The authors found that certain characteristics were associated with becoming long term recipients. Becoming head of household by having a child, nonwhites, high school dropouts, having many children and little or no work experience contributed to longer periods on AFDC. It is not surprising that these women have longer spells, because their poverty would be more severe and longstanding.

How do women leave or exit the program? The two major avenues enabling them to leave are marriage or an increase in earnings. About one-third leave because of marriage or reconciliation and another third leave because of increased earnings. Approximately 14% leave the program when their children grow up or leave home. Although marriage provided one of the most important means of leaving the program, Bane and Ellwood (1983) found that the probability of marriage is not the same for all women. Black women, those who entered the program when they became mothers, and high school dropouts have a smaller probability of marriage than other women on AFDC. In fact, black women tend to remain on AFDC for longer periods primarily because fewer of these women leave the program via marriage.

Once women leave AFDC, do they remain self sufficient? Since, about 40% of the women who leave have incomes below the poverty line, it is not surprising that one-third return to AFDC for another spell. The need for education and training for AFDC recipients is evident in these findings.

EFFECTS OF AFDC ON FAMILY STRUCTURE AND BEHAVIOR

A number of studies have looked at the effect of AFDC on family structure. Does the program encourage women to divorce or postpone marriage? Does it encourage nonmarital births? Ellwood and Summers (1986) looked at the relationship between the increase in female heads of household and the number of families on AFDC. They report that the number of children living in female-headed households began to increase more rapidly in the late 60s, and, at the same time, the number of children on AFDC also increased. However, after 1972, the number of children in female-headed households continued to increase from 14% to 20%, while the number of children receiving AFDC remained at approximately 12%. The trend can be more clearly seen by looking at black families. The number of children in female-headed households rose about 20%, while the number receiving benefits decreased by 5%. Why was there a decrease in the number of families receiving AFDC while their actual numbers were increasing? Again, as previously discussed, failure to index benefits and cuts in the program resulted in stricter eligibility requirements. As Ellwood and Summers (1986) point out, it is difficult to blame the program for the changes in family structure when the number of families receiving benefits was decreasing.

The effect of AFDC benefits has also been examined across states. It has been argued that states with higher benefit levels have further encouraged divorce and establishment of female-headed households. Cutwright (1973) and Ellwood and Summers (1986) found little relationship between benefit levels and divorce rates and nonmarital birth rates. Bane and Ellwood (1983) report similar findings. They found women in states with lower benefits tend to be on AFDC for a shorter time-period, but the length of time they were in poverty was as long as those in higher benefit states. There were minimum effects on divorce and separation. The major impact was on the living arrangements of young mothers who established their own household rather than continue living with their parents.

Other studies looking at the program's effect on family stability show mixed results. Sawhill, Peabody, Jones, and Caldwell (1975), Cherlin (1976) found AFDC did not encourage divorce or separation. However, several studies found significant relationships between AFDC benefits and marital stability (Hoenig, 1974; Ross & Sawhill, 1975; Hoffman & Holmes, 1976). Hoenig (1974) found significant effects for both blacks and whites in 1960 but for white women only in 1970. In the Ross and Sawhill study (1974) there was a significant relationship between AFDC benefits and marital stability for black women but not white women. The results of all these studies are inconclusive, and the conflicting findings may be the result of methodological problems. The difficulty is developing a model that separates benefit effects from other economic factors that may influence women's decisions concerning marriage (MacDonald & Sawhill, 1978). The alternatives for women (marriage, female head of household, AFDC benefits) have not been well-defined or included in many studies. Despite mixed results, there is little evidence to suggest AFDC has strong effects on marital stability. Garfinkel and McLanahan (1986) conclude that welfare programs did contribute to the growth of female-headed households but that the overall effect of these programs was small. MacDonald and Sawhill (1978) suggest factors other than government programs determine a couple's decisions concerning marriage; government programs do not seem to play a major role. They suggest that benefits may provide women with an alternative to a poor marriage.

Several studies have looked at the relationship between benefits and nonmarital births. Consistently, these studies have shown no significant relationship (see Cutwright, 1973; Bane & Ellwood, 1983). Moore and Caldwell (1976) using a national sample of over 4,000 women aged 15 to 19 found the level of benefits and the availability of AFDC benefits did not affect the women's decisions on sexual activity, conception, abortion, or marriage. This was true for both black and white women.

Most studies have indicated that AFDC has only small effects on labor force participation (see Ellwood & Summers, 1986). Danziger and Haveman (1981) suggest that transfers reduced work force participation annually by 4.8%. The labor force participation of these women would probably be small without AFDC because of the presence of small children, limited job skills, and lack of education.

It is hard to measure dependency on welfare; however, the study by

Bane and Ellwood (1983) suggests that most women are not long-term recipients and leave the program within two years. Within eight years, 85% have left the program. However, 17% do remain on AFDC for eight or more years. We have noted that most women leave the program through earnings or marriage and both are restricted or limited by the presence of children. In a recent study using PSID data, Hill and Ponza (1983, 1984) looked at the intergenerational effects of welfare benefits. Data provided information on the parent's receipt of welfare while the children were in the home, and then looked at the child's welfare dependence once he or she established a household. Only a small number of black (19%) and white (26%) women who had grown up on welfare were classified as being heavily dependent on these benefits (receiving at least 25% of average family income as cash welfare payments). Hill and Ponza (1983, 1984) also found receiving welfare had no significant effect on the labor force participation of black men. For white men, those coming from the most dependent families worked approximately seven hours less per week than other white men.

In summary, while there are methodological problems with many of the studies, and the results are tentative, the evidence does not imply that AFDC has strong negative effects on marital stability, nonmarital births, welfare dependency, or labor force participation. We conclude, therefore, that efforts should be directed toward improving the program and reducing the financial hardship of many female-headed families.

When the welfare of so many is at stake, can we continue to restrict eligibility and benefit levels? Can we continue to permit mothers and their children to live in extreme poverty? Benefits should be indexed to adjust for inflation. Creating a national minimum benefit level could reduce the inequity of the program (see Ellwood & Summers, 1986; Danziger et al., 1986). However, increasing cash benefits alone does not get at the root of the problem that lies in the poor education, lack of job skills, and apparent discrimination toward black males in the labor market. Programs to resolve black male unemployment are needed to make possible more stable relationships among black males and females. Education and job training skills are also important if we want female-headed families to become financially independent.

FINANCIAL RESPONSIBILITY
OF THE ABSENT PARENT

With the increase in female-headed families, and their corresponding poverty, the financial responsibility of the absent parent has received increased attention. Society and the government have become concerned as public costs have risen. Increasingly, we seem to feel the absent parent, usually the father, has a responsibility for his child and that this obligation should be enforced by the federal government. Despite legislation, the child support system has been ineffective in assuring that custodial parents receive support payments. In 1979, only 59% of the women who were eligible for support were actually awarded payments. Only 49% of these women received their full payment and 28% received no payments (U.S. Census, 1981). Only 11% of the fathers with children on AFDC paid any support (U.S. HHS, 1981). Furthermore the amount of payments varied according to particular judges and courts and have not been very equitable, especially for the mothers. Including child support payments, women's standard of living tends to decrease after divorce, while men's standard tends to increase (Ollerich & Garfinkel, 1983).

Legislation passed in 1975 and revised in 1980 and 1981 established the Child Support Enforcement Program. The states administer the program with major funding provided by the federal government. Under the provisions, the Internal Revenue Service has the power to collect child support for both AFDC and non-AFDC families, although the major emphasis has been on collecting payments for AFDC parents. IRS may also withhold tax refunds from parents who are delinquent in their payments. While it did not solve the problem, the legislation did increase the collection for child support payments (U.S. HHS, 1982).

In 1984, new child support laws went into effect. They take stronger steps to ensure that absent parents meet the financial responsibility of their child or children. With the new provisions, effects will be felt on all income levels rather than placing the most emphasis on AFDC families. For example, financial incentives have been included that encourage states to collect payments for nonwelfare families. The program also requires states to withhold child support payments from wages if these payments are one month late. Another provision of the law allows the first $50 of child support to be ignored when calculating AFDC benefits. This is to encourage AFDC mothers to identify the father and to encourage fathers to make support payments (Garfinkel & McLanahan, 1986). With these provisions, the government has taken additional steps to enforce child support payments by absent parents. This, in time should reduce the financial hardship for female-headed families not on welfare, especially white families. However, as previously discussed, it will do little towards helping families who receive welfare. Many black families, in particular, will not experience great improvement in their financial situation (Bane, 1986). According to Garfinkel and McLanahan (1986) the effects on most

AFDC families will be small, but it will enable a few to leave welfare. However, estimated support of female heads of household may increase by nearly $1 billion per year, although the authors admit that their estimate could be high or low depending on the efficiency of collection procedures and the development of a withholding system that enforces interstate payment.

The Family Support Act of 1988 provides additional regulations for improving child support payments and must be implemented between 1990-1994. Under this act, all support payments will be withheld from wages (the 1984 provisions only withheld payments when they were one month late). In addition each state must establish guidelines for the amount of child support the absent parent pays and courts and judges must utilize these guidelines in determining levels of payment (CDF Reports, 1990). Cases must also be reviewed periodically to update these payments. Clearly, the government and society have decided that the absent parent must assume responsibility for their children, and these laws help to bring about improved compliance.

EFFECT OF BUDGET CUTS ON AFDC AND OTHER CHILD WELFARE PROGRAMS

What has happened to America's children while society and politicians have grappled with issues of poverty? Between 1981 and 1984, federal funding was reduced for 25 programs providing services to children. These cuts were enacted during a period when poverty was increasing, resulting in a greater demand for services. Adjusting for inflation, the funding for these programs was cut by approximately 11%. The Reagan administration asked for larger cuts, but Congress consistently refused to go along with many of these proposals (Kimmich, 1985). States, localities, and private sources attempted to meet the growing needs of poor families, but in most cases, were not able to totally compensate for the losses. Cuts included changes in Medicaid that restricted eligibility and increased the costs of medical care and major reductions in funding for social services, especially daycare for the working poor. Cuts in education, employment, and income maintenance programs were large with most state and local governments making little effort to compensate for these reductions. The results were a reduction in services and/or increased costs to consumers for these services (Kimmich, 1985).

Kimmich (1985) and Burt and Pittman (1985) studied the effects of budget cuts, drawing information from four communities: Boston, Massachusetts; Wayne County, Michigan; Richmond, Virginia; and San Diego County, California. Staffs at the social service agencies in these communities were faced with budget cuts, increased demand for services, and reduced staff. They reported a reduction in thorough investigations and preventive services. Increasingly, they tended to focus on the most severe or crisis cases. There was an increase in reported cases of child abuse and neglect during the early 80s. It is difficult to determine if this increase in child abuse and neglect was the result of greater public awareness or increased poverty due to the economic recession and budget cuts. However, social service workers in the communities felt reductions in programs and services had increased the level of stress for many poor multi-problem families and most likely contributed to the increase in reported cases of abuse and neglect.

A major program affecting children is foster care. As a result of the Child Welfare Act of 1980, permanency planning is the major thrust of substitute care. The emphasis in permanency planning is on the limited use of foster homes. Supportive services for the families of children are an important part of the program. Instead of removing children from their natural homes, attempts are made to improve the functioning of the family so that the family remains intact or so that children may be returned to the home as soon as possible. Because of budget cuts, the development and implementation of supportive services has been curtailed. Nevertheless, three of the communities studied by Kimmich (1985) and Burt and Pittman (1985) reported a decrease in the number of children placed in foster homes, while requests for child protective services increased in all four cities. This means children may have been left in or returned to homes they would have been removed from in previous years. Thus, some of these children may have been in a high risk situation, and this could be a factor contributing to the increase in child abuse and neglect cases.

Cuts in the AFDC program had widespread effects on families who, not only lost AFDC benefits, but also access to other support programs such as Medicaid, daycare, and job training (Kimmich, 1985). Most cuts affected families in which the mother worked and also received benefits. This means the family income was probably just above the poverty level. According to Garfinkel and McLanahan (1986) the evidence suggests the cuts in AFDC substantially increased the financial hardships for mothers who worked and received benefits but resulted in only minor reductions in the number of welfare recipients and welfare dependency.

Kimmich (1985), using data from the four previously mentioned communities, reports that because of reduced availability of services and the higher costs of some services, recipients have increased their use of emergency programs such as general assistance, hospital emergency rooms, and supplementary food programs (WIC). Many of these programs are not designed to meet the specific needs of these families, which increased the hardship and stress for parents and children. And finally, because programs designed to meet their needs are not available, many do not receive help until their problems are severe or have reached a crisis level. The following report from a Wayne County Health Department worker in June of 1983 illustrates the problem. "When three local health centers were closed in Detroit, clients were left to find their own substitute health care. Other clinics were farther away, and transportation was often a problem. A Wayne County health department staff person summed it up: Six hundred pregnant women and 11,000 children were left to seek services elsewhere in the community. The Sisters of Mercy opened a private center to pick up some of the pediatric cases and, gradually, the maternity care too. But it wasn't nearly enough (Kimmich, 1985, p. 97)."

When considering the effects of the Reagan cuts on poor families, it is important to remember that little or no attempt was made to reconstruct programs to make them more effective. The policy was simply to cut funding; that meant agencies had to meet the same obligations with reduced resources. As previously mentioned, poverty increased during this period, putting additional strain on the agencies and their service (in the first three years of the Reagan administration, the number of children living in poverty increased by 21%; Burt and Pittman, 1985). The evidence strongly suggests that the reductions in funding created hardships for many families and increased the risk of child abuse and neglect. Furthermore, we do not know what the long term consequences of these cuts may be in terms of deferred health care, lack of employment, and increased pressure and stress for families.

The situation has not improved for children in the 90's. There was an increase of 841,000 children living in poverty in 1990; that means 13.4 million of our children live in poor families. In 1989, 19.6% of our children lived in poverty; in 1990 the rate increased to 20.6% (CDF Reports, 1991). These percentages illustrate "the nation's appalling neglect of children and its misguided public and private investment priorities," (CDF Reports, 1991, p. 1). The following facts highlight the seriousness of these issues (CDF Reports, 1991):

1. Approximately 9-11 million children and 10 million women of childbearing age have no health insurance.
2. In many major cities, half of the infants and toddlers have not received immunizations against childhood diseases.
3. Approximately 400,000 children drop out of school each year.

4. The number of children living in poverty increased during the 80's and continues to increase in the 90's with over 13 million living in poverty in 1990.
5. The negative consequences for children who live in poverty include health problems, poor performance in school, and teenage pregnancy.
6. Approximately 2.5 million children were abused or neglected in 1990 which represents a 147% increase from 1979.
7. Teenage pregnancy is more likely to occur when teenage girls have poor academic skills and come from poor families. Approximately 1 million teenage girls become pregnant each year and almost half actually give birth. In almost half of these cases, the mother does not receive early prenatal care.

There is little evidence to suggest that cuts in programs for families and their children have reduced welfare prevalence and dependency. In other words, the problem has not gone away, as a result of stricter budgets and limited programs. Instead, it appears that we have increased the hardships for poor families, who must struggle to get by on even less. The above figures suggest that they are not able to overcome the severe obstacles and stresses. As a society we need to determine if these cuts and the subsequent hardships on families are the most effective way to manage limited resources.

INCREASING THE EMPLOYMENT LEVEL OF THE POOR

We have looked at the positive effects of government transfers. We know they reduce poverty and relieve financial hardship for many families. However, transfers are meant to be used on a temporary basis until the family or individual can become self-sufficient. Gainful employment is the more successful long-term solution to poverty. According to Shiller (1980a), "subemployment" is probably the leading cause of poverty. "Subemployment" is a broad term referring to unemployed workers, discouraged workers who no longer look for jobs, and the underemployed who work in menial occupations while awaiting better paying jobs.

Since the 60s, the government has instigated numerous job training programs including the Manpower Development and Training Act (MDTA), the Youth Employment Demonstration Projects Act (YEDPA), the Public Employment Program (PEP), the Comprehensive Employment and Training Act (CETA), the Job Training Partnership Act (JTPA), and more recently Job Opportunities and Basic Skills (JOBS). These programs worked with various groups of individuals (minorities, youth, women, ex-addicts, unskilled) preparing them for participation in the labor market. At various times, public jobs have also been created to provide employment. However, despite considerable expense, most programs report only modest success (Bassie & Ashenfelter, 1986; Bassie, 1983; Masters, 1981; Danziger, 1981). Women and disadvantaged youth seemed to profit most from these programs; men experienced less significant gains. In CETA, for example, there were no significant increases in earnings for men. Several explanations have been suggested for the lack of improvement by men participating in these programs. For many women, increased hours rather than higher wages were responsible for increased earnings. As men tend to work more hours than women, an increase in wages as a consequence of additional work hours would be more difficult to accomplish. Secondly, programs appear to be more successful in preparing individuals for entry-level positions, which does not represent improvement for most men (Bassie, 1983; Bassie & Ashenfelter, 1986).

In their review of job training programs, Bassie and Ashenfelter (1986) cited two programs, Job Corps and Supported Work Demonstration as being very successful. Job Corps is a well-funded, intensive training program that works with a limited number of disadvantaged youth. Participants in this program have experienced significant increases in employment and earnings and a decrease in the use of welfare and criminal activity. The benefits appear to exceed the cost by approximately 40%. Supported Work trained several groups including ex-addicts, women receiving AFDC, ex-offenders, and young school drop-outs. Women and ex-addicts experienced the greatest improvement. The women increased their work hours and wages, while the major benefit for ex-addicts was a decrease in criminal activity.

Why haven't most job training programs been more successful? Part of the problem is related to funding. Financial resources for these programs are often limited so that a small amount is actually spent on each individual, and there is a time limit placed on participation in the program. Furthermore, funding for these programs has been reduced substantially since 1979. Another problem is that job-training programs have never been large enough to reach substantial numbers of the unemployed. The largest enrollments for CETA averaged one-twentieth of the unemployed (Bassie and Ashenfelter, 1986). According to Schiller (1980a), a critical element, which has a major impact on the effectiveness of training programs, is the availability of jobs once participants complete the training. If no jobs are available, training individuals will not solve the unemployment problem.

There must be a demand for labor, especially for less technical jobs, in order to decrease unemployment and poverty.

The fiscal and monetary policies of the government largely determine the demand for labor. It is important, therefore, for government to consider what type of economic policy will best benefit all sectors of the population. Schiller (1980a) argues that many of our policies have worked against the poor. We have consistently sought to decrease inflation at the cost of full employment. Blank and Blinder (1986) in their analysis found unemployment has a stronger negative effect on the poor than inflation, but the reverse is true for higher income families. It comes as no surprise that unemployment is unevenly distributed across age, sex, and race. Non-white, young workers suffer the most with nonwhite males experiencing the greatest negative effects. This coincides with our earlier discussion of the high unemployment rate of black males.

It appears that fighting inflation may be more beneficial for the middle class, and this could be a partial explanation for the government's continued interest in anti-inflation programs. Schiller (1980a) argues that low inflation and high employment are not necessarily incompatible, although based on the Phillip's curve, the government has consistently favored higher unemployment as a solution to inflation. If the government advocates policies that restrict demand for labor, training programs cannot be effective. This is the major reason the WIN and CETA programs were not more successful. Government economic policy during that time restricted the demand for labor; consequently there were few jobs available (for further discussion of this theory, see Schiller, 1980b).

Job training programs in conjunction with economic policies that increase demand for labor could reduce poverty. A more recent trend is the use of workfare requirements for women on AFDC (JOBS). Garfinkel and McLanahan (1986) indicate that initial costs for these programs would be high, but long-term effects could exceed the costs as these women leave welfare and become self-sufficient. California's more recent workfare program, GAIN, requires all AFDC recipients to participate. It not only includes intensive training but substantial resources have been provided for supportive services, especially daycare (Kirp, 1986). The Job Opportunities and Basic Skills program (JOBS), which states were mandated to implement beginning in 1990, also requires that states provide daycare as well as job training for AFDC recipients. Public jobs could also play a smaller role providing employment for those unable to acquire jobs in the private sector.

If we are serious about improving unemployment, training programs must be well-funded commensurate with current demand for labor, or at least the anticipated future demand for labor. The training must also focus on the job sectors that can absorb the trainees with their newly learned skills. Furthermore, if programs only reach a small number of the unemployed, we cannot expect a significant decrease in poverty. It will take considerable financial investment and changes in economic policy to make meaningful progress in employment for the poor. However, the severity of the problem for American families, especially minorities and female heads of household require our best efforts. The negative consequences of poverty weigh heavily on marital stability and the quality of life for children. We have large numbers of children who will spend at least part of their lives in extreme poverty. The long-term costs to society are enormous not only in financial terms but in the loss of productive citizens who can contribute to society rather than depend on it for welfare support. How much progress is made in this area depends, in large part, on the attitudes and willingness of the more affluent Americans to provide resources.

CONCLUSION

Looking at government attempts to improve the economic well-being of poor families, we see there are no easy, simple solutions. However the expansion in social programs since the early 60s did result in a reduction in poverty, although most of this reduction was the result of increased benefits and economic growth rather than an increase in earnings of the poor. The major focus of this chapter is the problems facing female-headed families whose numbers have increased so dramatically over the past twenty years. The two-parent family is no longer the statistical norm, a fact that requires reassessment of our attitudes and our social programs. A large percentage of female-headed families live in poverty. As almost half of our children will spend at least part of their lives in female-headed homes, there is concern about the high rate of poverty of these families both in terms of the negative effects on children and the increasing costs to the public. However, to the extent that the statistical norm has changed, but the societal attitudes based on old understandings about the meaning and functioning of the family have not, there is likely to be resistance to needed changes in public policy.

We have noted that funding for means-tested programs has traditionally been lower than for the social insurance programs. The real value of these benefits has declined since the early 70s because of inflation and budget cuts. These lower benefits have not resulted in a decrease in female-headed households or welfare dependency. As the effects of AFDC on marital stability, nonmarital births, and dependence appear to be small, increasing benefit levels are recommended as a more positive solution to an increasingly intractable problem in American society. Adjusting them for inflation and restoring cuts implemented by the Reagan administration and continued during Bush's term would reduce the financial hardship for many single-parent, and two-parent, families. More funding for supportive services such as education, job training, job creation, and day care could help many of these mothers and fathers become self-sufficient. In addition, the absence of medical care and health insurance for many poor families and children is intolerable and should be rectified.

We have stressed that the use of transfers should be continued but that they are only part of an effective program for the poor. Jobs with decent pay are needed to enable poor families to become self-sufficient. A growing expanding economy is the best solution, but government policies that attempt to offset the negative effects of slower economic growth would prove beneficial to the poor and diminish the ripple effects of poverty throughout society. Increasing minimum wage so that a family can meet their basic needs would enable many two-parent families to move out of poverty. We have stressed the plight of black males in the labor market. If we wish to provide opportunities for black families to improve their economic plight, we must address the issues associated with black male unemployment.

These are challenges that face us as a society. Solutions require long-term commitments and the allocation of scarce resources to programs that will benefit low income families and enable them to become self-sufficient, productive members of society. However, because of the severity of these problems, especially the poverty of female-headed families and the high unemployment rate of black males, there is a need to promote constructive changes in family policy to further these goals.

LOOKING TO THE FUTURE

Where do things appear to be heading in the future? What is the outlook for constructive changes in family policy? The outlook is decidedly bleak when writing this chapter. The news media are filled with doom and gloom and implausible proposals to set things right. In 1991, President Bush finally admitted the economy was in recession, without using the word. He even expressed a willingness to consider a $300 tax credit for every taxpaying American in the spring to encourage consumer spending and, reportedly, to shore up his sagging reputation in the opinion polls (Yang & Devroy, December 18, 1991). The U.S. Conference of Mayors reports "a growing crisis in hometown America," as indicated by a recent sharp rise of 26 percent in emergency requests for food and 13 percent for housing throughout the country (Rich, December 17, 1991).

How is the nation's leadership responding? They cut the already dismally low levels of welfare spending and with schemes to modify the behavior of the poor. Some are even billing these changes as "a blessing in disguise for the poor, because it is giving state officials an excuse to do what they should have done decades ago: transform AFDC from a longterm crutch to a short-term dose of behavior modification (Taylor, December 16, 1991, p. A-1). Lawrence Mead, the New York University political scientist and so-called intellectual father of the behavior-modification model of welfare reform, is giving second thought to the government's sudden, warm embrace of his theory. He is worrying about "a movement toward moralizing, big-government conservatism (Mead, as quoted by Taylor, December 16, 1991, p. A-1)." Clearly, it is a salve to the conscience of those who believe they must make drastic budget cuts to be able to cite the immoral behavior of the poor and to rationalize that reduced AFDC spending when coupled with behavior modification will ultimately help those whom they are immediately making more miserable. The transparency of what is happening is sardonically exposed by Senator Patrick Moynihan, a long-time student of welfare reform, "Look you smart-assed little 8-month old, I don't like the way your mother is behaving, and I'm going to show you! No more bottles, no more Pampers, no more nothing!" (Moynihan, as quoted by Taylor, December 16, 1991, p. A-8). In the presidential election campaign (November 1992), both President Bush and Democratic nominee Bill Clinton repeatedly emphasized the importance of family values and maintaining the family. Unfortunately, despite the rhetoric, neither candidate presented a well-developed program that would effectively address the complex issues of family policy and poverty in America. So our society, ignoring once more what we should have learned from the past, is lurching into the brave new world of the 21st century.

REFERENCES

Bakke, W. (1940). *Citizens Without Work*. New Haven: Yale University Press.
Bane, M. (1986). Household composition and poverty. In S. Danziger & D. Weinberg (Eds.), *Fighting Poverty, What Works and What Doesn't*, (pp. 209-231). Massachusetts: Harvard University Press.
Bane, M., & Ellwood, D. (1983). *The dynamics of dependence: The routes to self sufficiency*. Report supported by U. S. Department of Health and Human Services grant, Contract no. HHS-100-82-0038. John F. Kennedy School of Government, Harvard University: Author.
Bassie, L. (1983). The effect of CETA on the postprogram earnings of participants. *Journal of Human Resources, 18*, 539-556.

Bassie, L., & Ashenfelter, O. (1986). The effect of direct job creation and training programs on low-skilled workers. In S. Danziger & D. Weinberg (Eds.), *Fighting Poverty, What Works and What Doesn't* (pp. 133-151). Massachusetts: Harvard University Press, 133-151.

Bawden, D., & Palmer, J. (1984). Social policy: Challenging the welfare state. In J. Palmer and I. Sawhill (Eds.), *The Reagan Record*. Massachusetts: Ballinger Publishing Company.

Blank, R., & Blinder, A. (1986). Macroeconomics, income distribution and poverty. In S. Danziger & D. Weinberg (Eds.), *Fighting Poverty, What Works and What Doesn't*. Massachusetts: Harvard University Press.

Burt, M., & Pittman, K. (1985). *Testing the Social Safety Net*. Washington, D. C.: The Urban Institute Press.

CDF Reports (1990). Children generally hold their ground in the states. *The Monthly Newsletter of the Children's Defense Fund, 12* (4).

CDF Reports (1991). Leave no child behind. *The Monthly Newsletter of the Children's Defense Fund, 13* (2).

Center for the Study of Social Policy (1983). *A dream deferred: The economic status of black Americans*.

Cherlin, A. (1976). *Economics, social roles, and marital separation*. Preliminary draft, Department of Social Relations, The Johns Hopkins University, Baltimore, Maryland.

Cutwright, P. (1973). *Illegitimacy and income supplements: Studies in Public Welfare*. Paper no. 12, Prepared for the use of the Subcommittee on Fiscal Policy of the Joint Economic Committee, Congress of the United States, Washington, D. C.: U. S. Government Printing Office.

Danziger, S. (1981). Post program changes in the lives of AFDC supported work recipients: A qualitative assessment. *Journal of Human Resources*, 637-648.

Danziger, S., & Gottschalk, P. (1985). How have families with children been faring? Prepared for the Joint Economic Committee of the Congress. Author.

Danziger, S., & Haveman, R. (1981, May-June). The Reagan budget: A sharp break with the past, *Challenge*.

Danziger, S., & Weinberg, D. (1986). *Fighting Poverty, What Works and What Doesn't*. Massachusetts: Harvard University Press.

Danziger, S., Haveman, R., & Plotnick, R. (1986). Antipoverty policy: Effects on the poor and the nonpoor. In S. Danziger & D. Weinberg (Eds.), *Fighting Poverty, What Works and What Doesn't* (pp. 50-77). Massachusetts: Harvard University Press.

Ellwood, D. T. (1988). *Poor Support, Poverty in America*. New York: Basic Books, Inc.

Ellwood, D., & Summers, L. (1986). Is welfare really the problem? *The Public Interest, 83*, 57-78.

Ellwood, D., & Wise, D. (1983). Youth employment in the seventies: The changing circumstances of young adults. In R. Nelson & F. Skidmore (Eds.), *American Families and the Economy: The High Costs of Living*. Washington D. C.: National Academy Press.

Garcia, A. (1991). The changing demographic face of Hispanics in the United States. In M. Sotomayor (Ed.), *Empowering Hispanic Families: A Critical Issue for the '90s*. Milwaukee: Family Service America.

Garfinkel, I., & Holden, K. (1983). *Crises in social security and the welfare state.* IRP Discussion Paper.

Garfinkel, I., & McLanahan, S. (1986). *Single Mothers and Their Children: A New American Dilemma*. Washington D. C.: The Urban Institute Press.

Gottschalk, P., & Danziger, S. (1984). Macroeconomic conditions, income transfers and the trend in poverty. In D. L. Bawden (Ed.), *The Social Contract Revisited*. Washington, D. C.: Urban Institute Press.

Gramlich, E. (1986). The main themes. In S. Danziger & D. Weinberg (Eds.), *Fighting Poverty, What Works and What Doesn't* (pp. 341-347). Massachusetts: Harvard University Press.

Gramlich, E. M., & Laren, D. S. (1984). How widespread are income losses in a recession? In D. L. Bawden (Ed.), *The Social Contract Revisited*. Washington, D. C.: Urban Institute Press.

Haveman, J. (1982, October 23). Sharing the wealth: The gap between the rich and poor grows wider, *National Journal*.

Hill, M., & Ponza, M. (1983). *Poverty across generations: Is welfare dependency a pathology passed on from one generation to the next?* Paper presented at the Population Association of America meetings.

Hill, M., & Ponza, M. (1984). *Does welfare dependency beget dependency?* Institute for Social Research: Author.

Hoenig, M. (1974). AFDC income, recipient rates, and family dissolution. *Journal of Human Resources, 9*, 123-129.

Hoffman, S., & Holmes, J. (1976). Husbands, wives and divorce. *Five Thousand American Families, 4* (pp. 16). Ann Arbor, Michigan: University of Michigan, Institute for Social Research.

Kimmich, M. (1985). *America's Children: Who Cares?* Washington D. C.: The Urban Institute.

Kirp, D. (1986). Poverty, welfare and workfare: The California work/welfare scheme. *The Public Interest, 83*, 34-48.

MacDonald, M., & Sawhill, I. (1978). *Welfare policy and the family Public Policy.* Author.

Masters, S. (1981). The effects of supported work on the earnings and transfer payments of its AFDC target group. *Journal of Human Resources*, pp. 606-636.

McRoy, R. G. (1990). A historical overview of black families. In S. Logan, E. Freeman & R. McRoy (Eds.), *Social Work Practice With Black Families.* (pp. 3-18). New York: Longman.

Moore, K., & Caldwell, S. (1976). *Out-of-wedlock pregnancy and childbearing.* Working paper, Urban Institute, Washington, D. C.

Morganthau, T., Lewis, S., McCormick, J., Wolfberg, A., & Washington, F. (1991, December, 31). A tough winter. *Newsweek*, pp. 26-28.

Oelleirch, D., & Garfinkel, I. (1983). Distributional impacts of existing and alternative child support systems. *Policy Studies Journal, 12* 119-129.

O'Neill, J. (1986). Transfers and Poverty: Cause and/or effect. *The Cato Journal, 6,* 55-76.

Rich, S. (1991, December 17). 'Growing crisis' in cities cited. *Washington Post,* p. A3.

Ross, H., & Sawhill, I. (1975). *The Growth of Families Headed by Women.* Washington D. C.: Urban Institute Press.

Sawhill, I., Peabody, G., Jones, C., & Caldwell, S. (1975). *Income transfers and family structure.* Urban Institute Paper 979-03 (pp. 24-44). Washington, D. C.: The Urban Institute Press.

Schiller, B. (1980). *The Economics of Poverty and Discrimination* (3rd ed.). Englewood Cliffs, N. J.: Prentice Hall.

Schiller, B. (1980a). *The Economy Today.* New York: Random House, Inc.

Skoro, C., & Johnson, D. (1991). Establishing an updated standard of need for AFDC recipients. *Social Work Research and Abstracts, 27* (3), 22-27.

Tayler, P. (1991, December, 16). Welfare reformers seek to modify budgets and behavior. *Washington Post,* pp. A1, A8-9.

Tocqueville, A. (1835). Memoir on pauperism. Reprinted in *Public Interest,* Winter 1983, pp. 102-120.

U. S. Department of Commerce, Bureau of the Census (1981). *Child Support and Alimony: 1978.* (Current Population Reports Special Studies, No. 112, p. 23).

U. S. Department of Health and Human Services, Office of Child Support Enforcement (1982). *Child Support Enforcement Statistics–Fiscal 1981* (June).

U. S. Department of Health and Human Services, Office of Child Support Enforcement (1981). *6th Annual Report to Congress for Period Ending December 31, 1981.*

Wilson, W. J. (1984). The black underclass. *Wilson Quarterly, 8,* 88-99.

Wilson, W., & Neckerman, K. (1986). Poverty and family structure: The widening gap between evidence and public policy issues. In S. Danziger & D. Weinberg (Eds.), *Fighting Poverty, What Works and What Doesn't* (pp. 232-259). Massachusetts: Harvard University Press.

Yang, J. E., & DeVroy, A. (1991, December, 18). Administration considering tax rebate of up to $300. *Washington Post,* p. A1 & A18.

TECHNOLOGICAL ISSUES

Issues of Technology's
Possible Futures

Teresa Donati Marciano

KEYWORDS. Technology, Development, Ethics, Moral, Access, Power

INTRODUCTION: NATURE, HUMANITY, TECHNOLOGY, AND SCIENCE

Technologies are as old as life. They comprise all the uses of things, according to certain rules, to accomplish certain ends. A bee pollinating a flower is engaging in a "reproductive technology," just as the techniques

Teresa Donati Marciano is Professor of Sociology, Fairleigh Dickinson University.

[Haworth co-indexing entry note]: "Issues of Technology's Possible Futures." Marciano, Teresa Donati. Co-published simultaneously in *Marriage & Family Review* (The Haworth Press, Inc.) Vol. 18, No. 3/4, 1993, pp. 125-134; and: *American Families and the Future: Analyses of Possible Destinies* (ed: Barbara H. Settles, Roma S. Hanks, and Marvin B. Sussman) The Haworth Press, Inc., 1993, pp. 125-134. Multiple copies of this article/chapter may be purchased from The Haworth Document Delivery Center. Call 1-800-3-HAWORTH (1-800-342-9678) between 9:00 - 5:00 (EST) and ask for DOCUMENT DELIVERY CENTER.

(i.e., the process of employing a technology) of in vitro fertilization are a reproductive technology. Although we tend to think of technologies as devices of human initiation, many "human" technologies are simply attempts to control "natural" technologies. Beekeepers, for example, study and attempt to accelerate the honey-making technologies of bees.

All cultures possess technologies, ranging from techniques for making and preserving fire, to construction of shelters and of hunting and fishing traps, the making of clothing from varieties of raw materials, the planting, harvesting, and conservation of seeds in agricultural technologies.

"Modern technological societies," the term denoting what we call the "developed" world, should therefore be understood as expressing particular kinds of current technologies ("modern"), rather than as a condition in which technology has suddenly appeared and flourished. Technologies have preceded the sciences that eventually explained them. Procedures for making fire preceded the physics and chemistry of combustion. The modern assumption that science (theory, observation, and experimentation) precedes technology (applied science) tells us more about the status of science than about the historical reality of technology's presence in human cultures. The ongoing quest for new technologies, and the recovery of old technologies, as evidenced in recycling efforts around the United States, has us putting old items to new uses. Composting to fertilize the soil, the restoration of environmentally gentle cleansers to daily use, exemplify technological recoveries. They also demonstrate the ideological and ethical context of technological development and use. As elaborated later, no set of rules governing the use of things, exists apart from all the other sets of rules that currently hold sway in a culture.

No technology is "value-free." Even in a "scientific" age, moreover, the inventors and tinkers who look for ways to make life easier, to solve everyday problems such as opening jars or perfecting the proverbial mousetrap, continue their work. They may or may not apply "the latest scientific breakthroughs" to their devices, but what emerges are technologies in the form of gadgets and comfort items that fill mail-order catalogues, and cover the side walls of dime stores, notions and kitchen departments of large stores. The varieties of technology in our culture, then, seem to range, by analogy, from these "popular culture technologies" to "high culture technologies" that are more closely and obviously connected to science. This analogy is made with full understanding of the greater social value given to "science" than to "inventions," though profits from the latter may well exceed even the most generous grants and salaries of institutional scientific researchers. The rank order of the two is clearly a cultural value. Yet the role of science as a precursor of technological applications becomes more important when the technology, in order to be devised and used at all, must wait upon discoveries in science. The search for an AIDS vaccine (which is a medical technology) depends on locating the cause of AIDS, then isolating it and experimenting with its reactions. Only then can we find an application of knowledge to the technology that accomplishes a cure.

If "modern" technology means anything, then, it denotes the numbers of technologies that do wait upon science for their development and application. The ties that bind science and technology today are especially critical for the future in two fields: in life and health sciences; and in the employment structure as it affects the globalization of the work force and the quality of human life in and out of work. None of these technologies are or can be independent of the ethical and moral consciousness of their creators, and users, although our understandings of the social construction of reality show us how quickly technologies seem to escape human control. They become "objectivated," seeming to possess a life of their own, institutionalized as part of the ongoing environment around which we organize our lives (Berger & Luckmann 1966). In life and health sciences, the specific questions addressed in this context are those of reproduction and population control; for work force and family life, the questions of how technology aids or retards the care and education of children, and the life chances of children and their parents.

Because the larger ethical and moral issues are so entwined with the creation and use of technology, and because of technology's effects on such outcomes as equality and happiness, we must ask who "owns," and controls, the things we put to use, and the rules by which we use them, in living our lives. Raymond Williams' (1990, p. 10) comments are worth quoting in full for the way in which they frame the problem:

> . . . all questions about cause and effect, as between a technology and a society, are intensely practical. Until we have begun to answer them, we really do not know, in any particular case, whether, for example, we are talking about a technology or about the uses of a technology, about necessary institutions or particular and changeable institutions; about a content or about a form. This is not only a matter of intellectual uncertainty; it is a matter of social practice. If the technology is a cause, we can at best modify or seek to control its effects. If the technology, as used, is an effect, to what other kinds of cause, and other kinds of action, should we refer and relate our experience of its uses? These are not abstract questions. They form an increasingly important part of our social and cultural arguments, and they are being decided all the time in real practice, by real and effective decisions.

TECHNOLOGY, SCIENCE, AND THEIR VALUES

The global norm for all technologies is to be as useful as possible, as easily as possible. The global norm for modern science is to be "useful" for absolutely nothing. The "highest" science is "pure" science, theorizing and observing for no purposes other than themselves.

The debate over the "uses" of science for improving daily life is part of the history of education, especially from the nineteenth century to the present time. In the United States, highest status accrued to colleges and universities that were single-sex (male), where research was directed toward quantitative, so-called "hard" science, whose theorists explained natural and physical phenomena but whose work eschewed "social value" and application. This occurred in opposition to historically concurrent struggles of women to refute Darwinian notions of male biological superiority, and the involvement of women in such reform and social improvement activities as suffrage and child welfare (Rosenberg, 1982).

Meanwhile, science had seized for itself an explanatory role in culture. Cultures not only teach how to live, but also why people "should" live that way. The great meanings of life, death, success, affliction, are part of a culture's cosmology. What religion had almost exclusively claimed, science now counterclaimed: the tenets of belief and the supernatural order they expressed, were opposed by scientific theories based in connection, explanation, and prediction. Articles of faith were the antagonistic mirror of the scientific method. This is not to say that scientists could not be believers or religionists, but only that in a hierarchical cosmos where one God (monotheism) prevailed, there was only room for one entity at the top. Science and religion do coexist, but the social primacy of one or the other stems from the notion that certain paths lead to more "respectable" or more "certain" truths. The idea of coexistent, complementary forms of knowledge threatened both science and religion, and only today as we move toward holistic understandings has there begun to be some formal convergence of the two. The old antagonism was fueled by the presumed presence or absence of "values," as though anyone could be free of one's own culture. The political context of an intrusive German state that led Weber (1958) to defend the university and its disciplines as "value-free" domains, was forgotten until Gouldner (1962) demonstrated the mythical nature of the idea. Yet scientists still claim it. The idea of "value-freedom" persisted beyond the context that summoned it as a time-specific rationale for academic freedom.

Here exactly is the clue to the progress of science and technology: that the context from which science emerges, and technologies develop, is forgotten. These "children" of history begin to lead lives of their own.

Nor should anyone be surprised that science and technology, embodying hidden values, come to prevail in human life. Malinowski (1948) long ago pointed out that in any area of human endeavor where science advances, religion and magic recede in importance. The issue is one of control and certainty: assured outcomes of lagoon fishing and planting technologies increase the sense of confidence and control over those aspects of nature, and reduce the felt need for supernatural interventions. Only when uncertainty prevails do magic and religion also prevail, as with weather patterns in agriculture, or in preparation for seagoing travels with their perils to food supplies and life itself. Religion is, after all, a realm of faith and not of directly observable cause and effect. Malinowski's theories, based on tribal observations, certainly apply to much of our own everyday lives. Only when we are uncertain of a car's performance will we pray that it starts, runs properly, does not stall, and does not crash. But we do not pray over gasoline running from the pump to the fuel tank, or the new battery. Conditions of certainty dictate whether we will have recourse to the supernatural.

What needs to be questioned, however, is: of what are we certain, and do those certainties serve our evolving needs and wants? How do current "certainties" preclude the quest for other certainties? In other words, how does the structure of science and technology limit the possibilities for their serving us at all, and serving us better than we have been served?

An example of this is found in cartography and its revisionists; the latter question how and why we come to have maps that look the way they do. Note that the word revision means to see again, to see with new eyes, to see in a different way. Looking anew, they invite us to ask with them: why are the United States and Europe at the "top" of the globe? In what ways do projections of the round globe onto flat surfaces distort the sizes of various land masses, and in what direction of distortion? The Mercator projection makes Europe far larger than its actual proportional size to China, or Australia, or Africa. If "bigger is better," the mapmakers would be inclined to expand rather than contract the projection of their own continents (read "cultural homes") onto the pictures that represent the world. The result, however, is a value-hidden guide for our actual and intellectual travels.

What we find on most maps are the features that serve commerce: rivers, mountains, roads, elevations, airports, county lines, and major natural and human-made landmarks. Whose money is spent, for what purposes, in making the maps that are made? India was mapped to promote empire (PBS 1991). Oil companies emphasize roadways and insets depicting automobile access to different areas. Revisionist cartographers look at how maps might project other pictures of the world: states or smaller areas by rates of violent crime, by sex ratios, or by accessible school and shopping areas. Maps, however, tend not to be made to serve families, and therefore do not show the little parks for toddlers, or picnic areas, or free beaches. Technological access to family services is presented by phone companies, but only for those services that use phones; a new resident can phone a fast food delivery service more rapidly than find where children's parks and free beaches are located.

Revisionist approaches to science and technology have sprung from new consciousness of the capacity of knowledge to define "problems," and therefore to subordinate the interests of some to the interests of others. Thus, people of color, feminists, people of lower socially valued ethnic origins, have questioned the assumptions—and therefore the paradigms—of institutionalized science and technology. They have brought this questioning into all the academic disciplines, whether toward the 'canon' of literature, or the prevailing emphases and techniques of philosophy or history. Colonized peoples have wrought liberation ideologies (political revisions), out of previously unquestioned assumptions about overrule, "development," "progress," and "backwardness." These have been long struggles because ongoing patterned ways of life, of the rulers and the ruled, organized around belief systems, value rankings, and resultant feelings of efficacy and entitlement, are as resistant as any long-held patterns to large shifts, let alone radical change.

Systematic questioning of assumptions is the first step toward institutional shift, including science and technology. Organizing lives and responses in new ways, to meet new needs, further alters the system. The Montgomery bus boycott, the foundation of women's health clinics, are examples of organizing lives around new ideologies, each one responding to current technologies and their social and economic superstructures in revisionist ways. They show us that we can successfully ask: which technologies will we use at all, and how, with what outcomes for whom? The question for the future is: how can we shape the assumptions governing science, and those that create technologies, to meet our planetary and personal needs?

REPRODUCTIVE TECHNOLOGIES

The areas of birth and birth prevention challenge several basic assumptions of science and technology. It is frequently heard that the quest of science is the control of nature; technology must therefore be its instrument. The value systems of "science" and medical technology have additionally pursued the Frankenstein quest: to create life, in the form of as perfect a baby as possible, in any way possible. The impetus for these technologies has come from men, and brings to mind Gilbert and Gubar's comment (1985, p. 239):

> ... the novel's protagonist, Victor Frankenstein, not only usurps the creative function of God, he enacts the maternal role of a woman. ... as well as comments by Mary Daly (1968), that in Western cosmology Adam was the first mother.

If science and technology work hand in hand to control nature, then, who is doing the controlling, based on what values, for what purposes? The task for itself, "free" of larger value contexts–including the woman who is part of the larger context–centers on fertilization, implantation, surrogacy, fetal rescue.

The fetus is the task, and not the woman's body. The Baby M case expresses the value of a technology (surrogacy) for producing a man's genetic heir, wherein a fee is paid to a poor woman by a rich man, to obtain a desired product (the baby).

While birth-outcome technologies may help many couples who ardently desire a baby, the paradigm behind it is insufficiently examined. The fetal focus alienates the woman from her own body, for eventually every birth technology must make use of the woman's body to obtain eggs and to carry the fetus. The woman becomes vehicle to the technology, even aside from whether or not births-for-fees amount to peddling flesh. A fetus can be "rescued" by surgery, saved and birthed even when the woman is in a coma, "helped" by jailing an addicted or alcoholic pregnant woman–all of which, in Rothman's (1987) terms, shift us from the woman-centered maternal context to one in which woman and fetus are adversaries.

If this quest to control nature is so "good" and so "scientific," why are women denied control of nature via control of nature's own avenue, which is the woman's own body? What reproductive technologies imply and effect is the belief that science can only control nature by controlling the embodiments of nature, which are women. Women become nature, which scientists control.

This is not new. It simply answers once again the question posed by Sherri Ortner (1974): is female to male as nature is to culture? Explaining the universality of patriarchy, she shows that all cultures value culture over nature, and that women, by virtue of their reproductive functions (notably parturition and lactation) are equated with nature.

Religious ideologies, interestingly, also assert the claims of religion over nature, by defining nature as a product of divine creation, which in human form rebels against the divine plan for its exercise. The female is the most threatening human, most in rebellion, most in need of control. So say the male religious establishments, in the name of a male God.

While birth is promoted through unnatural interventions, and abortions condemned as unnatural interventions, there remains the question of contraception. Will women obtain the contraceptive capabilities that give them control over the outcomes of sex, without destroying or endangering their health? The easiest contraception is male contraception. Is the first contraceptive capability that of demanding condom use? Why does research focus its contraceptive aims on women when it is men who can so easily produce so many children? Women can only produce babies one at a time, with infrequent exceptions. Men can father as many children as there are willing and fertile women. Only in a system in which women are "stuck" and men free to depart with impunity, can a science and technology focus on the "woman's need" for contraception. All of these assumptions need questioning. Reproduction as a value, and as a kind of value, by sex, needs to be reexamined.

The future of reproductive technologies, and of the value of reproduction itself, depends on consciousness and willingness to organize around a raised consciousness. Why are poor women so likely to have so many children, beginning at so young an age? Does anyone care enough to so improve the quality of life of poor girls, to help them establish goals alternative to early motherhood, as to give them control over the course of their very lives? The answers for the future are the best answers of the past: true reform, true social welfare, which promotes and enhances the well-being of the disadvantaged. What could or will trigger such a movement? Visible possibilities that alternatives do exist and can work. Revolutions tend to begin after it is demonstrated that things can change, that conditions are not ordained by fate and out of human control. The French Revolution was a twin to the Enlightenment for that reason: that human agency can change things for the better.

WORK AND FAMILY LIFE TECHNOLOGIES

Work technologies serve corporations to enhance profits. Travel and communications technologies have been used to increase the speed and precision of directives, exchanges of ideas, and implementation of new programs. The global assembly line makes production more profitable by separating labor-intensive tasks from capital-intensive ones. Labor intensive work is performed in low-wage (periphery) countries, while capital-intensive production occurs in the already "developed" (core) nations. Whatever work, and wherever done, women are ever-larger percentages of the work forces, and children in ever-larger numbers require non-maternal care starting at ever-younger ages.

In the core nations, child care varies from very good (Scandinavia) to chancey (the United States); but all child care assumes that children are left, and then picked up, at the beginning and end of work and school days. Some one-site day care centers permit intermittent visits by parents during breaks. Otherwise, there is spatial and visual separation of parents and children.

Given the huge growth in surveillance activities of all sorts–to control employee theft, to test for and protect against drug use or sales, to prevent or identify and apprehend shoplifters, bank robbers, as examples–how is it that technologies for easy visual access of children to parents have not been developed? The home intercom is a commonplace; parents can hear a baby's cry in the nursery, or can give a child instructions to go to bed, from remote points in the house. Yet the center of parent-child locations is less the house, today, than the daycare center and the office. Can no similar, visual technology be developed? Teleconferencing saves travel time and expense, and is used to connect distant offices' executives. Could it not also connect distant parents and children?

The assumptions that govern these technologies are that they "pay," that they are profitable. The concurrent assumption, by neglect, is that family relationships do not pay in any quantifiable or identifiable way to benefit businesses. Yet the popularity of family leave policies shows how great the need is to find ways for families to transcend the boundaries of work day and work place, to connect with each other. The great numbers of single parents have particular need of this, yet their ability to make family needs a priority is limited by their single-earner family status, in a context of institutionalized resistance to "mixing family and business matters." While technology serves to transcend spatial and visual boundaries to promote enterprise, it serves by default to maintain boundaries between children and their parents.

WHAT FUTURES?

Short of a general strike, a revolutionary mentality, or a concerted grass roots movement to compel change through action such as boycotts, non-cooperation, nonsupport of resistant institutions, change is piecemeal and tends to serve first those who already have the most power.

REFERENCES

Berger, P. & Luckmann, T. (1966). *The social construction of reality.* Garden City, NY: Doubleday.

Daly, M. (1968). *The church and the second sex.* New York: Harper and Row.

Gilbert, S. M. & Gubar, S. (1985). *The Norton Anthology of literature by Women: The Tradition in English.* New York: W. W. Norton.

Gouldner, A. W. (1962). Anti-Minotaur: The Myth of a Value-Free Sociology. *Social Problems, 9*(3), 199-213.

Malinowski, B. (1948). *Magic, Science and Religion and Other Essays.* Garden City, NY: Doubleday Anchor.

Ortner, S. (1974). Is Female to Male as Nature Is to Culture? In M. Z. Rosaldo & L. Lamphere (Eds.), Woman, Culture, and Society. Stanford, CA: Stanford University Press.

PBS (1991). *Empire*, Part 4 of The Shape of the World.

Rosenberg, R. (1982). *Beyond Separate Spheres: Intellectual Roots of Modern Feminism.* New Haven: Yale University Press.

Rothman, B. K. (1987). Reproduction. In B. B. Hess & M. M. Ferree (Eds.), *Analyzing Gender.* Sage Publication.

Weber, M. (1958). Science As A Vocation. In H. H. Gerth & C. W. Mills, *From Max Weber: Essays in Sociology.* New York: Oxford University Press.

Williams, R. (1990). The technology and the society. In Tony Bennett (Ed.), *Popular Fiction: Technology, Ideology, Production, Reading.* New York: Routledge.

Technological Change, Sexuality, and Family Futures Planning

Robert T. Francoeur

SUMMARY. Planning for both future social, scientific and medical research and for the challenges and changes we will confront as a result of sexological research and reproductive/contraceptive tech-nology requires consideration of four areas of special concern: (1) contraception, (2) reproductive technologies, (3) gender differences, and (4) sexual relationships. In each of these four areas examples are provided illustrating the political, activist, and religious uses and abuses of data to promote partisan views and agendas. Planning for a more humane future requires continual, skeptical, careful, and open dialogue because it will often be impossible to anticipate or define the problems in advance, and weigh the likely costs and benefits of individual and societal options.

KEYWORDS. Adultery, Contraception, Gender difference, Gender orientation, Homosexuality, Human Genome project, Natural selection, Population control

---

Robert T. Francoeur is Professor of Biological and Allied Health Sciences, Fairleigh Dickinson University.

[Haworth co-indexing entry note]: "Technological Change, Sexuality, and Family Futures Planning." Francoeur, Robert T. Co-published simultaneously in *Marriage & Family Review* (The Haworth Press, Inc.) Vol. 18, No. 3/4, 1993, pp. 135-154; and: *American Families and the Future: Analyses of Possible Destinies* (ed: Barbara H. Settles, Roma S. Hanks, and Marvin B. Sussman) The Haworth Press, Inc., 1993, pp. 135-154. Multiple copies of this article/chapter may be purchased from The Haworth Document Delivery Center. Call 1-800-3-HAWORTH (1-800-342-9678) between 9:00 - 5:00 (EST) and ask for DOCUMENT DELIVERY CENTER.

135

INTRODUCTION

The history of contraceptive/reproductive technologies and of recent research on gender differences and sexual relationships contains many informative examples of how individual, societal, political, and religious agendas have radically affected our interpretations and applications of new knowledge and technologies. An awareness and appreciation of how such agendas and biases have worked in the past is vital to our planning for future research and to our management of the challenges and changes we will confront as a result of new research and technological advances. This chapter examines four areas of concern.

In the area of contraceptive technologies, our infatuation with science and technology led us to see the birth control pill as the primary factor in promoting the changes of the sexual revolution of the 1960s and 1970s and to ignore the more subtle and important factors of a shift to gender egalitarianism and a social acceptance of the right of every female and male to sexual fulfillment. A second lesson is evident in the self-interests that motivate some religious opposition to the use of contraceptives.

In the application of reproductive technologies, China's policy of one child per family illustrates how a social agenda can bring unexpected consequences which, in hindsight, we wonder how we did not anticipate because they are now so obvious. A brief examination of population policies in Romania, Poland, Germany and France adds perspective to this concern about how to plan for the future. In the near future rapid progress in the Human Genome Project will bring major conflicts between society's responsibilities to assure survival of the human race and the heretofore unquestioned right of individuals to have as many children as they want when they want them.

A third area of concern and insights for futures planning is illustrated by our resistance to accepting new research findings on real neurological differences between men and women. Instead of using the new data to redesign our pedagogical methodologies for more effective teaching, activists and advocates of gender equality rejected the new findings as dangerous and politically incorrect. In the area of personal development and relationship counseling this refusal to recognize real gender differences has led to articulation of unattainable goals. Again, planning for the future requires an awareness and avoidance of this temptation.

My final area of concern focuses on the social consequences of biases in our interpretations of research on sexual relationships in marriage and gender orientations. Defenders of traditional values that view heterosexual exclusive monogamy as the sole acceptable moral standard can claim their monolithic society actually exists as the dominant pattern because of our lack of solid data on the incidence of non-marital sexual relations. At the same time, gay rights activists use widely accepted but questionable data on the incidence of homosexual, bisexual, and heterosexual orientations as a powerful weapon in their quest for civil and religious rights.

FOUR CHALLENGES

1. The Biases and Social Consequences of Contraceptive Technology in Our Future

Science and technology are commonly said to be "value free," meaning they are supposedly based on the purely objective, unbiased pursuit of truth and knowledge of how things work and can be made to work better. Whether or not this objectivity exists, persons who do scientific research and develop new technologies are not "value free." As humans they have their biases and prejudices, their conscious or unconscious agendas and goals, their vulnerability to societal expectations, and their subjective values derived from the particular culture whose atmosphere they breathe.

In the 1940s, when John Rock and Gregory Pincus were looking for a research project they did not reach into a bowl of unanswered scientific questions and randomly pull out a slip suggesting they try to fill in a major gap in our knowledge about the hormone mechanisms regulating the female reproductive cycle. At the Worchester Foundation for Experimental Biology in Massachusetts, the idea of developing an oral contraceptive intrigued Pincus because of his ongoing interest in reproduction, but he was also sensitive to the fears of some that a simple, safe contraceptive could radically alter our sexual expectations and values, and maybe even produce a sexual revolution. John Rock, a researcher, gynecologist, and obstetrician, had to balance his concerns about overpopulation and helping women avoid unwanted pregnancies against his Roman Catholic background that condemned all forms of contraception. When testing of the pill began in 1954 and for many years after FDA approval in 1962, Pincus and Rock were praised for creating an effective, safe weapon to combat overpopulation and for giving women control over their bodies. They were also vehemently and widely condemned by those who saw this medical technology as an omen of cultural, moral, and spiritual disaster.

Because we are infatuated with science and technology, we tend to endow them with an exaggerated power to change social values and human behavior almost overnight, especially when they touch the sexual arena. For three decades, the media and many experts helped convince us that it was the contraceptive pill, and not a broad-based societal shift towards gender equality and personal autonomy, that caused the sexual revolution of the 1960s. But, as sociologist Ira Reiss (1990) points out:

> those who believe in the revolutionary power of the pill are presuming that before the sexual revolution of the 1960s women were ready and willing to have intercourse if only their worries about pregnancy were alleviated. That makes female sexual motivations much like a car with an engine running but blocked from movement by one obstacle, fear of pregnancy. Just remove the road block and it will surely push forward. But the major block for women was not their fear of pregnancy. Women throughout this century have been subjected to a restrictive sexual upbringing. Accordingly, they have been programmed by society to start premarital sexuality, if at all, cautiously and only with the justification of serious emotional commitment. The evidence indicates that this upbringing and not the fear of pregnancy is the basic cause of female sexual resistance. . . . [What women] needed in order to be sexually freer was a change in the equality and autonomy our society granted to women. Accompanying such egalitarian changes is the acceptance by one's friends and family of the right [of any adult] to have sex. That group support is the vital element needed for any lasting change in sexual behavior. (pp. 93-95)

At the same time, any discussion of the social consequences of the contraceptive pill technology would be incomplete without at least a passing comment on opposition to the pill, especially as articulated by the celibate hierarchy in the Vatican. In Offertenzeitung fur die katholische Geistlichkeit Deutschlands, a conservative periodical for the German Catholic clergy in October 1977, we find this revealing confession:

> In fact, it is quite certain that in the next ten to twenty years the "pill" will crush the growth of the Church, with all the consequences this will have for the next generation of priests and religious, as well as for the yield on church taxes. No more new church buildings will be needed. . . . What will happen is precisely . . . why people were warned against the propaganda for the "pill," namely: an alarming drop in the birth rate, a demoralization of society, a sexualization of public life, open propaganda for pornography and nudism. . . . Public contempt for chastity resulting in a decline in the social prestige of priests and religious . . . all in all a pollution of the spiritual environment on a scale hitherto unknown. (Ranke-Heinemann, 1990, p. 297)

The Vatican's distinction between "nature" and "unnatural" birth control that allows rhythm and Billings' methods and condemns the pill and condoms, has led to some frightening conclusions. In 1992, for instance, the dean of the Vatican's Institute on Marriage and Family Studies said that if one spouse has AIDS, the couple must practice total abstinence. However, if such abstinence might lead to adultery or grave harm to conjugal peace, then the couple may licitly have unprotected sex and risk a lethal infection (Gallagher, 1992).

Marciano accurately provides a much broader context for these political responses to contraception when she warns that "We must ask who 'owns,' and controls the things we put to use and the rules by which we use them in living our lives. . . . The female is the most threatening human, most in rebellion, most in need of control. Or so say the male religious [and political] establishments, in the name of a male God." In planning for the challenges and changes our contraceptive technologies will invariably bring us in the future, we have to remember that whenever a fascist, fundamentalist, sexist patriarchy controls a society's reproductive and contraceptive technologies, or any other technology, every individual in that society, but especially the women, are at great risk.

2. The Biases and Social Consequences of Reproductive Technologies in Our Future

Two current applications of our reproductive technologies are clearly going to present us with major research, forecasting, and planning problems. The first application and its problems are illustrated by China's attempts to limit its population growth and the attempts of Romania, Germany, France, and Poland to increase their growth. The second application focuses on our potential to prevent or cure hereditary diseases via the Human Genome Project.

China offers us a unique scenario for the future that illustrates how government leaders can use effective contraceptives and legal abortion to achieve a public good by restricting individual rights. In 1966 the government began a major effort to keep its population below 1.2 billion by the year 2000 (Jacobson, 1987; Ruan, 1991).

The effort began with simple steps. Contraceptives and abortions were provided without cost by the government. Premarital sex and courtship were discouraged. Government incentives encouraged Chinese women not to marry until age 25 and men until at least age 28. This minimum age was reduced to 22 for men and 20 for women in 1980, when the number of single people over age 30 increased significantly. Still, this restricts personal rights.

More important, the government instituted a policy of one child per couple. Couples who have only one or no children are given bonuses, priority in housing, and medical and educational advantages. Couples expecting a second child would forfeit 20 percent of their salaries unless the wife has an abortion. If a second child is born, the parents are taxed an additional 15 percent of their salaries until the child turns 7. Penalties for a third child were even more severe.

This policy has brought substantial progress, with the average number of babies per woman dropping from five or six in 1970 to 2.25 children in 1991. But with lax enforcement, China now expects to break the 1.2 billion barrier by 1995 and approach 1.3 billion by the year 2000. This expected growth is double what economists say is optimal as China struggles to modernize and increase its industrial base. The projection of 1.3 billion by the year 2000 is now triggering tougher enforcement as the number of women of child-bearing age increases dramatically.

The one-child per family policy has meant new hope for the country's long-term growth, but in a culture accustomed to large extended families, with many relatives sharing in the raising of the many children each couple had, the single child family policy has brought unanticipated problems. China now has a growing shortage of females. When limited to one child, four of five Chinese couples want a boy because they depend on sons for support in their old age. In some areas this policy has resulted in a birth ratio of five boys to one girl. According to China's 1990 census, about 600,000 infant girls, five percent of all females born in China each year, vanish without a trace. Demographers believe up to half the 600,000 infant girls may be given up for informal adoption and raised by other families. Parents may also send a first born daughter to live with relatives in other areas, or raise her without registering her birth. But female infanticide is also a reality.

A shortage of daughters also means Chinese men will be hard pressed in their search for a bride. The one child policy has also ruined marriages, intensified sexist attitudes and led to forced abortions, selective abortion of female fetuses in wealthy families, government harassment of offending families, bribery, abandonment, and countless battles between mothers and their daughters-in-law (Baringer, 1991; Bullough & Ruan, 1988; Francoeur, 1991, pp. 39-42; Kristof, 1991a, 1991b; WuDunn, 1991a, 1991b).

In rural areas where three-fourths of the population live, an estimated 100 million peasants are currently jobless. So far this has not led to major unrest, but with the number of unemployed expected to grow to 300 million in 1999, overpopulation and underemployment pose a significant threat to social stability. China's history is full of peasant rebellions including the 1949 Communist revolution.

China's unique policies on sex, marriage, and population growth remind us of problems other nations will face as they try to resolve the conflict between the individual's right to decide how many children to have and the state's responsibility to the common good and future generations by keeping its population within viable boundaries.

At the same time, some nations have implemented population policies to increase a birth rate that has fallen below replacement level and threatens the nation's future. Under Communist President Nicolae Ceaucescu, Romania criminalized abortion and promoted a high reproductive rate with what amounted to a "pregnancy police force." Thousands of children, abandoned by parents who could not raise them, were adopted by the President and raised in state orphanages. Their unquestioning loyalty to their father, President Ceaucescu, made them ideal members of the state secret police and military.

Similar political uses of pronatalist policies have occurred in Germany, France, and Poland. In Germany and France, during and after the First and Second World Wars, church leaders joined politicians in blaming the invasion and defeat of their countries on the selfishness of women who practiced "unilateral disarmament"–contraception–in the bedroom. In 1919, the Catholic Bishops of France warned that:

> The [First World] War has forcefully impressed upon us the danger to which [French women who practice contraception] expose our country. Let the lesson not be lost. It is necessary to fill the spaces made by death, if we want France to belong to Frenchmen and to be strong enough to defend herself and prosper. (Ranke-Heinemann, 1990, p. 290)

Under Poland's Communist government, contraceptives though scarce were subsidized. Legal abortions totalled 600,000 a year, roughly equal the number of live births. When the Communists lost control, the bishops and the Polish Pope immediately pressed parliament to outlaw all abortion and contraception. But in a nation that is 95 percent Catholic, 71 percent oppose any ban on abortion, 81 percent oppose any restriction on contraception, 61 percent reject the church's position on extramarital relations, and 63 percent reject its opposition to divorce. While the outcome in Poland is still in doubt, this and the other examples of nationalistic, militarist, and religious interests directing the application of our ability to control human reproduction deserves careful observation and analysis for insights into our own future.

The second crucial application of reproductive technology for the future involves the Human Genome Project. A dozen years ago, when scientists started discussing the possibility of identifying all the 50,000 to 100,000 genes carried on the 46 human chromosomes, no one suspected that we might complete this project in our lifetimes. We now expect to have all the human genes identified and decoded within a few years. Major breakthroughs in the sophistication and power of DNA probes and computer assisted decoding have brought us to the brink of being able to control individual genes in our hereditary package, detect and repair defective genes in the newborn or in the fetus, and even select "healthy" sperm and eggs for IVF and embryo transfer.

The potential of this knowledge is unlimited and wide open. The possibilities of misuse, abuse, and exploitation are awesome and frightening. Who has access to this information? Should employers have access to the results of genetic screening, or require genetic tests of prospective employees? Should insurance companies be allowed to use the results of genetic screening in deciding their rates for individuals, as they already do for heavy smokers and persons with high risk hobbies like sky diving and bunge jumping (Fletcher, 1974; Francoeur, 1977, 1984, pp. 89-105, 1987, pp. 61-71)?

Americans have a long tradition of naive enthusiasm for science and technology. A recent survey on public response to the Human Genome Project clearly illustrates this danger of our being manipulated. A 1992 March of Dimes Birth Defects Foundation poll of 1000 Americans revealed that the public is "extremely optimistic" and "deeply enthusiastic" about the progress of gene therapy and other experimental approaches to taming inherited diseases.

This naive enthusiasm ignores the fact that every scientific advance is a two-edged sword and can be used for good or evil. Americans may be excited by possible altruistic and humanitarian applications, but they are generally oblivious of the possible consequences of a hidden demonic technological imperative that can drive some applications. Commenting on the results of the March of Dimes survey, Dr. Jennifer L. Howse noted that, "There's a real anomaly between the public's overwhelming approval for gene therapy and its overwhelming lack of knowledge."

The risk for our future is obvious in several survey findings. Close to 90 percent approved gene engineering to thwart genetic disorders, yet 60 percent confessed they knew almost nothing about the technique. More disturbing was the 42-43 percent of those polled who approved gene therapy to improve the intelligence or the physical characteristics children would inherit. As for an individual's right to privacy, 57 percent said there should be no absolute right to privacy. Of this 57 percent, 98 percent said a spouse or fiance had a right to know the results of gene testing, 58 percent said an insurer had a right to know, and 33 percent said the employer has a right to know. This despite the experience of many people who have testified in Congress that they have been refused medical coverage when it became known that they carried a genetic predisposition for cancer or the gene for Huntington's disease that normally does not strike until a person is in his or her forties.

The need for all citizens to be involved in decisions affecting our future places an equal burden on the specialists to educate the public, and on the individual citizen to educate her or himself. Yet because monitoring technologies like the Human Genome Project requires some basic knowledge, the public increasingly leaves the application of technologies, especially in the health care sphere to the specialists who supposedly "know better." Unfortunately, the average American will continue to be blindly enthusiastic about our growing control over human reproduction until some application threatens him or her personally. Public education is essential, but we cannot expect any immediate effect other than blind enthusiasm.

That the past offers another example of the importance of being aware of who defines genetic diseases and who makes the rules regulating the use of knowledge gained from the Human Genome Project is evident in a 1936 meeting of Cardinal Faulhaber and Adolph Hitler. The Cardinal opposed Hitler's plan to prevent the "hereditarily diseased" from reproducing. Hitler claimed the best approach would be to sterilize the "hereditarily diseased." "The operation is simple," he argued, "and doesn't incapacitate them for a trade or for marriage" in the Third Reich. The Cardinal objected that sterilization is contrary to the natural law. The Cardinal suggested an acceptable alternative: "the State is not forbidden to isolate these vermin from the community, out of self-defense, and within the framework of the moral law." In the future, our much deeper knowledge of human genetics will undoubtedly confront us with much more perplexing questions than Hitler's debate with the Cardinal about the relative merits of castration versus concentration camps (Ranke-Heineman, 1990:330-332).

Resolving conflicts between society's rights and individual reproductive rights are bound to become far more complex and difficult in the years ahead. Will children born with a hereditary disability be able to sue their parents who conceived them despite knowing any child they conceived would be at significant risk for a specific genetic disease like cystic fibrosis? When will our courts have to decide the first "wrongful life" suit? How will we define and enforce the legal rights of the fetus to a healthy genome? How will we balance the rights of the fetus to a healthy genome with the right of individual adults to have as many children as they want when they want them? Will the common good be invoked to stop couples who want 6 or 8 children despite their one in four or one in two risk of having a child with Tay-Sachs, Huntington's, hemophilia, or another crippling (and costly) disease? Questions like these stir the specter of Nazi eugenics and ethnic cleansing. Despite the messiness of such questions, we cannot continue to ignore them. The human race as a whole and individuals alike share a responsibility of protecting the health, welfare, and future of all humans by keeping our population growth in balance with the limited resources of our earth that support our life.

Our current knowledge of human reproduction gives us a power unequaled in human history. That power will definitely grow in the years to come. In recent years, our power to control human reproduction has brought the realities of cesarean section operations forced by white male doctors on poor and minority women "for the good of their child." Women have been charged with fetal abuse. There has been a successful campaign to keep the RU 486 abortion pill out of the United States (Lader, 1991), a federal ban on abortion counseling in federally funded programs, withdrawal of federal funds from any foreign aid program that includes abortion as an option in controlling population, efforts to define the constitutional rights of the fetus from the moment of conception, and parental notification laws for minority women seeking to exercise their right to an abortion.

3. The Biases and Social Consequences of Gender Differences in Our Future

Research on the nature and causes of the differences between men and women necessarily involves both the biological and social sciences, and a long-standing tension between the social-constructionist and the biological-essentialist perspectives on gender. While the recent documentation of real biological differences in the neural systems and brain centers of women and men resolves this heated debate, our response to this research shows how our biases influence whether we accept or reject sexological research we find uncomfortable. Our response also illustrates how we can use and even distort science and technology to reinforce social attitudes rather than allow the facts to speak for themselves even when they force changes in our attitudes and moral values.

As the 1960s' concern with gender equality and personal autonomy for women matured into the feminist atmosphere of the 1970s and early 1980s, many scientists in diverse fields found one area of research both unpopular and dangerous. The politically correct view was that women and men are equal, meaning "essentially the same and differing only in their sexual anatomy and their resultant capacity to impregnate or gestate and lactate." All the gender differences beyond genital anatomy, it was stated, result from scripts for gender-stereotyped behaviors that are inscribed on the blank slates of our virginal minds after birth by a sexist, patriarchal culture.

In 1955, John Money, director of the Psychohormonal Research Center at the Johns Hopkins University, stated this gender neutrality/equality constructionist theory as follows:

> Sexuality is undifferentiated at birth and [only] becomes differentiated as masculine or feminine in the various experiences of growing up. (Moir & Jessel, 1991, p. 14)

Compare this belief with Milton Diamond's 1977 statement of the opposing, then politically incorrect, position that the prenatal wiring of the brain by male and female hormones makes the destiny of women and men different, giving them different priorities, ambitions, skills, and behavioral tendencies.

> He or she comes into the world with constitutional, genetic, and hormonally mediated . . . behavioral biases and innate patterning . . . (Moir & Jessel, 1991, p. 53)

Along the way, researchers were denied positions, grant funding, and tenure if their research suggested real gender differences. There is even evidence that the date in a famous gender case study was, deliberately or subconsciously, distorted and misrepresented by supporters of the politically correct gender neutrality hypothesis (Diamond, 1982, 1991).

The evidence, however, is now clear and undeniable that Nurture does not prevail over Nature, nor Nature over Nurture. Instead, Nature and Nurture interact at various critical periods in our development from conception to death. Scientific and clinical evidence now document that gender-different hormonal influences in the womb "wire" or "encode" male and female neural systems and pathways so that we are born with many gender-differentiated behavioral capacities and tendencies.

For two decades, activists, scientists and lay persons alike, have tried to ignore and deny the growing evidence of gender differences because they believed this would force us back into sexist exploitation. Sociologist Steven Goldberg and others, for instance, argue that millions of years of evolution and natural selection have created inherent differences between the male and female in mammalian and primate species that have made patriarchy–male dominance and control–"inevitable." To counter this argument, sociologist Cynthia Fuchs Epstein and others reject all evidence of gender differences drawn from neurological studies and from research on thousands of genetic identical twins raised apart.

Neither approach solves the problem. Recognizing the reality of gender differences does not mean we have to accept the exploitation and injustices of an "inevitable patriarchy." Denying real gender differences creates a dangerously counterfeited world, in which women and men compete in a world where male gender standards prevail and men and women are assumed to be essentially equal in all their attitudes, behavioral tendencies, and skills even though they actually differ (Diamond, 1982, 1991; Durden-Smith & deSimone, 1983; Goldberg & Epstein, 1991; McWhirter, Sanders & Reinisch, 1990; Reinisch, Rosenblum & Sanders, 1987; Tanner, 1990).

In her 1983 Presidential Address to the American Sociological Association, the distinguished Alice Rossi warned that attempts to explain human behavior and to design therapies to change behavior that ignore or deny the fundamental biological and neural differences between the sexes "carry a risk of eventual irrelevance against the mounting evidence of sexual dimorphism." Today, some advocates of gender equality still insist on denying the real differences between men and women. Their rationale appears to be a radical fear and confusion. They fear that any acknowledgment of the reality of biological and neural differences between males and females will inevitably lead to and cause gender inequality in the political, social and ethical realms. But, as Rossi points out, this fear confuses gender differences as a biological fact with gender equality, which "is a political, ethical, and social precept."

For those who accept the reality of gender differences but refuse to let it be used to defend the injustices of sexism, the challenge in the years ahead will be to reeducate men and women and use this knowledge to the advantage of both by working towards gender egalitarianism. Our knowledge of real differences in the ways women and men communicate can be used to facilitate communications and enhance human relationships (Tanner, 1990). Our knowledge of real differences in what men and women seek in their relationships can enhance relationships and make them healthier. It can expand the narrow male-biased priorities and objectives that prevail in the business and political arenas. Rather than continuing to maintain gender equality by telling the average female she can match any male's accomplishment in an educational system designed by males for male skills, our challenge will be to recognize real gender differences in learning skills and aptitudes and use this knowledge to redesign our educational system and methodologies to maximize the complementary skills of males and females (Holden, 1991; Gibbons, 1991; Gorman, 1992).

In planning for the future, for the challenges and changes we will meet in dealing with the discoveries genetics and neuroscience promise for the 1990s and the 21st century, we must be sensitive to and on our guard about the fears that often lie beneath the alleged objectivity of those who do the research in this area and of those who interpret, use and control this new knowledge.

4. The Biases and Social Consequences of Sexual Relationships in Our Future

Most Americans admit that our sexual attitudes and values have changed radically since the 1940s. In a 1991 nationwide survey reported in *The Day America Told the Truth*, Patterson and Kim (1991) found that premarital sexual relationships and nonmarital cohabitation are now part of the life of the majority of American families. One in five Americans loses his or her virginity by age 13 and half of all Americans have had sex by age 16. More than 50 percent of teenage girls are sexually active, up from 35 percent in 1973. Most of these teenagers have had two or more sexual partners, and one in 10 has had multiple partners within the previous six months. Ninety percent of college women were sexually active in 1989, the same as in 1975, but the percentage of sexually active 19-year-old males rose from 73 percent in 1979 to 80 percent in 1990. The average American now has seven sexual partners in his or her adult life.

Sociologist Annette Lawson (1988) found that 66 percent of the men and women in her survey group had extramarital affairs, and the urge was coming earlier, five years into the marriage as opposed to 13 years before 1960. Patterson and Kim (1991) found that close to a third of all married Americans have had or are now having an affair. This overall national average balanced extramarital behavior among the religious and rural with the fast-moving, anonymous life of our larger urban centers. In the past 50 years, the character of extramarital relationships has changed from the one-night stand to relationships that usually lasted almost a year. Three out of four married persons who were having an affair when the survey was done did not have any plans to end their affair soon. Two thirds of the men and 40 percent of the women had had more than one affair. More startling, almost two thirds of Americans believed there is nothing morally wrong with an extramarital affair.

These realities of life are reflected in the daily lives of church-going Americans. Some, seeking to hold the traditional line on sexual behavior, find comfort in fundamentalist conservative churches. Others increasingly press for reinterpretations and adjustments in what their churches quietly or openly accept and approve. The result has been a variety of work-study documents and statements by commissions in the mainstream churches.

A study of new directions in American Catholic thought, commissioned by the American Catholic Theological Society, gave cautious acceptance to some premarital and gay relationships (Kosnick, Carroll, Cunningham, Modras & Schulte, 1977). Though quickly condemned by the Vatican, the report's conclusions are commonly followed by liberal priests in their parishes.

A 1987 document from the Episcopal Church of Northern New Jersey called for the recognition of a variety of nonmarital relationships including gay unions (Thayer et al., 1987). Similarly, a call for the 1991 General Assembly of the Episcopal Church to bless gay unions and accept the ordination of active gay and lesbian clergy ended in a compromise that left the church's official stance on homosexual relations ambiguous at least for the three years until the next General Assembly in 1994. While the ordination of sexually active gay men and women remains technically against church policy, the blessing of gay unions and the ordination of non-celibate homosexuals is likely to continue and will probably become more frequent among Episcopalians in the future (Steinfels, 1991).

In 1991, the press reported that the General Assembly of United Presbyterian Church (U. S. A.) had overwhelmingly rejected the call for church recognition of responsible, committed premarital, extramarital, postmarital, gay and lesbian sexual relationships and the ordination of active gay men and lesbians to the ministry. In reality, the General Assembly did not vote to accept or reject, but rather to give the majority and minority reports further study and defer any decision to its next meeting (Presbyterian Church, 1991; Sheler, 1991; Steinfels, 1991).

While researchers try to document the realities of changing American sexual behavior and values, sexologists have been studying the nature and origins of gender orientations. These new insights have created pressure for the churches to recognize the naturalness of gay and lesbian orientations and lifestyles. The general consensus today is that our gender orientation–homosexual, bisexual, or heterosexual–is the natural result of neural tendencies encoded in the brain before birth and elaborated on and fixed by a variety of factors in the preadolescent and early adolescent years. Simon LeVay (1991) and others have uncovered significant anatomical differences in the limbic system of heterosexual and homosexual men, confirming the origins of our gender orientation in prenatal neural development. The factors behind these tendencies and their finalized expression are not known, but the conclusion is widely accepted (Barinaga, 1991; Gelman, 1992; McWhirter et al., 1990).

Since publication of Sexual Behavior of the American Male (1948) and Sexual Behavior of the American Female (1953), Kinsey's pioneering surveys have been the authority on what Americans are doing sexually. For 40 years, family specialists and sociologists have defended the value of Kinsey's data while acknowledging the limitations of his convenience samples and the fact that these data are now forty years old.

For ten years we have fought the battle against the AIDS epidemic using data on what Americans were doing sexually in the 1940s. In 1991 and 1992 Congress approved funds for social scientists to update these data with two nationwide, random sample surveys of adults between the ages of eighteen and fifty-four and teenagers.

Despite our desperate need for an accurate picture of what Americans are doing sexually in the 1990s, conservatives have managed to kill both surveys. A half a dozen conservatives won the day unopposed by the majority. Senator Jesse Helms (R-North Carolina) claims that these surveys are part of "the homosexual movement's agenda to legitimize their sexual behavior." Representative William Dannemeyer (R-California) claims these surveys are "a [public relations] game for the sexual revolution" and "wasteful government spending." Gary Bauer, president of the Family Research Council, says the teenage survey would be "an invasion of privacy and a waste of eighteen million dollars to study something that we painfully already know the facts about . . . [Since we] know many of our kids are having sex too early, too often and with too many people, we ought to be spending eighteen million dollars to figure out how to divert them from that conduct." Louis Sullivan, the Health and Human Services Secretary, claims that the teen survey would actually promote the idea that casual, promiscuous sex is normal (Francoeur, 1992).

Our out-dated data on American sexual behavior seriously cripples our dealing with the AIDS crisis. What percentage of Americans are homosexual or heterosexual? How many men including happily married husbands, are sexually active with both their wives and with men? What are different segments of our population doing that puts them at risk for HIV infection? Kinsey's data is not very helpful in answering these questions. We have long been aware of two major problems in Kinsey's data on this point: his limited operational definition of homosexual orientation and his necessary use of a convenience rather than a random sample.

Kinsey used two criteria, sexual attraction and sexual experience to orgasm, as the basis for his operational definition of sexual orientation. But we have long been aware of the limitations of this operational defini-

tion. Do we rate someone who has had one homosexual and 1000 heterosexual experiences the same as someone who has had one homosexual and
ten heterosexual experiences? Are both "Kinsey 1"–predominantly heterosexual but occasionally homosexual? Should we consider life-long
activity, or only activity within the last year, month, week, or decade? Do
we include or exclude adolescent experimentation and same-gender sex
activity in prisons that is never repeated in latter life? While Kinsey included both in his statistics, many today argue that we should exclude
both. Many also argue for a more realistic and clearer definition of gender
orientation that includes such factors as frequency, emotional/affectional
(limerent) orientation, fantasies, social preference, lifestyle, self-identifi-
cation, and the time factor (Coleman, 1990; Klein, 1990; Klein, Sepekoff &
Wolf, 1985; Moses & Hawkins, 1982). These considerations obviously
affect Kinsey's conclusion that roughly 50 percent of the adult male population is exclusively heterosexual ("Kinsey 0"), 40 percent are bisexual
("Kinsey 1-4"), and 10 percent are predominantly or exclusively homosexual ("Kinsey 5-6") in orientation.

Alongside this definitional problem, we have the problem of Kinsey's
convenience sample. Recent random sample surveys here and in Europe
suggest that the 40 percent bisexual and 10 percent gay figures are much
too high for the general population. A more accurate approximation, according to Diamond (1991) and others, would be 90 percent exclusively
heterosexual ("Kinsey 0"), 5 percent bisexual ("Kinsey 1-4"), and 5
percent predominantly or exclusively gay ("Kinsey 5-6"). Data from
these same random surveys suggest that the percentage for lesbians is
roughly half that of males, about 2-3 percent. Despite these new insights,
activists and advocates naturally continue to cite Kinsey's higher, more
impressive statistic of 40 percent bisexual males and 10 percent homosexual for obvious political reasons.

Our knowledge of biological and prenatal factors in gender orientation
support arguments that the biblical condemnations of homosexual behavior as unnatural are no longer valid. Our current research knowledge also
suggests good reasons why society and the churches should recognize
committed homosexual lifestyles and relationships, the rights of gay men
and lesbians to serve as ministers, teachers, and in the military, and at least
some forms of committed non-marital heterosexual relationships. However, the repeated use of questionable statistics on gender orientations and on
non-monogamous lifestyles–e.g., estimates on the incidence of extramarital affairs range from 25 to 70 percent or more–can backfire.

Thus my caution that, in researching and planning for social changes
that affect domestic partnerships and families, we must consider three

resources: (1) the on-going research of sexologists seeking to understand the nature and origins of gender orientations, (2) the research of social scientists seeking to document and understand both the changing patterns of sexual relationships and domestic partnerships (marital and nonmarital), and (3) the responses of activists and the various churches that play a considerable role in reforming the sexual values of Americans.

CONCLUSION

Whether we are dealing with basic research in contraception, population regulation, the Human Genome Project, the real diversities in American marriages and families, or the biological basis of gender differences and gender (sexual) orientations, we are dealing with powerful new knowledge and discoveries that directly and radically affect our human future. Planning for our future requires that society as a whole and every individual recognizes a radical new reality in human evolution: our increasing substitution of natural selection with human selection. Recognizing this radical new reality of our exploding control of human nature and our future, in turn, exposes a snowballing challenge: the unavoidable authority of specialists must be moderated and directed by the public who must have an effective voice in selecting our future.

Science fiction dysutopias like Brave New World in the 1930s and The Handmaid's Tale in the late 1980s carry a dire warning about allowing a select group to direct our increasing control over human nature and our human future. Unfortunately there is an understandable temptation for people to feel so threatened by radical changes on all sides that they gladly hand over the decision-making to supposedly wiser experts. Fundamentalism and fascism thrive on the fear of radical change. Yet, if the general public does not exercise its individual responsibilities for our future, others will gladly decide for us what our future will be, what our future roles will be, and who will benefit most from our increasing human selection.

To empower the masses so they can make the most humane choices in planning our future, natural and social scientists will have to bring to the surface the hidden values and biases behind all research, possible technological applications, and futures planning so they can be examined critically by the public.

Empowering Americans to select the most humane future also requires that citizens educate themselves so they can become involved in deciding what our priorities are going to be in the next five or ten years. Instead of leaving the decisions of priorities to politicians, social scientists, and activists seduced by the high visibility of headline making projects, the public needs to study possible scenarios before they seek to force a shift in our priorities. With the billions we pay for scientific research and health care, there is no justification for the United States ranking as low as we do in preventative medicine, basic prenatal and perinatal health care, and family support.

Given the many unpredictable factors in our technological future and the unforeseen consequences of any planning we might do, we can only hope to create a more humane future by constant efforts to educate the public in dedication and vigilance to the lessons of the past and the options our future seems to offer. In the decades ahead, our only hope lies in open, critical, on-going dialogue involving everyone affected by the future, and in daily vigilance against the potential for abuse of our growing reproductive knowledge by those who seek power and use knowledge to control others.

REFERENCES

Barinaga, M. (1991, August 30). Is homosexuality biological? *Science, 253*, 956-957.

Barringer, F. (1991, December 31). Birth rates plummeting in some ex-Communist regions of Eastern Europe. *New York Times*, p. A3.

Bullough, V. L., & Ruan, F. F. (1988, June 8). China's children. *Nation*, pp. 48-49.

Coleman, W. (1990). Toward a synthetic understanding of sexual orientation. In D. P. McWhirter, S. A. Sanders, & J. Machover Reinisch (Eds.), *Homosexuality/Heterosexuality: Concepts of Sexual Orientation*. New York: Oxford University Press.

Diamond, M. (1982). Sexual identity: Monozygotic twins reared in discordant sex roles and a BBC follow-up. *Archives of Sexual Behavior, 11*(2), 181-186.

Diamond, M. (1991). Bisexualities: A biological perspective. In E. Haeberle (Ed.), *Bisexualities: Volume 41*. Berlin: Walter de Gruyter.

Durden-Smith, J., & deSimone, D. (1983). *Sex and the Brain*. New York: Arbor House.

Fletcher, Joseph (1974). *The Ethics of Genetic Control: Ending Reproductive Roulette*. Garden City, NY: Anchor Press/Doubleday.

Francoeur, R. T. (1977). *Utopian Motherhood: New Trends in Human Reproduction* (3rd ed.). Cranbury, NJ: A. S. Barnes Perpetua Books.

Francoeur, R. T. (1984). Transformations in Human Reproduction. In L. A. Kirkendall & A. E. Gravatt (Eds.), *Marriage and the Family in the Year 2020*. Buffalo: Prometheus Press.

Francoeur, R. T. (1987). Reproductive Futures: 1964, 1984, and Beyond. In M. Marien & L. Jennings (Eds.), *What I Have Learned: Thinking about the Future Then and Now*. Westport, CT: Greenwood Press.

Francoeur, R. T. (1991). *Becoming a Sexual Person* (2nd ed.). New York: Macmillan Publishing Co.

Francoeur, R. T. (1992, August). Kinsey: Forty years later: The need to update. *Penthouse Forum*, pp. 48-53.

Gallagher, J. (1992, September 4). Rome's birth-control conceptions flunk real-world test. *National Catholic Reporter, 28*(38), 15.

Gelman, D. (1992, February 24). Born or bred: The origins of homosexuality. *Newsweek*, pp. 46-53.

Gibbons, A. (1991, August 30). The brain as "sexual organ." *Science. 253*, 957-959.

Goldberg, S., & Epstein, C. F. (1991). Is patriarchy universal and genetically determined? In R.T. Francoeur (ed.), *Taking Sides: Clashing Views on Controversial Issues in Human Sexuality* (3rd ed.). Guilford, CT: Dushkin Publishing Group.

Gorman, C. (1992, January 20). Why are men and women different? Sizing up the sexes. *Time*, pp. 42-51.

Holden, C. (1991, August 30). Is the "gender gap" narrowing? *Science, 253*, 959-960.

Jacobson, J. L. (1987). *Planning the Global Family.* (Worldwatch Paper #80). Washington, DC: Worldwatch Institute.

Klein, F. (1990). The need to view sexual orientation as a multivariable dynamic process: A Theoretical perspective. In D. P. McWhirter, S. A. Sanders & J. Machover Reinisch (Eds.), *Homosexuality/Heterosexuality: Concepts of Sexual Orientation.* New York: Oxford University Press.

Klein, F., Sepekoff, B., & Wolf, T. J. (1985). Sexual orientations: A multivariable dynamic process. In F. Klein & T.J. Wolf (Eds.), *Bisexualities: Theory and Research.* New York: The Haworth Press, Inc.

Kosnick, A., Carroll, W., Cunningham, A., Modras, R. & Schulte, J. (1977). *Human Sexuality: New Direction in American Catholic Thought.* New York: Paulist Press.

Kristof, N. D. (1991a, June 17). A mystery from China's census: Where have young girls gone? *New York Times*, A1, A8.

Kristof, N. D. (1991b, November 5). Stark data on women: 100 million are missing. *New York Times*, pp. C1, C12.

Lader, L. (1991). *RU 486: The pill that could end the abortion wars and why American women don't have it.* Reading, MA: Addison-Wesley Publishing Co.

Lawson, A. (1988). *Adultery: An Analysis of Love and Betrayal.* New York: Basic Books.

LeVay, S. (1991, August 30). A difference in Hypothalamic structure between heterosexual and homosexual men. *Science, 253*, 1034-1037.

McWhirter, D. P., Sanders, S. A., & Reinisch, J. Machover (Eds.). (1990). *Homosexuality/Heterosexuality: Concepts of Sexual Orientation.* New York: Oxford University Press.

Moir, A., & Jessel, D. (1991). *Brain Sex: The Real Differences between Men and Women.* New York: Lyle Stuart/Carol Publishing Group.

Moses, A. E., & Hawkins, Jr., R. O. (1982). *Counseling Lesbian Women and Gay Men: A Life-Issues Approach.* Columbus, OH: Charles Merrill.

Patterson, J., & Kim, P. (1991). *The Day America Told the Truth.* Englewood Cliffs, N. J.: Prentice Hall.

Presbyterian Church (U.S.A.). (1991). *Keeping Body and Soul Together: Sexuality, Spirituality, and Social Justice.* General Assembly Special Committee on Human Sexuality. Philadelphia: Presbyterian Church (U.S.A.).

Ranke-Heinemann, U. (1990). *Eunuchs for the Kingdom of Heaven: Women, Sexuality, and the Catholic Church.* New York: Doubleday.

Reinisch, J. M., Rosenblum, L., & Sanders, S. A. (Eds.). (1987). *Masculinity/ Femininity: Basic Perspectives.* New York: Oxford University Press.

Reiss, I. L. (1990). *An End to Shame: Shaping Our Next Sexual Revolution.* Buffalo, NY: Prometheus Press.

Ruan, F. (1991). *Sex in China: Studies in Sexology in Chinese Culture.* New York: Plenum Press.

Sheler, J. L. (1991, June 10). The Gospel on Sex. *U.S. News and World Report,* pp. 58-64.

Steinfels, P. (1991, July 20). Episcopal resolution on homosexuality offers an uncertain view. *New York Times,* p. A8.

Tanner, D. (1990). *You Just Don't Understand: Women and Men in Conversation.* New York: Ballantine Books.

Thayer, N. S. T. et al. (1987, March). *Report of the Task Force on Changing Patterns of Sexuality and Family Life.* Newark, NJ: The Voice (Episcopal Diocese of Northern New Jersey).

WuDunn, S. (1991a, June 16). China, with ever more to feed, pushes anew for small families. *New York Times,* p. A1, A10.

WuDunn, S. (1991b, July 4). Chongqing Journal: China's dismal truth: 100 million out of work. *New York Times,* p. A4.

FAMILY PROCESS
IN SHAPING THE FUTURE

Theoretical Issues in Researching
Problem Solving in Families

Irv Tallman

KEYWORDS. Definition of family, Problem solving, Tasks, Strategy, Scope, Awareness, Information, Evaluation

INTRODUCTION

One of the perplexing aspects of the study of human behavior is the tendency for the most common and frequently occurring behaviors to be the

Irv Tallman is Professor of Sociology, Washington State University.

[Haworth co-indexing entry note]: "Theoretical Issues in Researching Problem Solving in Families." Tallman, Irv. Co-published simultaneously in *Marriage & Family Review* (The Haworth Press, Inc.) Vol. 18, No. 3/4, 1993, pp. 155-186; and: *American Families and the Future: Analyses of Possible Destinies* (ed: Barbara H. Settles, Roma S. Hanks, and Marvin B. Sussman) The Haworth Press, Inc., 1993, pp. 155-186. Multiple copies of this article/chapter may be purchased from The Haworth Document Delivery Center. Call 1-800-3-HAWORTH (1-800-342-9678) between 9:00 - 5:00 (EST) and ask for DOCUMENT DELIVERY CENTER.

155

most resistant to scientific explanation and investigation. Nowhere is this more apparent than in the study of family problem solving. Gerald Patterson notes that, "Problem solving [in families] becomes most evident when it is absent. It is only when the debris of unsolved problems is everywhere that this omitted mechanism comes into focus" (Patterson, 1982, p. 230).

Patterson's observation has two important implications. First, problem solving, like the air around us, is so pervasive that it is barely detectable; second, most family distress and disorganization can be attributed to problem solving failures. Although the second implication may be overdrawn, there is nonetheless, a readiness among family scholars to attribute a broad array of individual and collective difficulties to poor family problem solving (Kantor & Lehr, 1975; Klein & Hill, 1979; Reiss, 1981; Spivak, Platt & Shur, 1976).

The relevance of problem solving as a factor in the everyday life of family members becomes even more evident when we consider how the family faces an unknown future. The rate of social, economic, and cultural change is so rapid that the only certainty seems to be that the future is uncertain. Couples entering marriage not only must take into account changing gender role expectations, they must confront a complex interplay between marital, parental, and occupational roles whose priorities and expectations are in constant flux. It is no longer clear who is supposed to do what in the home, on the job, or as parents. Nor is it clear what represents a fair division of labor or whose job has priority. Confusion as to role expectations is further confounded by a volatile economy propelled by an electronic revolution that allows for instant communication and obscures national political boundaries. Under such conditions couples cannot look to their own family experiences for effective role models. Indeed, parents today cannot rely on their life experiences or current social conditions as the basis for preparing their children for adulthood. The best they can hope for is to prepare them to be able to adjust to change and to be problem solvers so that they can effectively deal with change.

Given the ubiquity and relevance of problem solving in everyday life, the question is why has the study of problem solving in families contributed so little to our knowledge about how families function? This paper attempts to provide an explanation for this failure by analyzing the current state of affairs in family problem solving research. It then attempts to provide a solution to the problem by considering possible strategies for changing the current state of affairs. Finally, as an example of a useful strategy I provide a discursive summary of a theory of problem solving, part of which is currently being tested in research with couples.

POINT OF DEPARTURE

The range of topics to be covered under the rubric of problem solving opens the possibility of engaging in innumerable debates about issues that are tangential to the central thrust of the paper. It will be helpful therefore if I establish some epistemological constraints on these comments. The ideas presented here are addressed to students of the family interested in building a body of knowledge based on a set of procedures generally referred to as the scientific method. The paper does not address the ongoing debate between positivists and anti-positivists or between those who believe all knowledge statements are ideological and those who think the scientific method can be a protection against ideological bias. Even within these constraints, much that follows is likely to be viewed as debatable. Such a debate between people who share similar purposes is welcome and may even advance our collective effort to explain essential elements of family behavior.

There seems to be general agreement that the study of family problem solving is characterized by disparate theories and fragmented research programs (See, for example, Klein, 1983; Olson, Lavee & McCubbin, 1988). What is needed is a collective effort to systematize and expand this knowledge. This requires, in the first instance, greater consensus as to the meanings of fundamental concepts. It also requires an understanding of and commitment to the type of knowledge that can be cumulated. For knowledge to be cumulative the statements that make up our explanations must be communicated in a form that allows them to be expanded, modified, or falsified by subsequent investigators (Cohen, 1989, p. 293). The form in which the knowledge statements are combined should, therefore, follow some reproducible set of procedures. Finally to be cumulative the knowledge statements must be sufficiently generalizable so they can be transferable from one concrete situation to another (Freese, 1980). It follows that cumulative knowledge is theoretical knowledge.

The first necessary step in the endeavor to build theory is to develop a shared understanding of key concepts. Given the purpose of this paper, three concepts–family, problems, and problem solving–take on obvious import. In the following section I explore the meaning of family and problem. The definitions of problem solving and problem solving processes will be discussed in more detail in the section describing a specific problem solving theory.

DEFINITIONS

Family. There is no general agreement among scholars as to what is meant by "family." Elsewhere (Tallman, 1986), I suggested that the family has been variously defined as a social institution, a social organization, and a small group of interacting personalities. It also has been referred to as a kin group whose kinship is the basis for residing together in households (U.S. Bureau of Census, 1989); or an experiential milieu in which particular ways of perceiving and experiencing the world are forged (Berger & Kellner, 1970; Reiss, 1981).

Until recently, most family scholars believed that kinship was the one term that linked all of these conceptions of family. Kinship generally has been defined as a network of persons who are related by birth, marriage or adoption and who, because of that relationship, have a specific set of obligations toward one another (cf. Williams, 1970, p. 47 & 50; Eshelman, 1991, pp. 92-94). But even this conception has been challenged. For example, the argument is advanced that in Scandinavia cohabitation has become so institutionalized that it is comparable to marriage and, therefore, relevant to family (Manniche, 1989; Trost, 1979). Thus marriage, in the sense of a public, legal and/or sacred covenant, is no longer a necessary (and universal) component of kinship. Is kinship, then, restricted to birth ties? Gubrium and Holstein (1990, pp. 118-120) point out that in a period of increasing poverty and family disorganization the question of who is kin becomes obfuscated. They describe a number of situations in which kin terms are used not to designate blood ties but to acknowledge helping/dependency relationships. For example, a boy in trouble is brought to his "mother," a woman who raised him but did not give birth to him. There is no place for the child to go so the woman who cares for him considers herself and is considered by others as his de facto mother. The question is whether "mother" is a kinship term or a description of a role set? The fact that it is used both ways obscures rather than facilitates its meaning.

Another group of family scholars has posed a new and challenging conception of the family. Rather than considering its organizational and institutional aspects, the family is characterized as a unique set of relationships, experiences and characteristics. This set consists of: "affect, development, experience, rules, ethics, patterns, relationships, aspirations, values, and heritage that make up the familial part of the human experience" (Beutler & Burr, 1989). This is the "family realm" that is described as being basic and "natural." The uniqueness of the "family realm" is said to stem from its origins in the process of giving birth and being born (Beutler, Burr & Bahr, 1989). It is difficult to evaluate this new knowledge claim. Perhaps there is something that is fundamental, and universal about the bond that is formed between mother and child. It may be that the evidence of high rates of infanticide in many cultures, evidence of maternal desertion, the growing business of surrogate mothering and the readiness of many women to give their children up for adoption represent special cases under which the bonding principle is violated. To this point, however, the linkage between birth and the extended range of experiences described by Beutler et al. (1989), as unique to the family is little more than assertion by fiat.

It would appear that a definition of the family that is appropriate for this moment in historical time may not be appropriate over the centuries. Gubrium and Holstein (1990) illustrate how the meanings of the term "family" have changed over historical time. Even the term itself is a relatively new concept. They conclude that "Time has transformed family's imagery and discourse, changing the way we think and talk about communal life and social relations. Family's meanings and usage, then, are tied to their historical context." Moreover, Gubrium and Holstein (1990, p. 22) maintain that family meanings are " . . . situationally sensitive–that is influenced by their social and cultural circumstances . . . "

Thus there is good reason to conclude that meanings attached to the term "family" have changed as social conditions have changed. Indeed, except for the unsubstantiated claims of Beutler et al. (1989), there seems to be some general agreement that its meanings are constantly changing. If that is the case, if there is no core of behaviors or experiences that can be uniquely attributed to "family" at all times and in all places, then the term loses relevance for building a theory that will contribute to a cumulative body of knowledge.

Scanzoni, Polonko, Teachman and Thompson, (1989, p. 36) employ similar reasoning to conclude that the term has no scientific value and is viable only for lay persons who are able to tolerate the multiple meanings and inconsistencies of its usage. Scanzoni and his colleagues suggest that the phrase "close relationships" can absorb the essential meanings of family and can be defined with less ambiguity.

None of this is meant to imply that what goes on in the groups we call families is substantively unimportant. At this point in historical time the behaviors that take place in the settings and patterns of relationships that are popularly subsumed under the term family is of vital importance to the mental health of those involved and, in aggregate, to the well being of the social system. It deserves careful investigation. The unanswered question is how can we provide adequate explanations of these relationships?

The point I will be making in the pages that follow is simply that it is a mistake to try to base such explanations on *family* theory; rather, they are best derived from general, abstract theories about human behavior. Just as geologists draw on the laws of physics and chemistry to understand how the earth is formed and changes, so students of the family should rely upon general principles of human behavior to account for how such groups are formed, change and dissolve. The task for both the geologist and the family scholar is to understand the special conditions under which these principles operate. I return to this issue later in the paper when I discuss the requisites for building a theory of problem solving behavior.

To facilitate communication in this paper we need a working definition of what I mean when I use the term "family." For the remainder of this paper, family will refer to a group of people: (1) who are interdependent for goods, services, affection, information, status, social support, and income; (2) who are committed to one another for an extended period of time–usually a lifetime; and (3) whose boundaries are relatively impermeable, thereby creating a shared identity among its members. I make no claim to exclusivity for this definition; other groups beside families may also meet the above stipulations. I also make no claim for the definition's universality, it is not likely to hold for all families in all cultures and societies over time.

Problem. There seems to be general agreement among investigators interested in problem solving that a problem is *a state of affairs in which an actor's efforts to attain a given goal are disrupted or blocked and there is some probability (known or unknown) that this disruption or blockage can potentially be overcome by some physical or mental activity* (Agre, 1982; Kahney, 1986, p. 15; Newell & Simon, 1972, p. 72; Tallman, 1988). Thus a problem can be interpreted as a discrepancy between an actual and a desired state of affairs. It can exist for actors without their knowledge or awareness. A spouse, for example, may be unaware of his/her partner's dissatisfaction with aspects of their marriage until the partner is so dissatisfied that he/she breaks the relationship, or a family member may be dying of a disease that, if detected, could be cured. This stipulation allows us to include problem perception or awareness as an essential variable in the theory of problem solving to be discussed later. It is a variable that too often has been ignored in the problem solving literature.[1]

Because uncertainty exists as to whether a problem will be solved, and since uncertainty has been shown to produce stress (Janis & Mann, 1977; Lazarus, 1977), it can be inferred that problems are stressful events. However, since a problem can be solved or rectified, it differs from other stressful events such as crises, troubles and dilemmas (Tallman, 1988). For example, an earthquake can be both trouble and a crisis for a family but, since it is unrectifiable, it is not a problem. On the other hand, the restructuring of a family (rebuilding damaged housing, bringing injured family members back to health, and so forth) subsequent to an earthquake meets the definition of a problem.

A TAXONOMY OF PROBLEMS

It is axiomatic that the actions required to solve a problem are determined by essential problem characteristics (e.g., the goal to be attained and the barriers to be overcome). Thus if we can identify the range and types of problems people face, we might gain an understanding of the types of problem solving activities that are likely to be elicited. This has proved to be a formidable task. The difficulties of developing typologies of problems have troubled students of problem solving for years. Most have considered it an insurmountable task (Greeno, 1978; Kahney, 1986).

In 1974, perhaps out of naiveté, members of my seminar on problem solving joined with me in an attempt to construct a taxonomy of group problems (Tallman, Klein, Cohen, Ihinger, Marotz, Torsiello & Troost, 1974). What follows is a modified version of the original taxonomy. It is offered, not as a complete or even adequate categorization of the entire range of problems that people face, but rather, as suggestive of the kinds of issues that must be taken into account when contemplating an explanation of the problem solving process.

The taxonomy is constructed within three parameters, each posited as an essential part of any problem. These are: problem *source, task requirement and outcome control.* Outcome control pertains to key characteristics of the goal that is being thwarted, source pertains to the location of the barrier to attain the goal and task requirements to the type of group activity necessary to overcome the barrier.

The first parameter, *source,* identifies the point at which the problem originated. It provides an initial focus for gathering information about the problem. Two dimensions, *external-internal* and *impersonal-interpersonal* are identified.

Although there is general recognition that problems can be generated both within and outside the group or individual (Kelley & Thibaut, 1969), it has been difficult to identify and study internally generated problems. Virtually all problem solving research, whether with natural groups like the family or with ad hoc groups, has used problems created by the researchers. (See, as examples, research summarized in Abelson & Levi, 1985. See also; Aldous & Ganey, 1989; Reiss, 1981; Straus, 1968; Tallman & Miller, 1974; Tallman, Marotz-Baden & Pindas, 1983.)[2] Some investigators have systematically studied families with real life problems, but generally their research has focused on chronic problems in which the families studied have had a long prior history of problem solving failure. There is research on families with disturbed and aggressive children (Forgatch, 1989; Patterson, 1982), research that compares "distressed" families with "non-distressed" families in terms of different problem solving styles (Gottman, 1979; Hahlweg & Jacobson, 1984; Reiss, 1981; Spivak et al., 1976), and research with families in which a member has a chronic illness such as diabetes (Kieren & Hurbut, 1987). What is lacking is research on how internally generated problems emerge and how actors respond to these emerging problems as they develop.[3]

We know considerably more about how actors conceptualize, diagnose, and act when confronted with external problems. The theory and research emanating from cognitive psychology that focuses on how problems are conceptualized and represented in memory, the mental process of transferring and generalizing from one problem to another, and the use of analogues in problem solving, are all based on responses to externally imposed problems (see, as examples, Newell & Simon, 1972; Kahney, 1986; Mayer, 1983).

The second dimension under the source parameter is *impersonal-interpersonal*. Research on impersonal problems has tended to focus on the relationship between the structure of the problem (i.e., the initial state of the problem and the operations necessary to change that state), and the problem solvers' capacities to develop accurate cognitive representations of the problem structure. This linkage between the actor's cognitive interpretation of a problem situation and its objective conditions is the basis upon which problem solving strategies are assessed (Kahney, 1986; Smith, 1988). Solutions to impersonal problems are generally invariant and unambiguous: it is likely that there is only one solution available when an actor attempts to solve a puzzle or an anagram and, even if more than one solution is possible, there is generally clear, objective and incontrovertible evidence as to whether or not the problem has been solved. Under such circumstances it is relatively easy to distinguish between effective and ineffective methods.

Solutions to interpersonal problems, on the other hand, are not as easily identified and evaluated. They require introspective information as well as subjective assessments of the feelings, motivations, abilities and desires of the people involved in the problem (see Spivak et al., 1976; Jacobson & Margolin, 1979; Patterson, 1982). Despite these complexities, there has been a considerable body of research focusing on interpersonal family problems. Generally, this research has stressed the importance of communication as a source of family problems and as a means for resolving such problems (Fitzpatrick, 1988a; Gottman, 1979; Hahlweg & Jacobson, 1984; Noller & Fitzpatrick, 1988; Patterson, 1982). Recently, this body of research has identified the expression of negative affect in interpersonal communication as a primary obstacle to effective problem solving (Forgatch, 1989; Gottman & Levinson, 1988).

As important as this research is, it is likely that many, if not most, problems families face are impersonal (and external) in nature. Finding the best possible job, finding a house, balancing the household budget, fixing the furnace, finding money to send a child to college or to get a needed operation, determining and attempting to meet the nutritional needs of family members, are all important family problems. Moreover, the relationship between interpersonal and impersonal problems is such that one type of problem may influence the generation of the other. There are consistent data that suggest that families' failures to solve impersonal problems, such as those that produce economic hardship, contribute to the generation of interpersonal problems or vice versa (Conger, R. D., Conger, K. J., Elder, Lorenz, Simons, Whitbeck, in press).

The second parameter, *task requirements*, pertains to the necessary steps that must be taken to solve a problem. Under this rubric, problems are arrayed along three dimensions–*rule-boundedness*, *disjunctive-conjunctive*, and *simple-complex*. The *rule-boundedness* dimension focuses on the degree to which the solution requires discovering and following a set of rules or, at the other extreme, generating new rules. The rules may be procedural, analytical or regulatory or any combination of the three.[4]

It is likely that most problems faced by families are rule bound (e.g., balancing a budget, finding a job, building a house). Sometimes, the rules are not explicit and must be discovered in the process of problem solving. Learning to function effectively in new groups and organizations, for example, can require identifying implicit rules that are not formally stated. Other problem situations may require revamping, changing or altering existing norms, behavioral standards, and procedural rules. Some problems require developing new rules. Reiss (1981, p. 180) suggests that families traveling to foreign countries are often forced to establish novel patterns of behavior that are not necessary when they are at home. The resolution of some interpersonal conflicts can require that the persons involved modify or change existing standards or procedures.

Finally, there are problems that are so ambiguous that analytic rules may hamper the problem solver. Beisecker and his colleagues review data and report an experiment in which, under some conditions, negotiators perform better if they do not have knowledge about essential aspects of a bargaining situation (Beisecker, Walker & Bart, 1989). They interpret their results in terms of equity theory, but it is likely that the bargaining situation itself makes a spontaneous and non-reflective response an effective tactic simply because it catches the other party off guard.

Nemeth and Wachtler (1983) report experimental data showing that the presence of a minority viewpoint fosters independent creative responses. Problems with specific and unique circumstances cannot easily be solved with pat formulae. In such situations the contributions of parties with special knowledge and novel perspectives can be critical to a solution. The failure either to listen to or to contribute a minority perspective toward the solution of a complex problem contributes to "Group Think," a condition characterized by a false sense of security that the group decision making process is infallible (Janis & Mann, 1977). This sense of security is based on the reluctance of the group to consider the risks involved in a given choice or to consider reasonable alternative ways of thinking about a problem (Janis & Mann, 1977, pp. 130-133). Available research on parental and marital problems indicates that openness, flexibility, and tolerance for ambiguity are associated with effective problem solving (Kieren & Tallman, 1972; Gottman, 1979; Patterson, 1982, p. 230; Spivak et al., 1976, p. 161; Tallman & Miller, 1974).[5]

The *disjunctive-conjunctive* continuum is the second dimension included under the task requirement parameter. Disjunctive problems are problems that can be solved by any member of a group whereas conjunctive problems require the coordination of all members. Thus, fixing the family car when it breaks down is a disjunctive problem because it can be solved by a single family member. On the other hand, restoring family morale, maintaining the status of the family in a community, or reorganizing the family after the loss of a member are all conjunctive problems because they require the contribution of all family members. It can be seen that the best solution for disjunctive problems depends upon the abilities of the most competent person in the group, whereas the best solution for conjunctive problems depends upon the least competent (or least motivated) member of the group (Smith, 1989).

Some problems are best solved by a subset of the larger group. For example, sometimes interpersonal problems between siblings or between parents in a family are best resolved by this subset without involving the entire family. Similarly, problems such as fixing a plumbing leak may require the coordination of two family members because of the narrow space involved in diagnosing and repairing the problem.[6] We refer to this type of problem as quasi-conjunctive.

The third dimension, *complexity*, is concerned with the number of diverse elements that must be integrated to solve the problem. The most frequently utilized definition of problem complexity focuses on two key determinants, the number of elements in the problem and the number of interactions between those elements (MacCrimmon & Taylor, 1976; Volkema, 1988). Simple problems have few elements and few types of interaction. Generally, we can conclude that the more complex the problem, the greater the "information load" the actor has to process to reach a solution. Information load is frequently defined as the number of alternative behavioral routes available to solve a problem multiplied by the number of attributes that characterize the problem (Abelson & Levi, 1985).

There is a general tendency with complex problems to find some way to simplify the information load either by reducing the number of alternatives or synthesizing the number of attributes (Abelson & Levi, 1985; Schroder, Driver & Streufert, 1967). Consider how a middle class family might approach the problem of career planning for an adolescent. The options to be considered might be reduced by assessing the adolescent's abilities, interests, and family traditions regarding careers. This is linked to an assessment of real world opportunities for possible career routes. Generally, actors will conduct intensive information searches only after they reduce the number of alternatives, usually to no more than three options (Abelson & Levi, 1985).

The final parameter pertains to the degree to which the problem solution is under the control of the problem solver. Three types of problems are identified along this control dimension: *puzzles, strategies,* and *chance* (Anderson & Moore, 1960). Of these three types, the outcome of *puzzle* problems is most clearly under the control of the individual or group. This is because there is only one correct solution that is potentially discoverable by the problem solver. Success or failure in puzzle problems depends solely upon the actor's skills and resources. Much of the research in problem solving whether in ad hoc groups or families has focused on solving puzzle problems (Kahney, 1986; Reiss, 1981; Simon, 1978; Straus & Tallman, 1971). Daily family life is replete with puzzles ranging from uncovering the source of an unpleasant odor, to repairing a leak in the roof, or discovering the identity of a daughter's secret boy friend.

Unlike puzzles, the solution to *strategy* problems cannot easily be assessed in right-wrong terms. Strategy problems include those in which there is a conflict of interest between competing parties, or even more perplexing, there is a conflict between individual (or group) benefits and the welfare of the community. Prototypes of strategy problems are embodied in the various game theories including the enormous body of research on the "Prisoner's Dilemma" (see Tallman & Gray, 1990 for a review). Strategy solutions are evaluated in terms of the best results one can achieve under the circumstances. Outcomes must be weighed against the relative power of the opposing forces in the problem situation, and the short and long term payoffs involved. In strategy problems, the actor has only partial control of the outcomes since much depends upon the responses of opposing forces. Thus the level of uncertainty as to outcomes is greater than with puzzles.[7] Family strategy problems have been studied in the areas of child rearing (Patterson, 1982; Shure & Spivack, 1978), marital conflict (Gottman, 1979; Emmelkamp, van der Helm, MacGillavry & van Zanten, 1984; Jacobson & Margolin, 1979; Schaap, 1984), career planning (Tallman et al., 1983) and seeking consensus (Olson, McCubbin & Associates, 1983).

Chance problems can be assessed in terms of winning or losing. But, unlike puzzles the outcome is out of the actor's control. It is a gamble and the best that can be done is to estimate its probabilities. Research in this area has tended to focus on the heuristics and biases actors use when making such estimates (Tversky & Kahneman, 1982). The general tendency is to overestimate low probabilities and underestimate high probabilities. Probability estimates are also distorted if an event is observed (Tversky & Kahneman, 1982). For example, if a murder occurs in the neighborhood, there will be a tendency to overestimate the probabilities of the occurrence of murders in the area.

A critical issue when considering efforts to solve chance problems is identifying conditions under which actors are more or less likely to take risks. The prevailing evidence suggests that people are more likely to select risky alternatives to avoid losses than to obtain gains (Kahneman & Tversky 1984). To use an obvious example, most families seem willing to invest $500 a year in insurance to protect a home worth $100,000 even though they know the odds are a million to one that their home will not be damaged by fire or disaster. On the other hand, the same families are less likely to invest the same amount of money each year in a lottery at the same odds to win $100,000.

Chance problems in daily life are perhaps more pervasive than any other category in the typology. Efforts to solve chance problems include such common activities as dressing to avoid inclement weather, choosing the safest and/or quickest route to get to work, choosing one brand of soap over another when shopping. They also include less common activities such as trying to become pregnant, applying to schools or clubs for admission, or making financial investments.

Omitting the conditions of time and space that also affect problem solving[8] and simply dichotomizing the dimensions included under the three problem parameters yields 144 different types of problems–all of which are relevant to family life. Given this complexity and the changing meanings attached to the concept of family, it is probably not surprising that delving into research in this area is like exploring a jungle of contradictory data, ill defined concepts, multiple perspectives, and philosophical orientations that are rigidly maintained and rarely forsaken.

This raises the obvious question of whether it is possible to build a theory of problem solving that can be informative to students of the family? The question fits our definition of a problem: there is a goal (build a theory of problem solving for family behavior) and there are barriers to attaining the goal (poor data, no consensus as to the meanings of concepts, a complex and diverse subject matter). Using the above taxonomy, it is possible to classify the problem as "internal," "impersonal," "quasi-conjunctive," "non-rulebound," "complex" and "strategic." Since the problem is internal to our discipline, we alone must confront it and solve it. Because it is impersonal we should be able to employ objective criteria for determining a course of action and assessing our progress. Its quasi-conjunctive character suggests that we cannot solve the problem in isolation; but it can be solved by a subset of members of our discipline. It will not be necessary to gain the adherence of every sociologist or family scholar. The problem is non-rulebound so we must discover, create, or identify the procedural rules that should be followed for developing our theory. Finally, the problem is clearly complex and difficult and it requires a strategic approach. Given these conditions, the first task is to arrive at an appropriate strategy.

STRATEGIES FOR BUILDING A THEORY
OF PROBLEM SOLVING BEHAVIOR THAT CAN HELP
STUDENTS OF THE FAMILY

In the interests of clarity, I will restate the problem. We have a goal–the development of a theory that can help us in understanding family problem solving. There are barriers to attaining our goal–conceptual ambiguities, lack of consensus as to the meanings of key terms, diverse subject matter, and a confusing array of contradictory data and knowledge statements.

Our strategy must be directed toward overcoming the barriers described above. To accomplish this end we must address the following four critical questions:

1. Since there is great variability in what is considered theory (sociologists have been accused of treating anything that is not data as theory (Cohen, 1990)), what is the conception of theory we wish to employ? How do we establish conditions for testing the theory?
2. Given the definitional problems associated with the concept "family," do we want to limit our explanation to certain types of families, linked as they must be, to specific times and places? Alternatively, do we want to build a theory of sufficient generality and abstractness that it is relevant to problem solving processes in groups that include families?
3. Should our theory seek to explain generic problem solving processes or be limited to specific kinds of problems most like the ones that confront families?
4. Most theories of problem solving tend to be normative in the sense that they are concerned with how people learn to be *effective* problem solvers. On the other hand, most useful scientific theories of behavior tend to be descriptive or empirical, focusing on predicting what "is" rather than what "ought to be." Is it possible (or desirable) to build a non-normative theory of problem solving behavior?

Let us consider the first question: what do we mean by "theory" and what are its critical components? The discussion regarding the need for a cumulative body of knowledge provides us with criteria for addressing this question. First, the theory's concepts should be sufficiently explicit so that their meanings and operations are understood by other scholars interested in the topic; second, it should be relevant to family scholars; third, it should pertain to solving all problems or it should specify those problems to which it is applicable.

Finally, the theory should be precise enough and parsimonious enough to communicate effectively and unambiguously to an audience of interested scholars. At the same time, the principles (knowledge statements) must be able to penetrate the jungle of contradictory statements and account for an array of findings and explanations without leaving too much relevant knowledge unexplained.

To achieve this end, the statements that make up the theory should be sufficiently abstract to subsume large bodies of data as well as knowledge statements that seek to explain more concrete phenomena. For example, it is preferable for a theory of problem solving to incorporate principles that explain decision making as a generic process rather than seek to explain decision making in specific situations such as when a couple is considering a divorce. The advantage is not just that the former explanation has broader scope, it is also that decision making about divorce is embedded in an array of historically unique conditions linked to current cultural, economic, and social developments–conditions that will not be the same ten or a hundred years from now. Moreover, it is possible to move logically from general principles of decision making to explaining decision making in divorce situations by specifying the specific and unique conditions that make the latter a case of the former. It is much more difficult, if not impossible, to move from the specific to the general (Cohen, 1989, pp. 245-47).

The need for effective communication underscores the importance of formalizing theories. By formalizing I simply mean putting the theory's argument into some kind of established logical structure. This enables readers to understand the theory's purpose and implications by following the rules that link the explanatory statements one to the other. It also enables the reader to determine, at the logical level, whether the theory is true or false.

Finally, if the theory is to contribute to a cumulative body of knowledge it must be deductive rather than inductive. This is because, as noted above, we are unable to explain phenomena by moving from the specific to the general. Cohen (1989, p. 246) claims that, "Since Hume many thinkers have attempted to develop an inductive logic, but none have succeeded." Observations of specific events may well serve as a source of ideas but they cannot provide a basis for logical explanation. We have no way of knowing how unique the event is to a given time and place. In order to generalize about an observed event we would have to observe all instances of that event. It follows that theories cannot be tied directly to any particular set of data or, for that matter, to any single study (Walker & Cohen, 1985).

If the best way to build theory is through universal statements establishing relationships between abstract concepts, and if data represent temporally and spatially unique events, how can such statements be tested empirically? Indeed, contradictory findings cannot, by themselves, be sufficient to invalidate a theory. A leaf floating in air and ships rocketing through space are not adequate evidence for refuting the laws of gravity. According to Walker and Cohen (1985, p. 240), "It is always possible to uncover observations . . . that contradict . . . [universal] statements." What then can be done? Is it ever possible to have empirically useful theories?

The answer is, of course, yes–if we accept the important principle that all knowledge when applied to the empirical world is conditional (Cohen, 1980; Walker & Cohen, 1985). To test a hypothesis derived from a theory we need to specify the conditions that must be met for an observed event to be considered applicable to the theory. We also need to establish the conditions under which observations would be able to falsify the theory's prediction. For example, Emerson's (1962, 1972a, 1972b) statement, Pab = Dba (the power of A over B is equivalent to B's dependency on A) is testable only under conditions in which: (1) the distribution of some valued resource is such that "A" controls more of a resource x than "B"; (2) x is highly valued by "B"; (3) "A" is the only or the best prospect "B" has for obtaining units of x, and; (4) "B" is in a position to offer "A" some resource y in exchange for x. Note too that the theoretical statement is essentially structural in nature. It pertains to only two kinds of variables–resources and opportunities to obtain and exchange resources. Thus the predicted relationship between power and dependency does not take into account cultural factors such as traditional customs or values, ecological conditions establishing differential needs or expectations, and personality and biological differences. In fact, an adequate test of the principle would need to control these exogenous elements. In brief, a theory cannot plausibly be tested without explicitly establishing the conditions under which it can be falsified and the limitations of its applicability (Walker & Cohen, 1985).

Are these constraints so limiting that general theories are not useful in explaining family behavior? Such a conclusion is no more justifiable than concluding that the "Law of Falling Bodies" (which is based on the existence of a vacuum and the absence of friction–conditions that never occur in the real world) is of no use in the study of aeronautics. Actually the law serves as a guideline that directs the scientist to look for situations that minimize friction or develop measures of friction to estimate the rates of descent (the example is taken from Cohen, 1980). Similarly, Tallman et al. (1983) were able to use Emerson's power/dependence formulation as a basis for explaining the greater power observed among Mexican peasant wives as compared to United States white collar wives. The same principle was used to explain why power differentials found in observational data were different from those expressed in interviews.

I think that some students of the family have too quickly rejected a theory because they find some aspect of family life that is inconsistent with its principles (see for example, Beutler et al., 1989). Without specifying the scope conditions under which a theoretical principle is appropriately testable, we have no basis for either accepting or rejecting the utility of the principle.

In sum, I have attempted to show that an effective strategy for theory building entails developing universal (i.e., independent of time and space), principles that are arrived at deductively using a communicable logic and concepts that not only are clearly defined but whose meanings are generally shared by the relevant community of scholars. To test such a theory it is necessary to provide explicit statements establishing the scope of the theory's applicability and designating the conditions under which the theory can be falsified.

The second question relevant to a strategy for building theory pertains to whether the theory should be restricted to explaining *family* problem solving. This issue was discussed earlier when we explored the changing nature of family definitions. At that time I suggested that since our understanding of what is meant by the term "family" changes with time and situation, it is not a useful concept for building a theory that can contribute to a cumulative body of knowledge. A theory limited to explaining what happens in families is restricted to describing conditions at a given point in historical time.

The third question required that we choose between building a generic theory of problem solving or focus on a specific set of problems. This is a more difficult question to answer. Problem solving theory and research in the family that has focused on internal, interpersonal problems has produced significant and cumulative knowledge. The research of Patterson (1982) and his colleagues, the research on Behavioral Marital Therapy (Hahlweg & Jacobson, 1984), the work of Fitzpatrick and her colleagues (1988b), and the systematic research carried on by Gottman (1979), all center on problem solving in marital groups or in parent-child relationships. This body of work has been consistently driven by theory. Its origins are in social learning theory but it has been modified by communications and information theories, exchange theory and, most recently, physiological principles (Gottman & Levinson, 1987).[9]

This work undoubtedly will continue to contribute to knowledge of family problem solving but it could be augmented by theories of broader scope. For example, the interplay of internal and external problems is documented in the research of Kessler and McRae (1982) and others who have studied the effects of women's employment outside the home on intrafamily relationships. There is also evidence of the interaction between impersonal and interpersonal problems in the work of Elder and his colleagues demonstrating the interplay between socio-economic conditions and the characteristics of family members in dealing with the joint problems of loss of income and changing family functions (Elder, 1974; Liker & Elder, 1983). It is easier of course to advocate greater scope for theories than it is to construct such theories. The problem is to build a general theory that incorporates basic principles of the more specific theories without becoming so general as to be trivial and/or untestable.

There is some evidence that a general theory of problem solving is possible. Spivak et al. (1976), for example, list five criteria that contribute to what they call interpersonal cognitive problem-solving skills (ICPS). These are: (a) an awareness of the type and range of problems people face, (b) an ability to generate alternative problem solutions, (c) an ability to articulate step by step means for carrying out the solution, (d) an ability to anticipate the consequences of one's acts for oneself and others and, (e) an ability to understand the impact of one's feelings and actions on others. This formulation is not too different from the conception of "problem structure" or "problem space" developed by Simon (1978) and used to explain problem solving procedures in a variety of impersonal problems ranging from complex puzzles (e.g., the "Towers of Hanoi"), to chess, to business management (Kahney, 1986; Smith, 1988; Simon, 1978). The notion of problem space assumes that when confronted by a problem, people have some mental conceptualization of the initial state of the problem, they have some (clear or unclear) estimate of the goals involved, of the various stages involved in solving the problem, of the operations that are necessary, of the transformations necessary, and of the estimates of outcomes that result from taking the various steps in the process (see Kahney, 1986; Smith, 1988).

The final question posed for determining a strategy for building a problem solving theory applicable to families, asked whether the purpose of our theory should be normative (prescriptive) or empirical (descriptive)? Virtually all theories of problem solving are normative, focusing on helping people become better problem solvers. Given the purpose of this activity, it is clearly difficult to separate problem solving from the success or failure of the outcome. In fact, some investigators have maintained that to do so is illogical and/or trivializes the whole endeavor (Agre, 1982; Klein & Hill, 1979). Another position, the one I have adopted, holds that linking process to outcome confounds efforts to explain both phenomena. Are we to say that the poor problem solver does not engage in problem solving? If people engaging in problem solving can be effective or ineffective then the set of behaviors involved should be described independently of how the outcomes are evaluated. A further advantage of a theory that focuses on problem solving behaviors rather than outcomes is that it can provide a basis for differentiating those who engage in problem solving from those who avoid the process or make other coping adjustments.

It seems to me that the focus on normative theory has been a deterrent to developing useful knowledge about problem solving in families. The concern with effective or successful problem solving rather than with the generic processes relevant to all problem solving activity leads us back into the labyrinth of explaining specific outcomes at specific times and places. A theory of effective problem solving is premature–we must first be able to explain the essential nature of the behavioral processes involved whether they succeed or fail.

My colleagues and I have used the strategy described above to develop a general theory of problem solving processes (Tallman, Leik, Gray & Stafford, forthcoming). The theory uses universal principles drawn from behaviorist, social exchange, and decision theories. Because the formal theory is available elsewhere (Tallman, Leik, Gray & Stafford, forthcoming), what follows is a discursive discussion oriented toward demonstrating its utility for students of the family.

THE THEORY–A DISCURSIVE SUMMARY

We begin with two key definitions, one pertaining to the act of problem solving, the other to the problem solving process.

Definitions

The act of *problem solving* is defined as a *non-routine mental and/or motor activity undertaken under conditions of uncertainty as to outcome and oriented toward overcoming an impediment to goal attainment by circumventing, eliminating or removing a barrier or restoring previously established goal attainment routes.* There are two aspects of this definition that deserve mention here. The first is that problem solving involves an attempt to change a given state of affairs. Thus problem solving, as a behavioral process, is distinguishable from coping or other mechanisms of adjustment. The second aspect is that problem solving implies deciding between alternative courses of action. The key decisions to be made are located in the following problem solving process.[10]

The *process of problem solving* involves the following four stages:

- *Perceiving (awareness of) a situation as problematic.*
- *Searching for and processing information relevant to selecting effective problem solving activity (including deciding when to terminate the search).*
- *Deciding to engage in a problem solving activity.*
- *Evaluating the effectiveness of the activity that was undertaken. Was a solution reached? Is a solution possible with the current course of action? Should estimated probabilities be changed?*

The problem solving process is seen as sequential; it involves a series of decisions affecting whether the actor stays in a given stage, returns to a previous stage or goes to the next stage. The theory incorporates a decision model (Gray & Tallman, 1984, 1986) as one of its basic axioms. It then provides theorems establishing the antecedent conditions that influence decisions in each of the above stages. In essence the theory consists of a series of mini-theories designed to account for the conditions under which actors decide to move to the next stage in the problem solving process.

Scope Conditions

Four scope statements designate the domains of empirical applicability within which the theory can be tested and is falsifiable. The first statement restricts the theory to structural explanations, thus the key causal variables are resources controlled by actors and the opportunity to exchange resources. Second, it is stipulated that a problem is extant in the actor's environment. The actor need not be aware of the problem at a given time and may never be aware of it, but the problem exists (i.e., an objective observer with adequate knowledge using our definition would identify the situation as a problem). Thus the theory is not relevant to situations in which actors create problems out of whole cloth or engage in problem solving behavior when no problems exist.

The third scope condition limits problem solving activity to one problem at a time. The theory can explain why actors choose one problem to solve over others and why they will stop working on one problem when other problems of specific characteristics come into their awareness. But the theory is not relevant to situations in which the problem solver is working on more than one problem at the same time.

The final scope condition states that, "Relevant actors are entities capable of making and empowered to make decisions that can commit the entity to take action." Thus the theory is not relevant to family members such as infants or children who are incompetent or powerless to participate in decision making when the family is faced with a given problem. On the other hand, it is relevant to situations in which the group (family) functions as a decision unit.[11]

The Theory

The theory is based on the premise that the problem solving process is driven by decisions made under conditions of risk or uncertainty. Risk pertains to situations in which the outcome probabilities are known, such as when one invests in a lottery, buys life insurance or seeks admission to a prestigious university. Uncertainty pertains to situations in which the probabilities are unknown–for example, when considering marriage and estimating one's chances of living a happy life with a future spouse, or whether to get a fixed or variable rate mortgage, or settling a quarrel with a neighbor (see Lopes, 1987 or Tallman & Gray, 1990 for a more detailed discussion of the distinction between known and unknown probabilities). Most problems tend to involve more uncertainty than risk. In fact, as we shall see, part of the process of problem solving involves attempting to reduce uncertainty as much as possible.

The first part of the theory provides the essential elements involved in making decisions. The axioms and theorems in this section begin with the assumption that human behavior is oriented toward survival; that all choices, including decisions, take into account three critical variables– benefits, costs and probability of outcomes. These variables are combined in a decision making model that Gray and Tallman (1984) call the "Satis-faction Balance Model." The model specifies that actors faced with alter-native choices will seek to maximize satisfactions by considering (in ratio terms) the choices the actor anticipates will lead to satisfactions against those likely to lead to dissatisfactions. Satisfaction, as used in the model, is a relative term; it is possible to use the model to predict choices in which, under certain specified conditions, the actor will select a costly alternative over a beneficial one, or will choose between two costly alternatives (Tallman, Gray & Leik, 1991).

The second part of the theory uses the principles that underlie the decision model to derive theorems relevant to each of the four stages of the problem solving process. With regard to the first phase, the theory holds that the costs of engaging in problem solving are such that there exists an inertia that must be overcome before actors recognize a situation as a problem. This recognition or problem awareness is manifest simply by some conscious acknowledgment that a situation exists that requires changing.[12] The focus on change differentiates this response from coping behavior.

The theorems for phase one are intended to establish conditions for overcoming resistance to problem perception. They hold that the likeli-hood of perceiving a situation as a problem is a function of two interactive factors: (a) the degree to which the problem threatens the individual's or group's survival, and (b) the immediacy of the problem. Thus it is pre-dicted that families are more likely to be aware of situations in which there are external threats to their abilities to care for and protect their members and internal threats to their viability and functioning. For example, we would predict that families will be quicker to identify the danger of potential job loss for one of its members than potential loss of a possible promotion for that family member.

The immediacy theorem provides some theoretical basis for Aldous' (1971) and Weick's (1971) observation that families are generally faced with multiple problems and frequently must set aside one problem to deal with another. This theorem establishes immediacy as one critical criterion for establishing priorities among problems. For example, according to this theorem, parents engaged in a serious argument are likely to put aside that argument when confronted with a child who has just fallen off a bicycle.

Problem awareness need not imply that the actor will attempt to solve the problem (MacCrimmon & Taylor, 1976). Theorems establishing conditions that determine whether or not the actor will initiate the problem solving process and engage in information search propose first that the decision to proceed is based on the actor's estimates of the odds ratio of the benefits of action and the costs of nonaction compared with the benefits of nonaction and the costs of action. Thus, if a spouse finds certain behaviors in her partner annoying, her decision to attempt to change the behavior or stay with the status quo is based on: (a) the assessment of the advantages of the status quo, (b) a determination of just how disturbing the partner's behavior is, (c) estimating the chances that some kind of behavior on the spouse's part would produce change in the partner, (d) assessing the amount of effort and the negative consequences (e.g., anger on the part of the partner) of producing such a change, (e) estimating the relief or satisfaction resulting from the partner's changing his behavior, and (f) estimating the spouse's ability to endure the situation if no change takes place. Since problem solving always involves the possibility of failure, it follows that the magnitude of (b) and (e) would have to be quite high for the actor to engage in this process. The likely alternative to engaging in the process is adopting some kind of a coping response.

The second theorem relevant to this stage in the process predicts that actors will be more inclined to engage in problem solving to avoid losses than to seek additional gains. Thus, we predict that a family will invest more time and effort to avoid losing a home they own than to gain additional funds that might be equivalent to the value of such a home. Indeed we predict that actors will be willing to engage in problem solving to avoid serious losses even if their estimates of their chances of success are relatively low; whereas they would not take such risks if the problem focused on obtaining additional gains. Parents, for example, are likely to act to protect their children regardless of the odds of success.

With regard to the process of information search, our theorems predict that actors will not seek to find the best possible solution to the problem but will terminate their search as soon as they find a viable solution. We also predict that, other things being equal, the more serious the problem, the greater the effort the actor will make to gather information relevant to its resolution. This latter theorem, however, is modified by the complexity of the problem. Simple problems, or problems that are framed in simple terms, will rarely require an extensive information search no matter how serious they are. Problems that are framed in moral terms are usually of that sort (Tallman & Gray, 1990). Highly complex problems are likely to require a greater investment of time and effort in information search. However, complex problems are generally also difficult problems. Difficult problems may, under certain conditions, elicit great effort, but if these efforts are not successful they may be abruptly terminated. Therefore, we predict that the amount and persistence of information search is a non-monotonic function of problem complexity. Information search should increase with problem complexity up to some point at which negative feedback is so persistent that the actor abruptly terminates the search. Parents seeking to understand the hostile behaviors of a teenage child may initially invest great effort in trying to find out "what is wrong" and, after running into many blind alleys, throw up their hands in despair.

Most family experts know that the above example requires additional specification. There are clearly differences among parents in their ability to persist in their efforts to help their children. Following the work of Bandura (1986, p. 394), the theory holds that the actor's sense of self-efficacy is a key factor in actor's readiness to persist in finding solutions to problems even in the face of negative feedback. Our conception of self-efficacy is generally consistent with Bandura's notion. We have defined it as the " . . . self-evaluation of competence which results from the actor's history of reinforcements and punishments in a given type of activity" (Tallman et al., forthcoming). Thus, our theorem states that the probability that an actor will persist in attempting to solve a problem in the face of negative feedback is a positive function of the actor's self-efficacy with regard to such problems. The final theorem in this stage of the process holds that actors are more likely to terminate information searches if faced with another problem that is considered more threatening and/or more proximate. This theorem provides some explanation for the reported tendency of families to flit from problem to problem without reaching closure on any of them (Aldous, 1971; Weick, 1971).

The third stage in the process involves the evaluation of information and the decision to engage in some problem solving action. Here too we infer that if it is determined that no course of action is available, or the chances of success are so poor as to make any action excessively risky, the actor is likely to engage in coping rather than problem solving.[13] It follows that the probability that actors will choose to engage in problem solving is a function of their subjective probability estimates that at least one course of action can solve the problem.

There are a large number of theorems derivable from the principles underlying the decision model that are relevant to the final (evaluative) stage of the problem solving process. Most of these are intuitively obvious and do not require any extended discussion. Clearly if the problem is perceived as solved, the process is terminated. Similarly, if the problem is not solved, the decision to continue or abort the process depends upon the assessment of the magnitudes of the costs and benefits of the two options and the estimated probabilities that these outcomes will occur for each of the options.

There is one final theorem, however, that is less intuitively apparent. This theorem holds that the greater the resources invested in solving a problem the more likely actors will be to continue their problem solving activities. Thus, a couple with interpersonal problems who seek counseling help may persist on working on their problems regardless of the effectiveness of counseling; or an abused wife who has already invested so much in pain and effort to make the marriage work may stay in the relationship in the hope that her husband will change precisely because she has already invested so much that would go to naught if the marriage failed.

CONCLUSION

The sluggishness in the development of theoretical and research efforts to explain family problem solving behaviors is attributed to such factors as the limitations inherent in defining families and the inability to build and apply a theory of problem solving that can contribute to a cumulative body of knowledge. The problem is exacerbated by the broad array of problems families (as well as other groups) face. A taxonomy of problems is presented to illustrate both the richness and complexities involved in building a theory of problem solving behaviors.

I have tried to demonstrate that, rather than build a theory of *family* problem solving, the best strategy for understanding how families go about attempting to solve their problems is to apply principles drawn from general theories of behavior. Indeed, if one accepts as requisite the idea that theories should contribute to a cumulative body of knowledge, it is not possible to build such a family theory. I also attempted to show why, if the theory was to be useful, it should: (1) be deductive, (2) employ universal concepts that had constitutive meaning, (3) follow clearly stipulated deduction rules and, (4) provide scope statements that establish the limits of the theory's generalizability and the conditions under which it could be supported or falsified.

Given the conceptual and definitional problems discussed in the paper the question was raised as to whether it was possible to build such a theory. I attempted to provide an affirmative answer to the question by presenting the essential features of a theory of problem solving that met the above criteria.

Although I would like readers to seriously consider the content and potential explanatory power of this theory, my intent is not so much to advocate the advantages of this particular theory as it is to provide a framework for delimiting the debate about what constitutes useful theory for family scholars. Such a debate, if it focused on establishing shared definitions of critical constructs and evaluating the scope and usefulness of carefully constructed theories, could further the quest for a cumulative scientific body of knowledge. In my view, this kind of knowledge is necessary for an adequate and dynamic understanding of what goes on in families now, in the past, and in the future.

AUTHOR'S NOTE

Work on this paper was supported by a grant from the National Institute of Mental Health RO1 MH46828-02. The author wishes to express his appreciation to Marilyn Ihinger-Tallman, Lisa McIntyre and Jan Stets for their comments on earlier drafts of this paper.

NOTES

1. A significant exception is the recent study reported by Aldous and Ganey (1989).

2. A possible exception is the longitudinal study of Berkeley and Oakland children of the great depression reported by Elder (Caspi & Elder, 1988; Elder, 1974; Elder, Liker & Cross, 1984). Although this work identifies family problems as they evolve out of life circumstances, it does not directly address family problem solving activities and processes. Two longitudinal studies are currently underway that place specific emphasis on problem solving within families: one is directed by Rand Conger at Iowa State and one by the author and his colleagues at Washington State. The Iowa State study focuses on families with adolescents undergoing financial hardships. The Washington State study examines newly married couples' responses to problems as they develop in the course of their daily lives.

3. A possible exception to this statement is the work conducted forty years ago by Bales and his colleagues (Bales, 1950; Bales & Strodtbeck, 1951). Bales' research focused on identifying the roles necessary for dealing with any problem whether it was internal or external.

4. There is some correspondence between the notion of rule-boundedness and the distinction between well defined and ill defined problems (Kahney, 1986, p. 20). The two concepts are different, however, in important ways. Rule-boundedness is conceived as unidimensional. Well or ill defined problems are differentiated on several variables including the initial state of the problem, the clarity of the problem goals, and the procedures or rules necessary to solve the problem.

5. This is not to imply that the non-rulebound end of the continuum requires more creative solutions than rule-bound problems. Complex problems with multiple rules may require considerable creativity for successful solutions. The game of chess is an example.

6. These types of problems raise a number of issues that cannot be explored in sufficient depth in this paper. One of these issues is the particular decision rules used within a family at a given time (i.e., unanimity rule, majority rule, veto rule or dictatorial rule). Another is the fact that the decision rules can change as members of the family grow and learn. A third is that, for a number of developmental or social reasons, some members of the family may be defined as irrelevant decision makers for some types of problems (Judson, 1991).

7. The difference between risk and uncertainty will be discussed later in the paper. Briefly "uncertainty" refers to possible outcomes with unknown probabilities. Risk refers to outcomes in which the probabilities are known.

8. Tallman et al. (1974) identify two temporal dimensions, requisite time and allotted time, that influence problem solving behavior. Janis and Mann (1977, p. 51) claim that "Hypervigilance," a state of immobilization akin to panic, is created by the sense that the time available to solve a problem is running out.

9. Unfortunately space does not allow for a systematic review of this body of research. I should note here, however, that it has consistently progressed in refining the nature of interpersonal communications that foster or inhibit effective problem solving. As illustration this work has produced two key principles consistent with the theoretical perspectives used. One is that ineffective problem solving occurs when couples' responses become rigid or predictable; the other is that specific types of negative affect truncate the problem solving process.

10. See Tallman and Gray (1990) for definitional distinctions between the concepts of choice, decision and problem solving.

11. Elsewhere the author and his colleagues (Tallman, Gray & Leik, 1991) have developed a theory that provides a basis for quantifying the conditions under which individuals in a group are likely to combine to make unitary decisions. Briefly stated, the underlying principle is that the greater the interdependence of group members, the more likely they are to function as a single unit.

12. This definition of problem perception differs from some of the ways it is used in the literature. It is sometimes used to imply a more complex set of analysis

of the situation. Such definitions often use the term "problem definition" and imply a more detailed cognitive understanding of the nature of the problem (Aldous & Ganey, 1989). Unfortunately, researchers often require that subjects articulate their understanding of the structure of the problem. There is evidence that, with some kinds of problems, even effective problem solvers cannot always explain what was going through their mind while problem solving (Cohen, 1974; Straus, 1968; Abelson & Levi, 1985). Gottman (1979), among others, has shown that non-verbal communication is as important, if not more important, than verbal communication in marital problem solving.

13. The distinction between coping and problem solving has been discussed in detail elsewhere (Tallman, 1988; Tallman et al., forthcoming). Briefly, coping refers to adjusting to a stressful event, problem solving to changing the conditions that produce the stressful event.

REFERENCES

Abelson, R. P., & Levi, A. (1985). Decision making and decision theory. In G. Lindzey & E. Aronson (Eds.), *The Handbook of Social Psychology* (pp. 231-309). New York: Random House.

Agre, G. P. (1982). The concept of problem. *Educational Studies 13*, 121-141.

Aldous, J. (1971). A framework for the analysis of family problem solving. In J. Aldous, T. Condon, R. Hill, M. Straus & I. Tallman (Eds.), *Family Problem Solving: A Symposium on Theoretical, Methodological, and Substantive Concerns* (pp. 265-81). Hinsdale, IL: Dryden Press.

Aldous, J., & Ganey, R. (1989). Families' definition behavior of problematic situations. *Social Forces, 8*, 871-97.

Anderson, A. R., & Moore, O. K. (1960). Autotelic folk models. *Sociological Quarterly, 1*, 203-216.

Bales, R. F. (1950). *Interactional Process Analysis*. Cambridge, MA: Addison-Wesley Press.

Bales, R. F., & Strodtbeck, F. L. (1951). Phases in group problem-solving. *The Journal of Abnormal and Social Psychology, 46*, 485-495.

Bandura, A. (1986). *Social foundations of thought and action: A social cognitive theory*. Engle, NJ: Prentice Hall.

Beisecker, T., Walker, G., & Bart, J. (1989). Knowledge versus ignorance as bargaining strategies: The impact of knowledge about other's informational level. *The Social Science Journal, 26*, 161-72.

Berger, P. L., & Kellner, H. (1970). Marriage and the construction of reality. In H. P. Dreitzler (Ed.), *Recent Sociology #2* (pp. 50-72). New York: Macmillan.

Beutler, I. F., & Burr, W. R. (1989). A seventh group has visited the elephant. *Journal of Marriage and the Family, 51*, 826-28.

Beutler, I. F., Burr, W. R., & Bahr, K. S. (1989). The family realm: Theoretical contributions for understanding its uniqueness. *Journal of Marriage and the Family, 51*, 805-16.

Blood, R. O., Jr., & Wolfe, D. M. (1960). *Husbands and Wives*. Glencoe, IL: The Free Press.

Burgess, E. W. (1926). The family as a unity of interacting personalities. *Family, 7,* 39.

Caspi, A., & Elder, G. (1988). Emergent family patterns: The intergenerational construction of problem behavior and relationships. In Hinde & J. Stevenson-Hinde (Ed.), *Relationships Within Families Mutual Influences* (pp. 218-240). Oxford: Clarendon Press.

Cohen, B. P. (1980). The conditional nature of knowledge. In Freese (Ed.), *Theoretical Methods in Sociology: Seven Essays* (pp. 71-110). Pittsburgh, PA: University of Pittsburgh Press.

Cohen, B. P. (1989). *Developing Sociological Knowledge* (2nd ed.). Chicago: Nelson-Hall.

Cohen, B. P. (1990, August). *Sociological theory: The half-full cup.* Paper presented at conference on Formal Theory Construction: Past, Present and Future Tense. College Park, Maryland.

Cohen, R. L. (1974). *Social class differences in the problem solving process An integration of social organization, language, and non-verbal communication.* Unpublished Doctoral Thesis, University of Minnesota.

Conger, R. D., Conger, K. J., Elder, G. H., Lorenz, F. O., Simons, R. L., Whitbeck, L. B. (In press). A family process model of economic hardship and adjustment of early adolescent boys. *Child Development.*

Elder, G. H., Jr. (1974). *Children of the great depression.* Chicago: University of Chicago Press.

Elder, G. H., Liker, J. K., & Cross, C. E. (1984). Parent child behavior in the great depression: Life course and intergenerational influences. In P. B. Baltes & O. G. Brim Jr. (Ed.), *Life Span Development and Behavior 6* (108-58). New York: Academic Press.

Emerson, R. M. (1962). Power-dependence relations. *American Sociological Review 27,* 30-41.

Emerson, R. M. (1972a). Exchange theory part I: A psychological basis for social exchange. In J. Berger, M. Zelditch, Jr., & B. Anderson (Eds.), *Sociological Theories in Progress 2* (pp. 38-57). Boston: Houghton Mifflin.

Emerson, R. M. (1972b). Exchange theory part II: Exchange relations and networks. In J. Berger, M. Zelditch Jr. & B. Anderson (Eds.), *Sociological Theories in Progress V2* (pp. 58-87). Boston: Houghton Mifflin.

Emmelkamp, P., van der Helm, M., MacGillavry, D., & van Zanten, B. (1984). Marital therapy with clinically distressed couples: A comparative evaluation of system-theoretic, contingency contracting, and communication skills approaches. In K. Hahlweg & N. S. Jacobson (Eds.), *Marital Interaction: Analysis and Modification* (pp. 36-52). New York: The Guilford Press.

Eshelman, J. R. (1991). *The family.* Boston: Allyn and Bacon.

Fitzpatrick, M. A. (1988a). *Between husbands and wives: communications in marriage.* Newbury Park: Sage.

Fitzpatrick, M. A. (1988b). Negotiations, problem-solving and conflict in various types of marriages. In P. Noller & M. A. Fitzpatrick (Eds.), *Perspectives on Marital Interaction* (pp. 245-272). Clevedon: Multilingual Matters Ltd.

Forgatch, M. S. (1989). Patterns and outcome in family problem solving: The disrupting effect of negative emotion. *Journal of Marriage and the Family 51*, 115-24.

Freese, L. (1980). The problem of cumulative knowledge. In Freese (Ed.), *Theoretical Methods in Sociology: Seven Essays* (pp. 13-69). Pittsburgh, PA: University of Pittsburgh Press.

French, J. R. P., & Raven, B. (1968). The bases of social power. In Cartwright & A. Zander (Eds.), *Group Dynamics Research and Theory* (3rd ed.) (pp. 259-290). New York: Harper and Row.

Gottman, J. M. (1979). *Marital interaction: Experimental investigations*. New York: Academic Press.

Gottman, J. M., & Levenson, R. (1988). The social psychophysiology of marriage. In P. Noller & M. A. Fitzpatrick (Eds.), *Perspectives on Marital Interaction* (pp. 182-200). Clevedon: Multilingual Matters Ltd.

Gray, L. N., & Tallman, I. (1984). A satisfaction balance model of decision making and choice behavior. *Social Psychology Quarterly 47*, 146-59.

Gray, L. N., & Tallman, I. (1986). Predicting choices in asymptotic decisions: A comparison of two models. *Social Psychology Quarterly 49*, 201-206.

Greeno, J. G. (1978). Natures of problem solving abilities. In W. K. Estes (Ed.), *Handbook of Learning and Cognitive Processes*. Hillsdale, NJ: Lawrence Erlbaum Associates.

Gubrium, J. F., & Holstein, J. A. (1990). *What is family?* Mountain View, CA: Mayfield Publishing Company.

Hahlweg, K., & Jacobson, N. S. (1984). *Marital interaction: Analysis and modification*. New York: The Guilford Press.

Jacobson, N. S., & Margolin, G. (1979). *Marital therapy: Strategies based on social learning and behavioral exchange principles*. New York: Brunner/Mazel.

Janis, I. L., & Mann, L. (1977). *Decision making: A psychological analysis of conflict, choice, and commitment*. New York: The Free Press.

Judson, D. H. (1991). *Decision making in social networks: Models and simulation*. Unpublished manuscript. Washington State University, Pullman, WA.

Kahneman, D., & Tversky, A. (1984). Choices, values, and frames. *American Psychologist 39*, 341-350.

Kahney, H. (1986). *Problem solving: A cognitive approach*. Milton Keynes: Open University Press.

Kantor, D., & Lehr, W. (1975). *Inside the family*. San Francisco: Jossey-Bass.

Kelley, H. H., & Thibaut, J. W. (1969). Group problem solving. In G. Lindzey & E. Aronson (Eds.), *Handbook of Social Psychology 4* (2nd ed.). Reading, MA: Addison-Wesley.

Kessler, R. C., & McRae, J. A. (1982). The effects of wife's employment on the mental health of married men and women. *American Sociological Review 47*, 216-227.

Kieren, D. K., & Hurbut, N. L. (1987). *Arriving at a method to determine phases in family problem solving.* Paper presented at Pre-Conference Theory Construction and Research Methodology Workshop. NCFR Conference, Atlanta, Georgia.

Kieren, D. K., & Tallman, I. (1972). Spousal adaptability: An assessment of marriage competence. *Journal of Marriage and the Family 34*, 247-256.

Klein, D. M. (1983). Family Problem solving and family stress. *Marriage and Family Review 6*, 85-112.

Klein, D. M., & Hill, R. (1979). Determinants of family problem solving effectiveness. In W. R. Burr, R. Hill, F. I. Nye & I. L. Reiss (Eds.), *Contemporary Theories About the Family 1* (pp. 493-548). New York: The Free Press.

Lazarus, R. (1977). Cognitive and coping processes in emotion. In A. Monet & R. Lazarus (Ed.), *Stress and Coping.* New York: Columbia University Press.

Liker, J. K., & Elder, G. H. (1983). Economic hardship and marital relations in the 1930's. *American Sociological Review 48*, 343-359.

Lopes, L. L. (1987). Between hope and fear: The psychology of risk. In Berkowitz (Ed.), *Advances in Experimental Social Psychology.* San Diego: Academic Press.

MacCrimmon, K. R., & Taylor, R. N. (1976). Decision making and problem solving. In M. D. Dunnette (Ed.), *Handbook of Industrial and Organizational Psychology.* Chicago: Rand McNally.

Manniche, E. (1989). *The family in Denmark.* Uppsala, Sweden: The Family Studies Center.

March, J. G. (1986). Bounded rationality: Ambiguity and the engineering of choice. *Bell Journal of Economic Management Science 9*, 587-608.

Mayer, R. E. (1983). *Thinking, problem solving, cognition.* New York: Freeman.

Murdock, G. P. (1949). *Social structure.* New York: The Free Press.

Nemeth, C. J., & Wachtler, J. (1983). Creative problem solving as a result of majority vs. minority influence. *European Journal of Social Psychology 13* 45-55.

Newell, A., & Simon, H. A. (1972). *Human problem solving.* Englewood Cliffs, NJ: Prentice Hall.

Noller, P., & Fitzpatrick, M. A. (1988). *Perspectives on marital interaction.* Clevedon: Multilingual Matters Ltd.

Olson, D. H., Lavee, Y., & McCubbin, H. I. (1988). Types of families and family response to stress across the life cycle. In D. M. Klein & J. Aldous (Eds.), *Social Stress and Family Development* (pp. 16-43). New York: The Guilford Press.

Olson, D. H., McCubbin, H. L. & Associates (1983). *Families what makes them work.* Beverly Hills: Sage Publications.

Patterson, G. R. (1982). *Coercive family process.* Eugene, Oregon: Castalia Publishing Co.

Reiss, D. (1981). *The family's construction of reality.* Cambridge, MA: Harvard University Press.

Reiss, I. L., & Lee, G. R. (1988). *Family systems in America.* New York: Holt, Rinehart and Winston.

Rogers, R. (1964). Toward a theory of family development. *Journal of Marriage and the Family 26*, 262-270.

Scanzoni, J., Polonko, K., Teachman, J., & Thompson, L. (1989). *The sexual bond: Rethinking families and close relationships.* Newbury Park: Sage Publications.

Schaap, C. (1984). A comparison of the interaction of distressed and nondistressed married couples in a laboratory situation: Literary survey, methodological issues, and an empirical investigation. In K. Hahlweg & N. S. Jacobson (Eds.), *Marital Interaction: Analysis and Modification* (pp. 133-158). New York: The Guilford Press.

Schroder, H. M., Driver, M. L., & Streufert, S. (1967). *Human Information Processing.* New York: Holt, Rinehart and Winston.

Shure, M. B., & Spivack, G. (1978). *Problem Solving Techniques in Child Rearing.* San Francisco: Jossey-Bass.

Simon, H. A. (1978). Information processing theories of human problem solving. In W. K. Estes (Ed.), *Handbook of Learning and Cognitive Processes.* Hillsdale, NJ: Lawrence Erlbaum Associates.

Smith, G. F. (1988). Towards a heuristic theory of problem structuring. *Management Science 34*, 1489-1506.

Smith, H. W. (1989). Group versus individual problem solving and type of problem solved. *Small Group Behavior 20*, 357-366.

Spivak, G., Platt, J. J., & Shure, M. B. (1976). *The Problem-Solving Approach to Adjustment.* San Francisco: Jossey-Bass.

Stephens, W. N. (1963). *The Family in Cross-Cultural Perspective.* New York: Holt, Rinehart & Winston.

Stone, A. A., & Neale, J. M. (1984). New measure of daily coping: Development and preliminary results. *Journal of Personality and Social Psychology 46*, 892-906.

Straus, M. A. (1968). Communication, creativity, and problem solving ability of middle- and working-class families in three societies. *American Journal of Sociology 73*, 417-30.

Straus, M. A., & Tallman (1971). SIMFAM: A technique for observational measurement and experimental study of families. In J. Aldous, T. Condon, R. Hill, M. Straus & I. Tallman (Eds.), *Family Problem Solving: A Symposium on Theoretical, Methodological, and Substantive Concerns* (pp. 379-438). Hinsdale, IL: Dryden Press.

Tallman, I. (1986). Social history and the life course perspective on the family: A view from the bridge. In J. F. Short, Jr. (Ed.), *The Social Fabric: Dimensions and Issues* (pp. 255-281). Beverly Hills: Sage.

Tallman, I. (1988). Problem solving in families: A revisionist view. In D. M. Klein & J. Aldous (Eds.), *Social Stress and Family Development* (pp. 102-26). New York: The Guilford Press.

Tallman, I., & Gray, L. N. (1990). Choices, decisions and problem-solving. In *Annual Review of Sociology 16*, 405-33.

Tallman, I., & Miller, G. (1974). Class differences in family problem solving. The effects of verbal ability, hierarchical structure, and role expectations. *Sociometry 37*, 13-37.

Tallman, I., Gray, L., & Leik, R. K. (1991). Decisions, dependency and commitment: An exchanged based theory of group formation. In E. J. Lawler, B. Markowsky, C. Ridgeway & H. A. Walker (Eds.), *Advances in Group Processes 8*.

Tallman, I., Marotz-Baden, R. & Pindas, P. (1983). *Adolescent Socialization in Cross-Cultural Perspective*. New York: Academic Press.

Tallman, I., Leik, R. K., Gray, L. N., & Stafford, M. C. (forthcoming). *A theory of problem solving behavior.*

Tallman, I., Klein, D., Cohen, R., Ihinger, M., Marotz, R., Torsiello, P., & Troost, K. (1974). *A Taxonomy of Group Problems and Implications for A Theory of Group Problem Solving* (Technical Report III). Minnesota Family Studies Center. Minneapolis, Minnesota.

Trost, J. (1979). *Unmarried Cohabitation*. Vesteras: International Library.

Tversky, A., & Kahneman, D. (1982). Introduction. In D. Kahneman, P. Slovic & A. Tversky, *Judgments under uncertainty: Heuristics and biases*. Cambridge, Cambridge University Press.

U.S. Bureau of Census (1989). *Statistical Abstract of the United States 1989.*

Volkema, R. J. (1988). Problem complexity and the formulation process in planning and design. Behavioral Science *33*, 292-300.

Walker, H. A., & Cohen, B. P. (1985). Scope statements: Imperatives for evaluating theory. *American Sociological Review 50*, 288-301.

Weick, K. E. (1971). Group processes, family processes and problem solving. In J. Aldous, T. Condon, R. Hill, M. Straus & I. Tallman (Eds.), *Family Problem Solving: A Symposium on Theoretical, Methodological, and Substantive Concerns*. Hinsdale, IL: Dryden Press.

Williams, R. (1970). *American Society*. New York: Alfred A. Knopf.

Problem-Solving and Decision-Making as Central Processes of Family Life: An Ecological Framework for Family Relations and Family Resource Management

Kathryn D. Rettig

KEYWORDS. Problem solving, Decision making, Ecology, Resources, Rationality, Styles of perceiving, Choice

INTRODUCTION

The past decade has been a stressful one for families due to the complexity of rapidly changing economic, social, and technological environments. Many parents are now struggling to provide the human and economic resources necessary for their families. The task may be even more challenging in the future. It is difficult to be patient with family members

Kathryn D. Rettig is affiliated with the Department of Family Social Science, University of Minnesota, Twin Cities.

[Haworth co-indexing entry note]: "Problem-Solving and Decision-Making as Central Processes of Family Life: An Ecological Framework for Family Relations and Family Resource Management." Rettig, Kathryn D. Co-published simultaneously in *Marriage & Family Review* (The Haworth Press, Inc.) Vol. 18, No. 3/4, 1993, pp. 187-222; and: *American Families and the Future: Analyses of Possible Destinies* (ed: Barbara H. Settles, Roma S. Hanks, and Marvin B. Sussman) The Haworth Press, Inc., 1993, pp. 187-222. Multiple copies of this article/chapter may be purchased from The Haworth Document Delivery Center. Call 1-800-3-HAWORTH (1-800-342-9678) between 9:00 - 5:00 (EST) and ask for DOCUMENT DELIVERY CENTER.

when one is exhausted from working two jobs in order to make a living. Parents find that the universal intentions of making a living, creating a comfortable home, maintaining healthy bodies and minds, finding some enjoyment in life, and encouraging growth and development are goals that are more difficult to achieve with resources available in the current economic environment. Many well-paying production jobs have been lost and jobs in the service economy are providing lower incomes. The available money incomes for families affect, not only the current level of living, but also the investments that can be made in learning new skills. The problem-solving and decision-making abilities that are needed to meet these challenges are increasingly more important in a complex and rapidly changing world (Rettig, Rossmann, & Hogan, in press).

Family therapists have estimated that problem-solving and decision-making processes are significant problems for at least half of the couples they work with in therapy (Geiss & O'Leary, 1981) and that ineffective, indecisive, and disorganized joint problem-solving in a family is an obvious difficulty that frequently is the presenting complaint that leads to therapy (Wynne, 1984). Human development scholars recognize that competence in problem-solving is one of the most important factors contributing to resilience in children who overcome adversity (Masten, Best, & Garmezy, 1990). In view of the importance of these processes in contributing to the quality of both personal and family life, and the pervasiveness of difficulties faced by families in decision-making processes, it is important for family scholars to work toward integrative conceptual frameworks that will provide a meaningful organization of ideas for research analyses as well as for the practice of family life education (Arcus, 1987) and family therapy.

The socialization and economic functions of the family are experienced simultaneously in the everyday life of families. Parents intuitively realize that the instrumental and expressive activities of the family are interdependent and that the economic and social-psychological domains of family life are not separate spheres of existence. Family scholars may also realize the interdependence of instrumental and expressive activities and the interrelatedness of economic and social-psychological family domains, but too seldom have theories, research results, educational programming, or family therapy processes reflected this realization. The economic and socialization functions of the family have more often been viewed as separate rather than inseparable scholarly domains. There has been minimal communication, particularly across economic and social-psychological disciplines. The family economics and management literature are seldom cited in the literature of communication, family relations, family therapy, human development, social psychology, or sociology, despite common interests in the central family processes of problem-solving and decision-making.

Examples of disciplinary separations are indicated by separate literatures on family-problem-solving and decision-making processes that often use different languages and/or give minimal recognition to literature in parallel fields of study. Samples of work from these fields of study include: *communication* (Galvin & Brommel, 1986; Hocker & Wilmot, 1985); *family economics and management* (Deacon & Firebaugh, 1988; Gross, Crandall, & Knoll, 1980; Melson, 1980; Paolucci, Hall, & Axinn, 1977; Rice & Tucker, 1986); *family studies* (Hill, Foote, Aldous, Carlson, & McDonald, 1970; McDonald & Cornille, 1988; Settles, 1987); *family therapy* (Beavers, 1981; Constantine, 1986, 1984, 1983; Epstein & Bishop, 1981; Epstein, Bishop, & Baldwin, 1982; Haley, 1976; Olson, 1991; Reiss, 1981; Reiss & Oliveri, 1980); *psychology* (Brinberg & Jaccard, 1989; Gottman, 1979; Gottman, Notarius, Markman, Banks, Yoppi, & Ruben, 1976); and *sociology* (Aldous, Condon, Hill, Strass, & Tallman, 1971; Godwin & Scanzoni, 1989a, 1989b; Klein, 1983; Klein & Hill, 1979; Scanzoni & Szinovacz, 1980; Scanzoni, 1979; Tallman, 1988; Tallman & Gray, 1987; Weick, 1971).

One of the greatest challenges of the future will be the development of theories[1] and conceptual frameworks that can simultaneously give attention to the inseparable economic and socialization functions of families, expressive and instrumental activities, and to economic and social-psychological domains of family life. Some progress in the integration of economic and social domains of scholarship is evident in recent years and can be found in the examples of Becker (1981); Billings and Moos (1982); Constantine (1986); Epstein, Bishop, and Baldwin (1982); Foa and Foa (1980); Kantor and Lehr (1975); Lazear and Michael (1988); Olson, McCubbin & Associates (1983); Piotrkowski, Rapoport, and Rapoport (1987); Sen (1984, 1987); and Scitovsky (1976).

AN INTEGRATIVE FRAMEWORK FOR FAMILY RELATIONS AND FAMILY RESOURCE MANAGEMENT

Family resource management is a discipline in which integrative conceptual frameworks should be possible because it is an area of study that requires both an economic and a social-psychological approach to the study of the family. In order for an integrative conceptual framework to emerge in family resource management that could reach the mainstream of family theory, future scholars will need to (a) modify the existing frameworks to be more compatible with psychological and social theories, (b) integrate the literature of parallel disciplines more effectively in educational settings, research conceptualization, and theoretical publications, and (c) translate the language of other disciplines to the language of family management in an effort to call attention to common interests in family problem-solving and decision-making processes across disciplines.

The purpose of this paper is to take one first step in articulating a view of family resource management that departs from the existing conceptual frameworks in focus and emphasis and is more compatible with psychological theories of motivation and interactional theories of family studies and family therapy. The approach has worked effectively for at least five years in teaching at both undergraduate and graduate levels for students who are especially interested in human services occupations.

The presented viewpoint has several advantages for teaching family resource management in a family social science department. The framework (a) emphasizes the interpersonal dynamics of social decision conflicts that occur during problem identification and joint goal-setting processes; (b) focuses on personal perceiving processes as important in the stages of choice, particularly when two people are making one decision; (c) identifies individual as well as family decision styles; (d) expands the concept of decision styles to include perceiving, deciding, and actuating styles; (e) translates the family decision styles outlined by therapists into managerial language so that students realize common interests in the same decision processes; (f) integrates the overall problem-solving processes of management with the various decision processes (social, economic, technical) that are predominant at various phases of management; (g) articulates value conflicts that occur during various phases of management and decision processes; (h) conceives values and goals as the internal controls of managerial systems; (i) uses a systems organization of concepts, but an everyday language to describe the managerial processes of individuals and families; and (j) continues a consistent framework regardless of whether the decision maker is an individual, dyad, or family group.

Human relationships and managerial processes need to be viewed as interdependent rather than separate processes of family functioning since individual decisions impact the lives of those with whom the resources of time, money, energy, and space are shared. In some situations, individuals are free to choose a course of action; however, these decisions are made within a social context, influenced by cultural norms, and the decisions usually affect or involve others. The family environment is an important influence on individual decisions, and the family unit, in turn, is affected by individual choices. Family members also make joint decisions.

MANAGEMENT AS ADAPTIVE BEHAVIOR

Management is a thoughtful adaptation to the opportunities and de-mands of life. It involves problem-solving and decision-making, as well as carrying out actions to implement decisions. The consciousness of the deliberations that occur prior to decisions about how to use resources and the controlled implementation of decisions in order to reach valued-goals will distinguish management from other adaptive responses. The need for conscious problem-solving and decision-making is created because of changes that are wanted by individuals and families (proactive manage-ment) or because internal and/or environmental changes occur that require different responses (reactive management). The environment of families is broadly viewed to include the natural, human behavioral, and human constructed dimensions of human existence (Bubolz & Sontag, in press).

Problem-solving, decision-making, decision-implementation, and choice are central processes occurring during the adaptation behaviors that charac-terize family resource management. The definitions of these processes are needed in order to establish shared meaning. The following definitions are ordered from most comprehensive to most specific processes as outlined by Rettig et al. (in press).

Management includes the many processes through which families strive for goal achievement and for reduction of the degree of tension and disequilibrium as well as the processes through which they solve problems and plan for transcending their present dimensions (Liston, 1964).

Problem-solving includes the non-routine processes of removing, end-ing, or overcoming some barrier, obstacle, or impediment to attaining a goal (Tallman, 1988). Problem-solving processes may involve both physi-cal and mental activities and several kinds of decision-making processes.[2]

Decision-making is the process of comparing alternatives in terms of the actor's subjective estimates of the probable costs and benefits associated with each alternative and selecting the alternative that provides the best assurance of attaining the expected satisfaction (Tallman, 1988).

Decision-implementation is the process of putting decisions into action by planning and carrying out the plans for change.

Choice is the act of choosing one of the perceived alternatives.

The management of family resources requires an ecological perspective that assumes (a) adaptation involves the interdependence of human and envi-ronmental changes; (b) most problems are identified at the interface between person and family or between family and environmental systems and this gives rise to a decision situation; (c) the decision situation involves opportu-nities and constraints and suggests goals and resource needs; (d) resources for decision-making are simultaneously environmental, intrapersonal, and interpersonal; (e) climate, temperature, space, energy, and biological rhythms are important resources affecting perceptions of the decision situation and also the envisioned solutions; and (f) families are energy transformation systems that convert inputs of matter and energy into useful products and human abilities.

The family management perspective views the family as an economic unit because it has both goals and resources that are mobilized to reach those goals. An economic unit is defined as any unit that can maintain a set of goals (Diesing, 1976). The most important goal of the family system is the production of capable people. The production of capable people corresponds to the economic-socialization functions of families and is the most important output of the managerial subsystem of families. The resources available for reaching this and other goals are both human and economic. Family resource management assumes that problem-solving and decision-making are central processes in the management of everyday life and in the accomplishment of valued goals.

Management processes in the family function to maintain the strength of the family group, bring about nondisruptive changes, reduce tension levels, resolve conflicts, produce capable people, mobilize resources toward central life purposes, and enhance quality of life (Deacon & Firebaugh, 1988; Gross et al., 1980; Paolucci et al., 1977; Rice & Tucker, 1986). Rational decision-making requires some vision of a desirable outcome. An effective manager envisions a more desirable self, group, or environment and works to actuate those visions. Values, goals, and standards serve as guidelines for decisions about resource use and human resource development. To the extent they are goal-oriented, goal-seeking systems, families are controlled systems. The management subsystem, through problem-solving and decision-making processes, acts as the family system's control center.

The managerial subsystem of the family is similar to what Constantine (1986) called the "family paradigm, regime, and process" (p. 17). The family paradigm is an image of what the family can and should be and has also been called its meaning system (Kantor & Lehr, 1981; Reiss, 1981). Management language would call the paradigm or meaning system the family needs, values, goals, attitudes, and beliefs. A regime is the set of mechanisms by which a collective pattern in process is regulated (Constantine, 1986, p. 17). Managerial language would call the regime the processes families initiate to define goals, and mobilize resources for reaching them. Process would refer to the managerial processes of implementing decisions that are made.

MANAGEMENT SUBSYSTEM OF THE FAMILY SYSTEM

Social systems are conceptualized to have a "structure of interdependent component elements exhibiting coherent behavior as a unit" (Constantine, 1986, p. 50). The system also has some kind of boundary to separate the system from its environment, at least one function, various system processes, and also patterns of behavior that are representative of the system. The structural elements of the management subsystem of the family include: *decision situations (DS)* with current presenting problems or opportunities, resource availabilities, and risks; *decision processes (DP)* needed in the decision situation, whether economic, social, technical, or combinations of these processes; and *decision maker(s) (DM)* with unique styles of applying decision processes to decision situations.

The boundaries of the family's management subsystem are functional rather than physical or analytical.[3] The functions of the subsystem include all *conscious* problem-solving and decision-making processes and the *consciously controlled* implementation of these decisions. Unconscious behavioral adaptations fall outside the boundaries of the management subsystem. It is assumed that knowledge of the future is impossible and that most decisions are based on both information and intuition. Intuition is a legitimate part of problem-solving and decision-making as long as it is consciously acknowledged. In everyday life, rationality and intuition inform each other.

The management processes through which individuals and families create more desirable futures and adapt to internal changes and to changing environments involve three interdependent phases: *perceiving (P)* either a needed or wanted change or perceiving an environmental change requiring a new response; *deciding (D)* on a response to the change for oneself or with others, and; *actuating (A)* the decision. The individual or family as a decision-making unit must perceive the opportunities and constraints, decide what is to be done, and in some way actuate the decisions.[4]

These phases unfold sequentially in some decision situations, but there are an infinite number of feedback loops (processes of evaluation) that lead the decision-makers to move back and forth among them. Sometimes two people assume they perceive a problem in the same way, but when they try to plan what to do or when to act, they find their perceptions of the situation diverge significantly. They do not, in fact, agree on values, goals, priorities, or standards. These various conflicts require decision makers to use social, economic, and technical decision processes and to alternate among them in order to resolve the overall problem situation.

The patterns in the managerial subsystem of the family can be found in the unique perceiving, deciding, and actuating styles of the decision maker(s) whether individual, couple, or family group as they emerge over time across many decision situations. Decision styles are consistent patterns of perceiving and processing information and implementing choices during processes of problem-solving (Knox, 1983).

MANAGEMENT BY INDIVIDUAL DECISION-MAKERS

The structure, processes, and patterns of managerial systems can be demonstrated most easily by first assuming the perspective of an individual decision-maker. In order to do this, it is necessary to assume that the individual will have conflicts with others, which then involve joint decision-making processes.

Decision situations (DS). The first structural element of managerial systems is a decision situation (DS). The decision situation is the presenting problem, conflict, or opportunity. The decision situation occurs at the interface of environmental and decision-maker systems where changes initiate problems that are brought to the level of consciousness for the particular person(s) in that time and place. The presenting conflict or opportunity and the orientation, comprehensiveness, and content[5] of the problem determine the type of decision-making process and the human resources that are needed to resolve it effectively. Decision situations for individuals in family settings are most often *social (DSS)*, *economic (DSE)*, or *technical (DST)*. Legal and political decision situations, as identified by Diesing (1976), are sometimes possible for persons in family groups but have not been emphasized in this framework due to their infrequent occurrence. It is theoretically possible to discuss different kinds of decision situations as if they were pure types. However, in everyday life most decision situations include more than one kind of conflict or challenge and can be simultaneously social, economic, technical, legal, and political.

Each decision situation is specific to time, circumstance(s), and person(s). The decision situation has links to past decisions, current time constraints, interpersonal conflicts, resource availabilities, value conflicts, and different risks and consequences. Adaptive management behavior is not simply a function of the person(s) or of the environment(s) but exists as a codependent relationship of the interfacing systems. Opportunities or demands for change and personal interpretations of the circumstances are represented in the decision situation located at the interface of the decision maker(s) and environmental systems.

Social decision situations (DSS). The decision situation is a social one if the presenting problem involves a conflict with another person with whom one must make a decision and the conflict involves values, goals, standards, or roles. A social decision situation involves the challenge of mediating values, identifying value similarities, and agreeing on goals and policies that will integrate the group (Diesing, 1976). Social decision situations have previously been referred to as interactive and as "policy problems" when two people must agree upon which values are fundamental (Liston, 1966).

Economic decision situations (DSE). An economic decision situation is a presenting problem that involves allocating a scarce resource (such as time, human energy, money) among the demands of multiple competing goals. The problem results from too many alternative goals that cannot be satisfied at once due to scarce resources. An economic decision situation involves allocating scarce, measurable, interchangeable resources to meet as many of the important goals as possible. Liston (1966) called these presenting conflicts allocative problems. Economic decision situations can involve two people making one decision, but often the two individuals make contingent decisions. Resources that are jointly owned may be more easily allocated by joint decisions. Policy decisions about which goals deserve prime attention, which resources are available for use, and how much of the resource to allocate to each goal are examples of an economic decision situation.

Technical (DST), legal, political decision situations. When *one* goal has been identified as high priority and the presenting problem is how to accomplish this *one* goal with limited resources, then the problem is a technical decision situation that requires a technical decision-making process. Technical decision situations often involve organization, coordination, supervision, and control. Liston (1966) referred to these situations as integrative, interactional, and/or organization problems.

Diesing (1976) also identified legal and political decision situations. A legal decision situation involves an ongoing dispute between two parties of equal power. A neutral third-party decision maker resolves the dispute by applying specific rules that define the rights and responsibilities of the parties, usually in contract format (Rettig & Dahl, 1992). Political decision situations involve a conscious examination of the effectiveness of the decision making functions and procedures of a group.

Decision processes (DP). The second structural element of managerial systems includes decision processes (DP) that are needed in decision situations. Decision processes are the affective valuing and cognitive evaluations that occur prior to taking action and during the course of action to carry out established plans. The specific decision processes that occur within the perceiving (P), deciding (D), and actuating (A) phases of the overall management process will vary in relation to the decision situation as well as to the particular phase of the management process. The decision processes are *social (DPS)*, *economic (DPE)*, and *technical (DPT)*. It is important to mention that the complexity of making decisions in everyday life involves using social, economic, and technical decision processes within a short time frame, moving back and forth among these processes, and using all the processes to solve one problem.

Social decision-making processes (DPS). A social decision situation requires a social decision process in order for the conflict to be resolved effectively (Rettig, 1986). Social decision processes involve the two distinctly separate stages of problem definition and solution finding. The definition stage of the social decision process involves problem perception by uncovering interpersonal conflicts and their supporting factors, problem facing by gaining the cooperation of the other person to work on the problem, and problem definition by trying to understand the viewpoint of the other and stating the problem in terms of personal needs rather than preferred solutions. These processes are often intensely emotional because of value and standards conflicts. Therefore, social decision-making processes do not proceed in a linear, logical, sequential, efficient fashion or in a short period of time. There is a need for frequent time-outs and recycling of the processes. There needs to be a clear separation between the two stages of the process in order to make certain that the viewpoint of the other is understood. A rush to finding possible solutions endanger the effective resolution of the problem.

The solution finding stage of the social decision-making process involves mediating values to change desires, discovering value similarities, inventing creative alternatives, and collaborating to find solutions that meet the needs of all parties. The social decision making process *ends* with an agreement about value similarities, value priorities, and shared goals. Social decision-making is required during all phases of management, but is used more frequently in earlier phases (P) when family members detect environmental changes, perceive problems in divergent ways, and must converge in order to agree on value priorities and goals. A "good" social decision process views reason as creativity (Diesing, 1976). A rational social decision is one in which creativity has provided a solution to meet the needs of all parties and the result is integration of the group. The social decision-making process described above is similar to what is called a problem-solving process in other literature.

Economic decision-making processes (DPE). Once values and goals are agreed upon, the managerial process evolves to a decision situation that requires deciding how scarce resources like time, energy, and money can be allocated among multiple competing goals. The deciding phase of management (D) more frequently requires economic processes as the decision-makers struggle again to prioritize goals in agreed upon ways for resource allocation. Economic decision processes *begin* with known goals but first involve the difficult task of *prioritizing* them before the resources can be allocated. The deliberation process for economic decision making involves more obvious alternatives for which the decision maker needs to seek additional information and think through before making choices.

Prioritizing goals is a difficult task for individuals, but is an extremely complex process in families. Each role relationship (husband-wife, parent-child) involves goals for self, other, and goals that are shared. Self, other, and shared goals can be short-term, intermediate, and long-term. Goals multiply with the number of role positions one holds within the family and in the external environment. A "good" economic decision process views reason as calculation (Diesing, 1976). A rational economic decision is one in which careful calculation about which how many resources to allocate to goals results in clear understanding concerning which goals can be maintained and which ones are best sacrificed.

Technical decision-making processes (DPT). Technical decision-making processes require mobilization of a variety of resources for the accomplishment of *one* important goal. The goal could be a personal identity goal, a relationship goal, or a family work or recreation goal. Technical decision processes result in answering the questions of what? when? who? where? and how? and are more likely to occur in the actuating phase of management (A) when major policies and plans are implemented. Technical decision making requires planning, matching the resource limitations with standards for accomplishment, sequencing of activities, continuing evaluation of standards, checking and adjusting progress, supervising other people, and coordinating activities with others. A "good" technical decision process views reason as "efficiency" (Diesing, 1976). A rational technical decision is one in which the goal is accomplished in the most effective way with the lowest possible resource costs.

Decision makers (DM). The third structural element of managerial systems includes decision makers (DM) who have unique perceptions, goals, values, human resources, and ways of applying decision processes to decision situations. Decision makers are people who compare alternative courses of action by weighing the evidence and considering the multiple interacting variables in order to make a judgment about the course of action to select (Rettig & Dahl, 1992). Decision makers (when observed overtime) have *perceiving styles* (*DMP*) that involve preferred ways of accessing and interpreting information from the environment(s); *deciding styles* (*DMD*) that involve the consistent ways of thinking about and processing information; and *actuating styles* (*DMA*) that are the characteristic ways of acting upon situations and problems and implementing decisions. A husband and a wife with contrasting perceiving, deciding, and actuating styles may have a broader repertory for problem-solving and decision-making and also more frequent and intense interpersonal conflicts.

Perceiving styles (*DMP*). Individual perceiving styles involve preferred ways of *accessing* information or how individuals sense and feel in regard to the decision situation. Individuals have preferences for receiving information by visual, auditory, and kinesthetic modes that are reflected in the predicates of their sentences (Bandler & Grinder, 1975) and in the direction of eye movements (Bandler & Grinder, 1979). Kolb (1984) described information accessing preferences as watching, listening, feeling, doing, and thinking. Visual information accessing corresponds to learning by watching, auditory access is learning by listening, while kinesthetic information accessing includes feeling and doing.

The individual's preferred perceiving styles have a profound effect upon whether or not a particular change is viewed as an exciting opportunity or stressful and defined as a problem. Two individuals present in the same decision situation often perceive different problems and possibilities due to their unique perceiving styles, personal values and resources, past experiences, and psychological orientations. Psychological orientations are a consistent complex of cognitive, motivational, and moral orientations to a given situation that guide behavior (Deutsch, 1985). Each person in a decision situation has some information that is shared with others and some information that is uniquely personal.

A decision situation involving participants with different perceiving styles may lead to conflicts for them in the decision processes of defining the problem and in facing it. Problem definition is complicated because of differing spans of awareness (extensive scanning vs. intensive focusing); needs for stimulation and comfort; for conceptual distinctions (leveling vs. sharpening); and for categorizing ideas (broad vs. narrow). Individuals also have differing tolerances for perceptions that differ from conventional experience and preferences for separating problems from the context of human relationships (Knox, 1983). Problem-facing decision processes are complicated by differing individual preferences for reflection and action, time orientations, perceived locus of control, values, and other human resources such as risk tolerance.

Deciding styles (*DMD*). Individual deciding styles involve patterns of *processing* information, and range from the more general, intuitive approaches of the synthesist and idealist thinking style preferences to the more factual approaches preferred by analytical thinkers, and the rapid closure preferences of pragmatist and realist thinking style preferences (Harrison & Bramson, 1982). While individuals do use all five dimensions of processing information, some people have stronger preferences for particular styles. Persons with analyst thinking style preferences prefer: well-formulated, structured problems that can be solved; detailed, factual information; using formulas and objective methods for analyzing alternatives; logical, methodological analyses of problems; and cautious, predictive and factual planning (Harrison & Bramson, 1982; Rettig & Schulz, 1991).[6]

The present conceptual framework hypothesizes that the idealist and synthesist thinking style preferences would be more effective in social decision situations that are value-laden and unstructured; the analyst thinking style preference for economic problems that are structured and require calculation; and realist and pragmatist preferences would be more effective in technical decision situations that require adjusting resources and realities.

A decision situation involving people with strong preferences for different thinking styles may cause conflicts for them in the decision processes of information seeking and considering the consequences of alternatives. The information-seeking processes are complicated because the participants have differing preferences for types of information (detailed and precise vs. general), amounts of information (extensive vs. minimal), and forms of information (tasks vs. relationships and values and feelings vs. facts) (Knox, 1983). The process of considering alternatives is complicated by their differing preferences for closure (rapid vs. delayed), for organizing the analysis process (inductively vs. deductively), their rules of choice (objective vs. personal), and their interests in tactics and strategies.

Actuating styles (DMA). The actuating styles of individual decision makers in carrying out decisions represent patterns used in planning, organization, leadership, supervision, control, and coordination. The morphogenic and morphostatic planning styles as outlined by Beard and Firebaugh (1978), the goal-centered, resource-centered, and constrained planning styles described by Buehler and Hogan (1986) and the organizational styles of task assignment, task regularization, and task arrangement in regard to household work (Mumaw & Nichols, 1972) are examples of individual actuating styles.

It is recognized that decisions are situation-specific and that decision makers will respond to each situation in a unique way. However, the perceiving, deciding, and actuating styles of an individual decision maker may be somewhat constant over time and various decision situations. The repeated use of these personal decision styles can be identified by someone outside the system as the characteristic *pattern* of the management subsystem. The factors that influence personal decision styles have also been summarized by Jaccard, Brinberg, and Dittus (1989). When two or more people make joint decisions, the management subsystem becomes infinitely more complex. Decision styles of dyads have also been identified in previous research (Jaccard et al., 1989; Sillars & Kalbflesch, 1989). However, the present paper has excluded this discussion in the interest of length considerations.

MANAGEMENT IN FAMILIES AND BY FAMILIES

It cannot be assumed that patterns in the management subsystems of families can be observed in the same way as the management subsystem of individuals. It is more difficult to observe and classify family system behaviors than those of individuals. The patterns of the family management subsystem are the responses of the whole group over time, rather than the behaviors of individuals or dyads over time. Family decision-making processes, compared to individual processes, are far less explicit, organized, and self-conscious to insiders (Sillars & Kalbflesch, 1989) and are also less obvious to outsiders.

It is important to note those family members (insiders) who participate in problem-solving and decision-making processes may do so without a high level of conscious awareness. Family groups are unique in many ways because the ecology of family problem-solving differs from other groups who agree to meet at an appointed time and place. Family members seldom arrive at an appointed time, sit in straight-backed chairs, face-to-face around a table with notebooks in hand and ready to concentrate on the clearly-understood agenda. Telephones and crying babies are very likely to interrupt decision processes (Weick, 1971).

Family problems seldom receive a clearly-stated definition, concentrated attention on alternative courses of action, a consistent focus on one issue at a time, or a clear resolution of the problem. Many family problems are embedded in such a way that there is a stumbling to an incremental solution or a retrospective awareness that problem-solving occurred. Weick (1971) further explained the difficulties families have in deciding whether something is a growth-related phase that will pass or a problem that requires conscious intervention. Families are handicapped in problem-solving by unequal access to the important information, the lack of new viewpoints about how to attack unresolved problems, and the lack of cooperation of family members who can choose to be physically present, but psychologically absent during decision processes.

Families differ in their approaches to change and the resulting conflicts. The extent to which families engage conflict directly is the extent to which decision making is explicit, organized, and proactive. The style of avoiding conflict is associated with decision-making that is indirect, implicit, impulsive, and incremental (Sillars & Kalbflesch, 1988). An organizing and deliberate problem-solving approach is more likely for decisions of major consequence, even for families who have a more direct approach to conflict and a more proactive problem-facing approach. The diversity of family management approaches must be kept in mind for the following discussion.

Most the present knowledge about family problem-solving and decision-making patterns and processes has been obtained from *outsiders*, such as; family therapists (Beavers, 1981; Constantine, 1986, 1983; Falloon, Bryd, McGill, Razani, Moss, & Gilderman, 1982; Lewis, Beaver, Gossett, & Phillips, 1976); researchers who have designed laboratory studies (Reiss, 1981; Reiss & Oliveri, 1980; Straus & Tallman, 1973); an occasional study of participant observation in the natural setting (Kantor & Lehr, 1975; Steinglass, Bennett, Wolin, & Reiss, 1987); and some survey research (Hill et al., 1970). The scarcity of factual knowledge about family decision-making processes is a recognized limitation and an important area of needed research.

Family decision situations (FDS). All families must solve the same basic set of problems. They have to work out daily adjustments and make long-term plans for inevitable changes and possible emergencies. They must provide group security and still allow sufficient freedom for personal growth. It is important to adapt to change and to create change, yet it is also important to provide stability over time. Resources must be used to meet the needs of individual members and also retain the integrity of the family group. Families need to be reasonably self-sufficient and still be connected to the community. These challenges require daily adjustments by conscious management processes. Family management processes also involve the phases of perceiving (P) needed and wanted changes, deciding (D) on a course of action or decision process, and actuating (A) the decisions that are made. Families also face presenting problems, conflicts, and opportunities that involve *social decision situations* (FDSS), as well as *economic* (FDSE), and *technical decision situations* (FDST).

Family social decision situations (FDSS). Social decision situations in the perceiving phase of management occur at the interface of family and environmental and personal and family systems. The presenting problems of social decision situations involve *facing changes* that present challenges to family members concerning their agreed-upon values, goals, standards, and roles. The value conflicts that most frequently emerge at the perceiving phase of management process center around differing standards for the values of change vs. stability, variety vs. routine, excitement vs. security, stimulation vs. comfort, autonomy vs. connectedness, freedom vs. responsibility. The conflicts in standards involve questions like: How *much* freedom do you need? How *much* responsibility do we require? The value conflicts, priorities, and goals must be mediated and negotiated in social decision-making processes (Rettig, 1986). The conflicts occur as the family struggles to take a value stance on the issues presented by the cultural environment.

The changes faced by families challenge not only their basic value system and standards, but also force them to re-examine family policies, rules, and behavioral roles. The social decision issues often have to do with resolving different perceptions about: What are our family policies? What are our agreed upon value priorities? What are our shared goals? Who should do what at home and in the community? Typical questions that arise are: (a) How much do we encourage each other to try new things, go new places, explore different philosophies and lifestyles? (b) How much freedom do we have to do our own family things and how much responsibility do we have to our extended kin, friends, and community? (c) How much freedom does an individual have to pursue new opportunities vs. considering the needs of the other family members? (d) How interested and concerned are we in what goes on in the world around us compared to our own family world? How can we resolve our differences in perceiving styles?

The above decision situations are complicated by differing perceptions of individual family members. The most basic issues of perception on which people must agree are: "Is there a problem or not?" and, "Is this an opportunity for action or not?" This sounds obvious, yet in everyday life it is often difficult. Individuals who prefer high levels of stimulation and enjoy variety and change will find times of stability and quiet to be problematic. A family problem is created when other members of the family place higher value on stability, security, and comfort and experience frequent change as stressful.

Recognizing a "problem," "opportunity," or "decision situation" involves a value judgment. Is change a "problem" or an "opportunity"? How stressful is the change? Do we want this change or not? If *you* change (take this opportunity), then what will happen to *me*? Change involves both opportunities and constraints, but individuals have different standards for the values of change and connectedness depending on their past experiences, perceiving styles, present human and material resources, and the particular decision situation.[7]

Agreement on whether or not there is a problem is complicated from a personal point of view, because there are several ways the "other" person(s) may be "confused." S/he may see no problem when there really is one. S/he may see a solution when there is none, or s/he may expect an attitude change in addition to a simple behavior change (Watzlawick, Weakland, & Fisch, 1974). Unless there is agreement, the problem cannot be faced or solved. Once people agree on the existence of a problem, there next must be agreement on whether it is best to wait for it to subside or whether problem-solving efforts are needed.

Family economic decision situations (*FDSE*). The major problems in the deciding phase of the management process concern resolving different perceptions and standards about how the scarce resources of time, energy, money, space and goods should be allocated to individuals and shared by them. These are primarily economic decision problems that involve prioritizing goals, balancing needs and resources, and planning for the allocation of resources. Decision situations in the deciding phase of the management process can occur at the interface of family and environmental systems, but more often involve the interface of person and family systems. The decision issues often center around the differing standards for the typical value conflicts of: personal independence vs. group interdependence, individual uniqueness vs. group conformity, individual achievement vs. group solidarity, individual competition vs. group cooperation, decisiveness vs. ambiguity and explicit vs. implicitness in decision processes, factual vs. intuitive approaches to decision making.

The economic decision situations in the deciding phase of the management process often surface in questions like: (a) How can we find money, time, and energy to meet your goals as well as mine and ours? (b) When resources are scarce, whose needs must be met first and whose can be last? (c) When we can only do one thing, do individuals come first or does the group take priority? (d) Do we compete for scarce resources or do we continually seek new ways to cooperate in meeting needs? (e) How much freedom do individuals have in choices about time use and how much conformity to the group is required? (f) How much leadership is allowed for children in deciding about resource use? (g) Are the issues negotiated as in a democracy or dictated as in an autocracy? (h) How can we resolve our differences in deciding styles?

Family technical decision situations (FDST). The technical decision situations in the actuating phase of management occur at the interface of person and family and family and environmental systems and center around resolving different value, role, and standards conflicts of: democratic vs. authoritarian leadership styles; rigidity vs. flexibility of routine, standards, and implementation; individualistic vs. cooperative work orientations; task vs. gender-role divisions of labor; continual maintenance of order and organization vs. more flexible maintenance of order; and standards for coordination, control, and accomplishment.

The technical decision situations at the actuating phase of management involve issues such as: (a) Who will lead and who will carry out the decisions? (b) How closely should the workers be supervised? (c) How much routine is desirable and how much flexibility? (d) How rigidly should rules and routines be followed? (e) How will the work load be balanced among the members? (f) What standards of order and cleanliness are to be maintained? (g) How regularly must the standards be maintained? (h) To what degree must we work together at the same time or separately at a time we choose? (i) How well do we have to achieve to reach these goals? These are issues of leadership, supervision, roles, rules, planning, routines, schedules, and standards.

Family decision processes (FDP). The second structural element of managerial subsystems of families involves decision processes. The research observations of family decision processes in the natural setting are so few that family decision processes are difficult to describe. It is an aspect of the present model that will require more attention at a future time, but it is assumed from evidence in the literature that families engage in *social (FDPS)*, *economic (FDPE)*, and *technical decision processes (FDPT)* in response to these various types of decision situations.

Family managerial processes are complex with several interdependent decision processes occurring simultaneously, each of which may involve a different level of consciousness. First there is a valuing process that involves perceiving and identifying shared values (P), prioritizing shared values (D), and generating standards of behavior that are needed to act on those values (A). The family valuing part of the decision-making process is the most implicit and the least conscious for participants. Family members are more conscious of the goal-setting process that involves perceiving shared goals or developing an agreement about shared goals (P), deciding on goal priorities and allocating resources for their accomplishment (D), and actuating the goals by planning for their accomplishment and coordinating the work required (A).

Family social decision-making processes (FDPS). Social decision processes in families also involve processes of *problem definition* and *problem facing* that are what Hill et al. (1970) called identifying unmeet needs. Social decision processes in families *begin* with value, standard, goal, and role conflicts and *end* with agreed-upon values and goals (policies). The result of social decision processes in families is what McDonald and Cornille (1988) called meta policy. Meta policy was defined as the general family value system or primal family values that determine basic directions and aspirations (p. 251). Constantine (1986) referred to these values as the family paradigm. The family values arise from cultural norms and previous kinship generations, but have to be accepted and acted upon by the family in its current orientation. Often the value system is assumed and the social decision process involves articulating agreed-upon goals that represent these values. Family policy problems involve decision making processes about important values, goals, and general living conditions (Liston, 1966; Pershing, 1979).

Family economic decision-making processes (FDPE). The economic decision processes of families also *begin* with the goals as known. The challenge is to then *prioritize* the group goals, the individual goals, and the group vs. individual goals, obtain information about various courses of action, and think about resource possibilities and consequences of actions before making a decision about resource allocations. McDonald and Cornille (1988) referred to this process as policy formation because it involved the process of ranking. Value priorities are stable but not static so that changes and new commitments will require reprioritizing goals. The policy formation processes in families vary from "systematic and explicit to inadvertent and implicit" (McDonald & Cornille, 1988, p. 252) and hopefully result in choosing courses of action (Hill et al. 1970) and the development of family rules for prioritizing shared values and sharing scarce family resources. The economic decision process results in some kind of agreement about how to balance conflicting demands and preferences and how to structure the interdependence of their situation and shared resources.

Family technical decision-making processes (FDPT). Technical decision processes involve mobilizing and organizing resources for an important goal or implementing a decision that has been made that Hill et al., (1970) called "taking action." When family values and goals are initiated as implicit policies, they are usually implemented in a more explicit way in the form of rules or rule enforcement (Ford, 1983). The decision processes that involve implementing policy through rules and consistent lines of action were labeled "program development" by McDonald and Cornille (1988). Family policy decision processes translate the abstract values into concrete ways of behaving in everyday life. The technical decision processes clarify the issues of who must do what as well as when, where, how, how much, and how often.

Family decision-making also involves processes of evaluation that influence the way families make future decisions. The systems word for evaluation processes is "feedback" and McDonald and Cornille (1988) referred to this process as "impact assessment" in which programs were examined in light of the identified goals and values. The above examples demonstrate how the literature on family decision processes contains different words for the same processes and this creates conceptual confusion for students who often fail to recognize what the authors have in common.

FAMILY DECISION STYLES

The third structural element of managerial subsystems of families involves the unique ways in which family decision processes (FDP) are applied to family decision situations (FDS) by the family decision makers (FDM). Families develop their own ways of expressing priorities in fundamental value conflicts. The consistent choices of value priorities over time constitute family decision styles that a person outside the system can identify as patterns of the management subsystem. Families have *perceiving (FDMP)*, *deciding (FDMD)*, and *actuating styles (FDMA)*, each of which have differing value conflicts that must be resolved during decision processes. Family decision styles can be "observed" in the patterned behaviors represented by policies, rules, rituals, celebrations, power dynamics, roles, value priorities (Ford, 1983). The present conceptual framework has changed the organization of some of the ideas of Constantine (1983, 1986) and Reiss (1981) in order to separate perceiving and deciding decision styles. The labels of some of their concepts have also been changed in order to use management language. The actuating styles have been added in the present model because the implementation of decisions was not included in the descriptions of family decision-making by Constantine (1983, 1986) and Reiss (1981).

Family perceiving styles (FDMP). Families differ in their openness to change and the willingness to consider or access new information in the environments surrounding them.[8] Family perceiving styles are boundary issues and are indicated by the receptiveness of the family to change and the preferences for self-sufficiency or connections to the outside world. Family perceiving styles can be discerned by the value priorities consistently chosen in facing changes, challenges, new information, unfamiliar people, or connectedness in the community.

Value priorities of a family system are difficult to observe directly, but can be indicated by the implicit and explicit rules (Ford, 1983) and policies in regard to *change*, acceptable information, people, space, energy, money, time use, and family/community activities. Examples of these rules about change include: (a) information that may come in or must stay out, (b) people who are allowed in and those who should be kept out, (c) space areas that visitors may or may not enter, (d) how time, energy, and money are used to encourage or obstruct changes and connectedness. Do families encourage individual members to go out into the world and investigate different ways of living and personal growth, or do they approach this very carefully, expecting members to be "loyal to the party point of view"? Is continuous change a valued state of being or an inevitable (but undesirable) adjustment? How interested are they in the world around them? What kinds of community activities are preferred? What are the value standards for change and connectedness to the community? How much involvement do they seek in community affairs?

A policy that "every year we go to a different place for vacation" may suggest a value priority for variety over stability. The rule that "teenagers are to be entertained only in the family room" vs. a rule that "friends have access to any space in the house" may suggest differing standards of privacy and/or interpersonal connectedness. Definite rules about what children can read or watch indicates more filtering and control over new information that enters the household and perhaps a preference for stability. The total set of family policies and rules, along with their use of scarce resources, indicate value priorities.

The diversity of family perceiving style is recognized, and this diversity would make it impossible to describe the many variations that occur in everyday life. The range of styles would include preferences for security and stability at one end of the continuum and preferences for variety and stimulation at the opposite pole. The two hypothesized family perceiving styles are reported in Table 1 and will require research verification in the future for their managerial applications.

Stability/security-seeking family perceiving styles (FDMPS). Families with stability-seeking perceiving styles may prefer lower levels of arousal, more space between challenges, and may feel more threatened by change. They may be slower to explore new environments because of preferences for the comfort of lower levels of stimulation and a more "quiet" life (Scitovsky, 1976).[9] The value orientations of stability and continuity lead them to a time orientation that emphasizes the past and present more than the present and future, so they view change as stressful and would be likely to be more traditional in goal-setting. It is possible that they would

Table 1

Family Perceiving Styles (FDMP)[a]

	Stability-Seeking (FDMPS)	Variety-Seeking (FDMPV)
Value priorities	Stability, security, comfort, continuity, belonging	Stimulation, variety, change, freedom, excitement
Perception of change	"Change is a problem." Lower levels of stimulation preferred and higher levels of comfort	"Change in an opportunity." Higher levels of stimulation preferred and lower levels of comfort
Time orientation in problem-solving	Past and present more than future	Future and present more than past
Goal-setting	Traditional and with a group emphasis	Futuristic, speculative with an individual emphasis
Resource Awareness	Aware of obvious resources	Innovative scanning for resources
Information access	Controlled access to new information, people, experiences, environments, events. High interest in internal events	Receptive to new information, people experiences and environments, events. High interest in external events
Social contacts	Intensive, limited	Extensive

a   Hypothesized styles based on Constantine's (1986) conception of open and random family paradigms, Reiss's (1981) factor of configuration that exemplifies the family's mastery and their effective adaptability to new situations (Schulman & Klein, 1983), and Scitovsky's (1976) conceptualization of comfort vs. stimulation.

tend to use the obvious resources, rather to use extensive scanning to explore environments for possible resources. The parents are likely to prefer more control over information that goes to the children or the kinds of people with whom children can have contact. There is controlled access to new information, people, and experiences.

The stability-seeking family perceiving style may be indicated by the intensity of interest in internal rather than external events that shows in the time allocated to family-centered as opposed to community-centered activities. The community activities may center around the traditional institutions of church and school. It is possible that a smaller social network or a kinship network is preferred where the social contacts are more intensive than extensive in number.

Variety/stimulation-seeking family perceiving styles (*FDMPV*). Families with variety-seeking perceiving styles find change to be exciting and the stimulation it offers to be the preferred way of living.[10] They have a time orientation that emphasizes the present/future more than the past/ present. This time orientation leads them to be more speculative and futuristic in goal-setting and to be more innovative in scanning the environment for resources. Perhaps these families have more innovative ways of creating alternatives to mediate value conflicts, are more alternative minded, and are more resourceful in their approaches to problems.

Families with variety/stimulation perceiving styles are receptive to new information, people, experiences, and events. Their high interest in external events may be indicated by the extensiveness of their contacts with various social institutions in the community or their cross-cultural contacts. It is possible that the relationships with others in the social network indicate preferences for knowing and spending time with many people, rather than concentrating on knowing fewer people in greater depth.

Family deciding styles (FDMD). Family deciding styles in the present model can be contrasted by the degree to which individual and/or group goals are placed in priority when making decisions about scarce resources such as time, human energy, money, space, and goods. The decisions involve conflicts in standards concerning the values of independence vs. interdependence and cooperation vs. competition. The value priorities of family deciding styles can be observed in: (a) decision rules about whether scarce resources should be allocated by need, equality, or contribution; (b) goal priorities concerning individual and group concerns; (c) the extent of information sharing during decision processes; (d) the number of alternatives considered; (e) the speed of closure in decision negotiations; and (f) the decision-making roles of adults and children ranging from power dynamics of authoritarian to democratic and laissez-faire. The hypothesized family deciding styles also have many variations in nature, but the range of styles would include preferences for individualistic achievement goals at one end of the continuum to the midpoint of collaborative goals, to the preferences for accommodative solidarity goals at the opposite pole. The three hypothesized family deciding styles are reported in Table 2.

Individualistic family deciding styles (FDMDI). Families with individualistic deciding styles may use decision situations to demonstrate how each individual is independent from the family. When there is conflict of interest between group and individual goals, priority is taken by the individual who shows minimal concern for others or the group as a whole. Individuals place high priority on the values of uniqueness, independence, and personal achievement. Priority is given to individual rather than group goals. There is minimal agreement on goals, and few are shared. Group members are likely to agree that the goals of "self-discovery, identity, and self-awareness are of high importance" (Constantine, 1986, p. 167).

Table 2
Family Deciding Styles (FDMD)[b]

	Individualistic (FDMDI)	Collaborative (FDMDC)	Accommodative (FDMDA)
Value priorities	Independence, uniqueness, competition achievement	Independence and interdependence, cooperation, tolerance	Interdependence, conformity, loyalty, solidarity, unity, responsibility, self-sacrifice
Goal priorities	Individual over group goals or concerns	Balanced commitment to individual and group	Group goals and concerns over individual
Shared goals	Minimum agreement, but agreement on identity, self-discovery, self awareness	Agreement on group goals and on many individual goals	Maximum agreement and loyalty, belonging, stable nurturance
Information accessing	Individual information with minimal sharing	Maximum information accumulation and sharing	Informational access controlled by leaders and by age and gender. Information challenging basic assumptions is filtered or blocked
Information processing	Rapid closure with minimal information, loss of information, or continual information without closure	Deferred closure for individual and collective interests	Rapid closure for collective interests, minimum tolerance for diverse viewpoints, relativism
Consideration of alternatives	Few solutions are discussed, or many solutions are discussed without analyses or commitment	Numerous, imaginative solutions for meeting individual and group needs	Few solutions are considered; solutions are based on tradition or group continuity
Decision roles	Resistance of formal and explicit decision roles or procedures. Decisions often made independently by individuals	Rotation of expert power, egalitarian power structure with active participation of children in decisions	Parents as experts, authoritarian power structure with restrictive rules for child participation, explicit decision processes

b   Hypothesized styles based on Constantine's (1986) conception of random, closed, and open family paradigms and Reiss's (1981) concepts of coordination and closure and Olson's, et al., (1983) concepts of "enmeshed" and "balanced" family systems. Coordination refers to the solidarity of the family and the importance given to cohesion and cooperation. Closure is the openness of the family and the degree to which they delay their final decisions until they have all the evidence they can obtain.

Independence in decision-making is demonstrated by reaching decisions quickly (based on little information) or by "accumulating information indefinitely and refusing to come to closure until long after the others do so" (Reiss, 1981, p. 70). There is a lack of closure in these families on common solutions to problems. The way information is managed in the family system is also an important aspect of deciding styles. Individualistic family deciding styles are present when "much of the information remains with individual and is minimally shared with other family members so that communication is limited" (Constantine, 1983, p. 729). The alternatives that are considered in the decision process may be few or many, but they are minimally discussed and without analyses or commitment. The family group usually does not agree upon standards, or ways in which all could work together (Hess & Handel, 1959). When observed over time by an outsider, the family individualistic deciding style is often an erratic one.

Collaborative family deciding styles (FDMDC). Families with collaborative deciding styles are described as "open family systems" (Constantine, 1986) and as "balanced" (Olson et al., 1983). The collaborative deciding style is midway between individualistic and accommodative deciding styles and is characterized by more optimal balances in commitment to both individual and group goals. Open family systems seek goals of "practical effectiveness and constructive adaptability" (Constantine, 1986, p. 167). Information-seeking is less controlled and better communicated among family members. There is more openness to change, without fear of losing stability, and more tolerance for individual nonconformity. Families with this style are described as having high investment in closure and high tolerance for ambiguity that leads to deferred closure, maximum information accumulation, and common solutions. Collaborative conflict-resolution styles in families are characterized by assertiveness in reaching personal goals combined with high concern for the goals of others. Parties in collaborative decision-making go "beyond compromise to find creative solutions to maximize goal achievement for all" (Hocker & Wilmot, 1985, p. 42). The democratic involvement of children in decision-making processes is valued by families with collaborative deciding styles.

Accommodative family deciding styles (FDMDA). The accommodative deciding style in families is characterized by high levels of interdependence and by value priorities for conformity, unity, solidarity, and loyalty. Families with an accommodative deciding style would have goals of "security, belonging, and stable nurturance that would be held in high priority" (Constantine, 1986, p. 167). A conflict of interest in these families would mean that collective goals and group concerns would take priority over individual goals and personal preferences. There would be maximum agreement on many goals. Access to information is thoroughly controlled by parents and decisions are more likely to be handed down in a hierarchical mode. Alternative solutions considered are few in number and tend to be consistent with traditions in an effort to maintain continuity. Families with an accommodative deciding style often gain consensus early in the decision processes and would "ignore or distort additional information in order to justify the collective solution" (Reiss, 1981, p. 70).

There are different degrees of intensity among families who exhibit accommodative deciding styles. Olson (1991) described those with high levels of cohesion as "enmeshed." Enmeshed family systems may not have accommodative deciding styles, but can be problematic for individual development when any kind of dissent is considered intolerable, and close and uninterrupted agreement may be expected at all times.

Family actuating styles (*FDMA*). Family actuating styles are evident in decisions that indicate standards for the values of control and coordination. Actuating styles can be observed in: patterns of leadership, division of labor, coordination of work activities, methods of task accomplishments, and the standards for these accomplishments. How much control or flexibility is tolerated in implementing goal-oriented family activities? How rigidly are standards maintained in the execution of instrumental tasks? Family actuating styles are particularly affected by family structure and gender attitudes and numbers as well as stage in the family life cycle. Younger children, compared to older children, usually require a more definite routine in order to be comfortable. Larger families, compared to smaller families, require more coordination in order to function effectively since the work load is greater and the division of labor is more complex. The three hypothesized family actuating styles are reported in Table 3 and range from the extreme of controlled to the midpoint of flexible and the opposite extreme of random patterns of implementing decisions.

Controlled family actuating styles (*FDMAC*). Families carry out their activities with wide variations in the degree to which they try to control outcomes. Families with highly controlled actuating styles may engage in the kind of planning where parents decide what is to be done and who is to do the work. There are few deviations from goals and close supervision of work activity. The discipline of regular work routines is highly valued, work activities are carefully coordinated, and standards of accomplishment are achieved with regularity. There is high emphasis on task performance with less concern about the personal feelings that accompany the work process. It is an authoritarian leadership style that involves careful planning and supervision so that resources are used both efficiently and

Table 3

Family Actuating Styles (FDMA)[c]

	Controlled (FDMAC)	Flexible (FDMAF)	Random (FDMAR)
Value priorities	Control, order, coordination, regularity	Flexibility, cooperation, equality	Freedom, variety, independence, spontaneity
Standards of accomplishment	Definite and regularly achieved	Flexible and usually achieved	Changing standards and uneven achievement
Leadership styles	Authoritarian	Democratic	Laissez-faire
Supervision	Close, controlled	Moderate, flexible	Seldom present
Rules	Detailed, enforced	General, usually followed	Absence of rules
Planning	Goal-centered and detailed	Resource-centered and general	Absence of long-term planning
Roles	Traditional gender-based	Androgynous division of labor	Shifting
Work activities	Emphasis on task completion more than on relationships	Emphasis on relationships more than on tasks	Low task, low relationships emphasis
Responsibilities	Parent-assigned	Cooperative determination of responsibilities	Independent, irregular
Scheduling	Coordinated group work activities	Individual and group coordinated activities	No attempt at coordination of activities
Routines	Numerous, followed	Few and flexible	Absence of routines

[c] Hypothesized styles based on the planning styles described by Buehler and Hogan (1986) and Beard & Firebaugh (1978) as well as the differentiated roles described by Constantine (1986).

effectively. The work scheduling pattern indicates the implicit assumption that individuals will accommodate to group needs. This controlled family actuating style corresponds to the goal-centered planning identified by Buehler and Hogan (1986); morphostatic planning described by Beard and Firebaugh (1978); and the assigned, differentiated roles conceptualized by Constantine (1986).

Flexible family actuating styles (FDMAF). Flexible actuating styles have less emphasis on control over definite roles, rules, routines, and task performance. Goals change more easily in response to resource opportunities.

Standards are more flexible and achieved with less regularity because there is more concern for relationships than the standards of task accomplishment. This resource-centered planning style (Buehler & Hogan, 1986) involves a more flexible work pattern with fewer routines, less supervision, and less coordination. The work roles may be shared and alternated more frequently than in families with more controlled actuating styles. There is a cooperative determination of work responsibilities, and task accomplishment need not be completed by all members together at the same time as more often occurs in families with more controlled actuating styles.

Random family actuating styles (FDMAR). At the opposite end of the continuum are the more random patterns of actuating decisions in family systems with few agreed upon goals beyond having fun and supporting individual's rights for spontaneous expression. The leadership is random, shifting, and laissez faire. Roles are not as differentiated or clearly described or assigned. There is an absence of rules, regularity, and routine. Work schedules do not exist, and coordination is relatively absent. Standards of order and cleanliness are random and shifting. There is a low emphasis on task accomplishment and low emphasis on relationships concerning the completion of tasks. Despite the unpredictability, the work gets done, children advance in school, and bills are paid (Constantine, 1986, p. 109).[11]

COMPARISON OF FAMILY SYSTEMS CONCEPTUAL FRAMEWORKS

This paper has outlined a conceptual framework that can be used to understand problem-solving and decision-making by individuals and family groups, thus taking a first step in viewing family resource management in a way that is more compatible with the content in psychology, family relations, and family therapy. The present framework resembles that of Reiss and Oliveri (1980), and Reiss (1981) in giving attention to family styles of perceiving and processing information from the environment, but differs by giving attention to the entire management process, including the implementing of plans and decisions as well as the actuating styles of implementing family decisions. The framework shares Constantine's view (1986) of various management styles ("paradigms and regimes") that can be identified on the basis of their core images (value priorities) and goal-directed behaviors across time (p. 19). It differs by: (a) distinguishing among different decision processes needed at the perceiving, deciding, and actuating phases of the management process; (b) articulating the value conflicts that occur during various phases of the management process, and decision processes; (c) identifying specific perceiving, deciding, and actuating styles of individual and families; (d) using language specific to family resource management; and (e) excluding synchronous family paradigms because the regimes are not oriented toward the conscious control of family resources or activities.

The present conceptualization differs in focus and emphasis from the other family systems frameworks (Beavers, 1981; Kantor & Lehr, 1975; Lewis et al., 1976; Olson et al., 1983) in that emphasis is on controlled systems that keep at least one variable within a prescribed range (Kuhn, 1975) by recognizing conscious values and goals that influence decisions about resource use. There is less emphasis on the affective and cohesion dimensions of family life and more emphasis on the dimensions of flexibility (Olson, 1991) and power (Kantor & Lehr, 1975). These adaptability and power dimensions could be labeled the family's instrumental roles (Parsons & Bales, 1955).

Although the hypothesized decision styles are described in order to demonstrate theoretical constructs, families are not typed by styles as is the case in several other frameworks (Constantine, 1983, 1984, 1986; Kantor & Lehr, 1975; Olson et al., 1983; Olson, 1991; Reiss, 1981). It is recognized that managerial styles of the same family will vary by the problems faced, resources available, value conflicts present, phase of the management process, particular people involved in the decision situation, stage of the family life cycle, and changing environmental conditions. It is conceivable that a family system at the perceiving phase of management could respond to a presenting problem as an "open" system, decide what to do as a "closed" system, and implement its decisions using a more "random" response. Preferences for particular styles are recognized in this model, but families can be simultaneously of several "types."

The present framework places emphasis on the *processes* of problem-solving and decision-making in response to ongoing environmental changes. This interdependence of decision maker and environments that are identified as the "decision situation" make an ecological perspective necessary. The individual as decision maker and the family environment are interdependent (families as ecosystems) just as the family as decision maker and the larger environments are interdependent (families *in* an ecosystem) (Paolucci et al., 1977). The presented framework offered several advantages for teaching family resource management, suggested new hypotheses for researchers and therapists to examine, and also provided a different theoretical organization for research variables (Danes & Rettig, in press) that appears to work across some cultures (Danes, 1992). These advantages may stimulate increased communication about family problem-solving and decision-making across disciplines.

A major theme of the family research literature in the decade of the

1980s was the dynamic role of economic variables on marriage and family life, thus confirming that "changing economic conditions are intimately connected to the state of family health and welfare" (Berardo, 1990, p. 817). The issues of balancing work and family, diversity in families, and the complex milieu of families leading to stress were the other themes identified by Berardo (1990) in the decade review article. All of these themes will be present in the coming decade as we think about what the future will be like for families. The theoretical framework presented in this article can be useful in integrating: (a) the economic and social-psychological domains of family life in operationalizing research, (b) the instrumental and expressive functions and activities of the family in our teaching and therapy, and (c) the conceptual and practical reporting of our research to policy makers who need a better understanding of family needs.

AUTHOR'S NOTE

Research time was supported by the Minnesota Agricultural Experiment Station Project 52-054, "Family Adjustments to Economic Stress." Minnesota Agricultural Experiment Station Paper #16,548.

The following people have been particularly helpful in commenting on earlier drafts of the paper: Jean W. Bauer, Sharon M. Danes, M. Geraldine Gage, M. Janice Hogan, Paul Rosenblatt from the University of Minnesota; Linda Nelson, Michigan State University; Ivan Beutler, Brigham Young University; Judith Van Name, University of Delaware; and Mary M. Gray, University of Missouri. Patricia J. Thompson provided editorial assistance on an earlier version of the paper. The author also wishes to thank the many students who have asked important and searching questions that led to clarification of ideas.

NOTES

1. Theory consists of knowledge formulated in conceptual categories and patterns of relationships among categories (Brown & Paolucci, 1979, p. 79).

2. A problem is a situation that calls for analysis and action to produce a specific change (Tallman, 1988, p. 107).

Problem-solving processes involve nonroutine, mental or physical activities in which the actor attempts to overcome a condition that impedes goal attainment efforts (Tallman, 1988, p. 190).

Problem-solving activities can involve completing a task, bringing an end to a noxious situation, removing a blockage, or restoring an unstable situation to previous stability. These activities always entail some degree of risk that the problem may not be solved (Tallman, 1988, p. 190).

Decision-making is a conscious and nonroutine process of comparing alternative courses of action, selecting one of the alternatives, and making a commitment to the alternative until subsequent evaluation is made (Tallman, 1988, p. 113).

3. A system with a functional boundary includes all components that perform a specified function (Kuhn, 1975, p. 11).

4. The processes of perceiving, deciding, and actuating are based on Kuhn's model (1975) of a controlled system with the component parts of detector to receive and identify stimuli, selector to select a response to the stimuli, and effector to carry out the response (pp. 36-37). Kantor and Lehr (1975) refer to the system components as sensor, comparator, and effector.

5. Problems vary in terms of orientation, comprehensiveness, and content. The orientation may be preventative, remedial, or developmental. Comprehensiveness may be technical, elemental, or integrative. Technical problems involve how to do things and can often be solved by acquiring information. Elemental problems involve a segment of family life, such as food management or financial management. Integrative problems involve meshing several elements of family life into a balanced and satisfying whole. The content of a managerial problem may be organizational, allocative, policy, or interactive (Liston, 1966, p. 6-17; Rettig et al., in press).

6. A similar continuum of intuitive and analytical cognitive approaches has been reported by Owen (1985) in beta and alpha management styles and by Kiersey and Bates (1978) who described the dimensions of thinking vs. feeling; judging vs. perceiving ways of thinking that were originally conceptualized by Jung.

7. The gender differences in perceiving decision situations is represented in the work of Carol Gilligan (1982).

8. The family literature has labeled family boundaries by degree of openness (Constantine, 1983, 1984, 1986; Kantor & Lehr, 1975) or environmental sensitivity (Reiss, 1981) depending upon the permeability of the family boundaries and the collective view of the informational world. Owen (1985) contrasted some of these qualities of style and approaches to change as alpha and beta management styles.

9. The stability/security-seeking perceiving style corresponds to Constantine's (1986) paradigm of closed family systems that have a core image of stability, security, and belonging and have a regime that is continuity oriented, seeking to continue the past into the future (p. 20-21, 98-99).

10. The variety/stimulation-seeking perceiving style corresponds to Constantine's random paradigm. Random paradigms have a core image of novelty, creativity, and individuality with a regime that is discontinuity-oriented (p. 98-99).

11. Constantine reminds readers that all family paradigms can be enabled systems. An enabled system is one which (a) is able to meet its collective needs and goals, (b) on the average enables most of its members to meet most of their individual needs and goals, and (c) does not consistently and systematically disable particular members from meeting individual needs and goals (p. 26).

REFERENCES

Aldous, J., Condon, T., Hill, R., Straus, M., & Tallman, I. (Eds.) (1971). *Family problem solving: A symposium on theoretical, methodological, and substantive concerns*. Hinsdale, IL: The Dryden Press.

Arcus, M. (1987). A framework for life-span family life education. *Family Relations, 35*, 5-10.

Bandler, R., & Grinder, J. (1975). *The structure of magic*, Vols. I, II. Palo Alto, CA: Science and Behavior Books, Inc.

Bandler, R., & Grinder, J. (1979). *Frogs into princes: Neuro-linguistic programming*. Moab, UT: Real People Press.

Beard, D., & Firebaugh, F. (1978). Morphostatic and morphogenic planning behaviors in families: Development of a measuring instrument. *Home Economics Research Journal, 6*, 192-205.

Beavers, W. R. (1981). A systems model of family for family therapists. *Journal of Marriage and Family Therapy, 7*, 299-308.

Becker, M. (1981). *A treatise on the family*. Cambridge, MA: Harvard University Press.

Berardo, F. M. (1990). Trends and directions in family research in the 1980s. *Journal of Marriage and the Family, 52*(4), 809-817.

Billings, A. G., & Moos, R. H. (1982). Family environments and adaptation: A clinically applicable typology. *American Journal of Family Therapy, 10*, 26-38.

Brinberg, D., & Jaccard, J. (1989). *Dyadic decision making*. New York, NY: Springer-Verlag.

Brown, M., & Paolucci, B. (1979). *Home economics: A definition*. Washington, DC: American Home Economics Association.

Bubolz, M. M., & Sontag, M. S. (in press). Human ecology theory. In P. G. Boss, W. J. Doherty, R. LaRossa, S. K. Steinmetz, & W. R. Schumm (Eds.), *Sourcebook of family theories and methods: A contextual approach*. New York: Plenum.

Buehler, C., & Hogan, M. J. (1986). Planning styles in single-parent families. *Home Economics Research Journal, 14*, 351-362.

Constantine, L. L. (1983). Dysfunction in open family systems I: Application of a unified theory. *Journal of Marriage and the Family, 45*(4), 725-738.

Constantine, L. L. (1984). Dysfunction and failure in open family systems: II clinical issues. *Journal of Marriage and Family Therapy, 10*, 1-17.

Constantine, L. L. (1986). *Family paradigms: The practice of theory in family therapy*. New York, NY: The Guilford Press.

Danes, S. M., & Rettig, K. D. (in press). Farm wives' business and household decision involvement in times of economic stress. *Home Economics Research Journal*.

Danes, S. M. (1992). *Middle-generation Among couple decision-making patterns*. Presentation, Post Conference of the International Federation of Home Economics, "Household Resource Management Systems": Cross cultural approaches of Home Management, Geissen, Germany.

Deacon, R. E., & Firebaugh, F. (1988). *Family resource management: Principles and applications.* Boston, MA: Allyn and Bacon, Inc.

Deutsch, M. (1985). *Distributive justice.* New Haven: Yale University Press.

Diesing, P. (1976). *Reason in society: Five types of decisions and their social conditions.* Westport, CT: Greenwood Press.

Epstein, N. B., & Bishop, D. S. (1981). Problem centered systems therapy of the family. In A. S. Gurman & D. P. Kniskern (Eds.), *Handbook of family therapy.* New York: Brunner/Mazel.

Epstein, N. B., Bishop, D. S., & Baldwin, L. M. (1982). McMaster model of family functioning: A view of the normal family. In F. Walsh (Ed.), *Normal family process.* New York: Guilford Press.

Falloon, I. R., Bryd, J. L., McGill, C. W., Razani, J., Moss, H. B., & Gilderman, A. M. (1982). Family management in the prevention of exacerbations of schizophrenia: A controlled study. *New England Journal of Medicine, 306,* 1437-1439.

Foa, U. G., & Foa, E. B. (1980). Resource theory: Interpersonal behavior as exchange. In K. J. Gergen, M. S. Greenberg, & R. Willis (Eds.), Social exchange: Advances in theory and research. New York, NY: Plenum Press.

Ford, F. R. (1983). Rules: The invisible family. *Family Process, 22,* 135-145.

Galvin, K. J., & Brommel, B. J. (1986). *Family communication, cohesion, and change* (2nd ed.). Glenview, IL: Scott, Foresman and Co.

Geiss, S. K., & O'Leary, J. S. (1981). Therapist ratings of the frequency and severity of marital problems. *Journal of Marital and Family Therapy, 7,* 515-520.

Gilligan, C. (1982). *In a different voice: Psychological theory and women's development.* Cambridge, MA: Harvard University Press.

Godwin, D. D., & Scanzoni, J. (1989a). Couple decision making: Commonalities and Differences across issues and spouses. *Journal of Family Issues, 10,* 291-310.

Godwin, D. D., & Scanzoni, J. (1989b). Couple consensus during marital joint decision making: A context, process, outcome model. *Journal of Marriage and the Family, 51,* 943-956.

Gottman, J. M. (1979). *Empirical investigation of marriage.* New York: Academic Press.

Gottman, J. M., Notarius, C. I., Markman, H., Banks, D., Yoppi, B., & Ruben, M. E. (1976). Behavior exchange theory and marital decision making. *Journal of Personality and Social Psychology, 34,* 14-23.

Gross, I. H., Crandall, E. W., & Knoll, M. M. (1980). *Management for modern families* (2nd ed.). New York: Appleton-Century-Crofts.

Haley, J. (1976). *Problem-solving therapy.* San Francisco: Jossey-Bass.

Harrison, A. F., & Bramson, R. M. (1982). *Styles of thinking: Strategies for asking questions, making decisions, and solving problems.* New York, NY: Anchor Press.

Hess, R. D., & Handel, G. (1959). *Family worlds.* Chicago: University of Chicago Press.

Hill, R., Foote, N., Aldous, J., Carlson, R., & MacDonald, R. (1970). *Family development in three generations: A longitudinal study of changing family patterns and achievement.* Cambridge, MA: Schenkman.

Hocker, J. L., & Wilmot, W. W. (1985). *Interpersonal conflict.* Dubuque, IA: W.C. Brown.

Jaccard, J., Brinberg, D., & Dittus, P. (1989). Couple decision making: Individual and dyadic level analysis. In D. Brinberg & J. Jaccard (Eds.), *Dyadic decision making* (pp. 81-103). NY: Springer-Verlag.

Kantor, D., & Lehr, W. (1975). *Inside the family.* San Francisco: Jossey-Bass.

Kiersey, D., & Bates, M. (1978). *Please understand me: An essay on temperament styles.* Del Mar, CA: Promethean Books, Inc.

Klein, D. M. (1983). Family problem solving and family stress. *Marriage and Family Review, 6,* 85-112.

Klein, D., & Hill, R. (1979). Determinants of family problem solving effectiveness. In W. R. Burr, R. Hill, F. I. Nye, & I. R Reiss (Eds.), *Contemporary theories about the family* (Vol. 1, pp. 493-548). New York: The Free Press.

Knox, A. B. (1983). *Adult development and learning.* San Francisco: Jossey-Bass.

Kolb, D. A. (1984). *Experiential learning: Experience as the source of learning and development.* Englewood Cliffs, NJ: Prentice-Hall, Inc.

Kuhn, A. (1975). *Unified social science: A system-based introduction.* Homewood, IL: The Dorsey Press.

Lazear, E. P., & Michael, R. T. (1988). *Allocation of income within the household.* Chicago, IL: The University of Chicago Press.

Lewis, J., Beavers, W., Gossett, J., & Phillips, V. (1976). *No single thread: Psychological health in family systems.* New York: Brunner-Mazel.

Liston, M. I. (1966). *Management in the family group, syllabus and sourcebook.* Unpublished manuscript, Iowa State University, College of Home Economics, Ames, IA.

Liston, M. I. (1964). Management in the family as a social process. *Conceptual framework: Processes of home management.* Proceedings of Family Economics-Home Management Subject Section. Washington, DC: American Home Economics Association.

Masten, A. S., Best, K. M., & Garmezy, N. (1990). Resilience and development: Contributions from the study of children who overcome adversity. *Development and Psychopathology, 2,* 425-444.

McDonald, G. W., & Cornille, T. A. (1988). Internal family policy making and family problem-solving. In D. M. Klein & J. Aldous (Eds.), *Social stress and family development* (pp. 246-262). New York: The Guilford Press.

Melson, G. F. (1980). *Family and environment: An ecosystem perspective.* Minneapolis, MN: Burgess Publishing Company.

Mumaw, C. R., & Nichols, A. (1972). Organization styles of homemakers: A factor analytic approach. *Home Economics Research Journal, 1,* 34-43.

Olson, D. (1991). *Three-dimensional (3-D) circumplex model: theoretical and methodological advances.* Paper presented at the Theory Construction and

Research Methodology Workshop, National Council on Family Relations, Denver, CO.

Olson, D., McCubbin, H., & Associates (1983). *Families.* Beverly Hills: Sage Publications, Inc.

Owen, A. (1985). The application of beta management to family processes. In S. Nichols (Ed.), Thinking globally, acting locally: The balancing act. *Proceedings of the Family Economics-Home Management National Workshop.* Washington, DC: American Home Economics Association.

Paolucci, B., Hall, O., & Axinn, N. (1977). *Family decision making: An ecosystem approach.* New York, NY: John Wiley and Sons.

Parsons, T., & Bales, R. F. (1955). *Family socialization and interactions process.* Glencoe, IL: The Free Press.

Pershing, B. (1979). Family policies: A component of management in the home and family setting. *Journal of Marriage and the Family, 41,* 573-581.

Piotrkowski, C. S., Rapoport, R. N., & Rapoport, R. (1987). Families and work. In M. B. Sussman & S. K. Steinmetz (Eds.), *Handbook of Marriage and the Family* (pp. 251-283). New York: Plenum Press.

Reiss, D. (1981). *The family's construction of reality.* Cambridge, MA: Harvard University Press.

Reiss, D., & Oliveri, M. E. (1980). Family paradigm and family coping: A proposal for linking the family's intrinsic adaptive capacities to its response to stress. *Family Relations, 29,* 431-444.

Rettig, K. D. (1986). *Social decision-making.* Training manual. Minnesota Extension Service. St. Paul, MN: University of Minnesota.

Rettig, K. D., & Dahl, C. M. (1992). Impact of procedural factors on perceived justice in divorce settlements. *Proceedings, Theory Development and Research Methodology Workshop, National Council on Family Relations,* Orlando, FL, November 5, 1992.

Rettig, K. D., & Schulz, C. L. (1991). Cognitive style preferences and financial management decision styles. *Financial Counseling and Planning, 2,* 25-54.

Rettig, K. D., Rossmann, M. M., & Hogan, M. J. (in press). Educating for family resource management. In M. Arcus, J. Moss, & J. D. Schvaneveldt (Eds.). *Handbook of Family Life Education, 2.* Newbury Park, CA: Sage Publications.

Rice, A. S., & Tucker, S. M. (1986). *Family life management.* New York, NY: Macmillan Publishing Company.

Scanzoni, J. (1979). Social processes and power in families. In W. R. Burr, R. Hill, & F. I. Nye (Eds.), *Contemporary theories about the family.* (Vol. I, pp. 295-316). New York: The Free Press.

Scanzoni, J., & Szinovacz, M. (1980). *Family decision making: A developmental sex role model.* Beverly Hills: Sage Publications, Inc.

Scitovsky, T. (1976). *The joyless economy: An inquiry into human satisfaction and consumer dissatisfaction.* New York: Oxford University Press.

Sen, A. (1984). *Resources, values, and development.* Oxford: Blackwell and Cambridge: Harvard University Press.

Sen, A. (1987). *On ethics and economics.* Oxford: Basil Blackwell.

Settles, B. (1987). A perspective on tomorrow's families. In M. Sussman & S. Steinmetz (Eds.), *Handbook of marriage and the family* (pp. 157-180). New York: Plenum Press.

Sillars, A. L., & Kalbflesch, P. J. (1989). Implicit and explicit decision-making styles in couples. In D. J. Brinberg & J. Jaccard (Eds.), *Dyadic decision making* (pp. 179-215). New York: Springer-Verlag.

Steinglass, P., Bennett, L. A., Wolin, S. J., & Reiss, D. (1987). *The alcoholic family*. New York: Basic Books.

Straus, M. A., & Tallman, I. (1973). SIMFAM: A technique for observational measurement and experimental study of families. In J. Aldous (Ed.), *Family problem solving* (pp. 381-438). Hinsdale, IL: Dryden Press.

Tallman, I. (1988). Problem solving in families: A revisionist view. In D. M. Klein & J. Aldous (Eds.), *Social stress and family development* (pp. 102-128). New York, NY: The Guilford Press.

Tallman, I., & Gray, L. N. (1987). *A theory of problem solving applied to families*. Paper presented at the Theory Development and Research Methodology Workshop, National Council on Family Relations, Atlanta, GA.

Watzlawick, P., Weakland, J. H., & Fisch, R. (1974). *Change: Principles of problem formation and problem resolution*. New York: W. W. Norton and Company, Inc.

Weick, K. (1971). Group processes, family processes and problem solving. In J. Aldous, T. Condon, R. Hill, M. Straus, & I. Tallman (Eds.), *Family problem solving* (pp. 3-31). Hinsdale, IL: The Dryden Press, Inc.

Wynne, L.C. (1984). The epigenesis of relational systems: A model for understanding family development. *Family Process, 23*, 297-318.

Rethinking Family Decision Making:
A Family Decision Making Model
Under Constraints on Time
and Information

Roma S. Hanks

KEYWORDS. Family, Decision making, Choice, Planning

INTRODUCTION

This paper explores family decision making with a focus on the conditions under which decisions are made. The model presented in this article goes beyond rational choice to allow for the "real world" of family decision making: multiple decision makers, variable access to information, unpredictable outcomes, and individual and family variation along styles of inquiry and structure of knowledge. Examples of situations appropriate for the application of the model are drawn from the work place and from

Roma S. Hanks is Assistant Professor in the Department of Sociology and Anthropology, University of South Alabama.

[Haworth co-indexing entry note]: "Rethinking Family Decision Making: A Family Decision Making Model Under Constraints on Time and Information." Hanks, Roma S. Co-published simultaneously in *Marriage & Family Review* (The Haworth Press, Inc.) Vol. 18, No. 3/4, 1993, pp. 223-240; and: *American Families and the Future: Analyses of Possible Destinies* (ed: Barbara H. Settles, Roma S. Hanks, and Marvin B. Sussman) The Haworth Press, Inc., 1993, pp. 223-240. Multiple copies of this article/chapter may be purchased from The Haworth Document Delivery Center. Call 1-800-3-HAWORTH (1-800-342-9678) between 9:00 - 5:00 (EST) and ask for DOCUMENT DELIVERY CENTER.

medical treatment. The feasibility of decision support systems for family decision making is explored.

Research on family decision making has followed a reductionist model emphasizing micro process rather than macro influence. Much of the work on family decision making has examined congruence of spouses' perspective (Strodtbeck, 1951; Price-Bonham, 1977). The clinical practice of family therapy has focused on decision making as an arena for family communication (Kantor & Lehr, 1975; Olson, McCubbin, Barnes, Larsen, Muxen & Wilson, 1983). Family decision making has been explored from perspectives of power and gender roles (Blood & Wolfe, 1960; Safilios-Rothschild, 1970; Scanzoni & Szinovacz, 1980), and cognitive style (Rettig, 1987). Few researchers have incorporated contextual and process variables in the investigation of family decision making (Hill, Foote, Aldous & McDonald, 1970; Paolucci, Hall & Axinn, 1977). The prevalence of research on family decision making has assumed relative continuity across decisions and within the family system.

This paper attends to the complexity of family decision making in the context of family/organization linkage and technological change. In this article the family is viewed as a social organization interacting with other organizations that have dissimilar orientations about decision making. In the decisions included as examples, some elements of the decisions are under family control while others are under the control of other organizations. Understanding similarities and differences in family and organizational decision making orientations and processes, mechanisms for the exchange of information between families and organizations, and co-participation of members become relevant in developing a family/organization linkage perspective on family decision making.

Various models have been proposed to explain the interaction of family systems with complex organizations and with the environment more generally (Sussman, 1974; Broderick & Smith, 1979). Although most of the discussion around family/organization linkage is grounded in exchange theory (Sussman, 1974) and structural functional theory (Litwak, 1985), general systems theory has been useful in family therapy (Kantor & Lehr, 1975), family economics (Rettig, previous article), and in theorizing about family processes (Strauss, 1973). Family systems theory clearly relates internal family process to environmental factors (Broderick & Smith, 1979). The thesis of this paper is that research on family decision making needs to give more attention to the contexts of decisions, particularly in relation to control, information exchange, and decision making style/rules.

THE PROBLEM OF JOINT DECISION MAKING

The boundaries between families and organizations are becoming more permeable. The influence of family on organization can be seen in family-responsive corporate policies (Galinsky, Hughes & David, 1990; Stanley, Segal & Laughton, 1990) and in the implementation of mechanisms, such as ethics committees in hospitals by which organizations spread the liability for risky decisions. Increasingly, families enter organizational settings to participate in decision making that concerns health, education, or employment of family members. A recent Hastings Center Report, suggested that "medical decision making would be messier but better" if the concerns of the patient's family were given more weight and family members had a stronger voice (Nelson, 1992). Over two decades ago, Haug and Sussman (1969) noted that medical professionals needed to realize that clients and their families were often sophisticated consumers capable of seizing power from professionals who did not recognize the potential benefits of empowering clients in treatment processes. Much progress has been made in de-mystifying the client/professional relationship, particularly in the medical profession and educational organizations. Problems remain in facilitating family/organization linkages where there are differences in power, access to information, and level of decision making skill.

In many family/organization interactions, family members who are dual participants, holding family and organizational roles, draw on their knowledge of decision making processes in both settings. Other joint decisions involve family members who have no experience in the organizational context and bring to the situation only their relationship to the family member who is directly involved in the decision. These naive family participants have little knowledge of organizational decision making processes, rules, or goals. Conversely, the organizational participants have little knowledge of family decision making beyond the assumptions they bring from their own histories of family life.

Permeability of boundaries between families and organizations confined to the decision making occasion is problematic. According to Simmel, if families and organizations are to interact around decisions, they need to understand what may be their shared goals or superordinate goals both may desire (Wolff, 1950).

Family systems and complex organizations offer different kinds of decision making experience and training. Each has its own reality (Berger & Luckmann, 1967; Reiss, 1981). Family members who are members of complex organizations as well have been socialized to make decisions in both settings. Individual learning and decision making styles are mediated by family/organizational socialization but the influence is often reciprocal (Kolb, 1984; Rettig, 1987; Hanks & Sussman, 1990).

Within the family system, members' individual decision making styles influence decision processes and outcomes. Similarly, members of organizations bring individual styles to decision making. However, organizations are more likely to attempt to achieve uniformity of style among members by providing decision making training. The complexity of organizational decision making could be expected to dilute the influence of individual style on a specific decision. Still, individuals comprise families and organizations and collective decisions result from the interaction, negotiation, and compromise or consensus of members.

In families, especially extended families, one individual may become expert in one area. People specialize–mom decides about education or cars or "inside work." Uncle Joe may become the one to see about buying a car or Grandmother may have skills interacting with medical systems. This approach divides responsibilities. Some members may give over tasks they do not enjoy. Families often rely on other people who have had similar experience for knowledge. The stereotype of "over the fence" talk among neighbors has developed around this practice of information gathering. Most families do not have sophisticated information retrieval services. However, as computer technology is adopted into more homes, the possibilities grow. While it is now possible to retrieve information from encyclopedia, book airline tickets, and obtain current quotations on interest rates from a desktop computer in the family room or a laptop anywhere the modem can be connected to a phone line, the average family lacks the skills or access to these networks. This potential increase in the accessibility of information could be empowering to family, especially younger generations who are growing up computer literate, provided the data bases become easily used by ordinary people.

INDIVIDUAL DIFFERENCES AMONG FAMILY MEMBERS' DECISION MAKING STYLES

As family members interact in decision making, they create a shared system of inquiry that results in a structure of knowledge characteristic to that family (Reiss, 1981). In the model presented in Figure 1, individual differences in learning styles of family members impact directly upon perception of a decision, as well as being mediated by family variables. An experiential framework (Kolb, 1984) allows exploration of family decision making as a complex process that draws upon individual information gathering styles, the family system of inquiry, the family structure of knowledge, and dyadic and small group interactions.

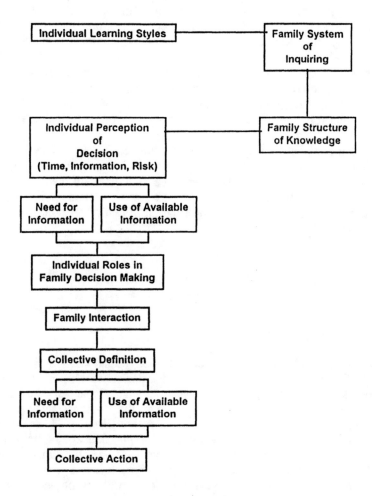

Figure 1. Conceptual Framework for a Structure of Knowledge
Model of Family Decision Making

Figure 1 presents a model of family/organization linkage in decision making incorporating individual style and socialization within family and organizational settings.

Variations in learning and decision making styles among family members can be viewed either as strengthening the family's ability to make decisions or as hindering the process by introducing a potential source of conflict. Individual family members have different roles in decision making (Rettig, 1987). Individuals differ in perceptions of the dimensions of a decision, e.g., time to make the decision, amount of information needed, and potential risk. The impact of any single dimension on a decision is determined in part by the role acted out by the individual presenting his/her perception of that dimension to the family. The family's collective definition of the decision results from the interaction of family members in their various roles with their various perceptions of the decision to be made.

Out of the collective definition emerges collective action. The family will either search for additional information or adopt a course of action. These collective actions may be interactive as the family discovers information needs while pursuing a course of action. It is at this point in the present discussion that the role of information in family decision making becomes critical.

FAMILY DECISION MAKING UNDER
RISK/UNCERTAINTY/IGNORANCE

Rational Actor Paradigm

Two important, but often not observable, determinants of individual or group decision making are: (1) the goal of the decision maker and (2) his/her understanding of the decision problem. Evidence is presented that, at least in political and psychological inference, the "rational actor paradigm" accounts for the goal of the decision maker (Brehmer, 1986). The actor is assumed to be making decisions in expression of rational processes. Goals are inferred from outcomes; decisions are presumed to be reflective of motives. The rational actor paradigm does not serve well to account for decision making behavior under conditions of uncertainty about outcome (Arrow, 1984). Those decisions "require the decision maker to rely on new and perhaps unique configurations of information" (Brehmer, 1986, p. 294). Kieren and Hurlbut (1987) suggest that defining and operationalizing rationality require clarification of the type of decision that is being made.

In a complex world of economic, demographic, and technological change, families make many types of decisions, often under conditions of uncertainty. Families can become confused by extreme constraints on information or they may be flooded with too much information, without the tools or experience to help them use that information. In addition, family decision making has an emotional dimension that gives weight to considerations that cannot be measured adequately using only rational criteria. Rational actor decision making models are of questionable utility in explaining family decision making, especially in situations that involve subjective assessments and value judgments.

Multiple Decision Makers

The existence of multiple decision makers in families requires the integration of information, perceived and presented to the decision making system from a variety of perspectives. This problem is compounded when the family interacts with a complex organization in making a decision. Families and organizational decision makers have different levels of education and experience with decision making. Without tools to help them organize and act on information, families are at a disadvantage. Information is often available, but not accessible to the family.

The remainder of this article introduces a framework for research on family decision making where limitations on the amount of time and information available are critical. Specific examples are given of family decision making that introduce elements of constraint on time and information. The examples are drawn from situations in which families are interacting with organizations in the decision making process. Decision making that involves family/organization linkage is susceptible to constraints on time and information due to differences in goals of the interacting systems, availability of information, and level of decision making skills.

A Work Place Example

Since the mid-1980s, American companies have offered early retirement incentives to increasing numbers of employees. The offers typically involve additions to age and service in pension calculations. Employees are asked to respond to the offers within a specified time period. These options are a particularly popular way of reducing middle management, but they have been used across occupational categories (Hanks, 1990a, 1990b). As an occasion for family decision making, the early retirement opportunity illustrates an important shift in control over life events. Retirement has been thought of by individuals and in the research literature as an individual decision, often made in consideration of family interests (Beehr, 1986; Szinovacz, 1987; Kilty & Behlig, 1986; Maddox, 1968). Current early retirement incentives are based on the assumption that the event of retirement is fairly flexible with regard to placement in the life course and that it can be seen as flexible in response to macro level, as well as micro level needs.

When responding to incentive offers, individuals and families have to make retirement decisions in very brief time periods, often with limited information about available alternatives. Although families may have planned for eventual retirement and participated in pension programs, they have not previously planned for early retirement because that option has not been encouraged on a broad basis (Hanks, 1990a, 1990b). Perceptions of the new retirement decision vary widely among employees and their families in companies that have offered early retirement incentives:

> As soon as I heard about the offer, I asked my boss if this meant me. He said no, but I told myself, I'd better rethink my relationship with this company.
>
> > –40 year old employee

> Oh sure, there were rumors, about retirement offers, but I never took them seriously.
>
> > –early retiree
> > (Personal Communication, April, 1987)

The younger person who was not in the target group for the retirement offer of his company perceived greater personal risk than the retiree who actually had an opportunity to respond to such an offer. The 40 year old employee:

- perceived risk,
- gathered information,
- presented options to the family,
- put in place a fall back plan.

Although he was not offered early retirement, he now has a plan of action and a consensus of family opinion about response to any similar offer his company may make in the future. He has increased both lead time and amount of information available to make a future decision. A macro level policy change has been presented to his family as a real event because of his high risk perception and early information presentation. He and his family still may lack information about future company policy, but they have other relevant information that will decrease their need for time to make a decision should an offer be presented that includes them. The family has increased decisional control by adopting a proactive stance.

Data from in-depth interviews with 60 families in which one or more family member took incentive-based early retirement from a corporation suggest that families tailored their decision making styles to their perception of the time and information constraints on their retirement decision. The potential for family control over outcome, the choice of options, and the risk involved were all considered (Hanks, 1990a, 1990b). For example, one retiree, who knew he wanted to retire and needed to decide if the incentive provided the benefits he wanted, used the following decision making style:

> I try not to take a stupid direction. I get information within the time frame, analyze, change direction. [Sometimes] where "there" is moves... Whether or not [to retire] was mine [my decision]; when and how–I consulted.

A Medical Example

A rapidly changing medical technology presents complex decision-making situations to both family members and medical professionals. Decisions often must be made quickly and without the ability to accurately predict conditions under which the same decision will be made in the future. Family members and medical professionals often are asked to act on the information at hand, recognizing that technological breakthroughs may offer new solutions, but bound by the time and information constraints of the current crisis.

One medical example is the treatment of imperiled newborns (Hastings Center Report, 1987). Historically, infants born prematurely or with severe anomalies were cared for in the home, where most were born, but little aggressive treatment was available. As new technologies increased the chances of survival for these infants, decisions about their care and quality of life became more difficult. Today the approaches to treatment vary, but fall into three general categories:

1. statistical approach–infants with statistical profiles that suggest unlikely benefit from treatment are not treated aggressively;
2. near certainty approach–treatment is begun for every infant and discontinued when death or severe impairment is certain; discontinuation of treatment being at parental discretion; and
3. individualized approach–periodic monitoring of prognosis allows termination of treatment when there is a high chance of severe disability; does not necessarily wait for certainty of death or disability.

Under all three approaches, family members are involved along with professionals in making decisions under conditions of extreme constraint on time. Furthermore, ongoing research and technological development provide changing possibilities for humane treatment of imperiled newborns with the accompanying possibility of regret and guilt feelings by family members involved in decision making. Most parents making decisions about an imperiled newborn have no previous experience with such decisions. Doctors often find themselves recommending experimental treatments.

A CONCEPTUAL FRAMEWORK

The decision in the work place and medical examples in the previous sections involve: multiple decision makers, unknowable outcomes of at least one option, short lead time, inadequate information to determine probability distributions for all outcomes, and costs for gathering information (Collingridge, 1980). These examples suggest that a perspective on family decision making that looks beyond process and role variables to the constraints on time and information surrounding the decision is appropriate. Macro level decisions are frequently made under conditions of uncertainty. Collingridge's model was developed for macro level decisions that had to be made quickly and often with the possibility of using experimental approaches. The application of this model to a conceptualization of individual and family decision making can be made where conditions usually examined only in discussions of macro level decision making can be shown to exist. Conditions of uncertainty are most likely to exist when family decision making is constrained in time and information. These conditions often accompany decisions in which: (1) families and other organizations make decisions together or (2) families make decisions in response to organizational initiatives.

A decision-making theory that can be applied to "decision-making under ignorance" (Collingridge, 1980) is particularly applicable to situations in which a variety of factors are influencing both opportunity and choice. This model is useful in situations in which families and other organizations share decision making responsibility and process. Families often make decisions under constraints on time and information. In addition to the previous medical and work place examples, decisions about education, long-term care, community development, and future financial security may require sharing of information and technology by families and organizations. Family and organizational decision makers have differential access to information about a decision topic. There are multiple decision makers in families and in other organizations with which they share decision making.

The contrast between Collingridge's model and models of simple decision making and decision making under risk and uncertainty merits a brief review of those models. More detailed discussion may be found in Collingridge (1980). Simple Decision Making:

- A single decision maker.
- The decision maker has a single objective.
- The decision maker knows all the options open to him/her.
- Is possible to measure the extent to which the decision maker's objective is reached.
- The outcome of each option is known and determines a value of the objective function.

Risk/Uncertainty Decision Making:

- Risk–where the outcomes of at least one option cannot be identified, but two or more possible outcomes exist.
- Uncertainty–where there is inadequate information to determine an objective probability distribution.

Both risk and uncertainty rely on decision making theory that is based on the Bayesian rule that the decision maker ought to optimize the expected value of the objective function.

Multi-variant decision theory approaches decision making involving a number of objectives and a number of decision makers. Game theory is an example of this kind of decision making. Collingridge questions the adequacy of any probability based decision theory to handle the inadequate factual information available for making decisions. He suggests a need to expand the decision making framework from "certainty:risk:uncertainty" to "certainty:risk:uncertainty:ignorance."

DECISION MAKING UNDER IGNORANCE

Proceeding under that model, Collingridge expounds a theory of decision making under ignorance, which he defines as "being prepared to correct decisions in the light of future information" (Collingridge, 1980, p. 37). The assumptions of his model are that:

- Decisions under ignorance cannot be justified.
- Rationality becomes the search for error and the willingness to respond to its discovery.
- Any decision made under ignorance may be discovered to have been in error.
- Decisions must be seen as process, not as point events.

The decision involves not only the selection of an option, but also a search for information in the future and a resolve to act on new information as it is found. That search and that resolve become rationality in the decision making process.

With those basic assumptions about decisions made under ignorance, Collingridge concludes that there are four characteristics of decisions that make them responsive to the possible need for flexibility for integrating new information:

- Decisions should be highly corrigible, i.e., they should be able to be corrected with minimal jeopardy to the desired outcome.
- Decisions involve the choice of systems that are easy to control.
- Decisions must keep future options open.
- Decisions should be insensitive to error.

Decisions made in response to the process of technological change and decisions made under conditions of severe time and information constraints fit the model of decisions made under ignorance. The Collingridge model of decision making under ignorance is an appropriate framework for the development of a family response model under conditions where information is insufficient to use a probability model.

In the example of early retirement incentive, the decision to accept a corporate incentive for early retirement is made in the context of a changing world market, changing demography of the work force, changing technological sophistication of the work environment, changing managerial styles, and changing organizational structures. In addition, most incentive-based early retirement involves limited time for making the decision. There are often multiple interested participants in the decision making process. Information about some of the economic variables may be inaccessible to family decision makers. The inaccessibility of information and the multiplicity of decision makers make it virtually impossible to accurately predict enough of the possible options and outcomes to use a probability based decision making approach.

In the medical example, the exchange of information between the family and the professional is the essential element. Families are responsible for sharing information about their values and beliefs, while physicians are responsible for communicating to the family any technical information about medical problems and procedures that may be understood and used in family decision making. Such information can be exchanged in a number of modes that vary widely in their technological sophistication and in their accessibility to non-professionals.

The decision making under ignorance model highlights the importance of access to information and lends itself to inclusion in a conceptual framework for joint decisions by families and other organizations. As Pepper (1942, pp. 44-46) points out in his discussion of the individual's use of knowledge:

> Common sense continually demands the responsible criticism of refined knowledge, and refined knowledge sooner or later requires the security of common sense support.

Families are often relied upon to provide the "common sense" components of decision making. The assumption is made that family members need less information than organizations because they have the knowledge of feelings and shared values. Organizations, on the other hand, must justify decisions on the basis of rational choice. In joint decision making, families and more complex organizations have less differentiated needs. Both organizational units in the decision making team need equal access to: (1) the information necessary to make a rational choice and (2) knowledge of the values and feelings that may make non-rational choice more appropriate.

Arrow (1984) suggests that subjective choice, rather than rationality, may be the basis for certain decisions made under conditions of risk/uncertainty. Choice is an important concept in decisions under uncertainty because those decisions are made with a range of possible outcomes. In Arrow's words:

> The immediate basis for a special theory of behavior under uncertainty is the subjective sensation that an action may not uniquely determine the consequences to the agent.... The meaning of uncertainty is that the agent does not know the state of the world. (p. 173)

Arrow earlier defined the concept of 'state of the world' as a description of the world so complete that, if true and known, the consequences of every action would be known. The agent who decides under uncertainty must be able to give value to different consequences and be able to envision the occurrence of different states of the world.

Families responding to organizational initiatives, as well as participants involved in family/organization team decision making, need to be able to understand the perceived values of outcomes that may result in differential weightings of those values by different decision makers. Increasing access to information about the decision makers and their respective cultures will help co-participants in decision making understand and predict weights of decisional components.

EXPANDING CHOICE

An innovative view of individual and family lifestyle choice is presented in Settles (1987) model. She views expansion of choice as a desired outcome of individual and family decision making and suggests several interactive dimensions of planning and group participation. Such mechanisms as education, multi-group participation, consciousness raising, and social change help families increase choices.

Expanding choice can be a way of adapting family decision making styles to meet the criteria for desirable decisions under risk/uncertainty/ignorance. Increasing flexibility and preparedness are logical outcomes of increasing the dimensions of choice. The family is constantly gathering information and increasing options so decisions can be seen as corrigible and future options are kept open. The proactive stance of long term planning rather than occasional responding prepares families to manage external initiatives that affect them and to interact with organizations in decision making.

The application of decision support systems to family decisions or family/organization co-decisions has not been made. An application of decision support to family decision making and long term planning is proposed in Figure 2.

The family faces an unexpected decision making event or opportunity to revise long-term plans. The family assesses the risk of acting on available information and decides either to act or to seek additional information. If additional information is deemed necessary, the family has several options for decision support: the organization involved in the decision, family members, experts, or the informal information network. The more readily available the information from whatever source, the more responsive the family can be to the conditions of the decision–constraints on time and information. Here the use of computer assisted technological decision support would be valuable. The family then acts and evaluates the decision outcome and process.

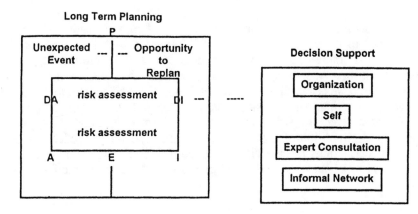

P = Planning
DA = Decision to Act
DI = Decision to Gather Information
A = Action
I = Information Gathering Activity
E = Evaluation of Action or Information

Definition of Terms in Decision Support System:

Organization - any formal organization (i.e., work; public agency; church)

Self - individual involved in decision and planning

Expert Consultation - professional or computerized

Informal Network - family; friends; community

Figure 2. Long Term Planning Model (With Decision Support)

Research is needed on the suitability of the concept of families using decision support systems. The current availability of information through personal computers and electronic text systems in use in private homes, libraries, and schools where families have access makes possible a new concept of family decision making that utilizes information gathering technology. Critical to such a concept is the ability of the family to identify the problem and to recognize the kind of decision that is to be made. In the case of team decision making, it is necessary to exchange freely accurate information about decision makers' values that might affect the decision as well as information that affects rational choice.

CONCLUSION

This paper has explored a conceptualization of family decision making that attends to the access to and use of information by family decision makers. This framework assumes that individuals and families can to some extent modify their decision making styles to the situation and that flexibility in style is a desired outcome of family life education in the area of decision making. The decisions that families and other organizations make together require a free exchange of information. Concerns over privacy and a tradition of professional supremacy inhibit that exchange. Those concerns must be carefully examined if free exchange is to occur. Technological advances available to large organizations must find family applications.

AUTHOR'S NOTE

This research was supported in part by the Department of Health and Human Services, Administration on Aging, Interactive Planning for Family Futures project, Barbara H. Settles, PhD, principal investigator.

REFERENCES

Arrow, K. J. (1984). *Collected papers of Kenneth J. Arrow, Volume 3: Individual Choice Under Certainty and Uncertainty.* Cambridge, MA: Belknap.

Beehr, T. A. (1986). The process of retirement: A Review and recommendations for future investigation. *Personnel Psychology, 39*(1), 31-55.

Berger, P. L., & Luckmann, T. (1967). *The social construction of reality.* New York: Anchor Books.

Blood, R. O., & Wolfe, D. M. (1960). *Husbands and Wives.* New York: The Free Press.

Brehmer, B. (1986). The role of judgment in small-group conflict and decision making. In H. R. Arkes & K. R. Hammond (Eds.), *Judgment and Decision Making: An Interdisciplinary Reader* (pp. 293-310). Cambridge: Cambridge University Press.

Broderick, C., & Smith, J. (1979). The general system approach to the family. In W. R. Burr, R. Hill, F. I. Nye & I. L. Reiss (Eds.), *Contemporary theories about the family* (pp. 112-129). New York: The Free Press.

Collingridge, D. (1980). *The Social Control of Technology.* New York: St. Martin's Press.

Galinsky, E., Hughes, D., & David, J. (1990). Trends in corporate family-supportive policies. In R. S. Hanks & M. B. Sussman (Eds.), *Corporations, Businesses, and Families* (pp. 75-94). New York: The Haworth Press, Inc.

Hanks, R. S. (1990a). *Family and corporation linkage in timing and control of incentive based early retirement.* Unpublished doctoral dissertation. University of Delaware, Newark, DE.

Hanks, R. S. (1990b). The impact of early retirement incentives on retirees and their families. *Journal of family Issues, 11*(4), 424-437.

Hanks, R. S., & Sussman, M. B. (1990). Where does the family end and the corporation begin: The consequences of rapid transformation. In R. S. Hanks, M. B. Sussman (Eds.), *Corporations, Businesses, and Families* (pp. 1-14). New York: The Haworth Press, Inc.

Hastings Center Report (1987), *17*(6). New York: The Hastings Center.

Haug, M. R., & Sussman, M. B. (1969). Professional autonomy and the revolt of the client. *Social Problems, 17*(2), 153-161.

Hill, R., Foote, N., Aldous, J., & McDonald, G. (1970). *Family Development in Three Generations: A Longitudinal Study of Planning and Achievement.* Cambridge, MA: Schenkman.

Kantor, D., & Lehr, W. (1975). *Inside the family: Toward a theory of family process.* San Francisco: Jossey-Bass.

Kieren, K. K., & Hurlbut, N. L. (1987). *Arriving at a method to determine phases in family problem solving.* Paper presented at the Pre-Conference Workshop on Theory Construction and Research Methodology, annual meeting of the National Council on Family Relations, Atlanta, GA.

Kilty, K. M., & Behlig, J. H. (1986). Retirement financial planning among professional workers. *The Gerontologist, 26*(5), 525-530.

Kolb, D. (1984). *Experiential learning: Experience as the Source of Learning and Development.* Englewood Cliffs, NJ: Prentice-Hall.

Litwak, E. (1985). *Helping the elderly; The complementary roles of informal networks and formal systems.* New York: Guilford Press.

Maddox, G. L. (1968). Retirement as a social event in the United States. In B. L. Neugarten (Ed.), *Middle Age and Aging: A Reader in Social Psychology* (pp. 357-365). Chicago: University of Chicago Press.

Nelson, J. L. (1992). Taking families seriously. *Hastings Center Report, 22*(4), 6-12.

Olson, D. H., McCubbin, H. I., Barnes, H. L., Larsen, A. S., Muxen, M. J., & Wilson, M. A. (1983). *Families: What makes them work.* Beverly Hills: Sage.

Paolucci, B., Hall, O., & Axinn, N. (1977). *Family decision making: An ecosystem Approach.* New York: John Wiley & Sons.

Pepper, S. (1942). *World Hypothesis.* Berkeley, CA: University of California Press.

Price-Bonham, S. (1977). Marital decision making: Congruence of spouses' responses. *Sociology Inquiry, 2*, 119-125.

Reiss, D. (1981). *The Family's Construction of Reality.* Cambridge, MA: Harvard University Press.

Rettig, K. D. (1987). *A cognitive conceptual family decision making framework.* Unpublished manuscript.

Rettig, K. D. (Previous article). *Problem-solving and decision-making as central processes of family life: An ecological framework for family relations and family resource management.*

Safilios-Rothschild, C. (1970). The study of family power structure: A review 1960-1969. *Journal of Marriage and Family, 32,* 355-362.

Scanzoni, J., & Szinovacz, M. (1980). *Family Decision Making* (Vol. III). Beverly Hills, CA: Sage.

Settles, B. H. (1987). A perspective on tomorrow's families. In M. B. Sussman & S. Steinmetz (Eds.), *Handbook of Marriage and the Family* (pp. 157-180). New York: Plenum Press.

Stanley, J., Segal, M. W., & Laughton, C. J. (1990). Grass roots family action and military family responses. In R. S. Hanks & M. B. Sussman (Eds.), *Corporations, Businesses, and Families* (pp. 207-224). New York: The Haworth Press, Inc.

Strauss, M. (1973). A general systems theory approach to a theory of violence between family members. *Social Science Information, 12,* 105-125.

Strodtbeck, F. (1951). Husband-wife interaction over revealed differences. *American Sociological Review, 16,* 468-473.

Sussman, M. B. (1974). Family non-family linkages. In M. B. Sussman (Ed.), *Source book in Marriage and the Family* (4th Ed.), (pp. 233-251). Boston: Houghton Mifflin.

Sussman, M. B. (1987). Family, kinship and bureaucracy. In A. Campbell & P. E. Converse (Eds.), *The human meaning of social change* (pp. 127-158). New York: Russell Sage Foundation.

Szinovacz, M. (1987). Decision making on retirement timing: Antecedents and consequences. Paper presented at the annual meeting of the Society for the Study of Social Problems, Chicago.

Wolff, K. H. (Ed. & Trans.). (1950). *The sociology of George Simmel.* Glencoe, IL: The Free Press.

Adolescents' Contributions
to Family Decision Making

Mary Lou Liprie

KEYWORDS. Adolescent, Family decisions, Critical thinking, Locus of control

INTRODUCTION

The need for adolescents to develop critical thinking and decision making skills suitable for a pluralistic society has been identified for some ten years in a variety of popular and scholarly reports (Boyer, 1983; Carnegie Council on Adolescent Development, 1989; Naisbitt & Aburdene,1990; National Commission on Secondary Vocational Education, 1984; Toffler, 1980). Likewise, a developmental task of adolescence is the development of independence. The process of reaching independence is gradual and involves the adolescent assuming more responsibility, including the making of decisions that were previously made by adults (Havighurst, 1972; Coleman, 1980).

Decision making ability has been thought to be a skill that is developed

Mary Lou Liprie is Associate Professor of Individual and Family Studies, University of Delaware.

[Haworth co-indexing entry note]: "Adolescents' Contributions to Family Decision Making." Liprie, Mary Lou. Co-published simultaneously in *Marriage & Family Review* (The Haworth Press, Inc.) Vol. 18, No. 3/4, 1993, pp. 241-253; and: *American Families and the Future: Analyses of Possible Destinies* (ed: Barbara H. Settles, Roma S. Hanks, and Marvin B. Sussman) The Haworth Press, Inc., 1993, pp. 241-253. Multiple copies of this article/chapter may be purchased from The Haworth Document Delivery Center. Call 1-800-3-HAWORTH (1-800-342-9678) between 9:00 - 5:00 (EST) and ask for DOCUMENT DELIVERY CENTER.

241

in the family. Decision making experience in the context of family life can foster competence in processes related to decision making and problem solving in other settings. Mann accordingly states, the "family environment is a major factor that influences adolescent participation in decisions, and shapes the opportunity to develop competence" (Mann, Harmoni & Power, 1989, p. 274). Continuing, Mann states that the family is really a laboratory in which the adolescent " . . . learns how to communicate and negotiate in order to influence decisions, and receives encouragement to make age-appropriate choices" (Mann et al., 1989, p. 274). Conger and Peterson (1984) concur that parents remain the most influential trainers of adolescent competence in decision making.

While there seems to be considerable support for adolescent participation in family decision making, most of the research on family decision making has focused on the marital dyad (Scanzoni & Szinovacz, 1980; Blood & Wolfe, 1960) or on parent perceptions of children's influence (Roberts, Wortzel & Berkeley, 1981; Mehrota & Torges, 1977). The few studies that have examined children's perceptions of their influence on family decision making have focused on consumer decisions rather than global decision making processes (Foxman, Tansuhaj & Ekstrom, 1989a; Foxman, Tansuhaj & Ekstrom, 1989b).

The data reported in this paper are based on the findings from a three year study of early adolescents' perception of their role in family decision making, as well as data from a limited sample of parents of third year participants focusing on parents' perceptions of family decision making. The suggestive nature of the data indicate that they represent early heuristic findings, subject to further refinement and testing.

THE EARLY ADOLESCENT

Adolescence, a major stage of development in the life cycle, witnesses the transition from childhood to adulthood. The period beginning roughly at 10-13 and ending at 18-20 with neither a clear beginning nor ending is marked by comprehensive physical, physiological, cognitive, social and emotional changes (Santrock, 1990; Fuhrmann, 1990). It is during the early adolescent period that young people often make decisions that will lead to productive fulfilling or nonproductive lessened futures. Intellectual growth and development are dramatic at this age, bringing the new capacity to think in more abstract and complex ways than in their past. It is well documented that adolescent thought is different from child thought and that adolescents are developing abstract reasoning and problem solving abilities. Adolescents can often entertain many possibilities while seeking a solution to a problem (Santrock, 1990).

Likewise, early adolescents face new and different conditions than those of earlier generations: drug and alcohol use and abuse, early sexual activity, or added home responsibilities due to family structure or adult work place conditions. In a broader sense the American economy is asking workers to think more creatively and flexibly as never before. Experimentation, inquiry, and curiosity are characteristic of early adolescence. The challenge is to channel the energy of early adolescents into thinking and decision making patterns that will be beneficial in the work and family worlds of the 21st century.

Critical Thinking

A flood of research interest in critical thinking has generated cross-disciplinary discussion about the importance of fostering critical thinking skills in early adolescents. Educators realize two important needs: (1) to "reengage families in the education of young adolescents by . . . offering families opportunities to support the learning process"; and (2) to teach young adolescents to think critically so they can meet later challenges of education and employment (Carnegie Council on Adolescent Development, 1989). Students must be able to identify new concerns and develop creative solutions. Global competition requires that students learn to examine their own thinking and decision making processes–to think about thinking–rather than learn externally generated responses to externally posed questions.

"Monological analysis [thinking] will not solve multilogical problems" (Paul, 1990, p. 19). Early adolescents in the 1990s live in a pluralistic society in which the value of diversity is being emphasized in their future work places, communities, and educational institutions. Citizens in such a world need to be taught how to think and how to generate new paradigms for thinking, problem solving, and decision making. A tenet of the philosophy of critical thinking is that the thinker, i.e., decision maker, constructs the problem as well as the solution (Paul, 1990). She or he participates in the formulation of the decision under consideration rather than choosing among prefabricated alternatives.

While emphasis on critical thinking has advanced in formal educational arenas, little has been done to examine the extent to which critical thinking is encouraged in family context or about the impact of critical thinking on early adolescent participation in family decision making. Perhaps the most interesting dimension of critical thinking for family interaction is the dimension of "responsibility for learning." In educational settings, "the student should be given increasing responsibility for his or her own learning. . . . The teacher provides opportunities for students to decide what they need to know and helps them develop strategies for figuring it out" (Paul, 1990, p. 27). The application to family decision making would suggest that families stimulate critical thinking by encouraging developing children to make decisions and providing experiences that foster the development of critical thinking skills. This process involves family communication about the way decisions are made, family encouragement of participatory learning and experimentation, and the practice of active involvement in decision making of individual and family needs.

Locus of Control

Locus of control, also referred to as self-efficacy has been related to decision making and to empowerment (Scales, 1990). Since Rotter's observation in 1966 that little work had been done to date on the social antecedents of locus of control and relationships between locus of control and other variables, many studies have been completed, however few have focused on adolescents.

The concept of locus of control has been widely investigated in social science literature in relation to stress and coping behavior (Glass, Singer & Friedman, 1969; Lefcourt, 1980), school performance (Harrison, 1968), childhood depression (Weisz et al., 1989), self concept (Eberhart & Keith, 1989; Marsh & Gouvermet, 1989), and some aspects of decision making (Wheeler & Davis, 1979) and interaction among family members (Strodtbeck, 1958; Wichern & Nowicki, 1977; Nowicki & Segal, 1974).

Locus of control is the perception a person has as being able to control environmental events and happenings, i.e., internal control; or as being subject to fate, chance, or the whims of others, i.e., external control. Internal control is related to the ability to delay personal gratification while external control is related to the need for have immediate gratification (Bialer, 1961).

Individuals act on their perceptions. They exercise control by attempting to change conditions in their world when they believe that they have control, or the power to exert control. On the other hand, if they feel that conditions they see are controlled by circumstances or by people or forces other than themselves, they may fail to act to change these conditions.

Studies using social learning theory appear to provide the general theoretical background for the concept of locus of control (Rotter, 1966). Citing that "as an infant develops and acquires more experience he differentiates events which are causally related to preceding events and those which are not" (Rotter, 1966, p. 2). Therefore it could be construed that as adolescents link behavior and outcome, they are reflecting cognitive growth and development by beginning to think in more critical and abstract ways.

In reviewing work on locus of control and cognitive activity, Lefcourt reported that those persons who were internally controlled sought and used information more than externally controlled people, even though they may have the same banks of information (Lefcourt, 1982).

In summary, Lefcourt (1982) points out that control is positively associated with access to opportunity. "Those who are able, through position and group membership, to attain more readily the valued outcomes that allow a person to feel personal satisfaction, . . . are more likely to hold internal control expectancies" (p. 31).

Study Description

An assumption underlying the study being reported here is that early adolescents may be more likely to participate in family decision making if they perceive themselves as being in control of what happens to them, especially if they believe that their input into family decisions may have some bearing on the outcome of the decision making process.

The primary objective of this study was to examine the relationship of early adolescents' perception of involvement in family decision making to perceived locus of control and critical thinking skills and parents' perceptions of their family decision making.

The sample and methodology included administration of a questionnaire to 939 early adolescents; 400 males and 539 females, ages 11-13 across the state of Delaware over a three year period. Ninety-five parents of the 214 third year participants served as the adult/parent sample.

Before reporting findings, it is useful the start with definitions of terms as they are used in this study. These were derived from theoretical perspective of the constructs and/or from scales and subscales within the data set.

Adolescent's Decision Making Role–The adolescent's perceived involvement in the family decision making process; includes what the adolescent believes he/she should and does have to say in family decision making.

Decision Making–Decision making involves the perceptions one has, as well as the activities and behaviors that are carried out, when making choices or selecting options and entails both the active and passive behavior(s) that are carried out to make the choice. Some decisions require advice; many require information; some require both. Some decisions are made individually; others are made collectively.

Early Adolescent–Youth ages 11-13.

Family–The adults with whom the early adolescent lives most of the time.

Locus of Control–The degree of perception of oneself as being able to personally control environmental events, i.e., internal control; or as being subject to fate, chance, or the whims of others, i.e., external control. Internal control is related to the ability to delay personal gratification while external control is related to the need to have immediate gratification (Bialer, 1961).

Parent(s)–The study subjects who, as parent or adult with whom the youth lives most of the time, completed the family form of the questionnaire.

ADOLESCENT DECISION MAKING IN THE FAMILY

Family Decision Making Strategies

Acting on the premise that the family context is where adolescents can obtain decision making experience, the teens and parents alike were asked to respond to a series of items that addressed the decision making process in their family. Adolescent reporting of family decision making strategies showed variety in the three years, with Years II and III more similar than Year I, as noted in Table 1. Adolescents and parents reported that their families often put off making decisions, and only about half of the sample, 43% to 48% considered both long-term and short-term consequences in their decision making. However, teens and parents alike who feel their families do not "put off" decision making have significantly higher critical thinking scores and are the most internal in terms of locus of control. Furthermore, teens and parents who believe their families think about both long and short-term consequences of their decisions are more internally controlled and have higher critical thinking scores than those who report their families think about only short-term consequences or neither.

The adolescents' perception of the family's internal control varied over the three years. Seventy-eight percent of first year, decreasing to 58% of third year subjects and 74% of the parent sample said their families felt they "do not have enough control over the direction our lives are taking" at least some of the time. Parents who felt their family had control most of the time had significantly higher locus of control scores than those parents who felt their family had little or no control.

TABLE 1
TEEN PERCEPTION OF FAMILY DECISION MAKING
PARENT PERCEPTION OF FAMILY DECISION MAKING

	Teen 1989 (n=318)	Teen 1990 (n=409)	Teen 1991 (n=214)	Parent 1991 (n=95)
Family...				
put off making decisions?				
Not at all	39.2%	41.3%	39.4%	27.4%
Sometimes	49.2	48.2	50.2	69.5
Fairly often	8.4	7.4	8.5	3.2
Almost always	3.2	3.2	1.9	0.0
When making family decisions...				
what does your family think about?				
Five years in the future	6.1%	9.4%	8.9%	25.4%
This year	26.2	23.7	25.8	61.3
Both	42.5	45.7	47.8	10.8
Neither	25.2	21.7	17.4	2.2
Family feel...				
don't have enough control?				
Not at all	22.4%	47.4%	42.3%	25.8%
Sometimes	50.0	41.2	44.1	61.3
Fairly often	15.4	7.9	8.9	10.8
Almost always	12.2	3.5	4.7	2.2
Decision making strategies...				
which does your family usually do?				
Get information ASAP	38.2%	51.9%	50.5%	75.5%
Change later	31.0	23.2	20.9	4.4
Make decision...available info	21.2	12.5	12.1	13.2
Wait as long as possible	9.5	12.5	16.5	6.6

There were a number of other consistencies between teen and parent data. Among others, both teens and parents reported the preferred decision making strategy of most families to be obtaining as much information as soon as possible before making a final decision. Other possible strategies were making a decision that could be changed later or waiting as long as possible to make the decision. On the other hand, a little over 12 percent of the second and third year teens as well as 13% of the parents indicated their families valued closure in decision making by their response that they preferred to "make the decision right away with the information available." (See Table 1.)

Teen Role in Family Decision Making

Teens and parents overwhelmingly agreed on the teens' primary role in family decision making. Of the 935 study subjects, 635 or 69% of the early adolescents saw themselves as involved in the family decision making process by expressing their opinion about the best solution. Most parents (79%) likewise saw their teens' role as being that of a participant in the discussion, as well as sometimes objecting to the final decision. These findings parallel the teen findings which held constant over the three years. At the same time, about 20% of the teens and only 11% of the parents indicated the teens' only involvement in family decision making was after the decision was made, when their family announced what had been decided. For 11-13 year olds, the role of participation in the discussion, and offering ideas for solutions would seem developmentally appropriate behavior. These are hallmarks of individuals whose intellectual growth and development are taking place as manifested through new abstract reasoning and problem solving abilities.

Family Members' Roles in Decision Making

The early adolescents and parents were both asked to identify family members who had specific roles and what their roles were in their family decision making. Collecting information, calling a family meeting and leading the discussion, making the final decision and carrying it out, were five of the seven roles identified by teens and parents that adults most frequently assumed.

While data revealed one adult usually assumes the leadership role in decision making, teens and parents agree that the mother most frequently gathers the information, while either the father, or mother calls the family meetings and leads the discussion. One or both parents make the final decision with one or the other parent carrying out the decision. If there was dissent regarding the decision, generally it was the children and/or mother that objected to the final decision. Data clearly showed that all family members with whom the teen lived were involved in decision making by assuming one or more roles.

While most teens were involved in the family decision making process, consistently over the three years, only about two-thirds as many teens thought they had "a great deal" to say about family decisions as those teens who thought they should have a "great deal" to say. Interestingly, more (44%) of the parents reported that they believe that their teen had "a considerable amount" to say about family decisions, while about one half (53%) of the parents indicated they thought their teen should have "a considerable amount" to say about family decision making.

In spite of the teens' perception that they have less influence over family decisions than they would like, when asked if the teens would change family decision making if they could, about one third responded that they would make no change, in other words they liked the way their family handled the decision making, i.e., "I wouldn't change anything because my family makes good decisions." Over the three years there was an increase from 29% to 54% of the teens indicating they would change the process by having more input themselves, i.e., "Include me in the decision and hope I get results," and "make my decisions and my brothers' decisions count more." Clearly adolescents wanted to have more influence than they currently have had over family decisions.

Several hypotheses were tested for relationships among the variables: adolescent perception of participation in family decision making, locus of control and critical thinking. A series of one way analyses of variances was completed.

In hypothesizing that there would be significant positive relationships among perceived locus of control, critical thinking and perceived role in family decision making of early adolescents, in all three years, it was found that the teen locus of control was significantly correlated with teen perception of participation in family decision making ($p < .001$). Similarly in year one, critical thinking was significantly correlated with adolescent perception of participation in family decision making ($p < .002$).

Another hypothesis suggested the mean locus of control scores of early adolescents who reported active participation in family decision making would be significantly different from those more passive participants. This was supported at the .0001 level of confidence.

Analysis showed that teens who feel in control of what happens to them take more active roles in family decision making, such as expressing their opinion about the best solution or gathering information to help the family make the decision. The relationship of locus of control to the teen's perception that the family encourage him/her to participate in family decision making was also statistically supported ($p < .001$). Lefcourt's position that control is positively associated with use of information and access to opportunity is strongly supported in this study.

Theoretical Model

The model presented in Figure 1 was developed by Liprie and Hanks as a result of the investigation being reported. The model builds on the classic decision making models to include issues identified as important by both early adolescents and parents.

A brief analysis of the model would indicate with any issue there is the

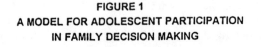

FIGURE 1
A MODEL FOR ADOLESCENT PARTICIPATION
IN FAMILY DECISION MAKING

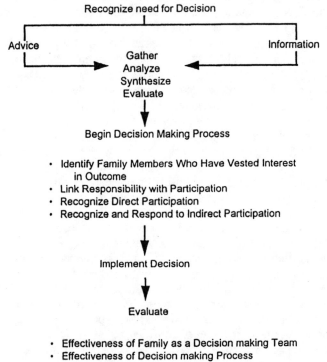

need for awareness for a decision to be made. The work reported by Settles and Foulke (1989), separates advice and information in adult decision making. This is especially applicable for early adolescents, as these youth are not emancipated and advice is a large component of their decision making. In family decision making it is important to identify all family members who have a vested interest in the outcome. It was found that those teens who were more internally controlled assumed more active roles in family decision making such as assisting in gathering information and actively participating in the discussion phase.

Indirect participation was interpreted to be coaxing on the part of the adolescent to get the parent or adult to change their mind before the final decision was made. While only 10% of the parents, approximately 75% of the early adolescents recognize this as a major part of decision making in their families. This could be viewed to reflect a power differential and might be seen as negotiation among adults of equal power.

Implementation of the decision and evaluation are components of classic decision models. Liprie and Hanks (1991) suggested that the evaluation include effectiveness of the family as a decision making team, the effectiveness of the decision making process and well as the more traditional outcome of the decision made. This model is seen as an interactive one and as presented could provide the underpinning for further investigations that deal with the interactive process itself.

CONCLUSION AND IMPLICATIONS

Results revealed that teens who feel in control of what happens to them, believe the family encourages him/her to participate in the decision making, as well as actually taking more active roles in family decision making, such as expressing their opinion about the best solution or gathering information to help the family make the decision. These internally controlled teens also feel they can coax the adults with whom they live to change their minds. This kind of coaxing may be part of the decision making process, at least from the teen's perspective, since the final decision is made after the coaxing occurs. Generally, the findings of this study support that early adolescents are eager to influence family decisions and that they are able to perform specific roles such as information gatherer and participate in the discussion. At the same time, adolescents and parents wanted the adolescents to have more influence than they currently have over family decisions. This needs to be further explored as parents and adolescents may have differing ideas as to how the teen is to have more influence.

Among the implications of these findings are the suggestions that adults with whom early adolescents interact in the home need to recognize and foster the development of skills that make adolescents more effective participants in decision making processes. Adult family members need to provide experiences that allow early adolescents to practice independent and group decision making so their perceptions of control and personal efficacy are strengthened. Adolescents who experience the adults in their lives performing "thought work: such as decision making and problem solving for them learn to respond to difficult tasks by turning to their superiors for the answers" (Claus, 1989). The family has been described as an important laboratory for decision making in which the adolescent learns about factors other family members take into account when making decisions, sees the effects of decisions made by others, learns how to communicate and negotiate in order to influence decisions, and receives encouragement to make age-appropriate choices.

The use of a model such as presented here brings our attention to the study of adolescent decision making and the family system and a need for research for average adolescents whose main challenge is simply growing up.

The demands of education and employment in the 21st century will be for skillful, critical thinkers who see themselves as effective decision makers and have a "track record" to support their perceptions.

REFERENCES

Bialer, I. (1961). Conceptualization of success and failure in mentally retarded and normal children. *Journal of Personality, 29*, 303-320.

Blood, R. O., & Wolfe, D. M. (1960). *Husbands and wives.* New York: Free Press.

Boyer, E. L. (1983). *High school: A report on secondary education in America.* New York: Harper & Row Publications.

Carnegie Council on Adolescent Development. (1989). *Turning points: Preparing American youth for the 21st century.* Carnegie Corporation of New York.

Claus, J. F. (1989). Renegotiating vocational instruction. *The Urban Review, 21*(4), 193-207.

Coleman, J. C. (1980). *The nature of adolescence.* London: Methuen.

Conger, J. J., & Peterson, A. C. (1984). *Adolescence and youth: Psychological development in a changing world.* New York: Harper & Row.

Eberhart, S. W., & Keith, T. Z. (1989). Self-concept and locus of control: Are they causally related in secondary students? *Journal of Psychoeducational Assessment, 7*, 14-30.

Foxman, E. R., Tansuhaj, P. S., & Ekstrom, K. M. (1989a). Family members' perceptions of adolescents' influence in family decision making. *Journal of Consumer Research, 15*, 482-491.

Foxman, E. R., Tansuhaj, P. S., & Ekstrom, K. M. (1989b). Adolescents' influence in family purchase decisions: A socialization perspective. *Journal of Business Research, 18*, 159-172.

Fuhrmann, B. S. (1990). *Adolescence, adolescents* (2nd ed.). Glenview, IL: Scott, Foresman, & Co.

Glass, D. C., Singer, J. E., & Friedman, L. N. (1969). Psychic cost of adaptation to an environmental stressor. *Journal of Personality and Social Psychology, 12*, 200-210.

Harrison, F. I. (1968). Relationship between home background, school success and adolescent attitudes. *Merrill-Palmer Quarterly of Behavior and Development, 14*, 331-344.

Havighurst, R. J. (1972). *Development tasks and education* (3rd. ed.). New York: David McKay Company, Inc.

Lefcourt, H. M. (1982). *Locus of control: Current trends in theory and research* (2nd ed.). Hilldsdale, NJ: Erlbaum Assoc.

Liprie, M. L., & Hanks, R. S. (1991, May). Teen decision making: A three year study. Paper presented at the meeting on Visions of Home Economics: 21 Century, Delaware Home Economics Teacher Conference, Dover, DE.

Mann, L., Harmoni, R., & Power C. (1989). Adolescent decision making: the development of competence. *Journal of Adolescence, 12*, 265-278.

Marsh, H. W., & Gouvermet, P. J. (1989). Multidimensional self-concepts and perceptions of control construct validation of responses by children. *Journal of Educational Psychology, 81*(1), 57-69.

Mehrota, S., & Torges, S. (1977). Determinants of children's influence on mothers' buying behavior. In W. D. Perreault, Jr. (Ed.), *Advances in consumer research* (Vol. 4, pp. 56-60). Atlanta, GA: Association for Consumer Research.

Naisbitt, J., & Aburdene, P. (1990). *Megatrends 2000: Two new directions for the 1990's*. New York: Avon Books.

National Commission on Secondary Vocational Education. (1984). *The unfinished agenda*. Washington DC: U. S. Department of Education, Office of Vocational and Adult Education.

Nowicki, S., & Segal, W. (1974). Perceived parental characteristics, locus of control orientation, and behavioral correlates of locus of control. *Developmental Psychology, 10*, 33-37.

Paul, R. (1990). *Critical thinking*. Rohnert Park, CA: Center for Critical Thinking and Moral Critique.

Roberts, M. L., Wortzel, L. H., & Berkeley, R. L. (1981). Mothers' attitudes and perceptions of children's influence and their effect on family consumption. In T. C. Olson (Ed.), *Advances in consumer research* (Vol. 8, pp. 730-735). Ann Arbor, MI: Association for Consumer Research.

Rotter, J. B. (1966). Generalized expectancies for internal versus external control of reinforcement. *Psychological Monographs: General and Applied, 80*(1), 1-18.

Santrock, J. W. (1990). *Adolescence* (4th ed.). Dubuque, IA: Wm. C. Brown.

Scales, P. (1990). Developing capable young people: An alternative strategy for prevention programs. *Journal of Early Adolescence, 10*, 420-438.

Scanzoni, J., & Szinovacz, M. (1980). *Family decision making: A developmental sex role model*. Beverly Hills: Sage.

Settles, B. H., & Foulke, S. R. (Eds.). (1989). *Family futures: A manual for peer leadership*. University of Delaware, Newark, DE.

Strodtbeck, F. L. (1958). Family interaction: Values and achievement. In D. C. McClelland (Ed.), *Talent and society*. New York: Van Nostrand.

Toffler, A. (1981). *The third wave*. New York: Bantam Books, Inc.

Weisz, J. R., Stevens, J. S., Curry, J. F., Cohen, R., Craighead, W. E., Burlingame, W. V., Smith, A., Weiss, B., & Parmelee, D. X. (1989). Control-related cognitions and depression among inpatient children and adolescents. *Journal of the American Academy of Child and Adolescent Psychology, 28*(3), 358-363.

Wheeler, R. W., & Davis, J. M. (1979). Decision making as a function of locus of control and cognitive dissonance. *Psychological Reports, 44*, 499-502.

Wichern, F., & Nowicki, S. (1977). Independence training practices and locus of control orientation in children and adolescents. *Developmental Psychology, 12*.

FAMILY VISION
IN CREATING THE FUTURE

Family Futures:
Possibilities, Preferences and Probabilities

M. Janice Hogan

SUMMARY. The potential for families to design their future is explored. Planning attitudes, goal setting and achievement, and preferences for role change are analyzed using data from a longitudinal sample of married couples. There is support for the concept of "family as futurists" among both husbands and wives. Educators and researchers are encouraged to further examine the futurist concepts and methodologies.

M. Janice Hogan is Professor, Department of Family Social Science, University of Minnesota, St. Paul, MN 55108.

[Haworth co-indexing entry note]: "Family Futures: Possibilities, Preferences and Probabilities." Hogan, M. Janice. Co-published simultaneously in *Marriage & Family Review* (The Haworth Press, Inc.) Vol. 18, No. 3/4, 1993, pp. 255-262; and: *American Families and the Future: Analyses of Possible Destinies* (ed: Barbara H. Settles, Roma S. Hanks, and Marvin B. Sussman) The Haworth Press, Inc., 1993, pp. 255-262. Multiple copies of this article/chapter may be purchased from The Haworth Document Delivery Center. Call 1-800-3-HAWORTH (1-800-342-9678) between 9:00 - 5:00 (EST) and ask for DOCUMENT DELIVERY CENTER.

KEYWORDS. Family futures, Husbands, Wives, Goals, Planning, Gender roles, Attitudes, Change

What is the future of families? In U. S. public opinion polls, respondents are concerned about the future of families. They paint a relatively pessimistic outlook for families but they express a positive outlook for their own family. This contrast between "our family" and "other families" lead me to an inquiry about family future perspectives. It is important that we talk to families about their own future–their goals, their preferred roles, and their resources. Do they envision successfully reaching goals and do they see changes that make them confident about their future? I argue that we need to engage family members in the discussion of their preferred future to establish a closer relationship between their perceived world and our understanding of it.

This provocative question about the future of families has been frequently addressed by social scientists. Their predictions of trends are based on extrapolated demographic data such as rates of marriage, fertility, divorce, remarriage, cohabitation, and extended family households. One of the underlying assumptions is that actions in the past create the future. In addition to demographic data, family researchers have conducted studies to examine the correlation of two or more conditions that may assist us in predicting trends. For example, what happens to marital satisfaction if there is more shared responsibility between the husband and wife for family work–across stages of the family life cycle, income levels, and cultural heritage.

Futurists, members of a professional field committed to predicting the future, inquire about the possibilities, preferences, and probabilities. Technology, human potential and information processing are central to their work. Futurist methodologies include scenarios, normative forecasting, futures wheels, extrapolation of demographic data, correlational trend analysis and surveys about preferences and probabilities of possibilities. They seldom focus on families–rather they scan the larger environment for new technological developments and trends in economics, energy, organizations, and the general population. Their time frame is often ten or more years into the future.

I believe that some futurist concepts can be helpful in probing family futures. Over a decade ago, I attended World Futures Society Conferences to learn more about their approaches and to co-present a paper on communicating the future in families.[1] At the same time, I wondered if families really want to think about the future, if they have goals, and if they want change. If "yes," the application of futurist concepts and methodologies could assist in the generation and transmission of knowledge about the alternative future(s) of families.

The questions about whether families think about and plan their future will be explored with a combination of futurist and family resource management concepts and survey data. Based on family resource management theory, the families that plan their future perceive themselves as decision-makers, capable of setting and reaching goals, and having some control over resources. In contrast, we theorize that some families are focused on their present family needs and they consciously avoid serious thinking about the future. They adjust to outside forces, perceive little control over most events in their lives, and use a constrained planning style.[2]

FAMILY AS FUTURISTS

Do family members have futurist attitudes? Are they optimistic about the future? Do families believe in planning for the future? To explore the idea of "family as futurist," I turned to the futurist literature for concepts.

Russell Ackoff (1974) proposed four types of planning attitudes: preactive, interactive, inactive and reactive. He proposed that these attitudes are mixed in varying proportions in people. Like primary colors, they can be mixed in many different ways to provide a wide range of secondary attitudes.

In his conceptualization, those with interactive and preactive attitudes believe in change but each has different views about the nature of the future. *Interactivists* believe that they are capable of controlling a significant part of the future and its effect on them; they want to invent flexible options and design a desirable future. They are not willing to settle for the past, the present or follow the trends into the future–they believe that intervention is required to improve the quality of life. *Preactivists* believe that the future is essentially unknown but that they can prepare to control its effect on them; they predict and prepare for the future using the best information for problem solving. They are reformers and seek change within the system.

In contrast, *inactivists* are satisfied with the present and seek stability; conformity and cohesion are desired so they do not seek new opportunities. *Reactivists* actively resist change by trying to recreate the past; they are nostalgic about the "good old days" and value tradition.

Are family members more likely to have the attitudes of interactivists, preactivists, inactivists or reactivists? Using the Ackoff conceptual framework, a random sample of 235 husband-wife couples[3] were surveyed about their planning attitudes in 1983. Data from a Likert-type scale[4] indicated that over 40 percent of the husbands and wives held the attitudes of interactivist planners. They identified with the statements: "We can make the next few years just about anything we want," "I like trying new ideas, planning new goals." Most respondents in the study indicated some support for these futuristic attitudes, albeit weak support (only about five percent rejected them).

Inactivism and reactivism attitudes were held by some husbands and wives but they received low or no support by the majority of respondents. In fact, about 60 percent of the wives and husbands responded that these attitudes were "not at all" their beliefs. Examples of non-futurist scale items are: "We ought to return to the good old days," "I have tried planning and it usually does not work," and "I do not believe in planning; I just take one day at a time."

There was partial empirical support for Ackoff's typology. Using factor analyses, three types were found among the wives: inactivists, reactivists, and futurists (a combination of interactivism and preactivism attitudes). Husbands also held the same futurists' attitudes as wives. A second group of husbands' attitudes included a combination of inactivism and reactivism statements–a single nonfuturist factor. Based on this survey, we can conclude that futurists (interactivism and preactivism attitudes) and nonfuturists (inactivism and reactivism attitudes) are present in families. Wives made a distinction between reactivism and inactivism planning.

GOAL SETTING IN FAMILIES

If families are to plan their family future, they will need to set and achieve some goals. This is a basic premise in both the futures and family resource management fields of study. We asked the wives and husbands in the study, "If you could have one goal successfully reached in the next few years, what would it be?" All but three percent responded with one or more goals. Approximately 100 different goals were stated by respondents–goals related to familism, financial security, employment, health, education, religion, housing, leisure or community environment.

The wives most often stated a goal related to familism–more closeness, love, unity or success in their marriage and family life and for their children to be happy, successful, and develop their potential. Next in order of frequency, wives' goals were about employment, financial matters, leisure, education, and housing.

Husbands stated financial goals most frequently. They are seeking financial independence, economic security, and are saving for retirement. Changing employment and pursuing leisure goals were a distant second and third in frequency for husbands. Familism, with special emphasis on goals related to their children's happiness and success, and housing goals were tied for fourth in order of frequency.

In 1989, 161 couples were interviewed again.[5] Over five years had lapsed and many of these families were in a different stage of the family life cycle. The priority of goals for wives and husbands had shifted in priority. Wives cited financial goals most frequently, followed by leisure, familism and education goals. Husbands continued to identify financial goals most frequently but leisure goals replaced employment changes as the second most frequent goal in 1989. Familism moved from fourth to the third most often cited goal for husbands.

It is interesting that in 1989 about 20 percent of wives and husbands had a goal related to improving family relationships, including happiness and successful outcomes for their children. For wives, the percentage was the same as five years earlier. However, the number of husbands with this goal had doubled from 1983 to 1989. This may be an indication of a priority shift for both husbands and wives–increased familism for husbands and increased economic goals for wives.

Of particular interest in the follow up study was whether the earlier goals were reached. Most of the husbands (62%) and wives (57%) indicated that the specific goal, restated by the interviewer, had been reached. About 20 percent of the husbands and 25 percent of the wives were still working on their goal; some had dropped the goal (8%). Others had modified the goal, sometimes due to a lack of resources. Again in 1989, about three percent of the respondents had no goals. On the basis of this longitudinal survey data, we concluded that most families set and achieve goals.

PREFERENCES FOR ROLE CHANGE

Futurists talk about preferences as important in designing the future. Do wives and husbands have preferences for change that would help them design a better future? We chose to study gender role change preferences. Which roles do husbands and wives prefer to have more responsibility, less responsibility and to stay the same–the nurturing role, resource management, provider role, housework or kinship exchanges? Wives and husbands were surveyed separately about their role preferences in 1983 and 1989.[6] What role changes, if any, did the wife want for herself and what role changes, if any, did she want her husband to make. Parallel questions were asked to husbands. We wanted to learn about changes that spouses preferred for themselves and for each other in order to determine if there were any patterns of preferences among married couples.

One of the most encouraging findings is that most of the couples have a complementary preference pattern (about 60%).[7] That is, the direction and the amount of role change that the husband and wife desire are similar. Frequently, she wants him to take more responsibility for understanding the emotional needs of family members, comforting upset family members, finding ways to reach family goals, and seeing and solving problems, and he also prefers to have more responsibility for these nurturing tasks. And, if he wants her to take less responsibility for housework such as preparing meals, cleaning, and planning how the housework gets done, she also prefers that change. However, he does not usually want more responsibility for housework.

One can ask about the probability of husbands taking more responsibility for nurturing and for housework. Because of their preferences for increased responsibility for nurturing tasks and because more husbands listed goals centered on familism, the probability of change in this area of roles would appear to be a reasonable hypothesis.

In general, wives want more role change than husbands. However, in many families there is agreement that husbands' level of family role responsibility should increase more than that of wives. Husbands prefer to have more change in their own roles than they desire in their wives' roles; wives agree. I suggest that this preference pattern of change in gender roles could lead to a better designed future for families.

But do husbands and wives discuss their family roles? In the 1989 follow up study, husbands and wives were asked how often they discussed responsibility for family roles. About 25 percent of the wives and 20 percent of the husbands responded that they discussed their roles often. Most respondents indicated that they occasionally discussed roles (57% of husbands, 52% of wives). Hopefully these discussions assist in an improved pattern of sharing role responsibilities.

Role change preference patterns do change over time. In this longitudinal study, both wives and husbands decreased their preference for role change for themselves and for their spouse over time. However, wives still want more role change than husbands. Couples in the younger stages of the family life cycle preferred the highest levels of change and those in the later stages with adult children or no children living at home preferred little role change.

CONCLUSION

There is support for the concept of "family as futurist" in this exploratory study of married couples planning attitudes, goal setting and achievement, and preferences for role change. Most husbands and wives have planning attitudes compatible with futuristic planning in their family. They indicate that they like to try new ideas, plan new goals, and believe that they can make the next few years just about anything they want. Most of these families could articulate goals and reach them. And, they have preferences for changes in their family gender roles that appear to be possible.

Many questions remain about the family as futurist. Do "mixed" planning styles, where one spouse holds futuristic attitudes and the other spouse believes in retaining their traditions, result in few common family goals? What are the planning attitudes and goals of step-families, single parent families, and families from different cultural backgrounds? What type of planning styles do children observe and use? Does too much planning and too much change combine to create stress and to engulf family members in conflict? How can too much change be avoided and a workable balance of change and stability be achieved? Over time do planning attitudes change and become more futuristic? How do family members work out their shared realities of the future?

Professionals committed to family research, teaching, and therapy may think of themselves as futurists. If so, you may want to consider discussing the questions above with your students, clientele group and colleagues to further understand the potential of families inventing their future.

AUTHOR'S NOTE

This paper is a revised version of a presidential address given at the National Council on Family Relations 52nd Annual Conference in Seattle, November 1990. Research was supported by the Minnesota Agricultural Experiment Station Project 52-42.

Appreciation is expressed to former doctoral students who assisted in the research design and implementation: Jo Anne Craven, Patricia Spaulding, Merideth Hanson, Judith Rommel, and Catherine Solheim.

NOTES

1. Jo Anne Craven, Ph.D., recommended that we submit an abstract for a presentation, "Communicating the Future in Families," at the World Futures Society's Fourth General Assembly on July 21, 1982 in Washington, D. C. There were a number of concurrent sessions but our presentation was the only one focused on family as futurists.

2. See C. Buehler and M. J. Hogan (1980 & 1986) for theory and research on planning styles of single parent families. The planning measure was not based on futurist concepts. However, there was empirical support for planning focused on creative strategies for reaching goals and another factor that centered on resource planning. Some of the single mothers and fathers used a constrained planning style—a sense of reactivity, constraint, and a present time orientation.

3. The sample of married households was randomly selected from the Minneapolis-St. Paul seven county metropolitan area. Both the husband and wife were required to participate in separate telephone interviews (20-30 minutes) about their preferences for changes in gender roles and adequacy of resources. Response rate was 62% of eligible couples. See Patricia Spaulding (1988) for information on sample selection and demographic data.

4. An eight-item scale was developed to reflect the four planning attitudes. Respondents were asked if each of the statements described them exactly, a lot, somewhat or not at all.

5. Attempts were made to contact all of the 235 couples five years later. Letters were sent to them offering a $10 incentive for completed telephone interviews. Only those couples who were still married to the same partners as in phase one were interviewed; widowed (N = 11), divorced and separated (N = 13) were excluded. Data were collected from 68% of the eligible couples. For detailed information on sample characteristics, see Solheim (1990).

6. A 16-item scale was developed. Reliability coefficients using Cronbach's Alpha for "Preferred Role Preference for Self" was .78 for husbands and .74 for wives in 1983 and .80 for husbands and .71 for wives in 1989. For "Preferred Role Preference for Spouse," reliability coefficients were .78 for husbands and .85 for wives in 1983 and .72 for husbands and .83 for wives in 1989. See Solheim (1990) for details of scale scoring and couple analysis.

7. See Spaulding (1988) for cross sectional analysis of the 1983 data and Solheim (1990) for analysis of the longitudinal data.

REFERENCES

Ackoff, R. (1974). *Redesigning the future: A systems approach to societal problems*. New York: John Wiley and Sons.

Buehler, C., & Hogan, M. J. (1980). Managerial behavior and stress in families headed by divorced women: A proposed framework. *Family Relations, 29*, 525-532.

Buehler, C., & Hogan, M. J. (1986). Planning styles in single-parent families. *Home Economics Research Journal, 14*, 351-362.

Solheim, C. (1990). *Couples' change in family work: A longitudinal study of preference patterns, resource adequacy perception, and conflict style*. Unpublished doctoral dissertation, University of Minnesota.

Spaulding, P. (1988). *Perception of family work roles: Couple preference patterns, contextual variables and resource adequacy*. Unpublished doctoral dissertation, University of Minnesota.

The Family Peace Connection: Implications for Constructing the Reality of the Future

Charles Lee Cole

Martha A. Rueter

SUMMARY. In this chapter, we describe how family professionals can help families promote world peace. We focus on efforts that promote internal peace, peace within individual family members based on positive self-esteem, a strong sense of mastery, and effective interpersonal skills. Families play a central role in establishing and promoting the internal peace of their members and family professionals can aid families in the development of the skills and abilities necessary to create internally peaceful members. The paper begins with a description of how internally peaceful family members influence the level of world peace. We also discuss the importance of developing constructive approaches to dealing with change, a constant threat to internal peace. Finally, we offer practical suggestions for how family professionals can help families capitalize on their fundamental position as internal peace builders.

Charles Lee Cole is affiliated with the Department of Human Development and Family Studies, Iowa State University. Martha A. Rueter is affiliated with the Center for Family Research in Rural Mental Health, Ames, IA.

[Haworth co-indexing entry note]: "The Family Peace Connection: Implications for Constructing the Reality of the Future." Cole, Charles Lee, and Martha A. Rueter. Co-published simultaneously in *Marriage & Family Review* (The Haworth Press, Inc.) Vol. 18, No. 3/4, 1993, pp. 263-277; and: *American Families and the Future: Analyses of Possible Destinies* (ed: Barbara H. Settles, Roma S. Hanks, and Marvin B. Sussman) The Haworth Press, Inc., 1993, pp. 263-277. Multiple copies of this article/chapter may be purchased from The Haworth Document Delivery Center. Call 1-800-3-HAWORTH (1-800-342-9678) between 9:00 - 5:00 (EST) and ask for DOCUMENT DELIVERY CENTER.

263

KEYWORDS. Peace, Family interaction, Internal peace, World peace

Efforts to promote the development of a more peaceful world have been many. Examples of the most visible attempts include the formation of treaties to reduce the number of nuclear arms, pursuing campaigns to alleviate world hunger, or calls for gun control and improved police protection. Each of these attempts to promote peace, sometimes called external peace efforts, focuses on changing the character of the *world* (Turner, 1988). By creating a more peaceful world, the hope is that people's perception of the world will become more peaceful, and in return, people themselves will act in a peaceful manner. There also exist what one might call internal peace-making activities (Turner, 1988). This type of peace-making begins with *people*. The attempt is to reduce the fear and anger in people's lives by helping them improve such things as their interpersonal skills, self-esteem, and sense of mastery. People who feel good about themselves, according to advocates of this approach to building peace, possess a peaceful internal self that induces them to perceive the world in a similar light. Since violent actions would be incongruent with a peaceful perception of the world, internally peaceful people are not likely to engage in conflictual or aggressive interactions. Instead, these people pursue actions which result in harmony between people and nations. In this way, internal peace expands outward to enhance world peace (Montessori, 1972; Turner, 1988).

Considering the ingredients of internal peace, self-esteem, a sense of mastery, and interpersonal skills, it appears families play a central role in establishing and promoting internal peace. In this capacity, families can make an immense contribution to world peace. Further, family professionals can help build world peace by using their expertise to aid families in the development of the skills and abilities necessary to create internally peaceful members. This paper, therefore, intends to describe how family professionals can help families promote world peace by improving their internal peace-making. We begin our task with a description of how internally peaceful people influence the level of world peace. This is followed by a discussion of the importance of developing constructive approaches to dealing with change. Building on these basic concepts, we offer suggestions for how family professionals can help families capitalize on their fundamental position as internal peace builders.

INTERNAL PEACE IN RELATION TO WORLD PEACE

If we are to help families promote peace, we must share some agreement on the basic processes by which internal peace generalizes to world peace and meaning of some important concepts. This section, therefore, describes the process by which we believe internal peace has its effect on world peace. We also use this introductory discussion to define several important concepts including the perception of reality, peace and what we call the world.

Figure 1 illustrates the way internally peaceful people can influence world peace. This model depicts the interplay between internal peace, the perception of reality, and world peace. It also shows the influences of change and the choice of coping responses upon one's perception of reality. As Berger and Luckman (1966) note, our perception of reality is formed through shared events that shape our assumptions about the world in which we live. Exchange of information among the members of a group in the form of dialogue serves to validate and confirm our perception of the world. In this sense, reality is perceived in the minds of the individuals engaged in the dialogue. Once formed, the perceived reality is held as a tentative explanation of the multiple phenomena occurring in that world at any one point in time.

A shared event that shapes our assumptions about the world might be a change in some element within the world. This new, unfamiliar phenomena to some extent nullifies the previous perception of the world. If the previous reality is sufficiently voided, established explanations no longer suffice. The lack of an explanation for current phenomena causes an upset in the level of internal peace felt by members of the world. The resultant distress motivates the deployment of coping mechanisms in order to make accommodating adjustments in the perception of reality. The coping

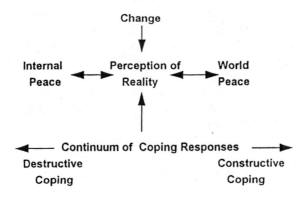

Figure 1. Change and World Peace

mechanisms chosen could range from constructive to destructive. Constructive coping serves to build the level of internal peace which in turn improves the peacefulness of one's perception of the world. Destructive coping, on the other hand, breaks down the level of internal peace and promotes a negative view of the world. Thus, if the response to a change is a constructive one, the resultant improvement in the perception of reality helps to bring about a greater level of peace in the world. A destructive response and its concomitant negative world view serves to reduce the peacefulness of the world (Staub, 1988; White, 1984).

WORLD PEACE DEFINED

Definitions of world peace vary. Some define peace as the absence of war. Others view peace as the existence of certain harmonious conditions (Montessori, 1972; Turner, 1988; Wagner, 1988). Those conditions include, for example, cooperation, concern, justice, empathy and understanding. Under the former definition of world peace, one could exist peacefully while possessing very little internal peace. Such is the case, for instance, when people feel oppressed although they do not rebel. Harmonious peace, on the other hand, requires internal peace. Few people can interact in a truly harmonious manner without both feeling good about themselves and possessing certain interpersonal skills. Since the focus of this chapter is upon the development of internal peace and the subsequent outgrowth of things like cooperation, justice, etc., it is evident the world peace we look for is a harmonious peace.

The world we live in can also be defined in several ways. A world can be as large as planet earth or as small as one's own body. In this chapter we will discuss three specific worlds or what we might call subworlds. Those three worlds comprise: (a) the international world, represented by the earth; (b) the national world, or the country where one lives; and (c) the familial world, one's family. Each subworld contains a whole host of elements which influence its level of peace. We identify four broad categories of elements. The economic elements and the ecological elements are primarily in the realm of external peace efforts. Bringing about greater peace by operating upon the social elements and the emotional/spiritual elements calls for internal peace efforts. The following descriptions further define these four categories of elements.

THE ECOLOGICAL ELEMENTS OF PEACE

The ecology of peace is defined as respect for the fragile balance of ecosystems necessary for survival of the planet Earth and all its inhabitants. Peace is dependent upon a balance of ecosystems that mutually reinforce and sustain each other. The environment of the planet Earth requires vigilance to ensure that clean air, water and soil are protected and readily available. A balance of natural environment must be maintained among rain forests, deserts, mountains, oceans, rivers, lakes, prairies, and marshes so that wildlife and flora may be balanced. At a national and international level, this means living interdependently and cooperatively sharing resources such as water and fuel that may be more prevalent in some regions than others. On the more micro level, the family creates an environment that is both responsive to the larger ecology that they live in and is instrumental in shaping and altering the ecological balance. The choice of where and how to live affects that family's interaction patterns and linkages to the outside world through community activities and cultural norms. Furthermore, the ecology of how the family embeds itself in the larger community structure influences and is influenced by the family.

THE ECONOMICS ELEMENTS OF PEACE

The economics of peace is defined as responsibly managing the investment and utilization of material and service resources. Similar to the ecology of peace, the economics of peace is based upon the assumption that interdependence of cooperation is preserved. Economics is the chief regulator of resources that determine the quality of life for individuals and families, communities, regions, and international organizations (Kresse, 1990). At the macro level, the international exchange of resources and distribution of goods and services provides access to needed commodities that provide a basis for interdependence and cooperation between nations. At the societal level, the distribution of resources is filtered down to the local communities and interconnects the various regions of the society. At the micro level, the family shares and manages economic resources which determine the quality of life they enjoy.

Up to now, we have focused on external forces that contribute to developing and maintaining peace. Now we will shift to two categories of internal elements. These are elements that come from within the individual and permeate out to the larger social systems of society and beyond to the international relations of the global world.

THE SOCIAL ELEMENTS OF PEACE

The sociology of peace is defined as the process of creating and maintaining a social structure that is based upon interdependence and cooperation. Peace is a by-product of how we are socialized and interact with others. On an international level, it is a function of increased social interaction where people get to know each other as human beings who share a common concern for survival and life. The diversity of life circumstances, cultural values and traditions provides an opportunity for increased growth and understanding that helps each side to see how much we need each other and various perspectives each contribute something unique to our common understanding of the nature of life and the meaning of peace. On a national or societal level, this means getting beyond the 'we-they' mentality of stereotypes associated with racial and ethnic groups or social class characteristics. On a family level, it means interacting peacefully and cooperatively with the other members of one's own family and mutually working to resolve conflicts and manage differences in a respectful manner that appreciates the contributions of each family member's unique life perspective and perception of reality.

THE EMOTIONAL AND SPIRITUAL ELEMENTS OF PEACE

One of the premises of this chapter is that for peace to be lasting, it must begin with an emotional and spiritual commitment to live in harmony with nature and those who share the planet Earth with us. Thus, the emotional and spiritual elements of peace include the development of an intentional life-style that can only come from being clear about one's own values and valuing existential commitments that give meaning and purpose to life. Diversity and valuing the unique contributions of each person is encouraged. There is a sense of connectedness and a permeating belief that others can be and should be trusted and appreciated. Being at peace with oneself means feeling less threatened and/or intimidated by the actions of others. The family is the natural arena for cultivating and maintaining the elements of emotional and spiritual peace. Thus, within the family system, this means family members encouraging family members to be comfortable with their feelings and intentions about life and to express themselves freely and openly.

The character of any world is determined by the relationships formed among these many elements. Ideally, the elements form balanced relationships such that the needs of all are met in an atmosphere of peaceful harmony. The optimal balance is different from one world to the next; no two worlds are likely to find the same best relationships.

The way each world meets its elemental needs is influenced by numerous factors (Leichter, 1979). Culture, history, politics, finances, environmental context, for example, are all potent factors. Idiosyncrasies in these areas prompt differences in perceptions of reality among nations, families, and individuals. With their varied perceptions, each world comes to deem particular approaches to establishing harmony appropriate while other avenues are rejected as ineffective or inappropriate. In other words, the optimal balance among the elements of a particular nation or family is self-determined and self-evaluated.

As family professionals, we cannot dictate elemental balance. What we can do is help families develop the skills necessary to bring about a peaceful balance between the demands of the social, ecological, economic and emotional/spiritual aspects of their existence. The most crucial skills to be developed are those that enable families to constructively cope with their constantly changing worlds. Developing skills to cope with change is important for two reasons. First, change is an ever present challenge for families (Mancini & Orthner, 1988), and second, change poses a constant threat to internal peace (Staub, 1988).

To illustrate the impact of change upon families, consider the Smith family. The Smith family is moving from middle childhood into the adolescent stage of their family career. For them, the changes taking place within the social elements of their family seem most salient. For instance, the children are beginning to make more demands for independence. This insubordination among the children leads the Smiths to begin to perceive their family in a different manner. Prior to the change, the Smiths saw themselves as a family whose parents were in control and whose children were reasonable and predictable. Now the kids seem moody and rebellious, and the parents feel at loose ends. The internal peace of family members is threatened.

The Smiths could undertake any number of responses to this new situation. They could chose responses that help to maintain or even improve the balance within their familiar world. By taking this constructive route, family members will likely come to believe that current events are manageable. Thus the Smiths preserve the ingredients of their internal peace (self-esteem, mastery, interpersonal relations, etc.). Further, their perception of their family will remain at least somewhat positive, and the overall peace of their familial world will survive. If, on the other hand, the Smiths respond with destructive coping, conflict, rather than balance, will likely ensue. As a result, the level of internal peace in family members deteriorates, and the Smiths begin perceiving their family in a disturbing light. As these perceptions become stronger, the Smith family finds engaging in hostile interactions easier and easier.

THE IMPLICATIONS OF A CONSTANTLY
CHANGING REALITY

This example shows that change itself does not destroy peace. In fact, as will be discussed later, change can furnish an impetus to augment the level of peace. Remember, however, that change results in an upset in internal peace. When families respond to the upset with destructive coping, change becomes a threat to both internal and world peace. An understanding of how change can pose a constant threat to peace sets the stage for a discussion of internal peace-making efforts.

As described earlier, people develop a perception of reality that explains current phenomena. If a change takes place, the current explanation no longer suffices. Staub (1988) points out that people have a tendency to respond to unexplained or strange situations with fear. He further explains that fear leads to anxiety and a valuation of the familiar as good and the strange as bad. This good/bad valuation allows the development of a superior/inferior orientation with strangers as inferior and those holding to the familiar among the superiors. Fear also motivates a selfish desire to maintain familiar surroundings. Having defined the familiar as good and the defenders of the familiar as superior, protection of the familiar through aggressive and violent acts is easily justified (See also de Rivera & Lairdo, 1988; MacMurray, 1962; and White, 1984).

Putting this sequence of events in the context of the Smith family, we see the potential for the following scenario: Recall the unfamiliar situation. The Smith children have become moody and rebellious while the parents feel at loose ends. In their prior reality, the Smith parents were seen as in control of family matters and the children were reasonable and predictable. The Smiths could easily perceive their new situation as strange and subsequently taint their internal peace with fear and anxiety. If so, they stand a good chance of undertaking destructive coping mechanisms with actions that attempt to recall the prior reality and thwart future changes. For example, the parents might define their past position of controlling family matters as the good and the current demands for independence made by the children as bad. The parents, the upholders of the familiar, come to view themselves as superior and in right in oppressing and restraining the children who are threatening the good. Inevitably, the children rebel and conflicts arise within the Smith family. Each new fracas leads to an escalation in conflict and no one in the Smith family feels either internal or familial peace.

Long ago Montessori (1972) described the results of this sort of "war between parents and children" in terms of its effect on people's perceptions and on overall world peace. According to Montessori, parents who oppress their children create children who themselves become oppressors. This happens because oppressed children, like all oppressed people, long for the power to overcome their oppressors. Both children and parents carry their desire for superiority with them into all realms of their interactions. By doing so, the inherent conflict of oppressor-oppressed relationships spreads to many other worlds. The resultant growth of antagonism hampers any attempt to bring about a harmonious balance between a world's elements and thus acts to break down world peace. Put in terms of the Smith family, the Smith children came to believe, like their parents, that one copes with disrupted internal peace by establishing a position of superiority and resisting all attempts at change. Since change is a continual part of all worlds, the Smiths lived in constant fear and in constant conflict with the elements of their worlds.

Constant change need not, however, pose a threat to world peace. In fact, change could be viewed as an opportunity to promote peace. The Smith family could chose to answer the children's calls for independence with actions that welcome yet guide these signs of growing maturity. For example, the parents could respond to their children's growing demands for independence by encouraging them to take greater responsibility for managing their own money and make greater choices regarding clothing and wardrobe. They might also encourage autonomy and independence by helping children understand the importance of clear boundaries in the form of members' rights to privacy. This could be exemplified in family members knocking before entering each others' bedrooms or bathroom. The parents could take further steps toward encouraging their children's growth by staying out of sibling quarrels and letting the children learn to work out their own solutions to problems through negotiation and compromise. In essence, the Smith parents could avoid the "war between the parents and the children" (Montessori, 1972) by creating an atmosphere that encourages the expression of individual differences and promotes a genuine respect for differences among family members with regard to values and interests.

Constructive responses such as these strengthen internal peace by building the children's self-esteem, sense of mastery and interpersonal competence. The parents also benefit. They enhance their own self-esteem and mastery and broaden the scope of their interpersonal skills to encompass effective interaction with adolescent children. When people improve these aspects of their personal lives, change becomes less fearful and inner peace becomes more durable. With their improved level of inner peace, the Smiths will likely perceive their family in a more positive, peaceful light. As a result, the Smith family experiences increasingly tranquil relations even in this most tumultuous period in their family's lifetime. Further, by avoiding the bitter fall-out of oppressor-oppressed relationships, this family brings internal peace and its concomitant improvements in interpersonal relations into other spheres and thus helps to build overall world peace.

The importance of the role families play in the building of world peace, therefore, cannot be overstated. Families provide the primary arena for the establishment of internal peace. By their manner of living, families provide the experiences that determine the level of self-esteem, mastery and interpersonal skills seen in their members. The manner in which families live is a reflection of their value system. When, for example, family values encourage respect for individual differences and a sense of responsibility for living interdependently in the larger society, the families help to sensitize their members to being world citizens who care for others throughout the world and also help them to feel a part of the world as a whole.

Attributes such as these form the basis of the mind set family members take with them as they move into wider spheres of interaction. Individuals with a peaceful, interdependent mind set will likely pursue harmonious relationships. Those with a fearful, power seeking disposition will likely engender oppression and conflict (Montessori, 1972; Turner, 1988). Figure 2 illustrates the way family peace and internal peace enhance one another and radiate outward to influence world peace. As one can see, internal peace and family peace support one another. A peaceful family is likely to be a family of internally peaceful members and vice versa. The family's peace, essentially a reflection of the synergistic quality of the individual members' interaction together, permeates outward to influence peace on a broader scale. Thus, a nation replete with peaceful families will likely be a peaceful nation, and since peaceful nations tend to pursue peaceful international relations the world itself becomes more peaceful. In short, the family is the key link between individual peace and the peace within society. In that context, the family is the primary agent for promoting world peace.

THE ROLE OF FAMILY PROFESSIONALS IN ENHANCING PEACE

Family professionals have the opportunity to play a key role in influencing the direction of reality change that will work toward the enhancement of peace. Family social scientists with backgrounds in sociology, human ecology, recreational and leisure services, etc., have a unique

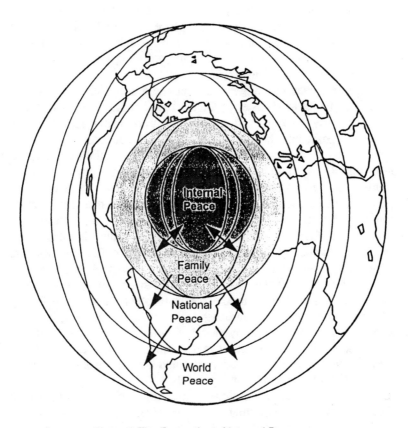

Figure 2.The Emanation of Internal Peace

sensitivity to the nature of the fragile balance of the larger ecology of the physical environment and the family system's social ecology. Advocating family responsibilities on a micro level helps to sensitize people to the need to maintain a vigilance for sustaining and protecting the environment so that the quality of water, air, and soil will be abundant. It also means sensitizing people to the power of families in working to protect the environment for the needs of wildlife and human beings alike.

Family professionals working in the economic sector have the skills necessary for helping families develop a financial plan and manage their resources effectively so they can share their resources meaningfully and invest in socially responsible ways that do not allow or encourage the exploitation of people from either this society or other societies. It also means encouraging and educating families of the value of investing in socially responsible areas that promote peace without feeding into the military-industrial complex and the concomitant arms race that has resulted from the military-industrial complex spiraling out of control for nearly 50 years (Perruci & Pilisuk, 1971).

Family professionals working in churches and other religious institutions have the opportunity to minister to the spiritual needs of families. In this capacity, they play a key role in shaping the moral conviction of people about war and peace and they can encourage the enhancement of efforts to promote and sustain the lasting peace that comes from within the individual. Likewise, family psychologists, marriage and family therapists, etc., work with families as a group and as individuals on issues related to the emotional well-being of its members. It is increasingly common to have family therapists being called upon to help family members deal with uncertainty and loss and the fear of war and destruction of the planet (Ptacek, 1988). Family therapists and family psychologists, etc., can help family members learn to communicate more effectively and build an atmosphere where trust and cooperation permeate the family system. In this sense, the self-esteem of family members can be enhanced and each member can sense the feeling of belonging and cohesive interdependence while maintaining separate identities and personal autonomy (Maslow, 1968; Satire, 1972). Family therapists and family psychologists can help empower families by sensitizing them to their potential to be advocates and active agents that promote peace on both the micro and the macro levels.

Family social scientists, sociologists, and others have the potential to use their expertise in group dynamics, social change and management of social conflicts to help families and larger systems within and between societies in respectfully working out their differences without the need of violence and war. Family life educators have the opportunity and expertise to teach family members how to live interdependently with respect for differences. In this sense, they have the unique opportunity to do preventive work to teach conflict resolution and communication skills. The consequences of teaching interpersonal skills for growth, promote behavior with increased levels of esteem for self and others and a true sense of security and satisfaction with life. In Maslow's (1968) view, if people are self-actualized and have the sense of belonging and security that can come from healthy family relationships, they will feel safe and have high levels of self-esteem and feel loved and appreciated. When this sense of security and esteem is fully developed, the threat of change and loss are manageable and people are better equipped to tolerate diversity and to appreciate differences. This in essence becomes a foundation stone upon which peace can be achieved, managed, and sustained.

Family professionals have the opportunity to help family members feel physically safe and secure and promote a healthy environment that protects the ecology of the ecosystem and valued elements such as clean and pure water and air. Teaching families about what they can do to help clean up the environment so they can be assured of having clean air and water is a part of family life education. Without a safe environment, the health of family members is constantly subjected to life imperiling circumstances which increase the level of family tensions and thus erode the possibilities for achieving and maintaining peace and harmony. Family professionals can play a role as advocates for peace. This advocacy role would address environmental and economic issues that threaten the stability and security of the family.

Families need to have access to economic resources to develop a quality of life that enables family members to live and grow. Enough money to purchase and maintain adequate housing, transportation, food, clothing and health care needs to be available to maintain a quality of life. Families need to have high quality education in order to prepare to live in an increasingly complex interdependent world. Knowledge of the diversity of cultural experiences within life and the development of a genuine respect for all people of the world is essential in order to build a lasting world peace.

Family members need to have opportunities to develop meaningful social relationships with others both within and outside the family. In order to feel secure and build a safe environment in which peace can be nurtured, people must feel connected and have a sense of belonging to the larger world of which each of us is a part. Family professionals need to teach family members the requisite interpersonal competence skills for interaction with others. These skills would include such things as communication, problem solving, conflict management and resolution, etc. Furthermore, family members need to feel centered and clear in their own values. A sense of spiritual connectedness that grows within the individual members of the family is essential in order to develop a lasting peace. Being emotionally mature and having a firmly developed sense of self esteem with a highly differentiated capacity to think and act both independently and in concert with others are outcomes.

CONCLUSIONS

In this paper, we have argued that peace is a process that is interwoven in the fabric of social relationships and springs forth from the inner nature of the spiritual and emotional aspects of the human condition. Peace is fragile and must be nurtured by encouraging the development of autonomous, whole persons who are highly differentiated and possess the capacity to be interdependently connected to the whole of humanity. The planet Earth is rich in resources that can help sustain life but they need to be zealously protected and nurtured.

Families are the vital link in building a world of peace because it is in families that people chiefly learn to cooperate and develop unique differences and strengths that become central to the survival of the family and the planet. In the model we developed for this chapter, it is clearly pointed out that the reality of peace is changed from within the perceived reality of family members. We have demonstrated how peace within the family has four interrelated elements (ecological, economic, social, and emotional/spiritual) that interweave through the family to the nations and on to international sectors of human relations.

The role of family professionals needs to be expanded to include the peace-maker trainer and advocate. In this capacity, family professionals must ask what their responsibility is to the larger society and to the world at large in terms of the development of structures that create opportunities for building a lasting peace. Who else is in a better position to develop the skills for cooperative living among family members? Who else is in a better position to encourage families to generalize their skills to life within the greater society?

There is also a need for research in the area of peace and the family that will no doubt have critical implications for the development of social policy. Future researchers need to explore the processes by which families resolve conflicts and manage differences and to investigate the linkages between the familial processes and the societal and global processes. We need more research on cooperation and the nature of interdependence within the family, as well as between societies and nations. More research could also be done on the nature of social structural components that contribute to the development of peace and cooperation within the family as well as between groups at all levels.

REFERENCES

Berger, P. L., & Luckman, T. (1966). *The social construction of reality.* New York: Doubleday Press.

de Rivera, J., & Laird, J. (1988). Peace fair or warfare: Educating the community. *Journal of Social Issues, 44*, 59-80.

Kresse, J. (1990, June). *Economic conversion to a peace-time economy.* Paper presented at the meeting of the Groves Conference on Marriage and the Family, Big Sky, MT.

Leichter, H. M. (1979). *A comparative approach to policy analysis: Health care policy in four nations.* Cambridge, MA: Cambridge University Press.

MacMurray, J. J. (1962). *Person in relation.* Atlantic Highlands, NJ: Humanities Press.

Mancini, J., & Orthner, D. K. (1988). The context and consequences of family change, *Family Relations, 37,* 363-366.

Maslow, A. (1968). *Toward a psychology of being* (2nd Ed.). New York: Van Nostrand Reinhold Company.

Montessori, M. (1972). *Education and peace.* (H. R. Lane, Trans.). Chicago: Henry Regnery Company. (Original work published in 1949.)

Perruci, R., & Pilisuk, M. (1971). *The triple revolution: Emerging social problem in depth.* Boston, MA: Little, Brown & Co.

Ptacek, C. (1988). The nuclear age: Context for family interaction. *Family Relations, 37,* 437-443.

Satire, V. (1972). *People Making.* Palo Alto, CA: Science and Behavior Press.

Staub, E. (1988). The evolution of caring and nonaggressive persons and societies. *Journal of Social Issues, 44,* 81-100.

Turner, J. (1988). *The arms race* (2nd ed.). New York: Cambridge University Press.

Wagner, R. V. (1988). Distinguishing between positive and negative approaches to peace. *Journal of Social Issues, 44,* 1-15.

White, R. K. (1984). *Fearful warriors: A psychological profile of U.S.-Soviet relations.* New York: The Free Press.

The Heart of the Story:
Mythology in Service
of the Past, Contemporary,
and Future Family

Kris Jeter

The story is "something lived in and lived through, a way in which the soul finds itself in life."

–James Hillman (1975)

LOOSE ENDS

Once upon a time, there was a creative, intelligent, and wise woman named Scheherazade. She and her husband, the sultan, lived in an erratic world with an unknown, and certainly an unpredictable future. The sultan, in his awesome position of power, felt particularly insecure. When his brother accused not only his wife, but all women of infidelity, the sultan sought a scapegoat to blame for his lack of ability to deal with the future.

Kris Jeter is Principal, Beacon Associates Ltd., Inc., Newark, DE.

[Haworth co-indexing entry note]: "The Heart of the Story: Mythology in Service of the Past, Contemporary, and Future Family." Jeter, Kris. Co-published simultaneously in *Marriage & Family Review* (The Haworth Press, Inc.) Vol. 18, No. 3/4, 1993, pp. 279-301; and: *American Families and the Future: Analyses of Possible Destinies* (ed: Barbara H. Settles, Roma S. Hanks, and Marvin B. Sussman) The Haworth Press, Inc., 1993, pp. 279-301. Multiple copies of this article/chapter may be purchased from The Haworth Document Delivery Center. Call 1-800-3-HAWORTH (1-800-342-9678) between 9:00 - 5:00 (EST) and ask for DOCUMENT DELIVERY CENTER.

He followed his brother's lead and chose the woman closest to him, Scheherazade. The sultan decided that in the dark of the night, when the future was most frightening, the unknown most terrifying, he would kill Scheherazade. Then, and only then, would he feel better.

Each evening for 1,001 nights, Scheherazade told the sultan a different story with the specific intention of distracting the sultan from his murderous plan. After 1,001 nights of telling legends and myths, although the state of the world was still erratic, the sultan felt more secure. For 1,001 nights, the sultan had been told ancient stories of how the universe was ordered. After hearing stories of how earlier human beings and their leaders had acted in times of chaos, he felt assured. The sultan was now confident in his ability to face the unknown future, or at the very least to make a story of his failures and successes and to continue onward with courage and a mature heart.

We today live in an erratic world, whose pace seems extraordinarily rapid and where the destination is exceptionally unimaginable. We professionals who study the family, may, at times, feel like the sultan. However, we can learn from the role model of the creative, intelligent, and wise Scheherazade. We can immerse ourselves in the ancient stories of the family to learn how to identify the patterns that connect human kin over time and space.

The family is conceptualized by researchers as a social group. The social group may extend empathy, intellect, intimacy, and reason. The social group may also inflict abuse, betrayal, chaos, and dismay.

In this essay, I define the family as a mythological story. The mythological story is the stable family–in humans since the beginning of the collective unconscious as well as the conscious memory. The task for professionals working with families is to facilitate the conscious choreography of the telling of contemporary and ancient stories with true experience and cathartic emotion. With the declaration of the family as the mythological story, the deeper meaning of life can emerge and instill faith in the future.

The remembrance and association of incidents in the mythological family with those of the day-to-day social family reveal significant patterns of connection that transform the mundane to the meaningful. When we preface the experience of our families as social units after the phrase, "Once upon a time," rapport with the human family over time is felt. Psychological vigor and wholeness emerge.

However, without the context of the human story, insecurity pervades our being. Information is readily available in democracies. News is broadcast, often as it is actually happening. During the Gulf War, government, as well as military officials, often admitted the source of their information was CNN Cable News! People worldwide stared at the screen, searching for friends and kin amid bombings, scud attacks, and troop movements, hoping minute by minute for the future of their family, and perhaps of the human family. The very unsoundness of the war reverberates from the satellite circling the earth down to our home "entertainment center."

The primary commercials that accompany the major network nightly newscasts–advertisements for backache, constipation, headache, and upset stomach–directly depict our apprehension of the present and fear of the future. Our insecurity is held taut, tense, tight within our bodies!

The sultan is alive and functioning today. Every 15 seconds in the United States, a person is abused by a member of her or his social group. During and immediately after the live television transmission of major football and soccer games, wife-abuse dramatically escalates; boys' play becomes men's war that must be won, at the stadium and at home (Steimetz, 1992).

Activation of the creative, intelligent, and wise storyteller, Scheherazade, is required. News told within the phrases, "Once upon a time" and "They lived happily ever after," could promote a rich context of meaning, empathy for the mortal condition, charity for humanity and universe, hope for the present and future.

PURPOSE

In 1974 Don Johanson found the nearly complete skeleton of a female hominid who lived three million years ago. The hominid was designated after a Beetles' song playing at the archaeological site, "Lucy in the Sky with Diamonds" (Johanson & Shreeve, 1989). Today, Lucy's biological typology is at the trunk of virtually all human biological family trees.

Johanson (1992) has often been asked, "When did we become human?" This is Johanson's answer. "It's my hope that we will become human. I think that we have evolved so quickly, we have diverged so rapidly from the natural world that we lived in two million years ago when our ancestors were living along that ancient lake in Olduvai, that technologically we are very advanced, but biologically, psychologically, philosophically in many ways we still have a long way to go before we really become human."

The family as a social group has likewise developed too hastily to provide a harmonious relationship. The family as a mythological story can be the archetype of balanced interaction for the future social group. The mythological story within the human unconscious is the staunch, steady family. Giving voice to present-day experiences and ancient stories assigns value to life and belief in the future. Perceiving and telling stories allows them to unfold and blossom forth into wisdom for facing the future with hope and fortitude.

What stories will assist the family as a social group to advance psychologically and philosophically, to become fully human? How does the expression of mythology succor and hinder the human family? What is the presentation mode of mythology that best serves the family of the future? Will a return to and a development of cosmogony and creation myths assist the family of the future to enter a world far beyond our imagination?

THE EXPRESSION OF MYTHOLOGY

*Once upon a time, in fact, just last week, at a nearby golf course, a gentleman played 18 holes of golf and returned to the club house to clean up. He emerged from the showers to find that his clothes were missing and all he had was one small, white, locker room towel! The gentleman could have put the towel around his waist, **but then there would have been no story!** So instead, the gentleman placed the towel around his head and walked out of the locker room, through the lobby, to his car.*

In the lobby, four women who were playing cards looked up to see the gentleman's departure. The first woman said, "My heavens, I wonder who that is." The second responded, "He is not my husband." The third agreed, "He is not my husband." The fourth added, "Well, he is not even a member of this club!"

–Joke
Juanita Kreps, U.S. Department of Housing Secretary, 1978

The need to tell stories–true and legendary, seriously and humorously–of the human experience is age old. The hyoid bone needed for linguistic capacity has been found in a Neanderthal grave in the Carmel Caves in Israel dating 120,000 to 35,000 years ago (Speirs, 1989). Since then, humans have given expression to their adventures, dreams, emotions, and sensual perceptions. They have even elaborated upon the original story, "putting the towel around the head," so that there would indeed be a story worthy of remembering and retelling.

The stories are living entities, having been repeated in the oral tradition, portrayed in art, and written as literature. With each telling, the images were recreated, the community was re-inspired. Stories were told to the rhythm of the beating heart–the grinding of grain, spinning of yarn, and tanning of leather. Today, we are privileged to have a legacy of legends and myths to arouse, provoke, and stimulate our individual selves, and moreover our social organizations, such as families, work places, communities, and nations.

The oral transmission of mythology over generations by kinfolk, especially to children at bedtime, is healing. When a child has heard parents tell myths of the cosmological parents, for both the story receiver and teller, the unity of the family over time is felt. The unconscious becomes an ever available protective harbor for understanding the family as a social unit. The dreamworld spawns an extended family of allies and guides available throughout life.

Likewise, the all-sensory transmission over generations of the myth by artists is restoring. For instance, in Indonesia, indigenous children and adults are always in attendance, sitting in the back, looking through the fence, grouped at entrances, during the performances of shadow plays and traditional dances staged daily for tourists. Moreover, every village in Bali has a community center for the celebration of each holiday (of which there are many) with the traditional arts. The 2750 year old epic, *The Ramayana* (1962), provides role models for marriage. Every male is Rama and every female is Sita. With every reenactment of the 3000 year old epic, *The Mahabarata* (the Great Story of the Bharata Family), known also as *Jaya* (Victory), different views of family conflict are integrated within the psyche. Restoration of the psyche occurs through myth.

The word mythology is derived from the Greek, *muthos*, which means word or speech. Mythology is the embodiment of the divine in words; it chronicles for a social community the origins, foundation, intentions, essence of the world. Mythology is the paradigm for action, enlightenment, sagacity, sapience for the cultural group. Mythology may be conveyed by action, art, location, or word.

Logos also means word; *logos* allows, indeed, even promotes controversy regarding the profane world. However, mythology is sacred story, the word accepted and presented as true.

Mythology gives each social group a sense of ancestry, identity, pride, purpose, strength, and uniqueness. I recollect the first time my family's pedigreed old English sheepdog, Baron, reared in the Rocky Mountains on a ranch with cattle and herding dogs, went to a gathering of old English sheepdogs and owners at a park in Denver, Colorado. Baron was overjoyed to see that he was not alone, that he had kin, if you will, a common cosmogony and shared story with other large, long haired, gleeful canine beings.

Yet, it is precisely the mythology that enhances differences between people that also separates the world's peoples and keeps us from becoming fully human. Eli Wiesel (1980, p. 21) writes passionately, "Jewish life was destroyed and blood was shed because of silly yet dangerous myths that were spread by so many enemies who had nothing in common except their hatred of the Jewish people." Irvin J. Borowsky (1991), Ellis Rivkin (1984), and others examine varied editions of the Christian Bible and are dismayed at the inaccurate translations. It was the political authorities, not Jews, who feared the possible political ramifications, not the spiritual credences of the charismatic teacher, Jesus, who ordered him crucified. Gershom Scholem (1971) has concluded that varied translations can only challenge the reader to "Go and learn Hebrew!"

Are literal words and mistranslations dismissing particular individuals, disrupting harmonious family relationships, inciting political warfare, keeping us from becoming fully human? Each mythology, each religion has suffered the ravages of mistranslation. For instance, John Temple Bristow (1988) found that when he translated the writings of Paul from English back into Greek, the Greek words and inherent messages were quite different between this translation and the original ancient manuscripts. Bristow believes that inaccurate translations of the Christian Bible have discouraged the full participation of women in their expression of Christianity. Furthermore, Elaine Pagels (1979) suggests, "It is the winners who write history–their way." Originally, there were many varied Christian beliefs, organizations, and texts, as evidenced by writings suppressed by the bureaucratic, masculine, orthodox church.

At times, literal quotes that do survive politics and time vie with the ways of the spirit. Words and actual practice may clash. Temples honoring Rama are the sites of recent violent clashes in India. On the five hundredth anniversary of the landing of Christopher Columbus on the shores of the Americas, there is a challenge to confront the discovery mythology with the re-writing of that history. The story, old or revised, is transforming of the human condition and spirit.

Some persons perceive the universality of the human condition within an age old story and act accordingly. For instance, during World War II, residents in French Protestant LeChambon and surrounding villages, located in the midst of a Roman Catholic territory in France, chose to shelter Jews from the Nazis. They immediately empathized because of two reasons. First, they and their ancestors were survivors of centuries of religious persecution. More important, they were reared with a knowledge of the Hebrew and Christian Bibles and reverence for ancestors ranging from their immediate parents back to Eve and Adam. Each host had a strong internal tranquillity and wholesome self-esteem. Enormous energy was expended to provide hospitality, yet, vitality was and is drawn from each person living according to one's personal belief system (Pierre, 1990).

Does the expression of empathy come from a two-fold belief in a universal story and a direct experience of prejudice? Can a story alone raise consciousness and change behavior? Researchers have a fertile ground for study; perhaps the story told below could be part of a research design on the development and actualization of active empathy, a skill of upmost value for families of the future.

In "The Legend of the Madonna," Ben Horovitz (1976), Yiddish author born at the turn of the century, humanized Mary of the Christian Bible and re-addressed the Marian miracles of Medieval Europe into a hope for equity. Realities are separated into polar opposites: the intellectual and the illogical, the practical and the idealistic, the physical and the emotional, the material and the celestial, the mortal and the divine, Christian and Jewish. Within the context of the story, these varied realties are presented as a unified whole. The listener's mind set is challenged to recognize the harmony of the universe despite, and, in fact, because of the multiplicity of options. Anything is possible within the orchestration of seemingly contradictory ways of being. I present "The Legend of the Madonna," a story of two families, with an updated ending. In my experience, each telling furthers empathy between Christian and Jewish listeners.

Once upon a time, Maria Dolorosa (in Latin, *the Grieving Mother*, a carpenter's wife, lived in a spacious home and was dressed in ornamental garments and rich jewelry. Maria Dolorosa felt uncomfortable because these were not clothes to which she was accustomed and so many people had only thin cloth.

Nearby lived Haya-Dina. (In Hebrew, with its varied, rich possibilities, Haya-Dina can mean *a Rare, Sweet Well of Water for Wild Animals* or *Living in Judgement* (Ilsen, 1992; Metzger, 1989). Haya-Dina, a Jewish widow of a judge, decided to go begging to obtain a dowry for her daughter, Miriam, betrothed to marry Aaron, an orphaned yeshivah student. Alas, money was scarce and no contributions were to be had.

As Haya-Dina was walking, a storm darkened the entire sky. Soaked, Haya-Dina took refuge in the only available shelter, a Christian church. Haya-Dina sat in the rear and a lovely young Jewish woman, who spoke with the compassion of a rabbi's wife or mother or a Rebbetsin, sat next to her and said, "Good afternoon." Haya-Dina responded with joy to see another Jewish woman in the Christian church.

The Rebbetsin said she was in search of her son. Haya-Dina said she was begging for a dowry for her daughter, Miriam. The Rebbetsin said that her name was Miriam and that she had un-needed jewelry that she would gladly give for the dowry of her namesake. Perhaps, she hoped, God would grant her finding her son. The storm ended, the women hugged, said blessings for the health and mission for each other, and took leave.

Haya-Dina bought Shabbos clothing for her daughter and her fiancee and also food for the Shabbos table. Joyful at their bounty, they went to the evening service. Abruptly, the service was interrupted by soldiers reading an announcement about a theft in the church and threatening immediate banishment of all Jews from the land. Calmly, Haya-Dina related how Rebbetsin Miriam had presented her with a dowry for her namesake. It was decided that all Jews and Christians would gather on Sunday at the church for a public return of the items by Haya-Dina.

On Sunday, the Jews were placed at the end of a parade, following the clergy, royalty, and Christians carrying banners, crosses, and relics. In the church, as Haya-Dina was returning the items, Rebbetsin Miriam, Maria Dolorosa, Mary, the mother of Jesus, walked from her throne toward the congregation, lifted her head and spoke. "I gave the dowry for my name sake, Miriam. It is hers."

The apparition of Mary profoundly changed the community. In my ending to this story, the similarities of spirituality and the human condition were recognized by both Christians and Jews. Each person was now free to engage in a chosen livelihood, to live in housing of any district, to worship according to the heart's path, to abide with neighbors in peace and harmony. Indeed, a new cosmogony was available for all.

COSMOGONY

The original myths of creation, cosmogony, may provide themes, contain ideograms, express contexts that can assist the family of the future to enter a new world. The conscious extension of cosmogony can assist the family as a social group to advance psychologically and philosophically and to co-create a world for the empathetic human. The word, cosmogony, is derived from the Greek words kosmos, the world, and gignesthai, to be born (Neilson, 1955, p. 601). Cosmogony is the study of the birth of cosmos, the balance, order, pattern, and symmetry of the world.

A number of themes are common in cosmogony (Bolle, 1987).

1. Mesopotamian mythology influenced monotheistic Hebrew, Christian, and Muslim creation stories. From absolute non-existence, the sky deity meticulously establishes and forms the earth.
2. Indian and Near Eastern mythology indicates that order arises from

disorder, the cosmos soars out of confusion. Chaos, often a dragon or water, is the energy that can be transformed into creation.

3. Myths from Africa, Greece, India, Japan, and Polynesia declare that the earth is born from the cosmic egg. Days, seasons, and years are coordinated with the fertilization, incubation, hatching, and caretaking of the global egg.
4. Babylonian, Egyptian, and Polynesian cosmogonies express stories that after the earth was initially formed, world-parents impersonally entwine. Without sexual consummation or parental interest, humans emerge. Dogon mythology tells of a cataclysmic schism and the hero who illumines society with sunshine and purpose.
5. Native American and other cosmogonies consider the earth to be the omnipotent womb, with dominion over all life. In a timely fashion, seeds grow upward from Mother Earth's core. At each internal layer of Mother Earth, the seeds deliberately amass, synthesize, unify before emerging from her body to be met by the masculine sun.
6. Some North American cosmogonies indicate that varied animals attempt and finally one succeeds to plunge into the chaos of water and fetch one grain of dirt. This molecule becomes the basis of the earth's formation. The earth-diver hero intends to institute a better world than the original deity.

Rudolf Otto (1923) in *The Idea of the Holy* identifies ideograms as images that manifest between thought and behavior. The ideograms of cosmogony deepen our understanding of the creation process.

1. Primordiality is the original essence of origins. The earliest entity may be the apathetic chaos or a cherishing womb.
2. The egg shell breaks; life bursts forth from the earth's womb. Ruptures occur between chaos and cosmos, confusion and systematization, passivity and energy, attachment and autonomy. Tension exists between dependence, independence, and interdependence.
3. Dualisms and binary poles facilitate power struggles, such as light and dark, day and night, death and life, deities and humans, dry and wet, female and male, good and evil. Each generation endeavors to achieve more than their ancestors and the possibilities for their progeny.
4. Ethics, the guiding principals of a society, may be rooted in the cosmogony. The mythology of origins often outlines norms for allocation of assets, respect of nature, confirmations and restrictions of behavior, practices for the soul, potentials for the spirit.

The balance, order, and pattern of the family are reflected in cosmogony. Family origins may be uncaring or loving. Ruptures and polarities provide opportunities for conflict management and growth. Social norms for behavior emerge from cosmogony. A re-creation of cosmogony by families, can assist the social group to, with compassion for the world as a human family, steadily approach the future with renewed ethical, psychic, and spiritual capacities.

Rollo May (1975) has analyzed mathematician, Jules Henri Poincaré's theorizing process to isolate the steps in the creation process. During periods of intense labor, a person may relax. Either during serenity or the time just between activity and placidity, a succinct point of wisdom appears. Enlightenment abruptly, blatantly, lucidly, indeed, forcibly penetrates a theory to which one is attached. The recipient immediately trusts this gift of knowledge. The human tapping of the creative source involves the ideograms of cosmogony: primordiality, rupture, dualism, and ethics!

Love making especially illustrates the creation process. A child may be conceived during sexual intimacy; vitality may be realized in exquisite intimacy, sexual or non-sexual. In an enduring relationship of abiding love, rapture bursts forth within the interplay of embracing and separating, entwining and disengaging, encircling and emancipation, fusing and releasing, uniting and liberating.

Dominican priest, Matthew Fox (1991) has defined the characteristics of creation and described the conception and activities of Creation Spirituality. The actualization of his theory is currently being experienced by families and communities around the world. The practice–based on the creation process and ancient philosophies–translates across cultures and religions and assists social groups to face the future with dauntless courage and progressive action.

Creation is a continual process of birth and death. The dominion and duration of creation is all encompassing. "It is the spiraling, dancing, crouching, springing, leaping, surprising act of relatedness, of communing, of responding, of letting go, of being." It is the first grace and every grace that has and ever will bless life. The word, spirituality, is derived from the Hebrew word, *ruah*. "To be spiritual is to be alive, filled with *ruah*, breathing deeply, in touch with the wind." The core of Creation Spirituality is the benevolence of creation.

Creation Spirituality has been practiced by aboriginals on each continent. In the Hebrew Bible, texts by the Yahwist or J author or those on prophecy and wisdom present a life enhancing cosmogony. Jesus' familiarity with these writings is evident in the Christian Bible; the parables sing of the equity of life. Matthew, John, Luke, and Paul draw on ancient creation centered concepts within their works.

Renaissance mystics lived, taught, and wrote of a view of all life as sacred. These include Francis of Assisi, Hildegard of Bingen, Julian of Norwich, Mechtild of Magdeburg, Meister Eckhart, Nicolas of Cusa, and Thomas Aquinas.

Matthew Fox recommends the use of four paths to find the Creator. For each path, he presents a commandment.

1. "Thou Shalt Fall in Love at Least Three Times a Day." On the Via Positiva, the positive path, the miracle of all life is venerated. The recognition of a flower, meditation upon a squirrel, being in awe of a child is active affirmation of creation.
2. "Thou Shalt Dare the Dark." On the Via Negativa, the negative path, we re-enter the primordial womb, listen to the stillness, look at the obscure, accept the agony, feel the void, dance with the shadow, brood while allowing life to pass.
3. "Do Not Be Reluctant to Give Birth." On the Via Creativa or creative path, we meet, grapple, acknowledge, integrate, and designate our archetypes. Together, we co-create the dream and the myth.
4. "Be You Compassionate As Your Creator in Heaven is Compassionate." On the Via Transformativa, the human with empathy for all life forms works for harmony and stability between opposing powers, even fairness for all. Kind, tenderhearted response to inequity is made.

Matthew Fox has observed that a human, family, and community who journey upon all four paths can consciously recreate the present and future. The cosmogony of joy, meaningful suffering, genesis, and equity best serves the social family throughout time.

Medieval Sufi author, Mohiudin ibu el-Arab, wrote eloquently about the life led in constant wonder and love in which the human consciously creates a cosmogony that best serves the human family. Ibn El-Arabi was called by Arabs Sheikh el-Akbar, the Greatest Sheikh. In the West, the Sheikh was entitled Doctor Maximus. His stories have guided Sufies, Christians, and others through the ever developing future of the past eight centuries. The words speak of the unity of humanity possible through love.

My heart can take on any appearance. The heart varies in accordance with variations of the innermost consciousness. It may appear in form as a gazelle meadow, a monkish cloister, an idol-temple, a pilgrim Kaaba, the tablets of the Torah for certain sciences, the bequest of the leaves of the Koran.

My duty is the debt of Love. I accept freely and willingly whatever
burden is placed upon me. Love is the love of lovers, except that instead
of loving the phenomenon, I love the Essential. That religion, that duty,
is mine, and is my faith. A purpose of human love is to demonstrate
ultimate, real love. This is the love which is conscious.

–Mohiudin ibu el-Arab

THE HEART OF THE STORY

The center, the heart of ancient maps depicts the known world, often
with an accuracy deemed remarkable by scientists of today who work with
the aid of computers and satellite transmitters. Yet, there was and will
always be the unknown. The original cartographers would indicate the
unknown world around the edges of the map with pictures of beasts,
creatures, dragons, and leviathans. Four large mouths blow forth the power of the wind, at whose mercy the mariner arrives or departs, sails or
drifts, lives or dies. The uroboros, the snake coiled, tail in mouth is poised
in the unknown, bidding and discouraging the explorer of the future.

We are all explorers of the future. Marie-Louise Von Franz (1972) has
written that "wherever known reality stops, where we touch the unknown,
there we project an archetypal image." As we attempt to bring the family
as a social group and a mythological story together into a portrait, the
archetypal image of the heart demands recognition. As we endeavor to
paint a picture of the family of the past, present, and future, the heart
challenges to be acknowledged. From the beginning of life, the newborn's heart presents itself as the primary link to the family of origin.

A fetus within the boundaries of the womb of a healthy woman is
generally tranquil. The soon to be born infant feels the heartbeat and love
of the mother. This experience of serenity is soon disrupted. The shock of
birth shoves the newborn to an agitated, aggressive, apprehensive universe. Upon being thrust into the world with a questionable future, life
becomes a struggle where needs are not always met. The baby responds
automatically. Through trial and error, the infant develops a set of genetically coded behaviors to satisfy needs as well as desires.

The infant requires love to thrive. In many indigenous cultures, the
baby accompanies the mother, skin to skin, throughout the first year of
life. In some societies, breast milk may be available on demand for several
years. The child brought up in security without fear will name everyone in
the vicinity as a friend. The child not tainted with prejudice loves purely.
Love, the innate, inherent impetus blends, harmonizes, orchestrates the
child's world. Adults can learn of unprejudiced love from the child.

Conscious human development and family living require venturing and exposing oneself to existence in unlimited, non-confined, boundless space and time; confronting the apprehension and suspense of the inconstant, obscure, and unpredictable. The task is to appreciate the individual human journey with certitude, confidence, and conviction; constantly to rediscover and cherish the flowering of the heart's garden. Bold fortitude allows one to choose to suffer the acute agonies of uncovering, revealing one's integral self, rather than dully accepting the dim pangs of the unconscious.

Love is an inherent stimulus, a synthesizing energy of human nature. With the development of the intellect–historically and individually–this primal faith has been replaced by a cognitive function called "falling in love." Choice of a partner in the West today is most often dependent upon falling in love with a projected concept of perfection, instead of an actual person, in order to satisfy individual needs and complete personal deficits.

After falling in love and losing one's equilibrium, the titillating excitement and romantic allure descends. The anticipated outcome is not realized. A partner may feel ensnared in a pit and either may sit entangled, emotionally dying; maltreat and oppress the partner; or bolt, quickly taking leave to repeat the process again and again. Infatuation and falling in love can be avoided by asking the universe to utilize the allurement appropriately and permit the relationship to evolve without the appeal of enchantment.

Love requires each person to be whole and complete. Lovers do not alter each other. Rather, they champion, forgive, and restore the partner. The energy of love can enter the open heart. Unconditional love comes from the Universe through spiritual practices, such as prayer and meditation, rather than a casual act of falling in love with a human. Love from the Universe is stable and counteracts fears of abandonment, loss, separation, and rejection. Love given freely without motive, claim, or requirement attracts the delights, marvels, and wonders of life.

By accepting the challenge of being in a loving relationship, one effectively enrolls in a school to learn lessons on listening to one's partner and communicating from one's own depths. Cessation of defense mechanisms and offensive assaults can occur through self observation and mindful attention. Expression of inner strength allows one to refuse to accept abusive and destructive behaviors and to return to the natural flowering of unconditional love from the Essential. In marriage, the incessant choices of each individual are choreographed into a dynamic dance. A committed relationship is one in which both persons feel the need for and clearly express shared communication, forgiveness, negotiation, and renegotiation. The union is strengthened by a joint intention to be of service to the world and the Universe.

Every human behavior is viewed as either an expression of love or a request for love. The act of forgiveness or "selective remembering" (Williamson, 1992) removes barriers between persons and promotes peace within the giver. Separation and divorce that occur after both partners have mastered the lessons of their unique relationship allows each to practice forgiveness and engage in different, and perhaps even deeper forms of love.

Love requires the duality of two individuals. Domination and submission indicate a shallow relationship. The deepest manifestation of love permits the autonomy and sovereignty of each while uniting them in felicity and pleasure. Each partner retains and expresses her or his simplicity, purity, fullness, and wholeness. The couple is strengthened by the sharing, reciprocity, and honoring of differences. They are best friends. In veritable love, there is no attachment to the beloved, the process, the outcomes, and love and liberty are merged. Thus, love becomes a surge of abundant delight in each other's natural and unique expression of soul and spirit.

The age-old stories of Isis and Osiris, Isolde and Tristan, Layla and Majnun, Radha and Krishna, Sita and Rama, plus The Song of Songs (Falk, 1990) tell of the love of a woman and man. Or, do they relate the journey of the soul to the universal source of love? Could love be a gift of creation? Can a couple consciously request bountiful love and give daily thanks to the Creator for the relationship with their human beloved on earth, which assists them in their realization of their celestial Beloved above?

The recitation of these age-old love stories has inspired generations of families across cultures to face the future with hope and courage. The storyteller creates cosmogonies applicable for each audience. The storyteller ennobles the virtue of love and exalts action of the heart by giving life to stories in which the family and the community enter a world far beyond all imagination, a future, and emerge victoriously. Deeds of the heart advance, psychologically and philosophically, the family as a social group toward becoming fully human.

THE ACTUALIZING HEART OF THE STORYTELLER FOR THE FUTURE

[As humans] advanced in knowledge and control over nature, the mystery and godhead of things natural faded into science. Only the

mystery of life, and love that begets life, remained, . . . utterly unex-
plained, and hence Aphrodite keeps her godhead to the end.

Jane Harrison (1922, p. 314)

PROLEGOMENA TO THE STUDY OF GREEK RELIGION

Love is creation in its purest sense. Through the giving of unconditional love, the vitality of love in the recipient is inspired. A metamorphosis occurs within the loved one and may well multiply. Love is the ultimate purpose of life. Bureaucratic, economic, governmental, legal, and social situations have been transformed by non-violent strategies and love, such as those furthered by Mahatma Gandhi. "Unconditional love combined with clarity of perception and spiritual strength form a trinity of experience which could become among the greatest gifts we might offer ourselves and others on this planet–and may very likely serve as our passport into the next millennium" (Chaudhuri, 1987, xvii).

Gerald G. Jampolsky (1979), Marianne Williamson (1992), and other teachers of *A Course in Miracles* (1975), believe that the opposite of love is fear. Most recently, Williamson has eloquently in personal appearances and in writing applied the theory to world conditions. "An entire world has been built on fear. Fear's system will not be dismantled in a moment. We can work on ourselves every moment that we live. The world is healed one loving thought at a time. Mother Theresa said that there are no great deeds–just small deeds done with great love."

As the world thrusts into the future, at a pace more rapid than ever before in history, we are being presented with many opportunities to transform fear into love. The storyteller, especially, propels the hearts of listeners toward loving actions that heal families and societies.

The storyteller brings humanity, imagination, intellect of the soul, passion, a three-dimensional to the blueprint of the myth. The inspired life force is freed from within the heart of the narrative. For the length of the performance, the storyteller is, in essence, saying–reiterating and repeating–"I love you." The beauty and continuity of the world are extolled. The audience is enjoined to suspend their belief systems, to return home at the story's end knowing that there is a greater power. Listeners are challenged to take that which they adore and treasure into the future.

Meanwhile, the dedicated storyteller acknowledges contributions of ancestral kin–familial, professional, as well as, universal. Sacrifices are made to the Muses in hope of tapping into their intonation of the memory of the past, present, and future. Ancient Hellenes called this expanded memory, truth, and all art was judged for its veracity. The discipline is practiced diligently in order to meet the Muses, to know the archetypal myth, to be the great exponent who carries the story to another age. From this age, other storytellers will carry the myth still further into a future age.

Storytellers utilize theatrical cunning to urge the audience to emotion, empathy, and social action. In Hellenistic and Greco-Roman theater, the most distinguished dramatic, scenery, stage, and Thespian device, *Deus ex machina*, was employed to introduce the deity. When calamity and catastrophe are at their height, and there is only despair for the future, a deity arrives in a spectacular exhibition of power to redeem the present and ensure the future. The deity is constantly present, and yet only comes when remembered and addressed.

In the master storyteller, William Shakespeare's (1969) last complete work, *The Tempest*, shipwrecked humans vie for power. Prospero, the legitimate duke of Milan undermines the rivaling contenders with futile excursions about the island in pursuit of utopian banquets. With the assistance of Ariel, a spirit of the air, and Caliban, a monster of the earth, the Tempest appears. The only thing humans cannot control is the Tempest. The Deity is indispensable; remembrance by humans of the Deity is required. Only with the strength of Providence, can the Tempest be handled and the gentle, beautiful world restored. Prospero forgives his opponents and conflict is gracefully managed.

This is the message of the story that has and will continue to assist the family as a social group to advance psychologically and philosophically. Praise of the omnipotent deity, the source of love, allows the disunity of the world to be met with mercy and positive social action.

For instance, when we are faced with loss, we find the events difficult to accept. We try to understand a mystery we cannot quite comprehend. We tell the story again and again. We use art, music, poetry, ritual, and story–metaphor–to grieve and slowly return to family and community life knowing that life as we know it will never be quite the same. The Muses believe that humans are frustrated about their mortal state; they sympathize with the human desire to be immortal by dancing to the triumph of nature and tranquillity over chaos. Through the Muses and deities, humans can experience a reprieve from their adversity and grief.

Likewise, when we are charmed, captivated, engaged, engrossed, absorbed by a story, it becomes an exemplary pattern, an archetype for our own life story. We tell and retell it to ourselves, and perhaps others. It becomes our theology in which we have faith.

In an erratic world, where the present is blared out in twenty-four hour news cable television and radio so that the future comes rumbling forcefully in disconcerting blasts of shock, we each are challenged to be our own storyteller, our own Scheherazade. With love, we can recreate our own cosmology, merging the family and society as social group and as mythological story.

Psychologist/philosopher Jean Houston (1992) has recently discussed therapy with survivors of incest. She questioned if some therapists are voyeurs listening to the client tell the story of abuse again and again. Houston described her work with functioning adults who experienced trauma and abuse as a child. The clients, through the process of guided imagery, become the guardian angel to themselves and their child. Whenever the negative past is remembered, the guardian angel enters and rescues the child, taking the young one to the land of delight. Here rich sensory experiences are presented that are larger than the trauma. The child is loved and empowered. The images of abuse are driven out. The field of memories is replaced by a field of dreams.

Houston indicated that a large number of persons speak of having inadequate parents. The mythological family can be recreated. The client can fully imagine a mother from the stage of the client's birth to adulthood. A wonderful mother would be seen with great concreteness–gardening, playing ball, telling stories, urging debate on world events. A marvelous father would also be imagined with precise clarity–cooking, helping with schoolwork, singing songs, asking for opinions on family life. Likewise, other family members could be completely developed as ideal characters within the mind set.

The family takes on an autonomous life and relates in a healthy, humorous, nourishing fashion. The story is told and retold, drawn, sung, enacted; all parts of the body sense it and the message becomes integrated within the heart. Houston reports, "The lousy history becomes a dream. In the brain mind system, there is not that much difference between the dream and reality. Therefore, the old realty becomes the bad dream and the new reality becomes the good dream." Love from the family as a mythological story conquers inadequate care from the family as a social group.

The retelling of the new story of the family can become a potent force for the transformation of the social order. Family units, legally established or created by the individuals themselves, are telling their stories and organizing around central issues related to their lifestyles and social concerns that affect all families. They are extensively using the various media such as television and radio broadcasting and organizational techniques learned from social revolutionaries and labor unions. Getting into the streets on marches to educate or confront the body politic on issues such as drug use, drunk driving, or destruction of the environment is a common occurrence.

Families and their kin-members are not passive or controlled, but are active, creative and are influencing large scale bureaucratic systems. They are taking charge of themselves and have become a potent force for the transformation of the social order. Family organizations will continue to flourish over generational time and will be the dynamic force in the twenty-first century (Sussman & Jeter, 1990).

With the energy and powerful expression of love, individuals and families can make a difference in the local and national world. Three social actions are described below which portray the actualizing heart of the storyteller of the present, for the future. Each project was started by a lone person responding to, telling the story of a family drama. Each action project has grown to affect in a positive way the life course of countless humans, families, and communities.

THE BANNER PROJECT

In the 1980's, Pecki Witonsky, a suburban Philadelphia author and mother, told the story of her son's substance abuse on the award winning CBS Sunday evening news show, Sixty Minutes. She then sought meaning for the story of her family as a social group within the context of cross-cultural mythologies. Her family is now actively being enlarged–into the "wider family" (Marciano, 1988; Marciano & Sussman, 1991)–through the establishment of a non-profit organization called *The Banner Project* (Witonsky, 1992).

Witonsky and others work with groups of children telling myths, such as the African, *Soldier And Dove*, and Native American, *Grandmother Turtle's Decree*. Together, they sing *Colors, Join the Resistance, Life is Like a Crystal in the Sea*, and other songs. Opportunities are provided for the children to act in skits, play games, and most important, tell their stories while being actively listened to by peers and adults. The children listen to and enact stories of *The Banner Project* that energetically affirm cooperation and avow that one person can definitely influence and make an impact upon the group and society.

The groups color, decorate, draw, paint, sew, write, and exhibit banners. Banners are publicly displayed in community centers, houses of worship, museums, and schools and carried by the singing artists in parades and rallies. Government officials and Hollywood stars, such as Mayor Ed Rydell and John Travolta, participate. In 1990, President George Bush was greeted with the banners on his tour through West Philadelphia. The powerful image of invincible Grandmother Turtle pulling colorful banners of children's stories, visions, and yearnings speaks loudly to communities and promotes courage to stand up against substance abuse. The arts replace drugs; love transmutes despair; hopefulness restores helplessness. Started by Pecki Witonsky and her friends, the idea is being actualized–panel by panel–through the involvement of children and adults, people of all colors, economic status, ethnicity, and religions.

THE NAMES PROJECT NATIONAL AIDS MEMORIAL QUILT

In August 1987, Cleve Jones, a community leader in San Francisco looked upon cardboard signs attached to a wall of the Federal Building stating the names of individuals who died of AIDS. Cleve Jones and Mike Smith decided to make a permanent memorial of a quilt, sewing together panels with people's names on them, and take them to display in Washington, D.C. in October. The word rapidly spread. In only six weeks, 1900 individual panels were created and carried to Washington, D.C. The Quilt is now so large and weighty, it is generally viewed in sections. In October 1992, the Quilt was once again displayed in its entirety on the Mall, blanketing the grassy park land between the Washington Monument and the Capitol in Washington, D.C.

The *NAMES Project National AIDS Memorial Quilt* has been called the largest community art project in history. Panels contain the rainbow colored remembrances and the shimmering golden dreams of a generation who have died before their time (Jeter & Sussman, 1989). Colleagues, friends, family members, and lovers create the panels. Also, people with AIDS construct their own panels as a way to face their own death while raising the collective consciousness. Panels display baby blankets and toys, stethoscopes, a priest's alb, photographs, playbills, T-shirts, union cards, Viet Nam medals, and other memorabilia. There are panels of organizations containing the names of members who have died of AIDS. Well represented are the fire and sheriff departments; dance and play groups; bands and orchestras; military units and the Peace Corps. And, there are panels of lovers, joined together on the quilt of design; joined together in death by disease. The AIDS Quilt travels from community to community. At each site, new panels are added. The Quilt allows us to educate, grieve, memorialize, remember, and try to understand an adamant and obstinate disease.

MAMA SAID

Helen Finner (Finner & Stewart, 1991) raised six children and currently is raising her three-year old granddaughter in the projects of Chicago. One day when Finner was walking outside her apartment house, she saw a young mother with two children crying. Finner listened to her problems, comforted her, told her stories of the mothering process. It occurred to Finner, that in the small towns in rural America, there is a sense of community; aunts and grandmothers tell young mothers stories of how it is to be a mother. In the city, there are mixed signals. The teenage girl is told by her mother to be dynamic, to get straight A's. Often, the mother is working long hours and is under great pressure to maintain her life personally plus keep her social family together. The adolescent girl is alone and gets attention (plus pregnancy) from a young man!

In 1991, Finner founded Mama Said. She sees young mothers and young grandmothers who have not benefited from hearing their kinfolk tell stories of the mother process. Finner believes that child abandonment, abuse, and infant deaths are due to the frustration of being alone physically, and moreover without the stories of how to be a mother. Finner's message is, "I had no one to help me as a single mother and I succeeded. You can succeed. Make up your mind that you want the best for your children." Social worker and mother, Tanya Stewart (Finner & Stewart, 1990), has joined and expanded Mama Said into three other projects. Girls join rap sessions and later life skills sessions. Mama Said is a form of initiation; a focus point is created and questions of "Where are you now?" and "Where do you want to be?" are asked. The wisdom and love of mothers across the ages are transmitted to young mothers, transforming them, their children, and society.

By the grace of the Muses and Fates we have centuries of stories, legends, and mythologies. The absoluteness of truth and legend, authority and mythology challenges us; what is real? Realities are often polar opposites: the intellectual and the illogical, the practical and the idealistic, the physical and the emotional, the material and the celestial, the mortal and the divine. Within the context of mythology, these varied realties can be presented as an integrated totality. The listener vicariously lives the story and perceives a reunion of the kinship of humankind. Possibilities are unlimited within the unity of ostensibly antithetical life ways.

We live in the family, concurrently as a social group and as a mythological story. We can face the unknown future with archetypal images, consciously re-creating our own cosmology, bravely telling our stories to transform fear into love. We can employ the ancient theater device, *Deus ex machina*, ourselves; the omnipotent will come to our aid when remembered, addressed, and thanked. We can be the archetypal Scheherazade and face the future with the wisdom of the story, knowledgeable that its eloquent contextual message integrates truth and legend, authority and mythology. The mythology that best serves the past, contemporary, and future family is a cosmogony, a narrative and action of the heart that advances courage, creation, empathy, loving kindness, and hope for all kin.

> *To Scheherazade*
>
> *Your unperturbed voice*
> *with a serenely repeated movement*
> *like the scimitar-stroke*
> *of a great bird's wing, lays open*
> *a rift of clear air*
> *through our silence, a coloured swathe*
> *engrossed with human action:*
> *debate, betrayal, ruse, justice.*
>
> *Through the page as through a pane*
> *we look out on a spacious real world*
> *where people say 'But Allah alone is wise' ...*
> *finding a baboon, an artist in calligraphy*
> *or the lost ring in the belly of a fish.*
>
> *In that saying, the imperturbable*
> *perspective: they are real*
> *to themselves in the same way*
> *as to us. In that, and the knowledge*
> *(on which especially your love is founded)*
> *that there is a story opening*
> *inside every other story,*
> *and that of these*
> *it is given us to know*
> *an infinite number,*
> *but still less than all.*

–Grevel Lindop (1988)
To Scheherazade

REFERENCES

Bolle, K. W. (1987). Cosmology: An Overview. In Mircea Eliade (Ed.), *The Encyclopedia of Religion* (Vol. 4) (pp. 100-107). New York, NY: Macmillan Publishing Company.

Borowsky, I. J. (1991). Forward. In James H. Charlesworth (Ed.), *Jesus' Jewish-*

ness: Exploring the Place of Jesus within Early Judaism. New York, NY: Crossroad.

Bristow, J. T. (1988). *What Paul Really Said About Women.* San Francisco, CA: Harper & Row, Publishers.

Chaudhuri, H. (1987). In Dionne Marx (Ed.), *The Philosophy of Love.* New York, NY: Routledge & Kegan Paul.

A Course in Miracles (1975) (Vol. 1-3). New York, NY: Foundation for Inner Peace.

Falk, M. (1990). *The Song of Songs: A New Translation and Interpretation.* San Francisco, CA: Harper.

Finner, H., & Stewart, T. (1991, November 14). CBS News Nightwatch on Mama Said. Interview by Christopher Matthews. Washington, DC: CBS News Division.

Fox, M. (1991). *Creation Spirituality: Liberating Gifts for the Peoples of the Earth.* San Francisco, CA: Harper.

Harrison, J. (1922). *Prolegomena to the Study of Greek Religion* (3rd ed.). New York, NY: Meridian Books.

Hillman, J. (1975). A Note on Story. In *Loose Ends.* Dallas, TX: Spring Publications.

Horovitz, B. (1976). The Legend of the Madonna. In Yenne Velt, *The Great Works of Jewish Fantasy and Occult* (Vol. II) (Joachim Neugroschel Comp. and Trans.), 102-113. New York, NY: The Stonehill Publishing Company.

Houston, J. (1992, March 1). *The Mythology of Meso-America* (Public Lecture). Port Jervis, NY: The Foundation for Mind Research.

Ilsen, E. P. (1992, January 26). Private Communication. Philadelphia, PA.

Jampolsky, G. G. (1979). *Love is Letting Go of Fear.* Millbrae, CA: Celestial Arts.

Jeter, K., & Sussman, M. B. (1989). Dedication. In *A Precious Tapestry of Rainbow Colored Remembrances and Shimmering Golden Dreams.* Pomona, NY: Foundation for Mind Research.

Johanson, D. (1992, February 6). *CBS News Nightwatch on Lucy's Child,* Interview by Charlie Rose. Washington, DC: CBS News Division.

Johanson, D., & Shreeve, J. (1989). Lucy's Child: The Discovery of a Human Ancestor. New York, NY: William Morrow and Company, Inc.

Lindop, G. (1988). To Scheherazade. In Peter L. Caracciolo (Ed.), *The Arabian Nights in English Literature: Studies in the Reception of The Thousand and One Nights into British Culture* (pp. xxix). London, England: The Macmillan Press, Ltd.

Marciano, T. D. (1988). Families Wider Than Kin or Marriage. *Family Science Review 1*(2), 115-124.

Marciano, T. D., & Sussman M. B. (1991). *Wider Families: New Traditional Family Forms.* New York, NY: The Haworth Press, Inc.

May, R. (1975). *The Courage to Create.* New York, NY: W. W. Norton and Company, Inc.

Metzger, D. (1989). *What Dinah Thought.* New York, NY: Viking.

Neilson, W. A. (Ed.), (1955). *Webster's New International Dictionary of the*

English Language (2nd Ed., Unabridged). Springfield, MA: F. & C. Merriam Company.

Otto, R. (1923). *The Idea of the Holy: An Inquiry into the Non-rational Factor in the Idea of the Divine and its Relation to the Rational* (John W. Harvey Trans.). New York, NY: Oxford University Press.

Pagels, E. (1979). *The Gnostic Gospels.* New York, NY: Random House.

Pierre, S. (1990, December 16). *Weapons of the Spirit* (Film). Wilmington, DE: WHYY-TV.

Rivkin, E. (1984). *What Crucified Jesus? The Political Execution of a Charismatic.* Abingdon.

Scholem, G. (1971). At the Completion of Buber's Translation of the Bible. In *The Messianic Idea in Judaism and Other Essays on Jewish Spirituality* (Michael A. Meyer, Trans.) (pp. 314-319). New York, NY: Schocken Books.

Shakespeare, W. (1969). The Tempest, or The Enchanted Island. London, England: Cornmarket. (Original work published 1674.)

The Ramayana of Valmiki (1962). In B. Sobel (Ed.), *The Theatre Handbook and Digest of Plays* (Vols. 1-3) (p. 503) (Hari Prasad Shastri, Trans.). New York, NY: Crown Publishers. (Original work published 1950.)

Speirs, M. (1989, October 27). *Paleolithic Picassos.* Philadelphia, PA: University Museum, University of Pennsylvania.

Steinmetz, S. (1992, March 31). Private Communication. Indianapolis, IN: University of Indiana.

Sussman, M. B., & Jeter, K. (1990). Marriage and Parenting in the United States. In S. R. Quah (Ed.), *The Family as an Asset: An International Perspective on Marriage, Parenthood and Social Policy* (pp. 170-171). Singapore: Times Academic Press.

Von Franz, Marie-Louise (1972). *Patterns of Creativity Mirrored in Creation Myths.* Dallas, TX: Spring Publications, Inc.

Wiesel, E. (1980). Myth and History. In A. M. Olson (Ed.), *Myth, Symbol, and Reality* (p. 21). Notre Dame, IN: University of Notre Dame Press, 21.

Williamson, M. (1992). *A Return to Love.* New York, NY: Harper Collins.

Witonsky, P. (1992). *The Banner Project.* Phoenixville, PA: The Banner Project.

EPILOGUE

Families in Time to Come:
Taking a Position on Trends and Issues

Marvin B. Sussman

INTRODUCTION

Writing on families in the future is intellectual play. The substance of
the messages stimulates the neural pathways of the brain. For a short time
the right side of the brain is stimulated. From deep in the unconscious,
there arise strong feelings and emotions on what the future world will and
should be like and what this means for families.

I am aware of the pathologies of human societies and cultures and the

Marvin B. Sussman is UNIDEL Professor of Human Behavior, Emeritus,
University of Delaware, and member of Core Faculty, Union Graduate School,
Union Institute, Cincinnati, OH.

[Haworth co-indexing entry note]: "Families in Time to Come: Taking a Position
on Trends and Issues." Sussman, Marvin B. Co-published simultaneously in
Marriage & Family Review (The Haworth Press, Inc.) Vol. 18, No. 3/4, 1993,
pp. 303-313; and: *American Families and the Future: Analyses of Possible Destinies* (ed: Barbara H. Settles, Roma S. Hanks, and Marvin B. Sussman) The
Haworth Press, Inc., 1993, pp. 303-313. Multiple copies of this article/chapter
may be purchased from The Haworth Document Delivery Center. Call 1-800-3-
HAWORTH (1-800-342-9678) between 9:00 - 5:00 (EST) and ask for DOC-
UMENT DELIVERY CENTER.

303

multitudinous frailties of humankind. Depressing as these are, in tandem with their increasing incidence in societies of growing complexity, I feel strongly that partial, and in some instances complete solutions, to current pathologies are possible. Consequently, this paper is an upbeat statement on solutions. Each perceived pathology is juxtaposed with a positive and often optimistic set of options. Judgments on what is have well-established empirical referents. The prognostications of the future are more problematic.

OVERPOPULATION

Overpopulation of the world will be a continuous phenomenon. Among the many societal consequences are reduced standards of living, frequent migrations, internal and external conflicts, and increased hunger, starvation, and morbidity within afflicted societies. Expanded population growth has been associated with high levels of misery and human suffering.

The United States will not experience a sharp rise in the growth of population in the 21st Century. Small size families will be the predominant norm with cultural minorities such as Hispanics and Blacks being the exceptions. Worldwide population growth will enhance migration and create pressures to change USA immigration policies. Families of diverse cultural, racial, ethnic, and class backgrounds will challenge existing practices of social and economic separation.

A new paradigm focused on coalescing minority cultures around superordinate goals will eventually become normative. Superordinate goals are those which are highly desired by two or more competitive groups but are unobtainable unless joint cooperation is obtained. Such collaborative undertakings do not guarantee peace and harmony among diversified ethnic and cultural groups. The potential to interact towards a resonated common goal, however, is a beginning to deconstruct the *in* versus *out* group norms and values that create conflict, tension, and often violence between groups and their members.

AGING AND THE AGED

Characteristic of societies of increasing complexity is the rising incidence of persons dependent for their lifeways upon the economically productive members of the society. This is especially the case of the older retired population and the very young. Reported for worldwide industrialized societies is the increasing earlier age of retirement from the workforce and the extension of time for the education and socialization of children.

The burden of support is upon the workforce, aged 15-65, those who contribute to the gross national product. Consequences of this burdening of the gainfully employed, are society wide transfers of economic value including: (1) increased taxation; (2) demands for higher productivity at lower labor costs; and (3) reduction or dismantling of various entitlement social service and health programs, e.g., Medicaid, Medicare, Headstart, in the United States.

In the coming years, members of families will be asked to spend more of their time, energy, and income to care for the chronically ill and disabled relatives. Laws determining filial responsibility have been enacted in 43 states and such legislation will occur within the next few years in the remaining jurisdictions. While such laws are not being vigorously enforced, they will be undoubtedly in the future as governmental bodies search frantically for monies to care for dependent populations.

Caring for one's own has had a long history and persists today in both expectations and practice. Family members are the major caregivers to their dependent members. The growing requests for care receivers come at a time when there is a paucity of women to assume traditional caregiving roles, because they are settled in careers and jobs. Also, fewer caregivers will be available as a consequence of the lower birthrate of the post World War II baby boom cohort. Ethical, moral, and legal issues regarding the extension of life of the older population; living without quality; care of the ill and disabled; best investment of dollars in medical care and social services will be assiduously debated in the following years.

ENERGY

As we move into the 21st century, the best guesses are that there will be very limited new sources of energy and that major savings will come from conservation. Population growth makes the energy issue one of the most critical ones in the coming decades. Even if new energy sources are found, there is likely to be difficulty in their use and distribution, because of the continuous conflicts over the possession and use of such resources.

The family's love of the automobile may be drastically modified. Currently, we may not be that far away from the rationing of fuel as during World War II or the shortages that occurred in the 1970s as a result of the fixed pricing by Middle Eastern cartels and Middle East conflicts. Families can go beyond relearning the paradigm of conservation. In addition to cutting back on the use of fuels, they can educate and socialize their members into the norm of parsimony, in the use of automobiles. Family education will include greater use of mass transit systems. New technologies will make such travel more energy efficient, convenient, and enjoyable.

CONTINUOUS GLOBAL CONFLICT

The energy issue is only one of the basic components of ongoing conflicts between the have and have-not nations. Highly developed societies are the major consumers of energy and most recently the Persian Gulf Conflict was motivated by the great need and concern for continuous cheap oil to power the needs of these societies. In addition to oil, the control and use of diminishing world water sources will catalyze nation state conflicts in the immediate future. Predictably the reduction or loss of water resources in any section of the globe will drastically affect the food chain and any development of human capacities. For example, in Jordan and Israel, the future growth of the population with any quality of life for families depends on the available water supply.

Conflict between ethnic and racial groups attests to the strong identity and ideology of members of such groups. During the period of the early 1990s the horrors inflicted on innocent individuals and families are beyond comprehension. The major victims of such conflicts are families, innocent ones, caught and trapped in undreamed carnage. Unfortunately, the leaders in power, scientific and professional elites, and protagonists of family well-being and values have offered little or no solutions to the wholesale destruction of families. The one and perhaps only solution of those families able to escape death and destruction is to migrate. The stories of such families uprooted and cast adrift, and often unwelcome by their host countries, are among the most tragic stories of this century. The "ethnic cleansing" is no more than developing new in-groups, to solidify, to organize, and to prepare for future conflicts with other ethnic distillations called out-groups. Unfortunately what is occurring today is highly duplicative of tribal warfare that has occurred throughout all of human history. It appears that humanity lives on the verge of readiness to kill. The task for the humanistically oriented social scientist is to work and experiment with ways to enable ethnic and racial minorities to live with themselves and with others. This may not stop the killing, but it might make a difference. Even if a handful of families are saved, it is worth the effort.

CLIMATE AND FOOD

For the first time in many lifetimes, more and more individuals are becoming concerned about the occurring climatic changes. Questions have arisen on how human uses of the land, water, air, and other nature's bounties create and affect such climatic changes. The destruction of the rain forest, the weakening of the ozone layer, the increasing incidence of high rates of pollution found in our urban areas have become central issues for debate, legislation, and even international accords.

The consequences for families are obvious. Farmers in Iowa who have experienced drought for four or five years are beginning to ask questions about this unexpected phenomenon, e.g., is it due to the depletion of the rain forest in Brazil? Some decide not to seek scientific answers but give up the farm and move to towns or cities in search of work in businesses and factories.

Climatic changes affect the oceans and the tides. An increase of even one to two feet will heap destruction on our coastlines as well as our inland lakes and rivers. The warming of the Arctic and Antarctic icecaps will result in the warming of the earth and severe temperature changes that will require complex and multitudinous changes in housing, lifestyles, and new behaviors for survival.

Foreseen is a continuous conflict between the advocates of an exportable worldwide sane environmental policy and those who speak for jobs by continuous exploitation of our natural resources. Families will be torn over their options attempting to live with this unique paradox. If we destroy our environment, jobs will be few. If we protect our environment, the economy may suffer. If we change the paradigm and integrate the best environmental practices with creation of industries using our high technology, the paradox of economy and environment can be sustained.

Changes in climate are obviously related to modifications of the food chain. Unfortunately, due to variations in climate and limited food supply, especially in its distribution, coupled with high fertility rates, the result will be rising hunger and starvation for tens of millions of families each year in the future. Major activities to modify this condition are (1) coordinated efforts to distribute food supplies through the emerging global economy; and (2) continuous and strengthened programs of child spacing and birth control.

A related program to be expanded would be health maintenance, especially pre-natal care. Pre-natal care is vital to enhance the survival of children. Such survival is critical beyond economic sustenance of family members in old age and is embellished in spiritual and ancestral worship systems involving members over generational time.

Another related concern is gainful and steady employment of providers in families. Security in jobs and possibilities for occupational advancement is another condition that lessens the need for a large sized family.

In sum, hunger can be reduced and families worldwide can experience some quality of life if food redistribution can occur through a global economy matrix; if fertility rates can be reduced; if health programs can be initiated to ensure the survival of children in small-sized families; and if steady jobs can be found for family providers.

THE GLOBAL SYSTEM

The world in the 1990s moved from being bipolar to being multipolar. Early political historians divided the world into component parts where nations like the United States, one-time Soviet Union, Germany and England had hegemony over less powerful nations. In this late period of the 20th century, there is a similar concentration of societies who are organizing around economic and other interests. The difference from previous times is that one nation may not be in power, controlling and dominating other nations in their geographical areas.

This multi-polar world is moving towards an impenetrable global system mainly due to improved and heightened worldwide communication. The communication revolution of the last two decades has effected rising expectations in all societies where there is increasing use of radio and television. The exchange and adoption and integration of cultural forms and soon to be followed, values, are a global process in spite of the efforts to isolate and secularize nation states. The earth has become a living organism; what happens in one part of the globe affects one, then two, then three . . . n events, organizations, economies. For families the concept of this process in mind-boggling. To grasp it requires acknowledging and understanding that one's own problems and those found in the larger society cannot be solved from a perspective of isolation. The earth, and before too long the cosmos, will have to be accounted as being part of our understanding and solution of the issues and problems. Families must overcome their cynicism about existing social institutions and begin to create new ones that have as their benchmark a global perspective. To be able to participate in this new world order will require renewed respect for science and technology and for demands on the part of families to have greater say in the use and outcomes of the discoveries of science and its endemic technology.

AIDS, CHRONIC ILLNESS, AND CARE

The incidence and prevalence of AIDS will rise each year into the future involving individuals and families of all racial and ethnic groups worldwide. The ultimate cure may be long in coming and foci will be upon prevention and treatment of this life threatening disease. It appears from the results of current research that appropriate treatment of the disease will postpone the deaths of AIDS victims. This prolongation of life will place increasing burdens on caregiving organizations and families.

The medical care system today with its current responsive ideology of viewing and treating physical dysfunctions as pathologies is unprepared to work with life threatening conditions that have strong social causation. Moreover, the heavy involvement of non-medical persons in the care and treatment of AIDS patients, especially family members and other significant service providers such as friends and lovers, portends serious conflicts and alienation between medical and non-medical caregivers. The current model of control empowers the physician who traditionally is in a superordinate position in the treatment hierarchy. The involvement of so many non-medical individuals in the treatment, care, and lifestyles of the afflicted individual requires a new model of care. It is difficult to determine at this point the best model. Suggested forms are partnership structures in which all those involved collectively determine the best program of care. Another possibility is to empower the victim of the life-threatening disease to the point where he or she can make the final decision on the treatment modalities and endemic care.

AIDS is but one example of chronic illness and attendant disability that are increasing in prevalence and incidence worldwide. We are entering the period of extended survival of individuals with severe disabilities who for the most part are dependent upon the gainfully employed population of the society. The increasingly negative evaluation of expanding institutional resources for the care of ill populations is noticeable in the United States. Government elites both here and in other developed societies hold the position that the society has reached its absorptive capacity for expansion of institutional organizations' services. They turn toward utilization of family members and other volunteers to do the day-to-day care with minimal financial support from societal institutions. Such individuals give of their time and energies without direct cost to the society, expend their own resources and those of the afflicted individuals. There reaches a point in the trajectory of the chronic illness and disability when such resources cannot meet the needs and tasks of care for the ailing individual, and the individual requires hospital care, including intensive care.

Nurturing a humanistic value embedded deep in our culture is to exercise heroic deeds to save the life of individuals at any age. No matter how deficient persons are in "normal" human abilities and function, the expectation is to love and care for these individuals knowing that few will experience a quality of life usually attained by individuals who are not so afflicted.

The moral and ethical issues of sustaining the life of humans severely limited in their normal functions will be a basic and critical issue in our society in the coming years and as we move into the 21st century. Concern and even modification of current moral and ethical postures on caring for the disabled and chronically ill may occur more quickly than we realize if the current economic patterns of federal and state support should change.

The availability and distribution of economic resources will affect the debates on the ethics and moral issues of such care. Families will enter into these discussions, especially when it appears that the resources accumulated over a lifetime are completely lost to pay for the costs of a few days of care or when the family will become bankrupt and radically alter its lifestyle because of the chronic illness of a member. They will look for resources outside the family such as provided by health care organizations in order to complement their primary care activities. If a health care insurance system is developed that will control costs and provide sufficient care, families will not lose their economic resources.

THE ECONOMY

In the remaining years of this decade, the economic and political system continues to be out of control with a burdensome debt and slow economic growth. Coupled with this inability to provide jobs for an increasing number of young people trying to enter the labor market will be soaring crime rates. These situations cast a shadow upon the future but can be opened to new values, paradigms, and practices vis-a-vis the creation of new scenarios.

In 1992 President Bill Clinton resonated the notion that the government should invest in jobs and not just in the bail-out of service and loan institutions. His scenario is to invest in rural and urban work corps in order to rebuild the infrastructure of our cities, rural areas, parks, and woodlands. Such work groups would be similar to those created during the Roosevelt administration, aimed to provide needed repairs of our roads, parks, bridges, and other public structures and also to stimulate the economy by increasing the demands for goods and services of participants in groups resembling Work Progress Administration.

Another scenario would involve an increasingly large number of citizens through political processes and "action in the streets" attempting to enhance and preserve our environment. Educational techniques of such groups usually are spontaneously formed and decentralized, working assiduously in their own or nearby communities. As we approach the 21st century action to preserve our forests, to reduce pollution, to eliminate radiation, could be aimed to create ecological sensitivity, and maintain respect and honor for the environment. Involving families of varied ethnic, racial, economic, and cultural backgrounds would become a potent political force in the coming years. The environmental movement is an example of a pattern of decentralization of power and increasing ability to implement well-reasoned objectives.

RELIGIOUS AWAKENING

Two dominant patterns of religious behavior for America have emerged during the 20th century. The first was a conservative fundamentalist movement whose members believe in the infallibility of the Bible and whose leaders were highly successful in using the mass media, especially television. Televangelists captured the hearts and minds of millions of people and only the human behavior of a few such as infidelity or unacceptable sexual behavior has limited their influence. This political right has made efforts to control appropriate behavior of families. Spokespersons have been leaders in the anti-abortion movement and work continuously to unify the American people to a single set of conservative values. Their power and influence have fluctuated. For example, the shift from a Republican controlled White House to a Democratic one may be a harbinger of a reduced conservative movement and a renewed interest in more liberal religious institutions.

Traditional Protestant religious institutions as well as Catholic and Jewish religious organizations have not experienced growth in numbers or influence in these past decades. However, a small but significant minority of individuals are creating new journeys of the spirit. Using a combination of religious tenets from far eastern religious traditions along with humanistic principles derived from the great philosophers of world societies, another new religious movement is emerging in which the spiritual journey not only encompasses individual transformation but also good community work.

Families today and in the future will be able to make a choice of one of these major religious systems. The basis of such a choice is problematic. The ultimate determinant will be the family's response to the exhortations of ideology, laws and legislation that shape religious behavior, and the inner motivation that guides the individual to behave according to her or his principles regardless of the consequences. A multi-modal religious system will exist in the future in American society, providing choices for families without being coerced by an authoritarian religious system.

THE GENDER REVOLUTION

There has been a growing awakening of consciousness in the twentieth century, and a number of revolutions in our ways of thinking and behaving. Many changes in legislation have occurred in meeting the requirements of the revolutionaries. The Blacks in the 1950s, students in the 1960s, and women in the 1970s engaged in activities pressing for enlightenment in place of the shadows of discrimination, intolerance, and prejudice. They were successful in creating new paradigms on how to feel and think, perceive and evaluate relationships. Although all that they desired to achieve was not obtained, enough occurred to redirect the course of the society from the traditional structures of power and control, and create a sustained driving force to work on the democratization of American society.

The gender revolution took as its prototype the Black and student movements of the previous decades but functioned less in the streets and more in the home. As family ideologies and practices began to change, men and women began to move more towards equitable relationships in the family. The consequences were felt throughout society. As more women entered the workforce they benefited from the efforts of earlier previous leaders of social and political change who had promoted legislation to provide equal opportunities for people of any gender, race, nationality, or creed. The trend is towards greater roles and power for women in American and other complex societies. Even if there is a shift from the current increasing incidence of women entering the workforce to one of election to being a manager of an evolutionary household, my definition of homemaker, the change in relationships within the family will not revert to the old superordinate/subordinate pattern. Equity and sharing will continue to dominate and grow in both prevalence and incidence in the coming years. Equity implies fairness and the portrait of the future of gender relations within the family is one of complementarity, fairness in the allocation of responsibilities and services. Partnership and empowerment of all family members is the predicted model that will influence the structure and processes of other organizations and institutions.

CONCLUSION

These views of the future of families focus on awakening and change; new paradigms and journeys for members of families. The question is whether enough members will take the risk and challenge and move out of encrusted old patterns and encapsulated egos.

Teilhard de Chardin expresses far better than I what is emerging from a deepened consciousness.

> Everywhere on Earth, at this moment in the new spiritual atmosphere created by the idea of evolution, there float, in a state of extreme sensitivity, love of God and faith in the world. The two essential components of the ultrahuman. These two components are everywhere "in the air," . . . Sooner or later there will be a chain reaction. (Russell, 1983)

AUTHOR'S NOTE

Individuals and families use their views of the future in committing to action. Dr. Hanks and Dr. Settles asked Dr. Sussman, the Senior Scholar among the editors, to provide his own assessment for the immediate future of families.

REFERENCE

Russell, P. (1983). The Global Brain (p. 179). Los Angeles, CA: J. P. Tarcher, Inc.